ESSAYS ON THE HISTORY OF PARLIAMENTARY PROCEDURE

8 February 2015 marked the 200th anniversary of the birth of Thomas Erskine May. May is the most famous of the fifty holders of the office of Clerk of the House of Commons. His continued renown arises from his *Treatise upon the Law, Privileges, Proceedings and Usage of Parliament,* first published in 1844 and with its 25th edition currently in preparation. It is known throughout those parts of the world that model their constitutional arrangements on Westminster as the 'Bible of Parliamentary Procedure'. This volume celebrates both the man and his book. Bringing together current and former Clerks in the House of Commons and outside experts, the contributors analyse May's profound contribution to the shaping of the modern House of Commons, as it made the transition from the pre-Reform Act House to the modern core of the UK's constitutional democracy in his lifetime. This is perhaps best symbolised by its enforced transition between 1834 and 1851 from a mediaeval slum to the World Heritage Palace of Westminster, which is the most iconic building in the UK.

The book also considers the wider context of parliamentary law and procedure, both before and after May's time. It constitutes the first sustained analysis of the development of parliamentary procedure in over half a century, attempting to situate the reforms in the way the central institution of our democracy conducts itself in the political contexts which drove those changes.

Volume 7 in the series Hart Studies in Constitutional Law

Hart Studies in Constitutional Law

Essays on the History of Parliamentary Procedure

In Honour of Thomas Erskine May

Edited by
Paul Evans

•HART•

FORD • LONDON • NEW YORK • NEW DELHI • SYDNEY

HART PUBLISHING
Bloomsbury Publishing Plc
Kemp House, Chawley Park, Cumnor Hill, Oxford, OX2 9PH, UK

HART PUBLISHING, the Hart/Stag logo, BLOOMSBURY and the Diana logo are
trademarks of Bloomsbury Publishing Plc

First published in Great Britain 2017
First published in hardback, 2017
Paperback edition, 2020

A catalogue record for this book is available from the British Library.

Library of Congress Cataloging-in-Publication Data

Names: May, Thomas Erskine, 1815–1886 honouree. | Evans, Paul, 1955- editor.
Title: Essays on the history of parliamentary procedure: in honour of Thomas Erskine May / edited by Paul Evans.
Description: Oxford [UK]; Portland, Oregon: Hart Publishing, 2017. | Series: Hart Studies
in constitutional law; 7 | includes bibliographical references and index.
Identifiers: LCCN 2017045634 (print) | LCCN 2017046434 (ebook) | ISBN 9781509900213 (Epub) |
ISBN 9781509900206 (hardback)
Subjects: LCSH: Great Britain. Parliament—Rules and practice. | Parliamentary practice—Great Britain—History. |
Great Britain. Parliament. House of Lords—History. | Constitutional law—Great Britain. |
May, Thomas Erskine, 1815–1886

Classification: LCC KD4354 (ebook) | LCC KD4354.E87 2017 (print) | DDC 328.41/05—dc23

LC record available at https://lccn.loc.gov/2017045634

ISBN: HB: 978-1-50990-020-6
PB: 978-1-50993-752-3
ePDF: 978-1-50990-022-0
ePub: 978-1-50990-021-3

Typeset by Compuscript Ltd, Shannon

To find out more about our authors and books visit www.hartpublishing.co.uk. Here you will
find extracts, author information, details of forthcoming events and the option to sign up for
our newsletters.

Preface

This book was originally conceived as a tribute to Thomas Erskine May, to celebrate the 200th anniversary of his birth, which fell on 8 February 2015. It has taken a little while for the idea to take shape in physical form. The staff at Hart Publishing have been very tolerant.

Thomas Erskine May (later and briefly Lord Farnborough) was the Clerk of the House of Commons, its most senior official, between 1871 and 1886. There have been fifty recorded holders of that office, but no others have achieved the level of immortality enjoyed by May. He is remembered by posterity not so much for what he did, but for what he wrote, and for only one book. As an ambitious young man of twenty-nine, still an Assistant Librarian of the House whose service he had joined at the age of sixteen, he published the first edition of *A Treatise upon the Law, Privileges, Proceedings and Usage of Parliament* in 1844. It was not the first (nor the last) attempt to distil from the soup of antiquity and then set down the principles which actuated and the rules which bound Parliament, but it has been the most enduring and influential. One hundred and seventy-three years later, the twenty-fifth edition of the *Treatise*, known throughout the world as '*Erskine May*', is under preparation. It still stands, without any serious rival, as the most authoritative text on the law and practice of the United Kingdom Parliament. It is often cited as one of the many written sources of the unwritten constitution of the nation. And its influence and authority is international.

So in part, this is a book about the forces that shaped a book, an effort to examine the *longue durée* of a set of ideas about how the central democratic institution of the United Kingdom derived its legitimacy and exercised its authority. It tries to place the much-restored, occasionally extensively overhauled, and now in places rather dilapidated Victorian monument that is the *Treatise* in the context of the particular era in which it was written, and in the context of what went before and what has come behind. It is not an exhaustive description of the history of the law and practice of Parliament, but a series of essays examining its state at particular moments, or its development along particular paths, or the drivers of change and adaptation at particular junctures, or the preconceptions that shaped it. We shape our rules and then our rules shape us.

This work is also a book about the people who wrote the book—the Clerks in the House of Commons. It is explicitly so in Part I, which looks at May himself and his milieu, as well as the current crop of his successors and the wider community of those who make Parliament work. It is implicitly so in many of the other chapters as well, where we are reminded from time to time that the *Treatise*, and the practices it chronicles and principles it derives from them, are the product of particular people with a particular culture and range of assumptions, and a training in a very peculiar discipline—parliamentary procedure—who do their work in the context of fiercely contested ideas of what the purpose of Parliament is. And in the process of compiling, reading and reacting to the *Treatise* these obscure public servants have helped shape the institutional memory of the organism which has had for centuries a central role in shaping the polity in which the citizens of the United Kingdom live. The digital age may bring the long reign of May's *Treatise* to an end eventually, as the notion of capturing the state of knowledge on a particular subject at one particular moment (subject to the whims of successive editors) may begin to seem insupportably old-fashioned. I hope this work will help to enlarge that institutional memory and to preserve the memory of how it is built.

Much of this book has been written by Clerks past and present. So I would like to dedicate this work to them and my many colleagues across the whole House of Commons service who have helped to make my nearly forty years there a stimulating if occasionally infuriating experience, but to whom above all I am grateful for creating such a collegiate and inquiring environment in which to spend the best part of a lifetime. And I must take the opportunity to apologise to my family, especially my wife Kate, for the state of distraction that the editing of this work has engendered.

Paul Evans
Crickhowell
August 2017

Contents

Part II: The Book

Part III: Procedural Development

Part IV: Select Committees

Part V: The *Lex Parliamentaria* Revisited

Notes on Contributors

Martyn Atkins is a Clerk in the Journal Office of the House of Commons and Clerk of the Procedure Committee. He has previously served as Clerk of the Political and Constitutional Reform Committee, as a Clerk in the Table Office and as the Clerk at the UK National Parliament Office in Brussels.

David Bagnall is Principal Clerk (Procedure) in the Office of the Clerk of the New Zealand House of Representatives.

Jean-Philippe Brochu is a Deputy Principal Clerk and Table Officer in the Canadian House of Commons. He joined the House of Commons in 2003 as a Committee Clerk and since worked as a manager in the Information Management Group, the Table Research Branch and the Journals Branch, as well as the Committees and Legislative Services Directorate. He was one of the managers in charge of the third edition of *House of Commons Procedure and Practice*, the key procedural authority on practices and precedents of the Canadian House of Commons, while also contributing to several of its chapters.

Emma Crewe is a Professor of Social Anthropology specialising in the study of political organisations. She has lectured at the University of Sussex and SOAS, and worked as a policy adviser, social scientist and senior manager within international grant-makers and NGOs. As a researcher at SOAS, her ethnographic research focuses on international NGOs and parliaments in the UK, Eastern African and South Asia. She also supervises doctoral students researching management at the University of Hertfordshire's Business School. Her publications include *Whose Development? An Ethnography of Aid* (with EA Harrison, Zed Books, 1998) *Lords of Parliament: Rituals, Manners and Politics* (Manchester University Press, 2005), *House of Commons: An Anthropology of MPs' Work* (Bloomsbury, 2015) and the *Commons and Lords: A Short Anthropology of Parliament* (Haus Curiosities, 2015).

Mark Egan is Greffier of the States of Jersey. He was a House of Commons Clerk from 1997 to 2015. His DPhil thesis was on the grass-roots organisation of the Liberal Party 1945–64 and was published in 2009 as *Coming into Focus: The Transformation of the Liberal Party 1945–64*. He has written extensively in the *Journal of Liberal History* (often under the name Robert Ingham) and has contributed numerous entries in the *Oxford Dictionary of National Biography* under that name. He co-edited the *Dictionary of Liberal Biography* (1998), *Great Liberal Speeches* (2001), *Peace, Reform and Liberation: A History of Liberal Politics in Britain 1679–2011* (2011) and *British Liberal Leaders* (2015). Editor of the *Journal of the Durham County Local History Society*, he has also contributed entries for the *History of Parliament 1832–68* on South Shields and Liverpool, and is currently working on New Ross. In a professional capacity, Mark contributed to the last two editions of *Erskine May's Parliamentary Practice* and the seventh edition of *How Parliament Works* by Lord Lisvane and Rhodri Walters.

Paul Evans is Clerk of Committees in the House of Commons. He joined the House of Commons service in 1981. His publications include: a chapter on "Privilege, Exclusive Cognisance and the Law" in the second edition of *Parliament and the Law* (ed Drewry and Horne, Hart Publishing, 2017); *Parliamentary Assembly of the Council of Europe: Context, Practice and Procedure* (11th edition, with Paul Silk, 2012); *Constitution by Committee? Legislative Competence Orders under the Government of Wales Act* (with Sue Griffiths); *Parliamentary Affairs* (2012); *Dod's Handbook of House of Commons Procedure* (1st–8th editions, 1997–2011); contributions to the *New Oxford Companion to Law* (2010); and chapters in a number of books published under the auspices of the Study of Parliament Group, of which he is a former Chair. He has contributed to every edition of *Erskine May's Parliamentary Practice* since the twenty-first.

Peter Fowler is Senior Clerk in the Chamber Research Office of the House of Representatives of the Federal Parliament of Australia. He is the Assistant Editor of the latest (7th, 2017) edition of *House of Representatives Practice* (the Australian equivalent of *Erskine May's Parliamentary Practice*), and has been Assistant Editor of five previous editions. He has been responsible for various Department of the House of Representatives publications and worked for some time with the Standing Committee on Procedure.

Oonagh Gay was a Clerk in the House of Commons Library from 1983 to 2015 and is a former chair of the Study of Parliament Group. Her publications include: *Conduct Unbecoming: The Regulation of Parliamentary Behaviour* (ed with Patricia Leopold, 2004); *Constitutional Watchdogs: At the Crossroads* (with Barry Winetrobe, 2009); a forthcoming chapter 'The Law and Conduct of Members of Parliament' in the second edition of *Parliament and the Law* (ed Drewry and Horne, Hart Publishing, 2017); a number of reports for the Constitution Unit of University College London and many research papers published by the House of Commons Library. She was a contributor in respect of electoral law to the 2011 edition of *Erskine May's Parliamentary Practice.*

David Howarth is Professor of Law and Public Policy at the University of Cambridge and a Fellow of Clare College, Cambridge. From 2005 to 2010 he served as the Member of Parliament for Cambridge. He was a member of the Wright Committee and of the Justice Select committee. Since returning to academic life his research interests have included the relationship between public law and politics, the role of lawyers in the House of Commons, and the jurisprudential and constitutional presuppositions harboured by senior UK civil servants.

Mark Hutton is the Clerk of the Journals in the House of Commons. He joined the House service in 1985. He was an Assistant Editor of the 23rd edition of *Erskine May's Parliamentary Practice*, and Deputy Editor of the 24th, a role he is reprising for the 25th edition.

Colin Lee is Clerk of Bills in the House of Commons and has served as a Clerk in the House of Commons for more than 28 years. He is the author of various articles and contributions to books on the historical development of parliamentary procedure and on financial procedure. He is Chair of the Study of Parliament Group.

Sir William McKay was Clerk of the House of Commons from 1997 to 2002. His publications include: *Parliament and Congress* (with Charles W Johnson, Parliamentarian, US House of Representatives, 2010); *Observations, Rules and Orders: An Early Procedural*

Collection (ed 1989); *Clerks in the House of Commons: A Biographical List 1363–1989* (1989, 2002); *Secretaries to Mr Speaker* (1986); *Erskine May's Private Journal 1883–1886* (ed 1984); ed *Erskine May's Parliamentary Practice* (joint ed 1997, ed 2004); *'Nothing Could Exceed the Badness of His Character, Even in this Bad Age': Comparing US and British Speakers* (*Parliamentary History Yearbook* 2010); *The Family Background of Sir Thomas Erskine May* (*The Table*, vol lii, 1984); *The Serjeant Complains About the Clerks: A Seventeenth Century Dispute* (*The Table*, vol lv, 1987); *The Origin and Sources of Henry Scobell's 'Memorials'* (*The Table*, vol lvii, 1989); *Question-time in Congress: Or Why President Truman Called Senator Fulbright 'An Over-educated Oxford Son-of-a-bitch'* (*The Table*, vol lxx, 2002). He has contributed biographies of Sir Thomas Erskine May and Sir Reginald Palgrave, Clerks of the House of Commons, to the *Oxford Dictionary of National Biography*.

David Natzler studied history at Cambridge, graduating in 1973. He has been a contributor to several books published under the auspices of the Study of Parliament Group and has contributed articles to *The Table*. He was the editor of the fourteenth and fifteenth editions of *The Houses of Parliament: A Guide to the Palace of Westminster*, the predecessor to the current official guidebook. He was appointed as the fiftieth Clerk of the House of Commons in March 2015 and is to be the Editor of the next (25th) edition of *Erskine May's Parliamentary Practice*.

Andrej Ninkovic is a graduate in Politics from the University of Hull who has worked in the offices of two Members of Parliament. He participated in the Speaker's Commission on Digital Democracy and has previously written on the regulation of the intelligence services.

Simon Patrick read mathematics at Cambridge and joined the House of Commons on graduating in 1978, where he was a House of Commons Clerk until his retirement in 2016. His last two posts were as Clerk of Bills (2009–13) and as one of the Principal Clerks of Select Committees (2013–16). He edited an unpublished work by the late Sir Edward Fellowes about the history of the Standing Orders 1833–1935, was one of the assistant editors for the last two editions of *Erskine May's Parliamentary Practice* (2004 and 2011), and contributed to the seventh edition of *How Parliament Works* by Robert Rogers (Lord Lisvane) and Rhodri Walters.

Eve Samson joined the House of Commons service in 1986 and is currently Clerk of the Joint Committee on Human Rights, having previously been Clerk of the European Scrutiny Committee, the Committee on Standards and the Committee of Privileges, and a Cabinet Office adviser on parliamentary procedure. She was a Commons Clerk on both the 1997 and the 2012–13 Joint Committees on Parliamentary Privilege. She has written on 'The Arrangement of Business' (in *Parliament in the 21st Century*, ed Nicholas Baldwin, 2004) and has contributed to *How Parliament Works* (Rogers and Walters, 2015). She is an Assistant Editor for the new edition of *Erskine May's Parliamentary Practice*, and a member of the Study of Parliament Group.

Paul Seaward is the British Academy/Wolfson Research Professor at the History of Parliament Trust. From 1988 to 2001 he was a clerk in the House of Commons, and from 2001 to 2016 was Director of the History of Parliament. His publications include an edition of Thomas Hobbes, *Behemoth* (Oxford, 2009), Edward Hyde, Earl of Clarendon *The History of the Rebellion: a new selection* (Oxford World Classics 2009), *The Restoration* (Macmillan,

1991), *The Cavalier Parliament and the Reconstruction of the Old Regime 1661–1667* (Cambridge, 1989) and other books and articles on seventeenth century politics and political thought and on Parliament in the twentieth century. He is the general editor, with Martin Dzelzainis, of an edition of the works of the seventeenth century statesman and historian Edward Hyde, Earl of Clarendon.

Jacqy Sharpe is a former Clerk in the House of Commons. She was Clerk of Legislation from 2011 to 2014 and Acting Clerk Assistant from October 2014 to June 2015.

Introduction

The Growth of Many Centuries

PAUL EVANS

PURPOSE

THIS BOOK SEEKS to trace some outlines of the history of the development of parliamentary procedure, partly through the records and manuals which embody and analyse that procedure, but also through accounts of its development in practice.[1] It uses as its fulcrum the work that has become the most famous and revered exegesis of the subject, *A Treatise upon the Law, Privileges, Proceedings and Usage of Parliament*, written by Thomas Erskine May, then Assistant Librarian of the House of Commons, and first published in 1844. The twenty-fifth edition of the work (hereinafter the *Treatise*) is now under active preparation. Part I looks at the man and the milieu in which his career took place, and examines the development of that culture. Part II looks at the precursors to, life of and descendants of the book which made him famous. Part III examines various themes in the development of procedure which began in or before May's time and continue to the present day. Part IV looks at aspects of the select committees of the House of Commons, which are generally regarded as outside the procedural zone of influence. Part V examines some aspects of the relationship between the law of Parliament and the law in general. May began the first chapter of the *Treatise* with the words: 'The present constitution of Parliament has been the growth of many centuries.' This book tries to capture some of the natural history of that evolution.

THOMAS ERSKINE MAY AND THE TREATISE

In chapter 1, Sir William McKay provides a brief biography of Thomas Erskine May's largely uneventful life. May joined the House's service as an Assistant Librarian (the

---

[1] The author is indebted to Dr Paul Seaward for many of the ideas and references in this chapter, particularly from his chapter on parliamentary procedure in Vernon Bogdanor's *The New British Constitution* (Oxford, Hart Publishing, 2006), and a lecture delivered in Leiden in 2014 on the *Lex Parliamentaria and the Sources of Parliamentary Procedure*. There have been numerous short surveys of the development of parliamentary procedure in Westminster, but Josef Redlich's 1903 work has never been surpassed for comprehensiveness: Josef Redlich, *The Procedure of the House of Commons: A Study of its History and Present Form*, trans A Ernest Steinthal (London, Archibald Constable & Co, 1908). Also worth noting are Gilbert Campion's introductory chapter to his *An Introduction to the Procedure of the House of Commons*, 2nd edn (London, Macmillan, 1947) and WR McKay's Introduction to the 23rd edition of the *Treatise*, as well as Paul Seaward's chapter noted above.

history of the House of Commons Library as an institution is described by Oonagh Gay in chapter 2) and rose through the ranks eventually to become its most senior official, the Clerk of the House. As chapter 7 traces, in the course of the nine editions of the book prepared by him in his lifetime, and at an accelerating pace after his death, the *Treatise* ceased to be the work of an individual author and became an expression of the collective wisdom of the Clerks, who formed the core of a permanent service of the House. These Clerks have a long history. In the 650-odd years since the first identified Clerk of the Commons was appointed, they have become a mix of administrators, facilitators, policy analysts, political advice givers and drafters—in a word, technocrats. But despite their increasingly diverse roles, they are centrally recognised, with particular relevance to this book, as the guardians of House of Commons procedure. Chapter 3 is an ethnographic study of the culture of this small and obscure profession by Emma Crewe, building on her earlier fieldwork amongst Members of the two Houses of Parliament. To an extent this book is consciously framed as not only an account of developments in parliamentary procedure, but also an account of the people who mostly recorded, systematised and influenced its development—the Clerks.

Procedure, put very simply, is the collection of rules and conventions which determine how and what the House debates, and how it reconciles disagreements and reaches decisions, delegates and mandates. It includes the rules and conventions which govern its relations with other constitutional decision-makers—in particular the Lords, the Crown and (to an extent) the courts.

THE AGE OF PRECEDENT

The seventeenth-century jurist, Sir Edward Coke, in his survey of the English common law first published in 1628, referred to the law and custom of Parliament as 'ab omnibus quaeranda, a multis ignoranda, a paucis cognita' [asked after by everyone, unknown to many, understood by few].[2] Coke's characterisation of parliamentary procedure as of immense obscurity is of a piece with his description of the common law itself as the product of centuries of refinement by generations of legal professionals, creating a system essentially inaccessible to those without specialist training. Chapters 4, 5 and 6 show how generations of scholars and practitioners struggled to put procedure into some sort of systematic form.

All these systematisers were vexed by the essential problem that the law of Parliament is what Parliament at any given time says it is, but must at the same time be governed by principles than put some limit on this apparent arbitrariness (in chapter 17, David Howarth asks whether parliamentary law really is a legal system). As Coke put it, the law of Parliament 'is so transcendent and absolute, that it cannot be confined, either for causes or persons, within any bounds'.[3] There is no external check, only the appeal to precedent and

---

[2] Sir Edward Coke, *The first part of the Institutes of the lawes of England. Or, A commentarie vpon Littleton, not the name of a lawyer onely, but of the law it selfe* (London, 1629) fo 11v (bk 1, ch 1, s 3). Coke uses a similar phrase at fo 110, bk 2, ch 10, s 164 where it is apparently attributed to the Parliament Rolls. Coke's main discussion of Parliament is in fourth part of the *Institutes*, published in 1644, where he devotes the first 52 pages to it, much more attention than is given to any other 'court'.

[3] ibid, fourth part, s 36.

antiquity. A frequently reprinted late-seventeenth-century guide to the *Lex Parliamentaria* claimed that the term 'cannot be meant or intended to signify any Prescription or Application of Laws to that power, which in itself is boundless'.[4] This indefinability is what gives the study of the law of Parliament its urgency and importance, while at the same time vexing it with complexity and contest of interpretations.

The concept of exclusive cognisance (that Parliament makes, interprets, judges and determines its own procedure and is answerable to no other authority for its decisions), generally claimed as an aspect of parliamentary privilege, can be seen to be derived from the concept of parliamentary sovereignty. May himself, in the first edition of the *Treatise*, offered a more liberal and democratic definition of parliamentary sovereignty, though not one that could be described as excessively hedged:

> The legislative authority of Parliament extends over the United Kingdom, and all its colonies and foreign possessions; and there are no other limits to its power of making laws for the whole Empire than those which are incident to all sovereign authority—the willingness of the people to obey or their power to resist. Unlike the legislatures of many countries it is bound by no fundamental charter or constitution.[5]

The important emphasis that May makes, as a liberal writing at the dawning of the age of mass democracy, is that Parliament is answerable to another authority—the people, who can bestow and withdraw their consent to its choices and decisions, and can ultimately decline to accept its claim of sovereignty. Respect for procedure can be seen to be an essential component in securing the people's assent to Parliament's exercise of its authority. The foundations of procedure are respect for due process, the acceptance of the rights of the minority, the need for clarity, and the necessity of keeping a true and agreed record of what has been done. Without these qualities, the willingness of the people to obey is likely to be unreliable. In 1796 the then Clerk of the House of Commons, John Hatsell,[6] wrote that:

> It has sometimes been advanced, that this expression of 'Parliamentary Law', or 'The Law of Parliament', is inaccurate; for that there is no such particular Law, distinct from the Common Law of the land. No such distinction has ever been attempted to be made: but, from the earliest ages of our history to the present moment, it has been uniformly asserted, by those best acquainted with these subjects, 'That the judicial proceedings in parliament are to be regulated, not by what are commonly and technically called, the Rules of the Common Law, but by their own customs, and the ancient practice of the two Houses of Parliament', and therefore, 'that the Law of Parliament forms part of the Common Law of the Land'.[7]

This reverence for the antiquity of Parliament's rules, and their essentially indefinable terms and extent, concealed numerous problems in practice. It did not mean that they were unchangeable: a procedural tract composed during the 1760s referred to as the *Liverpool Tractate* (discussed by David Natzler in chapter 5) notes several changes of practice, and even generally acknowledged absurdities in seventeenth-century practice which

---

[4] [George Philips] *Lex Parliamentaria: or, a Treatise of the Law and custom of Parliaments*, 2nd ed (1734) preface.

[5] Thomas Erskine May, *A Treatise upon the Law, Privileges, Proceedings and Usage of Parliament*, 1st edn (London, 1844) (hereafter, in all editions, *Treatise*) 29.

[6] He held that office for 52 years, from 1768 until his death in 1820.

[7] John Hatsell, *Precedents of Proceedings in the House of Commons with Observations* (in four vols 1776–1818, repr Shannon, Irish University Press, 1971) preface to vol 4.

still theoretically applied. But it did mean that an enormous stress was laid on precedent, and knowledge of precedent. The first edition of the *Treatise* explained the sources of parliamentary rules:

> The proceedings of Parliament are regulated chiefly by ancient usage. … Ancient usage, when not otherwise declared, is collected from the Journals, from history and early treatises and from the continued experience of practised members.[8]

As in the common law, any particular question was approached through establishing how similar cases had been resolved in the past. Parliamentary law, therefore, was largely a matter of knowing precedents. In chapter 4, Martyn Atkins describes the long struggle to bring some order to the records of the Commons (its Journals) and then to provide some sort of information retrieval system to them in the form of indexes.

There was impatience with precedent as a guide to the present long before May published his *Treatise*. Alexander Wedderburn protested in exasperation in 1770: 'Is there no rule to govern an assembly by but that of precedents? Is there no rule that results from the reason of the thing?'[9] The actual approach to the use of precedent was more complex and less reverential than the quotations above suggest. Precedents could be used as evidence of the settled practice of the House: outlying precedents or clearly poor ones could be ignored. In many cases, precedents were used as a way of backing what might in legal terms be called maxims, or what May might later call principles. And ultimately, a decision on how to proceed was in the hands of a majority of the House, which was perfectly free to ignore all argument from procedural propriety, if it wished to do so. Speaker Denison, in 1870, recalled 'Old Mr Ley' (probably John Henry Ley, Clerk in succession to Hatsell) saying: 'What does it signify about precedents? The House can do what it likes. Who can stop it?'[10]

So despite the way they were claimed to have been fixed centuries earlier, the House's procedures as they stood when May arrived were flexible and uncertain, and ultimately only as strong as the House's collective willingness to pay attention to them, and the powers of persuasion of those who were charged with maintaining them. This flexibility and adaptability has persisted into the present century—arguably it has accelerated to a pace that has left the notion of governing principles behind. The fact that, for a remarkably long time after they appeared to be obsolete, some of the earliest descriptions of parliamentary procedure described by David Natzler in chapter 5 continued to be cited and used was perhaps more due to a pride in Parliament's antiquity than to their practical value. But it also testifies to the lack of authoritative and persuasive guides to practice in the House of Commons until Hatsell made his great attempt to collate them (his work is discussed by Paul Seaward in some detail in chapter 6). Hatsell was the greatest systematiser of parliamentary procedure before May, in his *Precedents of Proceedings in the House of Commons with Observations*, published in four volumes between 1776 and 1796. While assembling his work, Hatsell observed pragmatically that:

> It is more material that there should be a rule to go by than what that rule is, in order that there may be a uniformity of proceeding in the business of the House, not subject to the momentary caprice

---

[8] *Treatise*, 1st edn, 131.

[9] PDG Thomas, *The House of Commons in the Eighteenth Century* (Oxford, Clarendon Press, 1971) 9.

[10] John Evelyn Denison, Viscount Ossington, *Notes from my Journal when Speaker of the House of Commons* (1900) 260. Ley echoes the Speaker in the 26 April 1675 debate: 'The House is no more bound by one order than another; you are masters of it as in Bills to be read by order, and the question put, and the day sometimes altered.'

of the Speaker or to the captious disputes of any Members ... it is not so material that the rule should be established on the foundation of sound reason and argument as it is that order, decency and regularity should be preserved in a large, numerous and consequently sometimes tumultuous assembly.[11]

Nonetheless, Hatsell believed it was only by a 'strict adherence' to precedent, the 'forms and rules of proceedings' that

the weaker party can ... be protected from those irregularities and abuses which these forms were intended to check, and which the wantonness of power is but too often apt to suggest to large and successful majorities.[12]

Curiously, Hatsell's work survives most visibly in the modern world in the form of Thomas Jefferson's *Manual of Parliamentary Procedure* (see chapter 8) which continues to hold some sway in the US Congress as a final authority on procedure. In the opening pages of the *Manual*, Jefferson quotes Hatsell quoting Speaker Onslow (Speaker from 1728 to 1761) to the effect that:

[N]othing tended to throw more power into the hands of the administration and those who acted with a majority of the House of Commons than a neglect of or departure from the rules of proceeding.[13]

The belief that the purpose of procedure is principally to protect the minority is one that did not necessarily remain the dominant view in the centuries that followed.

This appeal to precedent as the validating authority for procedure meant that for most practitioners the vast majority of parliamentary rules and practices had no easily discernible origin, and since they had never been deliberately formulated as a procedural code were largely inaccessible to the user. Like the common law, they had developed over centuries, and were supposed to have reached perfection through a long process of collective reasoning. As May observed in the first edition of his *Treatise*, 'step by step the legislature has assumed its present form and character; and after many changes its constitution is now defined by "The clear and written law, the deep-trod footmarks / Of ancient custom".[14]

Antiquity was presumed by the defenders of precedent to confer on Parliament's procedures an awe-inducing prestige. An 1816 review of the speeches of William Pitt and Charles James Fox related parliamentary procedure to the conservative but assimilative power of the British constitution:

Our constitution has in nothing so strikingly displayed its superiority over other systems, as in the counterpoise it opposes to a crude spirit of reformation, and in that happy union of forbearance with improvement which has marked every stage of its gradual development. The fury of change has always found in the details of parliamentary procedure those wholesome intervals which allow time for the re-action of cautious habits and sober inquiry.[15]

May came to this body of precedent as both an ambivalent admirer and (to begin with) a determined reformer. His work to repair and renew the procedures of the House is

[11] Hatsell (n 7) vol 2, 198.
[12] ibid, 171–72.
[13] Jefferson's *Manual* is reprinted as part of the *Rules of the House of Representatives of the United States* for each Congress. The quote is from p 1.
[14] *Treatise*, 1st edn, 1.
[15] 'Parliamentary Speeches of Mr Pitt and Mr Fox' in (1816) VII *British Review* 253–54.

documented by Sir William McKay and Colin Lee in chapters 9 and 10. May noted in 1854 (just before the publication of the third edition of the *Treatise*) that:

> [T]he antiquity of our Parliamentary forms, and the almost unvarying steadiness with which they have been observed for at least three centuries, is a remarkable feature of our Constitution. … There is a dignity as well as merit in this force of ancient custom, which secures a more willing and reverential obedience than any modern rules or byelaws.

But he went on to bemoan the lack of progress in making any permanent reform of the procedures of the House and laid the blame for this on the excessive piety for antiquity, which, he feared, 'had degenerated into fanaticism'. Despite the adoption of Westminster's forms throughout the world 'here again, the true faith has not been unmixed with idolatry; and to discontinue an old form was to cast down an idol'.[16]

Though broadly working within the same conceptual framework, Hatsell and May in some ways represent two contrasting approaches to procedure. It would be easy to read Hatsell's *Precedents* and come away with little or no idea how Parliament actually worked or why. In the introduction to his first volume, Hatsell warns that his readers must not suppose 'that the Observations upon the several cases are made with a view to declaring what the Law of Privilege is'. May, in contrast, was looking to derive principles and deduce general rules, 'preferring brief statements of the general results of precedents to a lengthened enumeration of the precedents themselves'. May was at heart a liberal and a moderniser who believed that 'organisation is not less essential in a senate than in a factory'.[17] But he was a cautious and tactical one, not above using precedent when it suited his modernising purposes. When seeking to justify the closure procedure, he reported in his diary that he had 'found what convinces the House of Commons more readily than any argument—I have found a precedent'.[18]

THE AGE OF CODIFICATION

Chapter 7 recounts briefly the history of the development of the *Treatise* from 1844 to the present, where it is still regarded with reverence. Chapter 8, written by an international cluster of Clerks, discusses its influence abroad, and recounts how the daughters of the Westminster Parliament found it necessary to shape their own procedures to their local needs, and to write their own bibles. It cannot, though, just have been May's skill and salesmanship, combined with the learning and piety of his successors, which has made the *Treatise* such an enduring authority in Westminster and abroad. May's life and career spanned a period of profound change in the representative politics of the United Kingdom, in the nature of Parliament, and in the role of government. He joined the House service three years before the passing of the Great Reform Act; he retired two years after the passing of the Third Reform Act. Parliament and parliamentarians were passing through what was, perhaps, the greatest upheaval in the institution in its history, aside from the period of the

---

[16] Thomas Erskine May, *The Machinery of Parliamentary Legislation* (London, Longmans, Green and Co, 1881) 4.

[17] ibid, 2.

[18] Cited by WR McKay in his Introduction to the 24th edn of the *Treatise*, 8.

Civil Wars and the Protectorate. The Commons was struggling to adapt to modernity, and May was there to watch, analyse and assist from his seat at the very heart of the Chamber (a Chamber in a Parliament building which had been created as a sort of neo-gothic Victorian cathedral dedicated to the British constitution). Chance placed him at almost the very centre of progress and change. The *Treatise* and the Palace of Westminster are perhaps two of the most enduring symbols of the constitutional settlement which took much of its shape in the Victorian era and still survives in great part to this day. Whether the *Treatise*, beneath the grandiloquent surface, is in as bad a shape as is the hidden wiring and plumbing and the roofs and cellars of the Palace is a question on which the readers of this volume, or the *Treatise* itself, may draw their own conclusions.

May took his chance to influence procedural change during this tumult of modernisation, as is chronicled by Sir William McKay in chapter 9. So what might be presumed to be the principal features of the 'Old Procedure' from which the Victorians, with Erskine May's help, made a so decisive a break?

The business of the Commons had been regulated by ad hoc motions rather than by any standing orders which could be consulted in advance and on which one might reasonably hope to predict the order and duration of the day's business. It required eighteen (or, according to some authorities, seventeen) debatable and votable motions just to get through the procedural stages of a Bill—excluding consideration of any amendments or clauses. The unsuitability of the House of Commons as a way of making serious and workable law became painfully obvious to anyone who actually saw it in operation and studied its products, rather than listened to the constitutional mythology. The value attached to the arcane forms of parliamentary procedure related partly to the way in which they placed obstacles in the way of those who wished to pass laws. The seventeenth century inhibited legislators as much as possible. It was a procedure that was stacked in favour of an opposition. Moreover, the House of Commons was frequently not only politically, but also procedurally and legislatively, chaotic and incoherent. Although from well before the 1832 Reform Act the House of Commons had spent much time discussing the procedural obstacles to effective government, its achievements in actually changing anything were modest.

It may to some have seemed a delightful if exasperating kind of anarchy. But the fact that the House had no systematic set of rules, clearly understood and set out, at least in relation to its mainstream public business, was clearly the source of some unhappiness even in the late seventeenth century. Hakewill in 1641 said that if the Commons followed the Lords' practice in having a simple list of rules and orders, it would save much time spent in debating what the orders were. Committees were set up in 1667, 1668 and 1674 to review the practices of the House, and in the words of the last of them, 'to consider the ancient orders of the House, and present such as are for the better decency, and orderly sitting, in the House'. During a debate in 1675, some regret was expressed about the lack of 'the records of your Standing Orders, whereas in the Lords House they have standing Orders and Rules'.

Did the existence of this state of cheerful chaos matter? Another factor in the formation of the House's culture which permeates the *Treatise* is the role of the Speaker and the reverence accorded to that office. The fact that Brand got away with his famous invocation of the closure in January 1881 is some evidence of his stature. May dedicated his first edition of the *Treatise* to the then Speaker, Charles Shaw Lefevre, and every subsequent edition has been similarly dedicated. The independence of the presiding officer is an important element of the House's procedures. It is supported by an elaborate theology of impartiality, which is in itself part of the treasure house of precedent, and which helps protect the House from any 'momentary caprice of the Speaker' against which John Hatsell warned. The third great source of the rules of procedure (alongside precedent, and the standing orders) are rulings from the Chair—the reinterpretation of rules, customs and conventions by the Speaker which helps to marry tradition to modern circumstances and to temper procedural propriety with an appreciation of that mysterious miasma, the mood of the House. The decisions from the Chair (as a series of privately printed records prepared by the Clerks and made available to the House during the later nineteenth and earlier part of the twentieth centuries was titled) could be of immense political significance. Evelyn Denison, Speaker from 1857, in his private journal agonised over the question in 1858 of whether an amendment to the order of the day for the second reading of a bill would be in order—mainly because his acceptance of the amendment, which was then carried, set off a chain of events which led to the fall of the government of Lord Palmerston. Procedural complexity reinforced uncertainty in a political context which was already uncertain enough as a result of the weakness of party ties, and placed the Chair in often agonising dilemmas in seeking to find a precedent that would lead the House out of yet another impasse or protect against yet another raid by the executive on its powers.

The slow change to a more formal procedural code for the House of Commons over the nineteenth century was the by-product of a gradual transformation in the House's procedures in the sixty years after the 1832 Reform Act. In some ways it mirrored the reforms which took place in common law procedure through the great commissions of the 1820s and 1830s. The organic or chaotic nature of Parliament's rules and procedures was analogous to the equally frequently criticised state of the English common law during the late eighteenth century.[19] The defenders of the common law against codification would argue that a system based on precedent provided flexibility and evolutionary change. The codifiers might have been more inclined to agree with another Clerk of the House of Commons, Courtenay Ilbert, who characterised the period after the century of revolutions in the following rather derogatory terms:

> The principles evolved in creative and revolutionary periods were laboriously reduced to form, and in the process life and growth were often arrested and tendencies were ossified into dogmas. Parliamentary procedure became a mystery, unintelligible except to the initiated, and the officials who formulated the rules were not anxious that their knowledge should be too widely shared.[20]

Procedural reform was not, however, debated either so vigorously or so rigorously as the reform of the law. But the resistance to change, largely arising from the reluctance of individual Members to abandon a flexibility that allowed them to raise almost any subject almost whenever they wished (and perhaps of Clerks to relinquish control over their inaccessible store of occult arcana), was not dissimilar to the claims of the opponents of legal reform. Reform took place steadily in the common law over the thirty or forty years after

---

[19] This provoked Jeremy Bentham's hugely ambitious attempt to create a legislative code. His attempt to make sense of parliamentary procedure, described briefly in chapter 9, is less well known.

[20] Redlich (n 1) Preface, xviii.

the Reform Act. But providing Parliament with a more certain procedural code was far less systematic and far less considered than that process: it was rather more a series of minimal responses to intense pressure until, finally, the pressure became so intense that drastic reforms became unavoidable.

There were outside forces driving change, as well as internal discontents. If the seventeenth century had been about subordinating the monarch to Parliament, the nineteenth was about subordinating Parliament to the people. That century was dominated by franchise reform and the increasing democratisation of the Commons. The pressure on Parliament in the early nineteenth century to respond to a growing and more engaged electorate, both through legislating and through articulating their concerns, was undoubtedly becoming intense. The emergence of the Commons as an active law-making institution was an enormous challenge to a set of procedures designed almost positively to discourage legislation.

In addition, by the early nineteenth century the government was itself becoming much more concerned than before to promote reforming legislation. This was the period in which the foundations of what is still recognisably the modern state were laid down by statutes regulating employment, housing and public health, establishing something approaching universal education, reforming the universities, and creating local authorities with extensive powers of their own, amongst many other social and economic reforms. And from the middle of the century, or certainly after the Second Reform Act, we begin to see the emergence of the political parties as national organisations. All these developments were to have a transforming effect on Parliament and the way it organised itself. The growth in the number of MPs wanting to speak, particularly in order to obtain publicity in their local newspapers, and the greater assiduity displayed by those elected for larger, more demanding constituencies has been well established.[21] Lord John Russell resisted in 1850 the claim that the government was responsible for the limited amount of time left to private Members by pointing out that:

> Another circumstance which appeared to him to stand in the way of speedy legislation at all times was this, that the more Members of the House turned their attention to public subjects, and the more Members there were who were capable of addressing the House on such subjects, the more time would be consumed in discussing any question. ... In these days there was far more attention paid, not only to the principle but to the details of every measure, and there was a far greater number of Members ready to address the House, and to enforce their views, than had been formerly the case. That was a change which had taken place quite independently of any Government or of any legislation.[22]

Under these pressures, the unsuitability of the House of Commons as a way of making serious and workable law became more painfully obvious. By the time of the first editions of the *Treatise* little change had been reflected in the permanent rules of the House, despite the best efforts of the reformers aided by the increasingly indispensable official, Thomas Erskine May.

It has been argued that there was a procedural revolution over the early nineteenth century, which chiefly consisted in the Cabinet gaining a large measure of control over

---

[21] Gary W Cox, *The Efficient Secret: The Cabinet and the Development of Political parties in Victorian England* (Cambridge, Cambridge University Press 1989) 54–56.

[22] House of Commons Debates, 12 August 1850, vol 113, cc 1029–43.

to a standstill, and helped precipitate a sea-change in the balance between the powers of the majority and the minorities.

The Irish Party's campaign of obstruction was first unleashed in 1877, and attempts to use procedural moves to block proceedings on certain Bills began to force drastic changes. A new standing order passed in 1880 created powers to exclude persistently obstructive Members from the House. The most notorious episode of obstruction was the sitting of 31 January 1881 which was only brought to an end when the Speaker refused to allow further Members to speak and the House agreed to a new set of rules known as the 'urgency procedure'. Further changes were brought in over the next few years. A regular time for the meeting of the House was fixed in 1886; standing committees were established in 1882 on a temporary basis, made into standing orders in 1888; a final resolution of the long-running issue of Members delaying the House going into Committee of Supply was achieved in 1882; there was a deliberate attempt to systematise the order in which private Members' Bills were taken. The closure was formalised in standing orders in 1887. Over the course of the 1880s the House's procedure was drastically reformed, putting enormous power into the hands of the majority. Some of the new procedures remained outside the pale of the standing orders: the guillotine—a draconian motion setting the times at which proceedings on various parts of a bill would be brought to an end—was introduced through rules brought in shortly after the urgency rule was established in February 1881, but was not incorporated into the standing orders for many more years. But with such few exceptions, when this reaction against the liberalism of previous procedure was consolidated in 1888 with the conversion of a series of previous reforms into standing orders, the House had effectively created for the first time at least part of a written and formally promulgated parliamentary code.

AFTER MAY

It was into this rather chaotic world that May had first launched his attempt to pin down exactly what the rules of procedure were and began to develop procedural science. Most of the changes described above took place during the period in which he produced his own nine editions. Since 1844 the *Treatise* has been the only true and complete record of the changing nature and interpretation of the rules, as the House of Commons struggled to find ways to address the huge variety of challenges it has faced in the last century and a half. The curious immortality of the *Treatise* in the hands of May's successors has entrenched its position so deeply that it cannot now be referred to in the media or almost anywhere else—where it is always known as 'May' or 'Erskine May'—without the accompanying phrase 'the bible of parliamentary procedure'. It was once quite regularly 'brandished' on the floor of the House at moments of controversy, though claims of alleged sightings of this activity are less common nowadays than they once were.

But contemporary seekers after guidance who have recourse to May might be disappointed if they hope for a clear and unambiguous statement of the rules by which the House conducts itself. As chapter 7 recounts, the *Treatise* as it now stands is the product of many hands and many revisions, and of many different views of parliamentary procedure, despite intermittent heroic attempts to tidy it up. Occasionally it plumbs unfathomable depths of ambiguity. To that extent it is quite like the Bible (and, as Emma Crewe notes in chapter 3, the Clerks have a certain priestly quality in their role in interpreting the law of Parliament). And as with the Bible, there are regular attempts to usurp its position as the sole repository of revealed truth. Its canonical status is certainly contestable, and its value as an aid to interpretation sometimes questionable. Chapter 17 offers a critique of this quality of ambiguity.

MODERNISTS AND METHUSELAS

The third part of this book looks, in different ways, at how procedure developed during and after May's lifetime, and sometimes seeks explanations for why it has taken the turns it has. Although most often driven by governments, change has also been contemplated by a long series of Procedure Committees, appointed either to solve a particular problem (which they only occasionally managed to do) or to engage in a vaguer but more wide-ranging process of modernisation. In chapter 12, Mark Egan traces the conclusions and recommendations of these committees since May's time. This record of the House's attempts to solve particular problems raises the wider question, for the more philosophically inclined observer, of the greater purpose of procedural reform. There appear to be two basic drivers of its development. The earlier forms of procedure, described above, were designed principally to keep the monarch, and subsequently the Cabinet, in check. As the modern age progressed through the nineteenth and twentieth centuries, the purpose of procedure came increasingly to be seen as to deliver the government's agenda—as efficiently as possible. Cecil Scott, writing in 1952, characterised these two tendencies as the Modernists and the Methuselas.[26] These two aims have remained constantly in tension. With the development of standing orders, by the beginning of the First World War, the procedures of the House of Commons were built around sustaining the party that could secure a majority in power, in order to deliver a manifesto programme of reform (or reaction to reform). And it was not just the statist-inclined radical parties that promoted this agenda—the Balfour reforms of 1902 were the major annexation of the time of the House by government. By 1908 there were ninety-six standing orders, all but five of which had been made after 1832.

What are the tangible procedural outcomes of these opposing philosophies? WH Greenleaf, in his book on *The British Political Tradition*, gave his own particular version of these two opposing views of procedure:

> The libertarian, wishing as he does to restrict the field of government action, will necessarily stress the need to revivify parliamentary powers of inquisition and control and to limit the flow of statute-making. On the other hand, the collectivist will tend to see Parliament as a legislative machine, a means of processing and legitimizing the ever more numerous proposals of the executive for the achievement of the general good; and in the last resort he will allow no procedural device or scrutiny to stand in the way.[27]

Or to put it another way, the organic, common law approach to procedure will tend to privilege decision over dissent, individual veto over the collective will. Or alternatively, the

[26] Lord Campion et al, *Parliament: A Survey* (London, George Allen & Unwin, 1952) 248.
[27] WH Greenleaf, *The British Political Tradition* (London, Methuen, 1987) vol 3, 763.

Methuselas see the purpose of Parliament as stopping the government doing things to us, while the Modernist will tend to see its primary purpose as being to enable the government to do things for us. The distribution of these two ways of thinking across the political spectrum from right to left is not quite as even as Greenleaf suggests.

In the USA there are a number of popular manuals which seek to apply what is called generically 'parliamentary procedure' to the meetings of associations, clubs, citizens' groups, and so forth—essentially any self-governing, voluntary organisation. Curiously, these manuals seem to have died out in the UK. One of these US examples is Alice Sturgis's *The Standard Manual of Parliamentary Procedure* which argues, with admirable clarity and assertiveness, the cheerfully collectivist view that:

> Parliamentary law is the procedural safeguard that protects the individual and the group in their exercise of the rights of free speech, free assembly, and the freedom to unite in organizations for the achievement of common aims. These rights ... are meaningless, and the timeless freedoms they define can be lost, if parliamentary procedure is not observed. ... The philosophy of parliamentary law is constructive—to make it easier for people to work together effectively and to help organizations and members accomplish their purposes.[28]

While the two philosophical camps might be able to agree, then, that Parliament is about the struggle of ideas, one prioritises actions and outcomes, the other deliberation and caution.

In 1906, Josef Redlich, an Austrian academic, liberal politician and intellectual, published (in German) his great work of observational anthropology on the parliamentary procedure of Westminster. He was on a mission to educate the continentals in the ways of democracy. He concluded that parliamentary procedure was 'no ordered scheme, planned by one powerful mind', and that 'the historic order of business of the House of Commons was never affected, either as a whole or in its separate parts, by juristic speculation or political theory', but that 'its origins and growth, the cautious, often imperceptible, transformations which it underwent, sprang from practical wants, expressed the actual facts of political power and of historic constitutional relations'.[29]

That appears to put Redlich firmly in the camp of those who saw the purpose of parliaments as to enable the creation of a modern and efficient state, privileging not opposition (or even that modern idea 'scrutiny') but effective governance. Indeed, he described his purpose in researching and writing his book as being to answer the question of how a parliament was to 'discharge the function of enabling the state to perform its regular work'.[30] Another, later-twentieth-century, more radical expression of this philosophy of procedural reform was perfectly encapsulated by a delegate to the Labour Party Conference in 1933, who declared that:

> Parliamentary procedure was ... devised to protect property from the King. It is being used now to protect property from the people, and socialism involves the transference of property and the abolition of the powers of property. We have got, therefore, to be prepared to recast the whole form of procedure by democratic government in order to carry through our programme.[31]

---

[28] Alice Sturgis, *The Standard Code of Parliamentary Procedure*, 4th edn (New York, McGraw-Hill, 2000) 2.
[29] Redlich (n 1) xxix.
[30] ibid, xxiii.
[31] Labour Party, *Report of the 33rd Annual Conference Held at the White Rock Pavilion, Hastings, October 2nd to 6th 1933*, 163.

And indeed, over the following eighty years pretty much the whole form of parliamentary procedure has been recast. The major waves of procedural reform have come from radical governments in a hurry to drive through major social reform: the Liberal government of 1905 and the Labour governments of 1945 and 1997; but Conservative governments have played their part and, generally, played along with reform. Writing in 1952, Gilbert Campion, a former Clerk of the House, argued:

> I have tried to show that the restrictive effect of the modern standing orders is confined to a part only of the field of parliamentary debate. They are devised mainly to benefit the Government which has by their means so far reduced opposition as to treble the speed of the legislative process during the last fifty years. But there remains a great block of business [which] retains the characteristics of the traditional practice of the House, free of restrictive standing orders and serving the purposes of the minority. ... It must be admitted that these opportunities have accrued to the organized opposition at the expense of the individual member, who is progressively deprived of the rights which the old procedure gave him. But it is worth noting that of the whole field of parliamentary business a considerable portion remains which is governed by the spirit of the traditional procedure rather than by the standing orders.[32]

However, the process of attrition which Campion had analysed in 1952 continued over the next fifty years. By 2010, all the time of the House was, at least technically, at the disposal of the government, with the exception of twenty opposition days and thirteen Fridays reserved for private Members' Bills. A member of the Cabinet, the Leader of the House, had the final say on its agenda. Writing in 1903, Josef Redlich, had let slip a rather wistful observation. He mused:

> However complete the reforms of the nineteenth century may have been, the procedure [of the House of Commons] remains a thoroughly English piece of construction, it has not lost the ancient Gothic style. Far from it; the rebuilding which has taken place has left the historic foundations untouched wherever they are capable of supporting the superstructure; it has left many a wing of the rambling fabric with scrolls and ornaments unmutilated; if we are to feel at home in the new mansion we must learn all about the plans of the old.[33]

It is perhaps more debatable whether the reforms of the twentieth century have left much of the historic foundations visible.

Take, for example, financial procedure, which is discussed by Colin Lee in chapter 15. The control of supply—that is, deciding how much money the government can raise through taxes and then deciding what it can be spent on—is, according to constitutional theory, the fundamental reason for the existence of the House of Commons. And yet we have moved a long way from the prolonged proceedings of the Committees of Supply and of Ways and Means under the Old Procedure. In 1900, the process of agreeing supply, already considerably simplified, took about a third of the time available to the House. Balfour's reforms of 1902 reduced this to twenty-odd days. In 1931, Winston Churchill described debates on the Estimates as 'the most worthless of any I have known in my career'.[34] Over the

---

[32] Lord Campion et al (n 26) 166.
[33] Redlich (n 1) xxxvii.
[34] Oral evidence to the Select Committee on Procedure on Public Business, 16 March 1931, HC (1930–31) 161, Q 1527.

following half-century the connection between the debates held on these days and the details of the public finances became increasingly tenuous. In the 1960s the ancient Committees were abolished, and in 1982 the House abandoned all pretence of a connection between the debates chosen by the Opposition and the control of finance, and created the modern 'Opposition Days'. We are now left with three 'Estimates Days' each session when, after a debate on a select committee report or two, only loosely connected with the national finances if at all, the House nods through the £700 billion or so of public spending. The House of Commons Procedure Committee recently described today's procedures for the approval of government spending as 'neither fish nor fowl'. The Committee went on to assert that:

> They are an unsatisfactory way of ensuring debates on matters of policy chosen by select committees rather than Government or Opposition, and they are an ineffective way of allowing all Members of the House an opportunity to voice their views on aspects of the Government's spending plans (whether their concerns are about efficiency, economy or effectiveness). They are baffling in their structure and purpose to anyone who is not well-versed in the complex mechanisms of parliamentary approval of Supply.[35]

But the reforms that led to this situation were a rational solution to the problem of voting supply and a pragmatic response to where the interests of MPs seem to lie. Although it took some time to complete the reform process, the scrutiny of expenditure has now been delegated, in practice, to the select committees of the House. But the result appears to have been to make the control of supply something in which no backbencher, or even opposition party, appears to feel it has any great stake, at least so far as debating it on the floor of the House goes. It is very difficult to trace the foundations of a profoundly important constitutional principle in the modern procedures.

More significant even than the control of supply is, perhaps, legislative procedure, discussed in chapter 13. At the beginning of this century a yet more comprehensive and 'rational' solution was introduced—'programming' of legislation—which essentially involves timetabling every stage of a Bill's progress after its second reading. This may be the rational and efficient reform that has had the most profound effect on the House of Commons Chamber in a century. It is still the subject of controversy, and many believe that the quality of the House of Commons' scrutiny of legislation in the era of programming is the strongest remaining argument for having a House of Lords.

Curbing of loquacity and prolixity has been a preoccupation of procedural reformers as long as they have been writing their books and pamphlets. In the last decade something happened which would once have been considered barbaric—the introduction of time limits on speeches in debate. Although the House proceeded gingerly with this notion to begin with, nowadays probably more speeches from the backbenches are time-limited than not. Whether the bargain struck these days—a lot of four- to six-minute speeches and wider participation—is better than fewer lengthy and often dull speeches, but with time occasionally to develop a complex argument other than from the front bench, is a matter for debate.

---

[35] Fifth Report from the Procedure Committee of Session 2016–17, *Authorising Government Expenditure: Steps to More effective Scrutiny*, HC 190, para 70.

However, in recent years there have also been some procedural developments which seem to go against the general direction of travel towards greater efficiency. In a concatenation of circumstances which began with the expenses débâcle of 2008–09, and ended with a coalition government, in 2010 the House took the first step in a century and a half to reverse the drift of the control of its agenda to the government. About a fifth to a quarter of the time available for debate was handed over to backbenchers, and a committee was elected to distribute the time. A startling and surprising feature of this reform was that there were very few restrictions placed on the kind of motions that could be debated at these times—in theory it is possible for the House's backbenchers, should they be able to assemble a cross-party majority, to amend its standing orders to reduce further the government's grip, or at least to do something in the face of government opposition. Previously, all the government needed to do was fail to find time for any inconvenient business. In practice, with a few notable exceptions (for example, on the EU referendum), the Backbench Business Committee has been quite conservative in its approach, and the 'Westminster Spring' which the most enthusiastic champions of reform had hoped for has not quite happened. Nonetheless, the simple expedient of asking backbenchers what they want to debate has certainly had a modestly revivifying effect on the Chamber, and seems to have engaged the attention of the electorate more effectively.

Another example is the parallel Chamber of the House (known, misleadingly, as 'Westminster Hall')—a concept that procedural traditionalists would once have said was inconceivable, as the House could not possibly be in two places at once. But the House has granted itself the gift of bilocation. As originally conceived, Westminster Hall was a vehicle for debating a whole range of potential matters, probably of a largely non-party nature, before referring them back to the plenary for decision. In practice, it has never been used for this. Although scorned by a significant part of the House as the epitome of a 'talking shop', in 'Westminster Hall', for three or four days a week, individual backbenchers, groups of backbenchers and select committees, operating in a discursive and non-decision-oriented procedure, raise many points of concern, ranging from the most local to the most wide and international, and they seem to enjoy the opportunity. Since 2015, one of these sittings has been put at the disposal of the revived Petitions Committee, which channels the enthusiasms and obsessions of the electorate expressed through e-petition to debate in the House.

The most famous of these procedural innovations is the departmental select committee system—now approaching its fortieth birthday. Although select committees are in fact as old as the House itself, pretty much, and have proved to be a very flexible instrument, the establishment of the departmental select committee system and its offshoots, which over the last thirty-odd years has grown massively in resources, professionalism and public esteem, has been the most profound change in Parliament of the last century. The notion of 'scrutiny'—a rather old-fashioned idea of checking government excess—has become a common term in the political lexicon. The centre of gravity of the House of Commons has certainly shifted dramatically from the Chamber to the committees. And, strikingly, in their purer form, as Mark Hutton recounts in chapter 14, select committees are largely rule-free zones, able to innovate and shape their ways of working to very different circumstances. They deliberate rather than debate, and they do it in private. In public, they converse (more or less politely and constructively) with the unelected in all shapes and sizes—not only the mighty but sometimes the humble and the meek as well. And the public seem to like

1

A Sycophant of Real Ability

The Career of Thomas Erskine May

WILLIAM McKAY

1850: NOT THE FITTEST MAN FOR THE POST

T HE DEATH OF John Henry Ley, the Clerk of the House, in the middle of August 1850, was unexpected and awkward. No plans had been made for the succession, though Mr Speaker Shaw Lefevre and Lord John Russell, the Prime Minister, agreed there was no question of promoting either the Clerk Assistant (who was the late Clerk's brother) or the Second Clerk Assistant, who was the late Clerk's son.[1] Indeed, Russell had vainly objected to the appointment of a Ley in 1841, arguing that two at the Table were enough.[2] There were other reasons for passing over the Clerk Assistant. The Speaker told Russell that 'poor William Ley is so nervous and incompetent that I fully expect to hear of his resignation now that he no longer has his brother to lean upon'.[3]

Filling the vacancy was not straightforward. The Clerk of the House was (and is) formally appointed by the Crown, on the advice of the Prime Minister. All appointments between 1748 and 1820, however, had proceeded on surrender of the patent by the outgoing Clerk in favour of a named successor. Consequently, nothing conclusive can be said about who had in fact named the successors, though since money usually changed hands these may have been private arrangements. In fact, when John Hatsell died in 1820 it was the first time since 1732 that the office had fallen vacant at a time when no one held a reversionary grant.[4]

In the early years of the nineteenth century, it must have seemed possible that the Speaker would informally acquire the right to appoint the Clerk of the House. In 1807 and again in 1812, Hatsell gave an assurance that he would not appoint a Clerk Assistant without the Speaker's assent, and in 1815 he surrendered his patent right to appoint a Deputy. In 1814

---

[1] In all, nine Leys were members of the department (not counting relatives), the first arriving in 1768 and the last departing 140 years later. In 1850 there were five: see WR McKay, *Clerks in the House of Commons 1363–1989: a Biographical List* (London, HMSO, 1989).

[2] P and G Ford (eds), *Luke Graves Hansard, his Diary, 1814–1841; A Case Study in the Reform of Patronage* (Oxford, Blackwell, 1962) 13.

[3] Russell Papers in the National Archives (RP)PRO 30/22/8d f 273, Shaw Lefevre to Russell, 3 September 1850.

[4] OC Williams, *The Clerical Organization of the House of Commons, 1661–1850* (Oxford, Clarendon Press, 1954) 100–01.

the Speaker secured the post of Second Clerk Assistant for his secretary, John Rickman, and six years later that of Clerk Assistant. In 1833, a select committee even suggested that the right to appoint the Clerk should be taken from the government and given to the Speaker, though in the event nothing was done.

Thus when JH Ley died in 1850 the situation was fluid. Shaw Lefevre's approach to Russell recognised the uncertainties. He disclaimed any wish to 'interfere in the slightest degree with any appointment which [the Prime Minister] might think it his duty to make',[5] but added that if the government had an internal candidate in mind, he 'most earnestly' wanted to be consulted before any appointment.[6] In short, if the government wished to appoint an outsider Shaw Lefevre could not stop them, but his views needed to be heard if there was an internal nomination.

The Speaker did not mention that he already had an internal candidate. Thomas Erskine May entered the service of the House as Assistant Librarian in 1831 at the age of sixteen, nominated by Mr Speaker Manners Sutton, at whose suggestion is unclear.[7] His family background is something of a mystery (see afterword) but it must have been at least comfortable. Between 1826 and 1831 he studied privately under the headmaster of Bedford School, and would have gone on to Oxford University, had he not (equally enigmatically) been 'suddenly called upon to renounce a career for which [he] had been destined'.[8] In the Library, he assisted in re-indexing the Commons Journals (see chapter 4). Shaw Lefevre claimed that May thereby acquired a sound knowledge of procedure, which underpinned his publication in 1844 of the first edition of *Parliamentary Practice*.[9]

What May had in mind in 1844 was very different from what the work became, both under his editorship and later. He wrote to the prospective publisher:

> I desire to write a concise work, explaining principles and laying down rules of practice in the shortest way, with marginal references to authorities. The citing of precedents at length makes a work very long.[10]

The Times called it a 'very lucid and valuable volume … a compact and compendious work'.[11] Shaw Lefevre thought it 'very valuable as far as it goes, and may be more complete when a new edition is published'.[12] Despite such faint praise, May's career gathered speed.

In 1847, he was appointed Examiner of Petitions for private bills, supervising the formalities of promoting private bills at the time of the railway boom, a duty which the Speaker told a select committee was 'by far the most laborious … about the House'.[13] The following year May assisted the Speaker in preparing evidence for a select committee on public business. In 1849, he published *Remarks and Suggestions … to facilitate the despatch*

[5] ERM/2/19, Mr Speaker Shaw Lefevre to Erskine May, 28 August 1850.
[6] Erskine May Papers in the Parliamentary Archives ERM/PA 2/16, Mr Speaker Shaw Lefevre to Erskine May, 22 August 1850.
[7] *The Biograph*, January 1882, 14–20.
[8] DCL Holland and D Menhennet (ed), *Erskine May's Private Journal, 1852–1882: Diary of a Great Parliamentarian* (London, HMSO, 1972) vi, 42.
[9] Since he worked on only the Journals to 1714, May's more up-to-date knowledge must have been otherwise acquired.
[10] ERM/10A/2, May to Charles Knight, 2 November 1843.
[11] *The Times*, 15 October 1844, 8.
[12] RP PRO 30/22/8d f 273, Shaw Lefevre to Russell, 3 September 1850. There were nine editions in May's lifetime.
[13] Select Committee on Private Business, 1st Report 1851 Q9 HC 1851 35 (PP 1851).

of public business.[14] The Speaker considered that May had more knowledge of the forms and practice of the House than any man since the death of Rickman.[15] Consequently, though others in the House had their eyes on the post, the 1850 vacancy could not have come at a better time for May, who improved his chances by taking the Speaker's advice to canvass Members.

The Speaker's backing was critical, but—unfortunately for May—not decisive. In part this was because he was simply out of luck. Russell had left London for the country, and before the Speaker's letter (drafted by May) reached him, he had received one from William Ley, the Clerk Assistant—the one man Russell did not want as Clerk of the House—informing him of the vacancy.[16] The Prime Minister's candidate was a senior civil servant, and Russell asked his political master to sound him out.

Sir Denis Le Marchant was the placid son of the dashing cavalry commander who had led the uphill charge of the heavy dragoons at Salamanca in 1812. Le Marchant had been everywhere—a lawyer, Brougham's secretary in the Lord Chancellor's office at the time of the Reform ministry, Clerk of the Crown in Chancery, a Whig MP, and a Minister at the Treasury and the Board of Trade[17]—and he trumped May's access to Shaw Lefevre by having been related by marriage to the Speaker. Personally, Le Marchant was keen to accept: the Clerkship was 'above all others the office which I should most wish to obtain'—even at the cost of a drop in salary.[18]

There were other advantages in appointing Le Marchant. If Speaker's Counsel replaced him at the Board of Trade, the former's duties would then be transferred to a Clerk at the Table, thus implementing the recommendations of a select committee in 1848. The Speaker was unconvinced, but by the time the House had sorted the matter out and another select committee had reported, Counsel had left for the Board of Trade and Le Marchant was Clerk of the House.

The Speaker was conscious of the appointee's shortcomings. He wrote to May years later that,

> with all possible regard for my old friend Denis Le Marchant, I thought Lord Russell's conduct in giving him the appointment (merely as a provision for a friend and an old supporter of the government) quite unjustifiable.[19]

There was, however, nothing the Speaker could do. Le Marchant was 'certainly *not* the fittest man for the post', but Shaw Lefevre could only assure Russell that 'if you are determined to appoint him, I will do my best to train him and make him a good clerk'.[20]

[14] House of Commons Paper 644 of Session 1847–48.

[15] WR McKay, *Secretaries to Mr Speaker* (London, HMSO, 1986) 11–18.

[16] Shaw Lefevre to May, 22 and 28 August 1850.

[17] D Le Marchant et al, *Three Early Nineteenth Century Diaries* (London, Williams and Norgate, 1952) and RH Thoumine, *Scientific Soldier: A Life of General Le Marchant 1766–1812* (London, Oxford University Press, 1968) 58.

[18] RP PRO 30/22/8E, Henry Labouchere to Russell, 25 August 1850 f 261 et seq; Le Marchant to the same, 26 August 1850ff. Other hats were in the ring: James Booth, Speaker's Counsel and Charles Romilly, who had been Speaker's Secretary (ERM/2/16, Shaw Lefevre to Erskine May, 22 August 185; 8/12, Sir J Brotherton MP to May, 24 August 1850; 8/14, Sir William Heathcote MP to May, 27 August 1850).

[19] ERM/2/75, Viscount Eversley to May, 31 August 1870. No one had become Clerk of the House after sitting as a Member since Thomas St Nicholas in the dark days of 1659.

[20] RP PRO 30/22/8E f 265, Le Marchant to Russell, 26 August 1850; f 265, Shaw Lefevre to Russell, 27 August 1850, same to May, 28 August 1850.

Members, too, were unhappy about the appointment of a Clerk with no procedural experience. In the debate expressing appreciation of the late Clerk, Joseph Hume, his name synonymous with economical reform and 'one of the biggest bores who ever left Aberdeen',[21] intervened to observe that:

> [O]ffices of this nature should always be filled up with a view to the public benefit, and when a vacancy occurs, due attention should be paid to the merits and capabilities of the party appointed to it.[22]

But it was too late.

1856: CLERK ASSISTANT

The Speaker tried to compensate May by dislodging the Clerk Assistant but William Ley, obstinate and obstructive, sat tight until 1856. When finally he agreed to go, he had the gall to propose his nephew Henry, then Second Clerk Assistant, as successor. The Speaker was outraged: he had to consider what was due to the House, but 'Mr Ley appears to look only to what he considers is due to himself'—an echo of John Hatsell's judgement on his Deputy, John Ley, whose idea was 'to make hay while the sun shone and nothing else'.

Ley's eventual departure brought to light a number of sensitive issues from 1850. In particular, Sir Charles Wood, Chancellor of the Exchequer, had written to the Prime Minister in August of that year recommending that the government should appoint all the Clerks at the Table.[23] Le Marchant was obliged to surrender his patent right to appoint the two Clerks Assistant. It was 'distinctly arranged' that these appointments should 'vest in the Crown': but there was no legislation, no revised patent. The Speaker, however, insisted and the government agreed that since the Clerks Assistant needed to be men upon whom he could rely, he should be given a veto on their appointments.[24] Thenceforward these were to vest in the Crown, exercisable by the Prime Minister on the advice of the Speaker.[25] The hole-and-corner nature of this transaction was well appreciated by the government, who carefully kept the details out of the newspapers.

Of course, once an appointment fell to be made, secrecy ended. A Treasury Minute of March 1856 blandly revealed everything. The new appointment had been made under the hugger-mugger arrangements of 1850 and not the statute of 1812. The government was obliged to push through Parliament an Act (13 & 14 Vict c1), belatedly amending the law on the right to appoint Clerks Assistant, and validating the most recent appointment.

---

[21] H Roseveare, *The Treasury: The Evolution of a British Institution* (New York, Columbia University Press, 1968) 145. This is an unjustified slur on the Granite City. Hume was the son of a master of a coaster trading out of Montrose, which burgh he represented.

[22] Parl Deb 1851 114 cc 138–43.

[23] Wood's proposals are in an insertion into a letter to Russell from Henry Labouchere dated 25 August 1850 (RP PRO 30/22/8E f 262). They included conferring on the Speaker the right to appoint Clerks at all lower grades, which fell by the wayside.

[24] RP PRO 30/22/8d, Shaw Lefevre to Russell, 3 September 1850.

[25] ibid f 345, Le Marchant to Russell, 24 September 1850.

been some flamboyant eccentricity in May's family background to lead one to expect such goings-on?

It is difficult to say: Erskine May's origins are a puzzle. On the one hand, contemporary records clearly identify him as the child of Thomas May, attorney (that is, solicitor) and his wife Sarah. On the other, a story was long current in his department that he was the son of Thomas Lord Erskine, Lord Chancellor, brilliant but erratic, who—dressed as a woman—went to Gretna to marry his mistress (and so legitimise their children).[63]

Parish register and census evidence confirm that Erskine May was born in Kentish Town and baptised in St Martin in the Fields on 21 September 1815.[64] His father was probably the Thomas May baptised in 1774 at Elham (between Folkestone and Canterbury) on the basis that Elham was where Erskine May's sister Lavinia died in 1886. Thomas May died probably between 1839 and 1843.[65] His wife Sarah has not been traced.

Erskine May's eldest sister, Maria Erskine May, is known to have been born in 1795 and her sister Lavinia May in 1797.[66] Anne Agnes May was born in 1802.[67] None of the girls has traceable birth records, so that the family relationships have to be pieced together indirectly. Erskine May did not include details of his parentage on his marriage certificate but when Maria married, her father was given as Thomas May; she was married from Erskine May's home; and he is a witness. The 1871 census describes Lavinia as Maria's sister. Anne Agnes died at Erskine May's house in Chester Square in 1847,[68] and her daughter Eliza Laughton lived with Erskine May and his wife as their niece until the latter's death. Finally, in his 1874 will May explicitly recognised Maria and Lavinia as his sisters, as Maria recognised him as her brother in her will.[69]

In 1839, May married Louisa Johanna Laughton, the daughter of a civil servant in Ceylon.[70] The preceding year, her elder brother Richard, a surgeon in the East India Company, had married Anne Agnes at Simla. The families had evidently been acquainted for some time, for in 1837 May had been appointed guardian of Louisa until she came of age[71]—and married her as soon as she did.

All this appears a straightforward family chronicle in which Lord Erskine makes—and need make—no appearance. May himself never seems to have claimed a Buchan connection, though he kept among his papers offprints of some of Lord Erskine's speeches. 'Erskine' as the middle names of two of Thomas May's four children might be simply admiration of a brilliant advocate: it may be by chance that Anne Agnes is the name of one of May's

[63] RG Thorne (ed), *The House of Commons 1790–1820* (London, Secker & Warburg, 1986) iii, 710–13.

[64] The entry was located by Lady Boulton; WR McKay, 'The Family Background of Sir Thomas Erskine May' (1984) LII *The Table* 96, n 3. In the 1871 census May is recorded as having been born in Highgate (see ibid, 96, n 4).

[65] A letter of 27 October 1839 from Revd George Mingaye of Chippenham refers almost certainly to May's parents (ERM/16/14) but by the time of Maria's marriage in 1843 the certificate shows her father as dead.

[66] ERM/16/33, Henry Duffell to Thomas Erskine May, 13 April 1867.

[67] May's birth in 1815 makes this a very long child-bearing period for their mother, but just within the bounds of possibility.

[68] *The Standard*, 8 November 1847.

[69] ERM/13/17.

[70] The Laughton family were descended from Revd George Laughton (1735–1800), rector of Chippenham near Newmarket. May seems to have taken a lot of social cover from the Laughtons and is buried at Chippenham. See also McKay (n 34) 2n for intriguing connections between the Leys and Chippenham.

[71] Nat Archives Prob 11, piece 1921, Arden ms 1–50 1840.

sisters and also of a sister of the eleventh earl of Buchan. Among Erskine May's papers, however, there are letters telling a different story. They were written by Sir David Erskine, an illegitimate son of the eleventh earl, and both Lord Erskine's nephew and his son-in-law. He begins in 1834 by addressing May as 'My dear Sir', which three years later becomes 'My dear Tom'. Sir David had news of Ann Agnes in India, wished to be remembered to another sister, described a Mr Erskine they had met in Melrose as 'our relation', and concluded 'long may [the sun] shine upon you, that you may revive the lustre of the Erskines at the bar of old England'.[72]

Reconciling the 'May' birth details and the 'Erskine' tradition is not easy. Lord Erskine married in the mid-1770s. His wife died in 1805 and they had eight children. Some time later he took up with Sarah Buck, a lady apprenticed to a straw-bonnet maker,[73] by whom he had four children. If he was Erskine May's father, one would have to suppose a liaison (with Sarah May the attorney's wife or anyone else) producing four more children, which began during his marriage, and continued for twenty years, overlapping with his relationship with Sarah Buck. It is possible but unlikely. A more watertight argument against Lord Erskine's paternity is that when in 1839 Revd George Mingaye summoned May to Chippenham, as his father-in-law was dying, he mentioned that May's father and mother were already there: but by then Lord Erskine had been dead for sixteen years.

Fewer difficulties arise if Sarah, the wife of Thomas May the attorney—Erskine May's mother—was a child of Lord Erskine. She may very well have been born in the 1770s before Erskine married, either before he left the army or when a little later he was studying for the bar in very modest lodgings in Kentish Town. But no evidence has so far come to light of who Sarah May's parents were.[74]

---

[72] ERM/16/9, 16/11, 16/12, Sir David Erskine to Erskine May, 23 July 1834, 8 and 23 July 1837.

[73] For Sarah Buck and Erskine, see McKay (n 64) 94 and *The Times*, 12, 14, 22, 24 July 1826.

[74] *The author would like to thank Gail Bartlett for her assistance in checking references to the Parliamentary archives.*

2

Slumber and Success

The House of Commons Library after May

OONAGH GAY[1]

THE BEGINNINGS OF THE COMMONS LIBRARY 1831–1914

T HOMAS ERSKINE MAY compiled and published the first edition of his *Treatise* while holding the post of Assistant Librarian of the House of Commons. Would May have recognised the Commons Library of today? The Library changed its name and acquired new functions in 2007 to reflect its broader roles within the House, and then divided in two in 2016. From the middle of the twentieth century the provision of rapid responses to a range of queries from individual MPs and the creation of pre-prepared briefings on current policy concerns became a core function, as well as the electronic indexing and preservation of parliamentary information and data. May's research which formed the basis of his *Treatise* was built on his experience assisting in the preparation of the systematic indexes to the Commons Journals. The main functions of the Library in the first decade or so of the twenty-first century expanded to include explaining the work of the Commons to a wider public. The importance of physical holdings of books, journals and newspapers is diminishing rapidly as internet-based storage has come of age, but finding accurate parliamentary precedents remains a vital role.

May's work as assistant Commons Librarian covered many of these functions, with the exception of public engagement, taken for granted as confined to a political elite in the early nineteenth century. After May's departure, the Library slumbered in its main functions for nearly a century. It recovered its drive and focus only with the pressure for parliamentary reform which gathered pace from the 1960s onwards. The next challenge is to see the full integration of staff within the broader corporate nature of the Commons, returning to the fluidity of function which enabled May to serve in differing posts across the Library and the Clerk's Department.

May began his career in House service as Assistant Librarian in 1831, aged sixteen. He had joined a relatively new entity within the House, as the Library had only been established since 1818. This event had taken place at the request of the Speaker, who had

[1] I am indebted to Priscilla Baines, Rob Clements and Christine Gillie, all formerly of the House of Commons Library for helpful comments. All mistakes and omissions are my own.

found the volume of acts, sessional papers and journals had accumulated to such an extent that they were not readily accessible, or being properly cared for.

The 1830s was an inauspicious decade in which to join the Library. The Librarian, Thomas Vardon, had been appointed to the post in 1831, after three years as Assistant Librarian, and was to remain in post for the next thirty-six years, still a record in Librarian terms. Two handsome rooms had been designed by Sir John Soane in the 1820s and opened in 1828, with books purchased with a £5,000 grant from the government. However, on 17 October 1834, Vardon beheld with horror the blackened remains of his Library, and the realisation that two-thirds of its stock had been lost in the great fire of Westminster Palace. Virtually all of the archives of the Commons had been lost.

The rebuilding plans for the Palace involved careful consideration of the needs of the Library and of Members. The first standing committee on the House of Commons Library had been constituted in February 1834, and was careful to exclude non-MPs from Library rooms as, astonishingly, acts and bills were being removed by lawyers anxious to find original texts. The Select Committee on Rebuilding the Houses of Parliament met in March 1835, agreeing that the Library should be given ample space in the new building. A temporary Library was established in the Long Gallery above the Public Bill and Journal Offices until the opening of the new Library suite in 1852 in the magnificent Pugin-designed Westminster Palace. From 1845 onwards the Library Committee occupied itself in selecting appropriate titles for the new holdings.

The Library suite occupied a prime location, a corridor away from the Members' Lobby and overlooking the Thames, with four spacious rooms, to which a fifth, the Reference Room, was quickly added. The design of the Library was meant to fit the dual function of a gentleman's or club library and a legislative library, with comfy leather armchairs and large desks combined with shelving from floor to ceiling. The views of Members on book purchasing became influential and by the turn of the century the Library book holdings had shifted in favour of a good club Library, and away from those of a legislative and parliamentary reference library.

Even by the 1830s some general principles had been established: firstly, that the Librarian should be paid enough for him to stay in post for some considerable time, and not be tempted to become a procedural Clerk as May did; secondly, that the Speaker should appoint the Librarian, assisted by a committee of Members, drawn from all sides of the House, which assisted with the establishment of an impartial service. These principles did not change in detail until the mid-twentieth century, when the internal structure of the Commons was modernised.

Thomas Vardon pointed out as early as 1835 that one of the main demands on his time was the provision of information to Members. He told the Library Committee in that year:

> There is no subject connected with parliamentary business, on finance or the forms of the House, or the progress of Bills or the contents of Acts, on which I am not called upon to offer instant information.[2]

This would ring true to the research Library Clerk or public outreach officer of today.

It is clear that Vardon and May spent much of their time indexing the Journals, the Public Acts and the Private Local and Personal Acts, and this work enabled May to get to grips

---

[2] Select Committee on Rebuilding the Houses of Parliament HC 104, 1835 Evidence, 13.

with the historical and legal precedents in the Journals from 1547 onwards. The first edition of the *Treatise upon the Law, Privilege, Proceedings and Usage of Parliament* was published in 1844, while he was still Assistant Librarian. The Librarian in the mid-nineteenth century had close associations with the Speaker and other senior parliamentary staff, and the Library was the primary source of information on precedents. Yet this tradition disappeared by the turn of the century.[3] May's promotion to become Examiner of Petitions for Private bills and then Taxing Master for both Houses of Parliament in 1846 may well have contributed to the diminished role of the Library.

As we learned in the preceding chapter, May became Clerk Assistant in 1856 and then had to wait fifteen years before attaining the Clerkship. In the meantime, the post of Assistant Librarian remained unfilled for two years after May's departure, until Hon George Waldegrave was appointed in 1849. He proved a worthy successor in terms of networking, becoming Secretary to Speaker Denison in 1857 and an MP in 1864.

The death in office of Thomas Vardon in 1867 after nearly forty years in the Library marked a turning point in the fortunes of his creation. May, as Clerk Assistant, took immediate advantage, moving into the vacated residence of the Librarian on the principal floor. Thereafter, the drive and impetus behind the improvement of the Library and its services to Members seemed to disappear. The new Librarian was George Howard, who had served as Assistant Librarian after the departure of Waldegrave. Denison consulted both Disraeli and Gladstone on the appointment, offering £1,000 a year, in part consideration of having lost a residence. After twenty years in post, Howard retired in 1887 and was succeeded by Ralph Charles Walpole, himself retiring in 1908. The Library had settled into being a pleasant retreat for gentlemen MPs, rather than a source of precedent. That role had been ceded to the Clerks who took on the role of indexing the Journal with the death of Vardon.

SLUMBER AND FRUSTRATION: THE EARLY TWENTIETH-CENTURY LIBRARY

Change began after the First World War, when an advisory committee of Members was established in July 1922 to assist the Speaker in the management of the Library. MPs were clearly frustrated at the state of the Library stock, which lacked up-to-date reference material and a focused approach to acquisitions. One MP, George Benson, noted: '[A]s a backbench Member in 1930 I was appalled to find the House of Commons served by a Library which had hardly progressed since 1850.'[4] A weighty voice was added by Ivor Jennings, Reader in Law at University College London, in the 1934 first edition of his influential book *Parliamentary Reform*, where he devoted a whole chapter to the inadequacies of the Library as a source of relevant information and research assistance for MPs:

> It should be one of the functions of Parliament to inform its own Members. The Library staff should therefore be able to produce information on any topic with which the House or a committee thereof, is dealing. If, for instance, the problem under discussion is local taxation, the Library should be able to produce a memorandum referring to official statistics, the reports of the numerous

---

[3] D Menhennet, *The House of Commons Library: A History*, 2nd edn (London, HMSO for the House of Commons Library, 2000).

[4] Second Report from the Estimates Committee 1960–61, HC 168 Evidence from Sir George Benson MP, 1–2.

commissions and committees which have investigated the problem in the past, reports on foreign experience, and the investigations of private research workers.[5]

The stock was in hardly better condition than the services. By 1930 the shelves were groaning with leather-bound volumes which were slowly disintegrating in situ. Double shelving had become endemic. The 1930s, however, was not a decade in which to propose additional expenditure, even for the benefit of Members, and no improvements occurred until after the Second World War. Plans were set out in 1944 for reforms, the evacuation of the Commons following the devastating bombing of May 1941 offering an opportunity for a rethink of parliamentary services, an opportunity that may come round again shortly. Most of the Library stock had been evacuated during the war (although the Library suite itself was not evacuated) and this concentrated the mind. The major factor was undoubtedly the mood of reconstruction and reform. Even before the general election in July 1945, a select committee had been appointed in April 1945 to inquire into the present state of the House of Commons Library. The chair was George Benson, whose scathing comments have been quoted above. The Librarian presented a detailed memorandum written originally for the Speaker in December 1944.[6]

TOWARDS A PROFESSIONAL SERVICE: THE 1940s TO THE 1970s

Real progress followed the select committee appointed in October 1945, which produced two reports in November 1945 and March 1946. It returned to the original vision of the Library set out by Vardon in recommending that the Library produce precise and detailed information and specialist advice to all Members. Unsurprisingly, MPs also signalled that they would require instant responses to their queries. They recommended new positions of research assistants at the same grade as clerks, and with the same status.[7] From the seven staff in post in 1945, under the Librarian John Kitto, a rapid expansion led to twenty in 1949, of whom seven were senior staff. The position of graduate Library Clerk had come into being. Evidence from the first Library handbook for Members published in 1950 showed how these principles had begun to take root. A new statistical section with two qualified statisticians existed to answer enquiries from Members and a research department also with two staff produced a wide range of bibliographic material. The shift to more analysis in research outputs was yet to come. The 1945 select committee authorised the purchasing of books to be borne on the House of Commons Estimate, an initiative which became increasingly important in expanding Library material. The stock was renewed extensively with the help of a government grant, and comprehensive author and subject indexes were compiled. The number of daily national newspapers taken increased from one in 1946 to 100 in 1950.

Most of the new Labour MPs of the 1940s and 1950s did not have independent means, and with no research assistance and very little office space available within the Palace, the Library therefore became an essential base at Westminster. The first Librarian who benefited from the embedding of the principles of library, research and information as interlinked

[5] Ivor Jennings, *Parliamentary Reform* (London, Gollancz, 1934) 162.
[6] HC 98 1944–45, Appendix A.
[7] HC 35 and 91 1945–46.

functions was Strathearn Gordon (a former Clerk) who was appointed in November 1950. Gordon instituted manuals and rules, as befitted his military background, but was a consolidator rather than innovator.

His eventual successor, David Holland, was responsible for innovative strip indexes that allowed MPs to see at a glance the progress of a bill or a committee, or a series of parliamentary documents on a similar subject. These first appeared in 1955 in the Reference Room, fitted out with newspaper chest and periodical holders. The staff complement by 1960 was thirty-two, with an annual expenditure of £40,000.[8] Further growth in status and staff took place in the 1960s, as the reform of Parliament moved up the political agenda. A career structure was created with the appointment of two Assistant Librarians and two Deputy Assistant Librarians in 1962. The Advisory Library Committee, which had been meeting since 1922, recommended a formal select committee to control Library policy in its evidence to the 1965 Palace of Westminster Select Committee.[9] This committee had been established to determine the next steps following the transfer of control in 1964 over accommodation at Westminster from the Crown to Parliament (for the Commons in the person of the Speaker). The incoming Prime Minister, Harold Wilson, had been faced with pressure from backbenchers to improve the inadequate accommodation at Westminster. A decade before, a select committee chaired by Labour MP Richard Stokes had pressed unsuccessfully for involvement by Members in the running of the Commons and a reform of governance.[10]

The need for better office accommodation for MPs and their staff was to be the main driving force behind backbench demand for effective Commons management for the rest of the twentieth century. The expansion of services for Members from 1960s onwards required reforms in internal governance, although such changes emerged only slowly. The internal structure and working arrangements at the Commons had emerged piecemeal since the nineteenth century. At this stage, the Commons was notable for its complexity, lack of transparency and absence of formal governance and accountability mechanisms which were developing elsewhere in the public sector. Now Wilson moved to establish a Services Committee for the Commons, with four sub-committees including a Library sub-committee with the Librarian in attendance. The sub-committee lost no time in recommending more staff, particularly following the 40 per cent increase in enquiries in the Research Division between 1961 and 1965. A small Scientific Section began operation within the Research Division in 1967, bringing the number of Library Clerks to eight. Most important of all, in the eyes of Strathie Gordon, was the creation of the Library as a separate department of the House from 1 August 1967. He retired a month later, his ambition met.

His successor as Librarian, David Holland, was a warm and cultured man, who had survived a prisoner of war camp during the Second World War. Under his leadership the Library blossomed. Research desks were installed in Room C of the Library suite, positioned close to the Commons chamber, enabling research staff to take face-to-face enquiries from Members and build the Library's reputation for research. The Speaker agreed in 1967 to make over his private Library situated in the current Room D to form part of the Library

---

[8] HC 168 1960–61, Evidence, Appendix B, 12–13.
[9] HC 285 1964–65. Evidence, 54–56.
[10] Report from the Select Committee on House of Commons Accommodation, 1953–54 HC 184.

Suite, which became the new quiet room for MPs. From 1968, there were four sections within the Research Division: Economic Affairs, Statistics, Home and Parliamentary Affairs, and Science, plus an International Affairs section within the Parliamentary or Reference Division. The Library was beginning to take its current shape.

The 1970s were a time of rapid growth for the Library as pressure for parliamentary reform became stronger and MPs became more professional and more demanding. The squirearchy and the trade union stalwarts were being succeeded by keen and able candidates whose primary career interest would be in the Commons, whether as minister, Shadow Cabinet or backbencher. The Library began systematic monitoring of the passage of legislation, producing reference sheets for each major government bill which became more analytical in style as the decade progressed. Enquiries from individual MPs doubled in volume. The Information Age had begun, and the Library was experimenting with computer indexing from 1968 onwards, with some government resourcing. There was cooperation with the UK Atomic Energy Authority at Culham in producing electronic current affairs indexing. Dr David Menhennet, Holland's deputy, became Librarian in 1976 and oversaw a steady expansion of services until his retirement in 1991. During his tenure, the Library was very successful in gaining and retaining new users, both within and without Westminster, as well as in obtaining the necessary resources to develop its services. The Study of Parliament Group (SPG), founded in 1964, played an influential role in emphasising the importance of information, as illustrated by its publication *The House of Commons: Services and Facilities* in 1974.

The Library had to respond to two much larger and rather different groups of customers in the same decade. In 1974, it established a branch library for the use of Members' research assistants, who were treated as a separate client group from the prime target of Members. It also set up a Public Information Office to meet the growing need to respond to telephoned enquiries from the public to House departments, ranging from procedural queries to historical enquiries about former Members, and general advice about accessing government services. Its publications included the *Weekly Information Bulletin* and the *Sessional Information Digest*, bizarrely produced quite separately from *Votes and Proceedings* and the *Sessional Return*, published by the Clerks in the Journal Office. The various House publications had overlapping content and represented the victory of the separate departmental approach, rather than a customer-focused approach. A small bi-cameral Education Unit was established in 1978 to offer a service for school visits.

The Library remained small in comparative terms. While the Commons Library had 76 staff in 1975, the parliamentary libraries in Canberra had 187 and Ottawa 180, with significantly fewer Members to work for. The Libraries at Westminster remained separate, with the House of Lords Library having an additional role as legal library to supply the Law Lords with authoritative sources for their judicial role. The Lords Library developed in tandem with the Commons in the early nineteenth century, and there has been increasing sharing of stock, but research services remain resolutely independent in each House. Peers grew jealous of the greater research specialisation in the elected chamber, but until thorough reform of the upper House occurs, amalgamation remains unlikely.[11]

---

[11] Menhennet (n 3) 104.

Two major developments in the 1970s significantly affected the future development of Library research services for the next few decades. They were first the rapid expansion of personal staff for Members, and secondly decisions on the staffing of the new system of departmental select committees from 1979. As a result priority was given to answering enquiries from individual MPs and their staff, and Library assistance to other House services was correspondingly affected. The UK model of parliamentary library began to differ significantly from its European neighbours, whose institutions prioritised work for committees.

At first the specialist Library service seemed set to dominate in terms of briefing Members. A Committee on Assistance to Private Members chaired by William Van Straubenzee in 1975 had concluded that the Library represented the best public expenditure option, given its specialist reach. Personal assistants employed by MPs themselves would have only generalist knowledge and a lack of familiarity with the sources. Since 1971 Members had been able to claim for research assistance to help with their parliamentary duties out of their secretarial allowance. Initially only £300 was available from a total of £1,000 per year, but by 1975 the Top Salaries Review Body was recommending £3200 per annum, to be used either for secretarial or research assistance. The Library Sub-Committee set a limit of 100 passes for such staff to use Library facilities in 1975.

Van Straubenzee pointed out that employing more Library researchers would enable backbench MPs to have a wide range of specialist advice, which would also help with the burgeoning constituency caseload. As MPs resigned or were defeated, the turnover of expertise among their parliamentary researchers was a wasteful use of public money. The Committee pursued a two-pronged approach of recommending the doubling of Library specialist resources as well as allowing all MPs to have personal assistance. The report itself was never formally debated by the House, but the overall strategy was adhered to, and both Library research and personal assistance for individual Members grew rapidly into the 1980s.

The Library management of the time was well aware of the dilemma. It would be more efficient to restrict the flow of public money to the personal assistants of MPs, and instead to offer a bespoke specialist research service. However, MPs wanted their own staff and in fact the staff came to be strong supporters of the Library, which provided a discreet and confidential service, enabling them to offer a fast and responsive service to their Members. However, the expansion of personal staff left MPs in effect running their own small businesses without any training, and their assistants were not given access to House development or human resources advice. These issues remain to be addressed by the House.

The Library's Education and Social Service Section was formed in the early 1980s to respond to the growing number of constituency queries handled by research assistants. Such work is valued greatly by MPs. Significant increases in personal assistance to MPs resulted from a 1990 Top Salaries Review Board report which recommended that each backbench Member should be able to employ up to three staff. The improvement in office space for MPs as result of the new buildings opposite the Treasury enabled some of these staff to be housed at Westminster, rather than in constituency offices.

Secondly, the creation of a greatly enhanced system of departmental select committees from 1979 onwards took place without a formal role for Library research staff. This was to prove a decision which limited the role of the Library within the House for forty years.[12] In view of Professor Bernard Crick's well-crafted polemic, *The Reform of Parliament*, published in 1964, which had commented on the potential for the Library to provide specialist advice for select committees and the added value that developing research expertise would bring to all Members, some attention should be paid to how this decision was made. A Treasury Organisation and Methods team had reviewed House services in 1967, concluding that Library research clerks should service select committees on a regular basis, and in fact this did occur until the mid-1970s when the growing workload led the Library to prioritise its services for individual Members over assistance to committees. This was to prove a fateful decision. The Procedure Committee noted in its seminal 1978 report advocating departmental select committees that the Library provided 'the only existing pool of full-time expert staff directly under the control of the House ... this expertise can be put to valuable use in providing background information for select committees particularly at the beginning of new enquiries'. It concluded, however, that 'it would not be right for such assistance to be provided at the expense of the Library's services to individual Members'.

There was limited enthusiasm elsewhere in the House service, a product of the cultural divide and departmentalism that marked the development of this service until the 1990s. The Library was thus thwarted in its attempt to offer research services across the whole of the Commons. The spirit of Erskine May did not live on. These two factors led the research element of the Library into a role which was more focused on the individual MPs and their constituency workload. Work for select committees took a lower priority and the Clerk's Department began to recruit its own specialist advisers for individual enquiries. Eventually these posts were augmented by full-time specialist staff and some interchange between Library and select committee specialist advisers began in the first years of the 2000s.

THE HOUSE OF COMMONS (ADMINISTRATION) ACT 1978: A HOUSE SERVICE

The SPG has had an important but largely unrecognised role in fostering parliamentary reform. It was formed in 1964 from academics with a serious interest in Parliament, and from senior clerks and Library clerks, who were anxious to ensure that reform proposals were practical and achievable. The involvement of Library staff had significant input into the growing pressure to reform the Commons, and modernise employment conditions. This meant that the SPG's focus could be more broadly based than simply procedural reform. Pressure from the Group was one of the factors that ultimately led to the first stage in the development of a more modern system of governance for the House, the House of Commons Administration Act 1978.

The immediate background to this Act was a revolt by MPs and senior staff against an attempt to create permanent Treasury control over the finances of Parliament. A small team from the Civil Service Department, led by Sir Edmund Compton, a former Comptroller and Auditor General, carried out a review of the administrative services of the Commons in 1974. The report became known as the Compton Report and was the first to propose a chief executive model for the Commons, recommending that the separate departments become

---

[12]   Procedure Committee First Report, 1977–78 HC 588, lxxxll.

a unified service.[13] The recommendation was before its time and was effectively shelved for forty years. Compton noted how the House of Commons Offices Act 1812 was hopelessly out of date, with the Commission it established failing to meet for years at a time. In reality, the government controlled the finances of the Commons, as apart from the Speaker, all other Commission members were Cabinet Ministers. Compton favoured abolition of the Commission altogether, but MPs and senior staff fought back, deprecating attempts to hand over its functions to the Chancellor of the Exchequer rather than a revitalised Commission.

In 1975 another select committee chaired by Arthur Bottomley recommended the creation of the House of Commons Commission as a substitute for Compton's Chief Officer, ensuring Member control of essential Commons services, and preserving the separate departments with direct access to the Speaker, rather than operating through a chief officer. The official Opposition and backbenchers would be represented on the proposed Commission. The trade unions within the House added their voice for reform of employment practices. The legislation to establish the Commission was passed in 1978 by a determined Michael Foot as Leader of the House, ensuring modernised terms and conditions for House staff (but not staff employed directly by Members).[14]

The Act confirmed in statutory form the agreement that formally dated from 1970 whereby the pay and conditions of staff should be kept 'broadly in line' with those in the Civil Service, the Commission would be the formal employer, and the role of Accounting Officer would be held by a member of staff (the Clerk of the House). The Act also gave the Commission power to increase or reduce the number of House departments and allocate functions to departments.

THE LIBRARY IN THE 1980s AND 1990s

The House as a whole was a relatively late adopter of information technology but from the late 1970s onwards, IT became crucial to the development of the Library into a wide-ranging information service. Initially, the services were developed for Library staff to use on Members' behalf, but gradually those services became available online throughout both Houses; later the internet enabled the department to extend its reach worldwide. During the 1980s, major resources were devoted to an electronic indexing service, the Parliamentary On Line Information System or POLIS, initially for parliamentary questions and later for bill and other proceedings and individual Members' debate contributions. The indexing was done by professionally qualified librarians in order to ensure that the material was systematically indexed. For the first time it became possible to analyse in detail the parliamentary activities of individual Members, although initially this information was used internally with only limited public access through the Information Office. As its applications became more widely understood, POLIS subsequently spread from the Library to other House departments and thus contributed in a limited way to the integration of House services.

---

[13] Review of Administrative Services in the House of Commons July 1974, HC 254.
[14] Bill Proctor, 'Implementing Ibbs' (1992) 60 *The Table* 66; detail on developments before the House of Commons Administration Act 1978 is given in M Lawrence, 'The Administrative Organisation of the House of Commons' (1980) 48 *The Table* 68 and in 'The Autonomy of Parliament' in Dawn Oliver and Gavin Drewry (eds), *The Law and Parliament* (London, Butterworths, 1998).

In 1988 the Clerks created a separate database of Early Day Motions to which the Library added subject indexing, and in 1984 POLIS was used to provide copy for the printed indexes of *Hansard* and for sessional indexes to parliamentary papers.

DEPARTMENT OF INFORMATION SERVICES: THE 1990s TO 2015

From the late 1990s the Library's focus became broader, particularly under pressure from the House's Modernisation Committee which championed the improvement of the House's services for the public and the development of parliamentary outreach. Like other House departments, the Library also had to adapt to changes in the House's sitting times and Members' growing preoccupation with their constituencies. The creation of the Parliament and Constitution Centre (PCC) in 1999 was designed to bring together Library research and outputs on Parliament itself. It combined the reference work on Parliament carried out in the main Library suite with the information presented to the public from the House of Commons Information Office, and offered quality research and interpretation on Parliament. From the beginning the Centre was focused outwards on building academic links, and publishing its standard briefings on the internet.

The Public Information Office underwent a name change to the House of Commons Information Office in 1998 to clarify its focus, and the emerging new technology enabled it to expand its services to the public, via 'find my MP services', publicising forthcoming business and tracking legislation, including statutory instruments. The Education Unit also began a visits programme and launched an exploratory website at the same time. In the early 2000s the House began to focus on public engagement. It made sense for the department for information to lead the way on promoting and supporting public engagement, with an expanded website which would make the Commons much more visible to a wide range of public, whether public bodies, constituents or specialist organisations. The Modernisation Committee's reports in the first years of the 2000s saw the provision of additional resources for the Library's existing services as the most effective way to promote public engagement.[15] The Modernisation Committee validated the increasing constituency work of MPs, as well as encouraging more meaningful scrutiny work, both in the chamber and in committee.[16] In 1996 the Top Salaries Review Board (now SSRB) noted that 'work in the constituency has increased immensely in the last 20 years or so'. These observations were repeated in its reports on MPs' pay and allowances in 2001 and in 2004.[17] With the decline in the two-party system, concerns about retaining the volatile support of the electorate led many MPs to focus on local issues and resolving local constituency problems. Their demands for advice fed through to the Library research service.

John Pullinger, a former senior government statistician, became Librarian in 2005 after the first external competition. He had no experience of House service, but arrived with a strong focus on public engagement and learning. The Education Service underwent a

[15] Modernisation Committee First Report 2003–04 HC 368, Connecting Parliament with the Public.
[16] Modernisation Committee First Report 2006–07 HC 337, Revitalising the Chamber: The Role of the Backbencher.
[17] See Oonagh Gay, 'MPs Go Back to Their Constituencies' (2005) 76 *Political Quarterly* 57 for background on the motivation for constituency work.

large expansion, and a new dedicated education building was finally created in ground adjacent to the House of Lords. This ended years of indecision. The number of visits by schoolchildren increased to nearly 50,000 a year, and state schools were heavily targeted.[18] An Outreach service was quickly established to contact external groups throughout the UK and explain how they could engage with Parliament. The UK Parliament web content became more integrated, so that parliamentary reference material, including bill trackers, visitor and media services could be found from one portal, and research briefings, online *Hansard* reporting and subject-specific topics all became readily available.

The 2010 Parliament was marked by increasing demands on research services, and by a push towards co-working by staff of select committees and Library researchers, a development that had been gathering pace since the early 2000s. The physical distance between the Committee Office and research services was, however, a significant barrier. In 2015, in a building near Westminster Abbey, Committee Office staff were mingled with Library research sections, according to subject.

Will co-location lead to a joining-up which will reverse the separation that has widened since May's time, when he established his reputation as a proceduralist while in the Library and took his deep knowledge to the Table of the House? While the functions of the two groups of staff are complementary, there may be significant resource issues that would need to be addressed for real co-working. There is a tension between flexibility and specific skills.

The Commons Library suite would be familiar to May if he were to wander the corridors of Westminster again. The Oriel Room still looks out over the Thames and offers magnificent views, as well as Pugin-style fitments, even if computer terminals now occupy significant space within the adjoining rooms. The spirit of scholarship, pragmatic political assistance, impartial service to all comers, and commitment to the central democratic institution of the nation are as present in the staff of the contemporary Library as they were in May's day.

---

[18] See House of Commons Commission Annual Report 2013–14, 6.

3

Magi or Mandarins?

Contemporary Clerkly Culture

EMMA CREWE[1]

CLERKS AS A PROFESSIONAL GROUP

IN ERSKINE MAY'S time the profession of parliamentary clerking was confined almost entirely to Westminster, though recognisable cadres of clerks had begun to emerge in his lifetime in the British colonies.[2] Clerks serve legislatures across the world, but they still constitute a small professional group with a shared focus on the rules and conventions of political processes as well as the administration of the institution of Parliament. Those working for the Commonwealth Parliaments, whose precedents and traditions owe much to Westminster, have their own society to share good practice through meetings, attachments to sister Parliaments and their own journal *The Table*.[3] Reading their journal makes it obvious that although the formal aspects of clerking may be constant across Parliaments, the politics varies in each, which in turn moulds the job of the Clerks into contrasting forms and substance. The variation in politics is relevant to understanding Clerks because, as we see from May's life, although they are the main vessels of procedural knowledge, they are also deft political observers and operators. As Clerks in different Parliaments (or even within different Houses, such as the Commons and the Lords in the UK) respond to the contrasting politics, their work and culture emerges with variation. So while we could see Thomas Erskine May as an archetype of the profession, and perhaps its most prominent role model, Clerks, like all individuals, also act in response to their particular time, as the philosopher Colapietro explained:

> Whatever counts as an individual, is historically situated. While nothing seems easier than abstracting recognizable individuals from the situations in and through which they exhibit their unique

[1] I would like to thank following Parliamentary Clerks and officials for their observations and comments: the editor of this volume Paul Evans as well as John Benger, Rob Cope, Oonagh Gay, Tom Goldsmith, Tom Healey, Philippa Helme, Sir Malcolm Jack, Robin James, Andrew Kennon, Colin Lee, Lord Lisvane, Lucinda Maer, David Natzler, Eve Samson and Hannah White. I have only named Clerks with their written consent, otherwise all informants have been anonymised unless their speech is already in the public domain. I am also grateful to Cleo Vester for her copyediting. I am responsible for all errors.

[2] For a historical account of the clerking profession at Westminster, see OC Williams, *The Clerical Organization of the House of Commons* (Oxford, Clarendon Press, 1954).

[3] <www.societyofclerks.org/SCAT_Home.asp> accessed 24 March 2015. There is also a world-wide Association of Secretaries General of Parliaments which meets under the auspices of the Inter-Parliamentary Union.

recognisability, nothing is more dangerous. Abstracting them from these situations, fosters the illusion that such individuals are related to these situations only in an external and adventitious manner. Whatever else they are, human agents are situated beings whose modes of expression, striving, and reflexivity are inescapable functions of their historical situatedness.[4]

So May was clearly a creature of his time, as were his illustrious predecessors and successors, but it is not merely, or even mostly, the heads of the profession who make its culture. The number of people working in the House of Commons nowadays who describe themselves as 'Clerks' is over 100. They are not only vastly greater in number than in May's time; they are also far more diverse in background and character. This chapter considers clerkly culture in the House of Commons as observed during the 2010–15 Parliament, with its own specific rhythms, ethos and development.

When researching politicians and political institutions the best source of reflection is to be found in conversation with the Clerks and other staff who work in Parliament. If they trust you to treat their views sensibly, then they reveal more about MPs than MPs ever could themselves. Politicians are the most skilled performers of representation; they are supremely accomplished at winning support rather than reflecting on the nature of their work. In contrast, the officials with the closest ring-side seats to MPs' work in Parliament, the Clerks, are reflective and fascinated by their own workplace. Although they take great care to appear discreet, if they believe you will not betray their confidence, and you understand what is confidential, then Clerks throw light on what goes on away from the public gaze and interpret behaviour with a shrewd sense of both culture and politics.

It was during an ethnographical research project to find out about UK MPs that I encountered Clerks who not only shed light on their mistresses and masters, but became intriguing to me in their own right.[5] In September 2012 I was interviewing a Clerk, let's call him Harry, in the atrium of Parliament's newest building, Portcullis House, asking about what it was like working with MPs. This atrium has, since the beginning of this century, almost entirely displaced the lobbies of the old Palace as the central marketplace of gossip and informal exchange. A prominent Conservative MP walked up to us and saw we were having an informal meeting—we had only coffee and no notebooks in front of us—and he started joking with the Clerk, pretending to treat him as if he was unstable. 'Did you know I am his psychotherapist?' he said to me, 'H-o-w a-r-e y-o-u d-o-i-n-g ...?' he asked loudly, as if to someone unhinged and deaf. Harry kept trying to intervene and finally managed to say: 'Do you know Dr Crewe from the University of London, who is doing an academic study of MPs?' The MP appeared visibly shocked and in a second shape-shifted from jovial, chatty mate leaning over our table into an upright, straight-backed, highly dignified important person offering to help with my research project. In a blink his face was transformed from a huge smile and twinkling eyes to sombre formality.

The MP departed swiftly and I asked Harry, 'What on earth was all that about?' He laughed and explained that he had been Clerk to the MP's committee and they had been on an overseas trip together, one of the main ways that Clerks and MPs get to know each other well. He was joking around, as he always does with Harry, because he saw that I had

[4] Vincent Colapietro, 'Situation, Meaning and Improvisation: An Aesthetics of Existence in Dewey and Foucault' (2011) 11 *Foucault Studies* 20.
[5] Emma Crewe, *House of Commons: An Anthropology of MPs at Work* (London, Bloomsbury, 2015).

an officials' pass, so he assumed I was an insider. As soon as he realised that I was not only an outsider, but an academic on a serious mission who was planning to write about MPs, he changed his tune from warmth to formality, politeness and reserve. It is perhaps what anyone has to do in a place of work when adjusting between close colleagues and strangers. But on discussing this encounter with Harry, I realised that MPs have to switch between performing different roles and guises on the turn of a sixpence multiple times a day and that Clerks see them more clearly than anyone else (although MPs' own staff may know the individuals they work for even better as individuals, their knowledge tends to be confined to their specific boss and party group). I began to realise that the skill of Clerks was far more complex than the technical content of procedural expertise implies. If you ask Clerks what it means to be clerkly they are inclined to say, 'precise' or 'concerned with rules' or, more disparagingly, 'pedantic', but to be a Clerk entails far more. They have to be shrewd observers, researchers and mediators. They mediate between MPs (via the Chair) during proceedings in the Chamber or committees and between MPs and others: MPs and peers, MPs and witnesses or visitors, MPs and the media, MPs (and others) in Parliament and government, and Parliament and the judiciary.

During the 2010–15 Parliament I formally interviewed eighteen clerks (twelve male, six female) by appointment (up to three times in some cases) and had hundreds of briefer informal conversations with Clerks either in Westminster or within meetings of the Study of Parliament Group, a network of academics and parliamentary officials. I observed meetings in the Table Office, Journal Office and Committee Office of the House of Commons and attended a professional training day for Clerks. I worked with some Clerks on a project that involved mainly middle-ranking officials interviewing MPs to get their feedback on services provided by the administration. When I followed the passage of a bill through Parliament, including through pre-legislative scrutiny by a select committee, I spoke on several occasions to the Clerk of the Committee. Finally, I gave written (and sometimes oral) evidence to the Administration, Liaison, International Development and Governance Select Committees.

Clerks are professionally distinct (even if not exclusively so) in being keen observers, utterly discreet, and wordsmiths of political texts. They are socially distinct as well. Traditionally, clerkly manners are courtly and cautious, universally polite to outsiders but sharp and witty to those they know well. Their background until the 1990s tended to be predominantly private school and Oxbridge-educated, white men with a smattering of grammar school redbrick graduates. Although becoming more diverse, they remain behind the rest of the Civil Service. While the senior Civil Service had 36.7 per cent women in 2011 and 5 per cent ethnic minority staff, the House of Commons had only 30 per cent and 0 per cent, respectively, at a senior level in 2012. In the old days when there were very few women Clerks, they used to meet regularly to give each other moral support and referred to themselves as the 'coven'. By 2015 this had changed quite considerably, partly because more recently women and men have entered the profession in almost even numbers. In the past the vast majority of Clerks entered Parliament straight from university as 'fast-stream' Clerks on passing Civil Service exams. It was a caste-like group—tightly knit and difficult to break into for non-Clerks. Their identity is reforged by various means. Clerks have seminars about procedure and an annual professional training day on procedure for Clerks; the one I went to encouraged creative thinking about possible innovations as well as an exercise in prioritising the most important standing orders (the compulsory rules that govern much of parliamentary business in the Chambers). Clerks meet for dinner occasionally and those of roughly the same level tend to eat lunch together, if they have time to stop for something to eat. However, the need for professional development and maintaining a collegiate way of working has the unintended effect of excluding non-Clerks. The requirement for procedural experience for senior posts, and the informal way of promoting Clerks, has disadvantaged non-Clerks until recently and, arguably, continues to do so. But the boundary between Clerk and non-Clerk is becoming more porous. More recently staff have been transferred to become Clerks from the Library, from technical specialists who advise select committees, from administrative staff in the Committee Office, from *Hansard* and the Parliamentary Office for Science and Technology. Nonetheless, the perception of non-Clerks is that Clerks can be aloof and it remains difficult to become a Clerk, despite an acceleration of change in the last few years.

Clerks are generally polite about each other irrespective of their background. According to one woman Clerk:

> The people are fantastic, one of the best things about working here is that all of the clerks tend to be people who have very odd interests, quite a few of them have done PhDs and you find people who in their spare time are writing books on bridges or the history of Newcastle or whatever it might be so, they're all very supportive and they're a great bunch of people to work with really.[6]

But a handful of Clerks feel out of place and some feel Clerks are dragging their feet as far as innovative HR practices are concerned. Parliamentary hours, a culture of being always on-call, inflexible rules about when Clerks can take leave and difficulties with ensuring that those returning from maternity leave get interesting jobs, make clerkly work challenging for those with childcare responsibilities, particularly if they wish to work part-time. Other departments in the House of Commons seem to have advanced further in offering flexible working and job sharing.

It seems to be assumed by some MPs, and a few Clerks, that real Clerks are refined people who have been to private school, studied Latin or Greek, and hail from privileged backgrounds. 'I'm not a real Clerk', one state-school-educated Clerk told me, 'and this doesn't really feel like my building. I'm only part English so it is not my history.' The number who fit the courtly stereotype was never that great and is shrinking, especially below the most senior levels, and diversity is clearly on the increase and moving upwards. So although clerkly culture is one of a kind, Clerks within it are different from each other but also changing gradually as they become more diverse and Parliament itself evolves.

In functional terms Clerks fulfil three main roles: (a) clerking for the parliamentary chambers, (b) managing the committees, and (c) administering Parliament. In all these roles they act as both supporters of politicians and upholders of rules. They tend to circulate around the House so that any senior Clerk will have had experience of all three of these. In the time of Erskine May the House was a relatively simply organism, employing few people, with unpaid MPs devoid of research assistants, in a single and relatively new building and with far less focus on the constituencies where the franchise was far more limited. In the last half century, managers have been brought in from outside to lead on, for example, finance, HR and IT, but Clerks still get involved in all departments. Since these roles are not unique to Clerks, my focus will be on their work on specifically parliamentary business in

[6] <http://beyondthephd.co.uk/audio/details.php?id=95> accessed 15 March 2015.

Chambers and committees. The content of this work is described in *The Table* and other learned journals. But what lies beneath these functions, that is, what goes unsaid publicly about the work of Clerks? To get at this question I will consider whether the work of Clerks is similar to Magi priests protecting Parliamentary rules and knowledge or mandarins managing rulers. Which are they, if either?

KNOWLEDGE AND WORDS: MAGI OF THE SACRED RULES?

Clerks 'at the Table' sit up to three abreast at a table on the floor of the House (between the government and opposition benches) and advise MPs on the rules. They are experts on the procedure of political debate and privilege. Their knowledge of rules is more than a form of scriptural accuracy; it only has meaning in specific contexts and applications. Since all MPs' work is political in the broad sense of the word—putting or opposing proposals, forming coalitions and opposing factions and arguing about decisions (especially concerning money)—the rules become political. So when an MP seeks guidance the Clerk will advise about how to gain the advantage, but if another from the opposing side comes two minutes later to ask about how to get the better of opponents in the same debate, then the Clerk will be just as ready to sabotage his own previous advice. One Clerk gave an example:

> I experienced this at its most extreme when clerking the xxx bill. ... I counted it as a measure of my success that I think those I dealt with in the Public Bill Office on both sides of the argument had a sneaking suspicion (though no certainty) that I was in fact on their side of the argument because my advice on achieving the outcomes they wanted was helpful.[7]

Or, if one MP asks how to organise a procedural ambush followed by another asking how to anticipate an ambush, each piece of advice given must be equally honest, thoughtful and considered. Clerkly advice will focus on how to use procedure to achieve the MP's political aim whether the Clerk likes or dislikes the aim; they may believe that their role is to be impartial or, if more philosophically aware, understand that their political partiality must never influence their advice for the purposes of manipulation. So they are apolitical in the sense of striving to sit on the fence and never taking sides, but they are intensely political because they have to understand the politics and motivations underlying different groups and individuals well enough to guide MPs about how to navigate the maze of political procedure. At the core of their work is a process of improvisation with endless finely judged responses to the specific configuration of actors, goals, mood and ritual context.

Lord Lisvane, formerly Sir Robert Rogers and Clerk of the House/CEO 2011–14, describes their work as follows:

> It isn't just about knowing about the standing orders or what the rules are ... I always summed it up to my colleagues, and latterly, to my more junior colleagues, as the woodcraft of Parliament ... in the sense of tracking through the forest—the combination of the learnt, the known, the instinctive. ... If there is one sentence which sums up this process or this skill ... it is helping members achieve most nearly in parliamentary terms what they want to achieve in political terms.[8]

---

[7] By email, 14 April 2015. PBO refers to the Public Bill Office.

[8] As quoted by Peter Hennessy, <www.civilserviceworld.com/articles/interview/lord-hennessy-meetssir-robert-rogers> accessed 19 March 2015.

Clerks aim for an air of impartiality and act as if they do not have favourites. However, they react to individuals—thinking 'Oh God, it's him or her', or 'What a pleasure to deal with x'. They either disguise this inevitable human reaction to different Members or, in some teams they might agree to deal with each other's bête noire. When MPs approach Clerks they tend to get a more negative response if they have a fixed idea about how to pursue their aim but they elicit more comprehensive advice if they ask for it in an open way. If an MP asks, 'Can I get a debate about nationalising x industry by doing this and that?', some Clerks (and especially those they do not know well) will reply, 'This won't work for this reason and that will run into various obstacles' and stop there. If an MP asks them an open question—'How can I get a debate on nationalising x industry?'—then any Clerk would be easily able to discuss the full range of possible procedural strategies and processes. For new MPs the key information to get from officials is not a whistle-stop tour of all procedure, which takes years or decades to learn, but knowledge about where and how to get advice (from, for example, the Table Office for questions or the Public Bill Office for queries about bills); and by explaining their political aims rather than seeking approval and defending tactics or plans.[9] (They will find equally knowledgeable experts in the Library but while a few researchers know about parliamentary processes, such as Oonagh Gay who writes elsewhere in this work, the expertise of most concerns policy issues—the content rather than the process of politics).

Some MPs realise that Clerks can be a key political asset; others fail to appreciate the nature of the Clerk–MP relationship and do not ask for advice at all. For some MPs the embarrassment of admitting their ignorance—especially if they have been in Parliament for a while—can deter them more than the problems caused by trying to muddle through. Those who are not content simply to take their procedural advice from the Whips may be bold enough to seek on-the-spot advice from Clerks at the Table or venture into the 'Table Office', where a small team of these brainy proceduralists are on hand to advise about the best tactics for what they wish to achieve. This extension of the operation of the Table can be found beyond the corridor behind the Speaker's Chair and consists of a tiny room with a rota of Clerks and one assistant who dispense advice but also get MPs' oral and written questions into good shape. In May's time the 'Table of the House' was where procedures happened, advice was sought and given, and plots hatched and traps laid. Questions were once 'tabled' at the Table in the Chamber but as the volume increased, this became difficult. So the physical Table has become a metaphorical one through the creation of a room that represents the Table and its purpose, and contains more Clerks, but in a different space. So this metaphorical Table has expanded into a large department, with its own strong subculture within which accuracy is highly prized and mistakes greatly feared.

A narrow-sighted MP will assume that these Table Office Clerks block any feisty questions by stripping out any radical language because they are conservative, tradition-bound pedants. A broad-minded MP will realise that these Clerks are determined to hone every question into a weapon of scrutiny, getting government into a place where it might become more difficult to evade the question. As the late Gwyneth Dunwoody MP told the Procedure Committee in 2002:

> [T]here is discipline in Members having to table their own questions. Frankly, there is also an advantage to the Member because one of the functions that the clerks fulfil with enormous diplomacy

[9] See Crewe (n 5) 42–43, 159–62.

is the ability to deal with the question that has just been put by Mr Quinn. If you are physically in the office and you have framed the question badly and you have put it down to the wrong minister, they will gently persuade you that you would get a much better reply if you sent it to this particular department because that is what you really want to know. They will not put it to you in quite those terms but over the years the clerks' department has saved more Members of Parliament from making fools of themselves than almost any other organisation in the world.[10]

Foolish MPs fail to see that Clerks have considerable powers of observation and political savvy. They do not see this because Clerks disguise both. They ration their advice, so as not to appear presumptuous, and present it as politically neutral. But they are only too aware of the political sensitivities and subtleties of different strategies. If an MP presents a fuzzy or tendentious question, then a Clerk will correct it. If an MP goes and asks, 'How can I ask this question in the most awkward way for government?', the Clerk will obligingly advise. Above all, Clerks are discreet. Often they cannot explain why they are advising the way they are—it would reveal what they know about other players and parties—and consequently MPs tend to underestimate Clerks' knowledge to their own detriment. However, even some Clerks claim that some individuals can be reticent about giving fulsome advice and some clerkly rules and practice can be unhelpful. Sometimes Clerks are encouraged to ask MPs for the 'basis' of a question, and some consider this kind of scrutiny goes beyond an appropriate role (as long as the question is neither disputatious nor accusatory). It is a matter of contention between Clerks the extent to which it is appropriate to challenge MPs.

Clerks are wordsmiths, crafting text to give words as much power as possible for the MPs using them. An example is found in their editing of parliamentary questions, whether they are for answer in writing or orally in the Chamber. The journey that a question takes once submitted by an MP is exhaustive. First of all, when questions arrive at the Table Office the Clerks check they are 'admissible', that is to say comply with a number of rules relating to their orderliness (these rules reflect decisions by the House or Speaker's rulings, and are not invented by the Table Office as some Members are inclined to believe). If not—if it is, for example, vague, misaddressed, offensive, fails to press for action or information and/or does not engage ministerial responsibility—then the MP is sent a postcard or email so that she or he, or someone from their office, can discuss it with the Office.

In the case of oral parliamentary questions, there are always more Members wishing to participate than there is time in the Chamber so their questions are then sent to the Upper Table Office for the 'shuffle'. This was once done manually on the large Upper Table Office table. Now they put the MP's name and question number into the computer and once all the questions for a particular day have been entered, the computer randomly selects a manageable amount. Then they retrieve the hard copies and return them to a Clerk for editing. Her edits make the language consistent, removing redundant words. Oral questions are expected to be briefer than writtens, to prevent Question Time getting bogged down. MPs cannot ask about discussions between civil servants. Argumentative questions are out of order. The initial question has to be in neutral language, but if a Member complains about this, the Clerk will point out that it is merely paving the way for a supplementary question, of which no notice is given, and which can be as politically barbed as the Member wants.

---

[10] House of Commons Procedure Committee evidence, <www.publications.parliament.uk/pa/cm200102/cmselect/cmproced/622/2030503.htm> 5 March 2002 Q 61, accessed 28 August 2015.

Usually, when a Clerk explains changes he has made to various questions, it becomes clear that these correct imprecision, vagueness or argumentativeness. The most common edit is designed to minimise a minister's room for evasion.

A sample of changes made by a Clerk to a particular set of questions tabled in 2012		
Original phrase	**Edited version**	**Reason**
1. Being silenced	Not discouraging whistle-blowers from coming forward	Less contentious
2. Delay	Time taken	More specific
3. When government will legislate	When Parliament will legislate	Parliament legislates, not government
4. Action	Steps	Reduces scope for vagueness
5. General impact for unspecified period	Effect of a specific intervention over specific time period	Reduces scope for vagueness
6. Very long time period	Much shorter time period	Would have been too costly

The written questions are forensically investigated for flaws at a hurroosh,[11] a meeting of Clerks to check the questions one last time and then approve. I asked Lord Lisvane where the word came from and he told me he first heard it in the 1960s from the lips of fellow Clerk and former army officer Frank Allen, who had served in Burma, who used it to mean palaver. Lord Lisvane and colleagues applied it to the 'wash-up' meeting. According to one web forum it is an old colonial word meaning, '*a general process of bureaucratic disturbance, confusion, fear, suspicion and agitation … initiated by the nabob at the apex of the administrative pyramid in reaction to the incompetence or political incorrectness of an underling or underlings*'.[12] The hurroosh I watched was relaxed and laced with arcane knowledge and jokes about the pedantry of Clerks, whether or not the nabob—Paul Evans, the then Principal Clerk in this instance—was present.[13] But the word nevertheless captures something of the urgency of the Table Office getting it right.

When MPs vote in the Chamber it always used to be only Clerks who noted who was passing through which division lobby—two recording the 'ayes' (yes) and the other two the 'noes'. Since the number of desks was increased from two to three in each Lobby, the group of staff who can do this work has been widened to include non-Clerks. There are now three desks—alphabetically divided A–F, G–M and N–Z according to Members' names— and the division Clerks on A–F have to contend with being tucked in at the side, unable to see Members approaching until they are suddenly upon them. The Members congregate in the lobby, talking about who is planning an early day motion, or whatever, and you can see who is being collared by the Parliamentary Private Secretary or Minister and which MPs are lobbying ministers. Then you can see the lonely ones; the non-clubbable MPs looking like wallflowers at a party. One Clerk told me that although this is the easiest duty in the

---

[11] There is no agreement on the spelling. Other Clerks have suggested it should be Harouche or Haroosh.
[12] Crewe (n 5) 61.
[13] This meeting took place on 5 September 2013.

world—after all you are merely marking names—the stakes are extraordinarily high. First, MPs can be bad-tempered if you remind them to confirm their name: the self-important ones assume that they should be recognised, while the most famous can sometimes be the most polite. But secondly, and worse, if you make a mistake then the consequences are awkward. The recording of the names of those voting in the division will be wrong and once the result is announced, it is embarrassing to make a correction. Some MPs have gone as far as complaining to the press when their name was recorded in the wrong division lobby.

In most contexts mistakes made by Clerks are rare but they can have serious repercussions. One former Clerk of Printing told me that a bill was printed with a whole section missing because the Parliamentary Counsel forgot to include it and the Clerk did not notice. As another example, an Appropriation Bill was passed in 2002 in which the sums missed out one column and since it was not noticed until after some accounts had been audited, further legislation had to be passed in the next session to correct the error.[14] The Clerk responsible, who has since become one of the world's leading authorities on parliamentary scrutiny of finance, commented:

> [O]ur organisation and culture is very supportive to mistakes which are occasional and out of character. Making a mistake with wider resonance and implications creates sympathy and warm feelings. This is an encouragement to learn more and do better. I think such tolerance would not apply to mistakes which are systematic or which other colleagues could not see themselves making. It is the rarity value which makes them a positive experience.[15]

It is perhaps partly this collegiate attitude to error—a contrast to the ferocious blame culture of many modern bureaucracies—that helps to reduce the likelihood of mistakes.

Clerks in the Public Bill Office have a book in which they write mistakes. This is referred to as the 'Black Book', although in rather typical parliamentary fashion the latest version is actually red, and also nicknamed, 'The Book of Shame'. This has the advantage of junior Clerks seeing that even those who have progressed to great heights have made errors. Mostly these mistakes are minor and easily reversible, such as: 'I wrongly advised the Chairman of the Standing Committee for the Hunting (recommitted) Bill that an opposition amendment could not be called for a division after the fall of the knife'; and 'Gave x incorrect advice about Queen's Consent so that he had to make last minute arrangements to find a Privy Counsellor.' This book is rarely used and mostly Clerks will inform their manager if they have made an error. It is a relatively small sin to give the wrong advice about procedure, but it is a terrible crime to fail to discuss it with anyone. When a junior Clerk failed to table an amendment, mistakenly thinking that the MP was not going to raise it, the MP then raised it on a point of order in the Chamber. The Table Clerks had not been warned by the junior Clerk, so were unable to advise the Speaker, and were furious with their colleague.

In nearly all instances, Clerks can work around small mistakes. Sometimes the Chair or Speaker will cover a Clerk's back. For a rule-bound organisation to operate effectively, the trust between the 'consigliere' figure of the Clerk and the political enforcer (Speaker, Chair

[14] HC Debates, 3 December 2002, col 865.
[15] By email to Emma Crewe, 14 June 2015.

or whoever) is fundamental. For instance, the then Clerk of the Journals in the House of Commons, Liam Laurence Smyth, recalled that:

> [A]s a fairly new Table Clerk, I whispered to the chair that I had accidentally pressed the timer too hard, giving a member extra speaking time. The Deputy Speaker replied that if anyone queried it, he'd blame the error on a digital malfunction—'but, Liam, we won't let them know whose digit it was!'[16]

Clerks mind especially about errors in parliamentary documents, such as minutes and Journals, that might then become precedents. Failures to follow the standing orders and other irregularities in procedure that are revealed in texts can undermine the rules. In contrast the majority of Members simply want to pursue their political outcomes without being personally embarrassed in front of other Members in the chamber by their lack of knowledge of parliamentary procedure. So it is mainly Clerks, and to a lesser extent the Speaker and Deputy Speakers, Chairs and Members on the Procedure Committee, who continually review whether the rules are working.

Although you can find the parliamentary rules and conventions in various books—principally in the volume that is the subject of this book, Thomas Erskine May's *Treatise* (called May for short by Clerks) and the Standing Orders—the interpretation of these rules reveals a vital elasticity in certain aspects of procedure, which is examined elsewhere in this volume. To adopt a well-worn cliché, procedure is an art not a science. The books have little meaning unless you are steeped in the culture, traditions and assumptions of the House. As one Clerk wrote to me when commenting on this chapter: 'May the book has no existence except through the interpretive efforts of the Clerks. Those who take its nostrums literally will soon find themselves going down a cul-de-sac or up a garden path.' For this reason Clerks learn procedure over years and years of practice, like learning a craft or language. An example in the twenty-fourth edition of May serves to illustrate:

> By a convenient and necessary elasticity of practice, the standing orders which prescribe a limit to the time for the transaction of business are not so strictly enforced as to prevent the House from completing, when the fixed hour arrives, the proceeding on which a decision is in process of being taken.[17]

One of the country's top proceduralists explained that there is a distinction between (a) most Standing Orders that have to be applied rigidly, and (b) a few Standing Orders and plenty of other rules that are subject to interpretation according to political circumstances. As examples, when advising a chair on what 'adequately discussed' might mean in Standing Order No 68, or whether to ever publish written evidence to a select committee before it is reported to the House, or the extent to which the subject for an adjournment debate needs to engage the responsibility of ministers, requires judgement. Some rules, as we see elsewhere in this volume, derive from ancient practice, others derive from Speaker's Rulings. Of course, 'ancient practice' is itself a highly contestable social construct: much of what went

---

[16] Stephen Reynolds, '"You Have Committed a Great Offence and Have but a Weak Answer to Make for Yourself": When Clerks Make Mistakes' (2013) 81 *The Table* 13. <www.societyofclerks.org/Documents/The Table_2013.pdf> accessed 25 March 2015.

[17] William McKay, *Erskine May's Treatise on the Law, Privileges, Proceedings and Usage of Parliament*, 24th edn (London, LexisNexis Butterworths, 2004) 312.

before has been discarded and what remains is deemed to serve a purpose. The more recent the Speaker's Ruling, the more weight the latter has. It takes practice to understand where there is leeway and how far it stretches. A new Clerk observed:

> [I]t is hard to understand procedure in the abstract; you have to understand it empirically and it is much easier to learn as part of a group. So it is very important that others explain things but also that you see it for yourself.[18]

The learning of procedure is achieved, therefore, through practice and discussion as a group. New Clerks are like apprentices, learning the craft of advising on procedure through improvised practice, mentoring and continual evaluation. For more senior Clerks, mentoring turns into a collegiate process of collective reflection on procedure through regular discussions.

Clerks are like priests in the sense that they know the sacred knowledge of parliamentary rules more thoroughly than anyone else and mediate between the Speaker and politicians as they perform and communicate with each other, or prepare to do so, by ensuring the rules are followed. They play a particular role when MPs are introduced to the House, like priests presiding at baptism and confirmation, although permanent departure from the Commons demands less ceremony than death due to the unpredictable nature of elections. Like the priesthood, they belong to a tight-knit group with a hierarchy; train each other in the sacred knowledge; and are on hand as the experts of process during the rituals of debate, committee hearings and the various stages of law-making. Until recently they wore distinctive clothes to mark them out from others. As one member of staff explained in relation to the wigs Clerks wear: 'I sort of see them as a depersonalising mechanism—it doesn't matter who the person is sitting at the table, what matters is the office that they hold.' Clerks still wore until February 2017 eighteenth-century court attire when sitting at the Table in the debating Chamber and when wandering the corridors of Westminster, giving them the air of lawyers (or priests of the court). When some MPs see the wig it can confirm in their minds an assumption that Clerks embody traditionalism and an excessive affection for the past. While some newer Clerks see the uniform as giving the false impression of conservatism, other Clerks (mostly older ones) describe their uniform in more complementary terms, suggesting that it creates a sense of stability within which change becomes more possible. For example, Lord Lisvane told me:

> [F]or as long we are in a chamber that looks like a 14th century church, the wigs fit in. The wigs are part of a settled framework, which allows us to change other more important things in the middle. They are part of what creates an emotional harbour. … Formal clothing and a degree of ceremony (which many people outside Parliament like) create a safe and predictable space in which the hurly-burly of politics, and important rather than superficial change can take place more easily.[19]

However, Lord Lisvane's successor, David Natzler, swept away most of these distinctive elements of dress in 2016, retaining only the gown and bow-tie. Somehow a point was felt to have been reached where the distinctiveness and tradition were outweighed by the risk of archaism—a constant problem with parliamentary tradition, and where currently the push is all on the side of relevance. But polarising Clerks into two camps—rational

[18] Interview held by Emma Crewe, 27 November 2014.
[19] Interview held by Emma Crewe on 28 February 2012 and email sent on 15 May 2015.

modernisers and traditional ritualists—would be misleading. In clerkly culture, and even in the minds of individual Clerks, you can find a creative tension arising from the value attached to both change and continuity at the same time. The wigs may have gone, but the gowns remain.

Despite some similarities, unlike priests Clerks interpret the rules (without concealing the fact), and most of them push gently for continual reform and innovation, even putting forward proposals for change to Members. As we see elsewhere in this volume, Thomas Erskine May, whose book has become the 'bible of parliamentary procedure' was himself an energetic moderniser, as were many of his successors. Clerks and priests respond in different ways widespread public cynicism towards politicians and an analogous decline in membership of the Church in the UK. The relationships between MPs, and between MPs and citizens, is going through a transformation which brings them closer together both in constituencies and through social media and the rituals need to catch up. But Church congregations are drifting away, leaving few options for priests to coax them back. Priests offer sympathy to their 'flock' for the suffering that God apparently fails to prevent, whereas Clerks keep their distance but argue for change. The procedural work of Clerks is to try and make sure that the conflicts between politicians are expressed fairly and are resolved in ways that are seen as legitimate. It is perhaps the mix of improvisation, innovation and interpretation that sets Clerks apart from priests. Clerks believe in accuracy and fairness but know that truth is in the eyes of the beholder.

POWER AND INNOVATION: MANDARINS MANAGING MEMBERS?

At the heart of the Clerks' job is their relationship with politicians. Commons Clerks serve MPs or 'Members', as they call them. To understand Clerks' work, you have to consider what politicians do. When politicians perform, their aspiration is usually to win support for themselves, their parties and their causes through interviews, canvassing, whipping, speechifying, debating and writing in public. Writing now means not just in print but also email, tweets, blogs and websites. Endlessly transmitting images of themselves looking busy to constituents and other potential supporters has become compulsory since the rise of constituency work since the 1970s. Clerks, and others who manage Parliament, are focused on winning support not for themselves but for the institution and Members of it. They rarely speak in public and when writing or editing texts, their names are usually absent unless it is an academic piece, in the journal *The Table* for example, or part of educating the public about how Parliament works. Their goal is to make politicians and Parliament look good and the authorship of their performance is usually invisible.

One Clerk told me she thought of the servants in the television series *Downton Abbey*—a portrayal of a wealthy family and the servants employed by them—as she sat in attendance on MPs at a committee. Aristocrats or politicians will speak candidly in front of servants or Clerks, as if they were not there, because they know that those serving them are utterly discreet. Like servants, Clerks gossip about the Members among themselves, and perhaps a few trusted associates, but almost never to the media or to other MPs. Although this is now changing, traditionally Clerks join the House service straight from university and many will not leave until retirement. Some Clerks point out that their skills are not readily transferred elsewhere. The result is a relationship of trust but also, at times, abuse by politicians.[20] In contrast to the exquisite politeness reserved for potential supporters, MPs can be abrupt, even ill-tempered to those closest to them: parliamentary staff, their own staff and other MPs who they deem to be obstructive. Clerks witness MPs at their worst and they are inclined to see some of them as self-important and ill-disciplined. Their stories to illustrate this are not in short supply.

An essential element of the clerkly culture in the Commons is the recognition, forcefully socialised in new recruits, that 'election' confers a power and authority that mere appointment can never confer. Elected Members are, through the anointing of the polls, fundamentally different beings. There is, inevitably, a contradiction between this deeply held ethos and the realities of daily human contact with the individuals who can never live up to these democratic expectations. Clerks stress the diversity of manners among MPs. Some are thoughtful and considerate while others are demanding, irrational, and inclined to talk at great length during political debates or committees about their pet issue or constituency matters, ignoring the concerns of other committee members. They reserve thorough irritation for those committee chairs and members who grandstand, divert a course of questioning to pursue their own personal political agenda or grab attention in the media for themselves rather than the whole committee or the issue, or those that bully staff (especially junior ones). If a junior Clerk or other member of staff is bullied, a senior Clerk will speak to him or her about it. The morally reprehensible MPs leave some Clerks, and especially the longer-standing ones, somewhat disdainful if not cynical, even if they remain fiercely loyal to Parliament as an institution. For the younger ones, the experience can be bruising. Clerks remind themselves continually that they serve Parliament not individual MPs: 'It is to the office that I must give my loyalty, not to the individual', in the words of one but the sense is conveyed by many.

On the other side of the coin, how do MPs view Clerks? Their respect for the intelligence and efficiency of Clerks is nearly universal, but the evaluations by some MPs are coloured by their politics. Critical MPs on the left tend to see Clerks as private-school educated, privileged and conservative, while those on the right complain that Clerks are bureaucratic, rule-bound and risk averse. Modernisers perceive them as an impediment to change. When a Clerk was travelling with a very senior MP, the latter introduced the former to his wife saying, 'This is x, my wife. She is a Labour supporter which very few Clerks are.' This Clerk was firmly on the left but kept quiet because as a Clerk his views must remain unknown, even if those ascribed to him were the product of prejudice rather than observation. Impartiality does not mean that Clerks have no political opinions; several told me that they collectively probably span the whole political spectrum with a tendency towards being socially liberal and reform-oriented. If anything most Clerks complain about the innate conservatism of Parliament themselves, especially when the Commons and Lords try to work together. But at the same time their role is designed to point out hazards when MPs seek advice on a plan or tactic; the senior ones have seen the results of so many ruses, it is hardly surprising that they are disposed to warn about unintended consequences. The MPs read this as caution or even resistance to change.

---

[20] This alleged bullying by an MP is not the only example I heard about during the 2010–15 Parliament: <www.dailymail.co.uk/news/article-2136772/Hacking-probe-MP-bullied-harassed-women-Commons-But-insists-smear-discredit-findings-weeks-report.html> accessed 30 March 2015.

Clerks work closely with Speaker and Deputy Speakers (just as they do with Chairs of committees). The top three Table Clerks and the Speaker with his/her three Deputies meet every morning for a 'conference' to discuss the day's proceedings. The Clerks will advise about potential complications and how to handle them. They explain the pre-prepared brief detailing what needs to be said by the Speaker/Deputy at what point in the debate. When a Speaker or Deputy is new, they will get advice about how to chair parliamentary debates. One Clerk told me: 'Being in the Speaker's Chair is like being a driver. You can be a good and careful driver of a car but it is difficult to explain every movement to someone else. Or you can just drive the car and it will go.' Some of their job requires repetition of key phases that are needed in the ritualised debate, for example when a division is called and they call out, 'Lock the doors!' But most of the time good chairing requires a sense of what is needed and desired by the collective of Members, 'the sense of the House'; before deciding how long to give to different items and who to call. Both Speaker and Clerks at the Table need to pay attention to the mood of the House—whether ratty and sniping or lively and buzzing or desultory and disengaged. Some Clerks are better at this than others; it requires complex skills of observation and analysis of MPs' emotions and reactions to each other.

Some Clerks use distinctive body language to send signals to the Speaker or Deputy Speaker. If one particular Clerk inclines his head, it means he is worried; if he turns around, then someone is 'way out of order'. The Revd Ian Paisley gave an example when paying tribute to former Clerk Sir Donald Limon:

> [W]hen the Speaker, or the occupant of the Chair, leaned forward to talk to the Clerks, I was on good ground, because the Speaker was not sure whether to call me to order or not. But when the Clerk turned round and initiated a discussion with the Speaker, I knew that I was in for trouble. Therefore, the Clerks have always been my guiding star.[21]

The Deputy/Speaker can sometimes repeat the Clerk's exact words of advice on occasion so they have to be careful what they say. The Table Clerks are in an exposed situation but mostly MPs pretend they are not there. On one occasion an MP said during a debate: 'I heard what the Clerk said and I completely disagree.' This was shocking, according to the Clerk, Sir Malcolm Jack, like interrupting the performance of an actor in mid-flow and asking 'Why are you saying it like that?' MPs are not supposed to interrupt the Clerk's invisible performance within the parliamentary ritual in that way. The MP apologised to the Sir Malcolm later the same day.[22]

Part of the role entails standing up to Members—after all, even if they are attentive to individual freedoms, they serve the whole House and not individual Members. When Clerks refuse to allow something, generally MPs accept it and, if not, then the Speaker will seek to ensure that the Clerks are respected partly because their advice is usually accompanied with suggestions about how to achieve the MP's goals.

Clerk: 'You can't table that?'

MP: 'Why?'

Clerk: 'It doesn't relate to the ministerial responsibilities.'

---

[21] Sir Ian Paisley, HC Debates, 18 December 1997, col 491.
[22] Interviewed on 17 October 2011.

MP: 'So how can I raise it?'

Clerk: 'Like x, y, z ...'

While most MPs play along with the intentions of the usual channels during debates, and do not know enough about procedure to sabotage them in any case, occasionally a truly skilled proceduralist MP outwits those who think they are in control. For example, David Heath (Liberal Democrat and then an opposition MP) foxed the government with a little-known manoeuvre. During a debate on the membership of the Independent Parliamentary Standards Authority he moved 'the Previous Question'—which takes the form: 'That the Question be not now put.' The subtlety is twofold: first, the Speaker has no choice whether to allow the 'previous question' to be debated, and second, that although its ostensible purpose is that if it is agreed to, the House proceeds to the next business; if it is not agreed to, the issue under discussion must be decided immediately. The Liberal Democrats' opponents wanted a decision and therefore called, 'No!' when the previous question was eventually put for decision. The Liberal Democrats did not call 'Aye'. This meant the House had disagreed to the previous question and was therefore agreeing to proceed immediately to the decision (which meant that the amendment which the Liberal Democrats' opponents wanted to move later and which might have been agreed was forestalled). But there was a certain amount of grumbling that the Clerks had not been forewarned—even if sworn to silence.

Some Clerks argue that unnecessarily obscure procedure can be maintained by the whips for the purposes of confusing backbenchers. For example, if you wish to call a snap vote, then you can say: 'I beg to move that the House do now sit in private'; or in the past the more poetic 'I spy strangers', which can easily be stopped by the whips simply shouting, 'No!', as long as there is no dissent. (On one occasion, in 2001, a new whip, surprised by the manoeuvre late at night, simply forgot to shout 'No', so the motion was unopposed and the House had to complete the rest of its sitting in private.) However it can only be done once a day. On Fridays, when customarily various devices are used to kill Private Member's Bills, MPs get this out of the way at the start of the sitting so that it cannot be used to sabotage a particular bill or use up time which would otherwise be available for debate. Some Clerks told me that such obscure rules, those that tend to be understood only by traditionalists, whips and some ministers, are maintained to reduce backbenchers' opportunities for causing trouble. Other Clerks paint a less conspiratorial picture, arguing that procedure is continually changing but that the pace of reform should be sufficiently gradual to allow MPs to stay in touch with what is in and out of order.

Clerks have been instrumental in what Speaker Bercow has called the Doctor Who-like regeneration of the House of Commons, especially in changing the rules of debate, select committee membership and use of parliamentary time in favour of greater control by backbenchers. In 2009 Robert Rogers (now Lord Lisvane) compiled a briefing with seventy-five possible reforms to the rules governing the business of the House, drawn upon by all ten candidates for the Speakership.[23] Speaker Bercow, who was elected shortly afterwards, prioritised the taking of a far larger number of Urgent Questions and the backing for more

---

[23] <www.theguardian.com/politics/blog/2009/jun/19/commons-reform-plan-speaker> accessed 30 March 2015.

extensive outreach and public education. The work of Clerks also changed as a result of the then Prime Minister Gordon Brown's desperation to appear positive after the MPs' expenses scandal of 2008–09, with the 2010 election looming, which led to his announcement of the Wright Committee. The then Clerk of Committees, David Natzler (Clerk of the House of Commons from 2015), took charge of clerking this committee partly because he knew it would be influential but also because it had to work fast and through the recess.[24] He had the support of a specialist researcher, Lucinda Maer, who was seconded to the Committee from the Commons Library, and Dr Meg Russell of the Constitution Unit, who was appointed as the Committee's specialist adviser. They provided ideas for the Committee, facilitated a seminar, which drew in a number of external experts and organisations, and provided advice on what was achievable and realistic for the committee to agree on and achieve. Many of the Committee Members had considerable expertise themselves, either as experienced backbenchers, select committee chairs or former government ministers and whips. The Clerk and specialists knew which Members were particularly influential, in the sense that they were close to their party leadership, and when they drafted sections of the report they had to bear in mind not just the perspectives of their committee but allow them time to consult others. As they do on any procedural matter, their skill was in dealing with the contradictory imperatives of individual freedoms and collective interests: the need for the elected government to get its way and for backbenchers to have their say in meaningful ways.

Once the politicians approved most of the Wright Committee's proposals, the then Principal Clerk of the Table Office helped the Members to work out how the new Backbench Business Committee would operate in practice. With the Clerk's guidance its new Chair, Natascha Engel MP, created this entirely new committee. For the first time in the modern history of the Commons, backbenchers had control of some time within the debating Chambers. They worked out criteria and rules, unhampered by old procedure, that ensured that the whole process of allocating time to backbenchers was transparent, flexible and topical. Those MPs pitching their ideas for debates to the Backbench Business Committee had to be cross-party, they decided, and should do so in public. As the Committee started its work, refinements emerged in an iterative way in discussion with the whips. The usual channels tried to put up whips to answer the debates, claiming it was good practice for them, but the Backbench Business Committee Members complained until the whips were replaced by ministers.

Clerks perceive innovation as an integral part of their work. The rituals within a church may change slightly, with the updating of the language of texts, for example, so that congregations can understand them more readily, but the purpose is merely to bring people closer to God, not to transform the relationship in any way. The purpose of rules in a Parliament is quite different from a church because the relationships being regulated are in a constant state of flux. As a few examples, between 2010 and 2015 Clerks worked with reform-minded Members to introduce various new rules aiming to revive the House following the expenses scandal of 2008–09. They assisted the House in introducing and implementing rules for electing chairs to select committees, ensuring party and gender balance in Deputy Speaker elections and establishing and running a new Backbench Business Committee that

---

[24] Interview held with Emma Crewe, 8 August 2012.

allocated time to backbench debates controlled by a cross-party committee. The system of government in which the executive sits within the legislature (as found in Westminster) creates a constant tension between the role of MPs as supporters (or opponents) of the executive and their role as representatives of the nation against an over-mighty government. The tension is reflected in the Clerks at well.

At the Table in the debating Chambers, and when the House sits in Public Bill committees to discuss the detail of proposed legislation, the emphasis is on procedure within the context of politics. As in a judicial court, the *process* of law-making is important because the legitimacy of the law depends on correct procedure and the resulting text contains society's rules—until they are changed again—with the full weight of the state to enforce them. In select committees it is the opposite; for Clerks, the emphasis is on politics within a procedural framework, but a framework which is committed to holding the Executive to account, not enabling it to have its way. The fault-lines of such politics do not necessarily fall along predictable political party lines, although some committees do some of the time and particularly those concerned with current political debates, but they are political in a broader sense nonetheless. Whether scrutinising the record of a government department by questioning a minister, conducting pre-legislative scrutiny or listening to witnesses when undertaking an inquiry, select committees may consider swathes of conflicting evidence. With the assistance of their staff team, led by a first and usually a second Clerk, they debate these strands of evidence and make political judgements about what seems most persuasive and publish their conclusions.[25]

This means that Clerks have to have a sense of the politics of their committee, even more than knowledge of procedure, when planning and guiding meetings as well as drafting reports. As one Committee Clerk put it: 'You have to be adept at picking up minute agreements and disagreements so that you can reflect the views of the whole group when it comes to writing reports.' Committee Clerks tend to encourage the chairs to take account of the whole committee, encourage the quieter members to speak up, and obtain formal approval for reports from all the members. Some chairs are insensitive or indifferent to the perspectives of some of the members of the committee; Clerks try to compensate for the inability of a few obstinate chairs to carry the whole committee along with them. Clerks have to tread a difficult path with insensitive chairs. If they anger the latter by trying to persuade them to take on board the views of other members of their Committee, it can make their relationship fraught. They guide on finding ways through disagreements and on learning from the past where possible. But on most occasions it is the Clerks, rather than MPs, who push for reflective learning about the past. While Members are under huge pressure to respond to the everyday pressures from the media, their parties and their constituencies, Clerks take the longer view, coaxing committees towards greater effectiveness in seeing the bigger picture, or at least seeing it from many angles.

To conclude whether Clerks are mandarins or servants requires a consideration of the power relations between Clerks and MPs. The formal hierarchy claims that the MPs in government have executive power, MPs as a collective (or in small groups such as committees) act as a check on that power, and Clerks do no more than guide in the *process* of mediation and refereeing of political contests. The informal power relations between the two are

---

[25] Crewe (n 5) ch 6.

messier and more changeable than this suggests, as I have tried to convey in this chapter. Both individual MPs and Clerks vary in their skill at navigating politics and procedure. But also the opportunities for Clerks to influence the rules of the political game shift—for example, the period after the MPs' expenses scandal was a time when Clerks were unusually influential, crafting many of the reforms that were recommended by the Wright Committee. If taking a relational view of power, rather than viewing it as if it is a commodity or structural position, then the informal power of Clerks to influence process continually rises and falls depending on relationships between individuals and groups at a specific time. It is difficult confidently to categorise Clerks as mandarins, because their invisibility and the endless fluctuations of power relations mean that, as a professional group, consolidation and recognition of their power is always out of their reach. Their commitment to the messy unpredictability of democracy and debate, while it may be at war with their urge to order and regularity, precludes power-seeking as a professional ambition.

CLERKING: PRACTICAL JUDGEMENT MISRECOGNISED AS TRADITION

In this chapter I have described the work of Clerks in the roles they play that are unique and central to their parliamentary setting with a focus on the key locations of debate: the Chambers and the committees. Clerks also hold many of, and the top, management positions responsible for administering Parliament. The management style of Clerks can be flexible and creative, unusual for any organisation in modern times, plagued as most are by the bureaucratic demands and inefficiencies of managerialism.[26] This has arisen partly because Parliament is unlike any other institution, and the job of parliamentarians is unique, and also because Clerks are in a class of their own with their own distinct culture as well. They may be out of step with the more pernicious prevailing trends within organisational management in three ways. First, their flexible approach to work prizes improvisation and can be innovative and unconventional. While most organisations are drowning in superfluous documents and discussions to respond to the demands of corporate strategy, planning, performance management and audit, Clerks and other Commons officials have developed a culture that tends to eschew these symbols of managerialist bureaucracy. The usual public sector audit bureaucracy—annual staff performance and time recording forms—are encroaching, but it is against the will of many Clerks. Their strategy, plans and risk registers are relatively lean even if all these demands are becoming more onerous.[27] Secondly, despite the dominant management discourse elevating outcome above process, Clerks focus on high-quality process as much as on outcomes because in a democracy due process is a key outcome in earning the trust of the governed—though there will be some conflict between the ritualised work of the Chambers and the more informal world of committees. Thirdly, while performance management systems in many organisations focus on either corporate or individual performance, the House of Commons has retained a dimension lost in many

[26] See Marilyn Strathern (ed), *Audit Cultures. Anthropological Studies in Accountability, Ethics and the Academy* (London, Routledge, 2000). For more about management of the House, see Richard Kelly and Ed Potton, 'The Administration of the House of Commons', House of Commons Library Standard Note, 2014, SN/PC/6976.

[27] 2013–17 strategy, <www.parliament.uk/documents/commons-chief-executive/Strategy-for-the-House-Service-2013-17-(leaflet)WEB.pdf>; and 2014/15–16/17 corporate business plan, <www.parliament.uk/documents/commons-commission/Commons-Management-Board/CBP-2014-WEB.pdf> both accessed 30 March 2015.

institutions: collegiate working. By nurturing a collegiate style of working, and not just highly individualised motivation, Commons Clerks provide support and constructive criticism to each other. One staff member who previously worked in a government department reported a marked contrast in atmosphere and relationships in the Commons. While Clerks are supportive and collegiate, managers in the government department were authoritarian and inclined to blame their juniors for their own mistakes.

How have Clerks managed to deftly sidestep these fashions and trends? They may derive a stubborn confidence through the difficult business of managing unruly politicians over decades. Or it may be that their habit of critical reflection on their own practice, and that of government departments through select committees, makes them wary of unnecessary bureaucracy or polarising choices between traditionalism and modernity. But above all, a surprisingly large number of parliamentary staff stay in the addictive world of Parliament for decades. They develop a feeling of belonging to something more than a workplace— a community and an institution. Rather than damage their relationships with colleagues, and therefore jeopardise their place in this community, they take care to avoid aggressive competition and conflict. They reduce the potential for competition by circulating Clerks when vacancies come up, rather than inviting people to compete for posts as is usual within most public-sector organisations. Having said that, rivalry is a feature between Clerks partly because some can be intellectually competitive but also because there is a limited number of senior positions. Competition in a collegiate style is thus intrinsic to clerkly culture. This culture often excludes non-Clerks, so the challenge for the future is how to retain collegiality and embrace others into it.

Meeting this challenge became the focus of a bitter argument within the House of Commons about who should replace Robert Rogers when he announced his retirement as Clerk of the House and Chief Executive Officer in 2014. A recruitment panel set up by the House of Commons Commission, and chaired by the Speaker, announced the offer of appointment as Clerk to a parliamentary officer in the Australian Parliament. It was alleged that some MPs wanted to redress the elitism and male dominance of the Clerks by appointing her because she was female, despite her lack of experience as a parliamentary Clerk. Others thought she might bring experience in management and bring about innovation and change. The consternation of Clerks was leaked to the media, directly and indirectly by politicians who were allies, so the Prime Minister held back from recommending the candidate to the Queen. The recruitment process was paused and a select committee established to consider the matter. In the ensuing exchange of claims and counterclaims, the 'culture' of the Clerks was often characterised as backward looking, tradition bound and opposed to innovation, and Clerks blamed for poor management. Frank Doran MP argued:

> I think one of the perennial problems of people who reach the top in this institution—and I say that advisedly—is that there is a lack of outside experience. That has been shown over the decades. We are very slow to move things forward and custom and deference are a big part of the problem as well.

Peter Hain MP complained about the Clerks' culture of aloofness.[28] On the other hand, Sir Kevin Tebbit, who conducted a review of the management of the House of Commons

---

[28] <http://data.parliament.uk/writtenevidence/committeeevidence.svc/evidencedocument/house-of-commons-governance-committee/house-of-commons-governance/oral/15556.html> (Q319), and <www.publications.parliament.uk/pa/cm201415/cmselect/cmgovern/692/692.pdf>, 32–33, accessed 30 April 2016. Frank Doran is mistakenly referred to as Frank Dobson in the report.

in 2007, warned: '[T]here is an alchemy here—a curious combination of effects which produces a unique result—and you tamper with it, to some extent, at your peril.'[29]

During this process Clerks were not at liberty to criticise MPs or their decision-making publicly. It was for this reason that I gave evidence to this committee:

> [R]ecognition of the complexity of Parliament would be useful, because there is a lot that officials cannot say publicly. They cannot be rude about MPs. They cannot talk about the inevitable conflicts that go on within organisations. They cannot take credit for things, because they are always giving credit to MPs. They cannot explain the delays that happen, which I know happen particularly between the House of Lords and the House of Commons. Also, when MPs get involved, they cannot blame the MPs for those delays; they have to take the blame themselves. So I think some recognition of all that would be helpful for morale.[30]

The committee deliberated on all the evidence and decided to keep the Clerk of the House as the most senior position.

The expertise involved in clerking, like any form of phronetic knowledge that can only be learned through years of practice, has innovation sewn into its core. Innovation (or lack of it) does not emerge due to a specific clerkly personality type, ideology, culture or management practice; it is an inevitable part of the process of applying expertise. As the pragmatic philosopher, John Dewey explains:

> You and I may keep running in certain particular ruts, but conditions are provided for somebody else to foresee—or infer—new combinations and new results. The depersonalizing of the things of everyday practice becomes the chief agency of their repersonalising in new and more fruitful modes of practice. The paradox of theory and practice is that theory is with respect to all other modes of practice the most practical of all things, and the more impartial and impersonal it is, the more truly practical it is.[31]

The process of exercising Dewey's version of practical judgement through experimentation and reflection on experience means that continuity and change are always in a paradoxical and dynamic relationship in any organisation. On the one hand innovation is built into such a process, but at the same time some enduring traditions and practices make us who we are and allow us to recognise each other.[32] This is true of the practical judgement required in clerking work as much as any other expertise based on learning through practice. So Clerks innovate as much as any other professional group, and certainly more than priests, but exercise caution about abandoning the rules that govern process. Democracy requires an obsessive focus on process, or trust in Parliament will be lost.

In this chapter I have challenged, as have the accounts of procedural history elsewhere in this volume, the assumption that the culture of House of Commons Clerks is resistant to change. 'Organisational culture' is often represented in management literature as an entity separate from the everyday practices and relationships of people at work, or a process that obstructs reform. But the implication that it is separate from the people making it or that

[29] ibid, 44.
[30] <http://data.parliament.uk/writtenevidence/committeeevidence.svc/evidencedocument/house-of-commons-governance-committee/house-of-commons-governance/oral/15827.pdf> (Q648) accessed 28 April 2016.
[31] J Dewey, *Essays in Experimental Logic* (Chicago, Chicago University Press, 1916) 441.
[32] Chris Mowles, *Managing in Uncertainty. Complexity and the Paradoxes of Everyday Organizational Life* (London, Routledge, 2015) 102.

it can ever stand still reflects an outmoded understanding of culture from the perspective of anthropology, sociology and cultural theory. Culture in communities or organisations is a process (and not a social object) of doing and relating through a mix of shared and contested values, emotions, aspirations, norms and rules. The creation of culture never stands still and can be harmonious or conflictual, occasionally egalitarian and more often hierarchical. As Mowles puts it, culture is 'written on the body and is a disposition to think and act in a particular way' and 'can provoke highly emotive responses in us of mutual identification, but can also promote division as "we" unite against "them"'.[33] Within Parliament there are various cultures and one of them, I would argue, is created by and between Clerks. It will be no surprise to anyone that clerkly culture is neither global nor static—it is specific to each parliament or chamber and continually changing—but it is also interweaves with other cultures created by the whole population of officials working in Parliament and, still broader, everyone in the 'Westminster village'.

So assumptions by some MPs that Clerks are conservative and risk-averse turn out to be a misrecognition of their work and culture. Honneth's work on *The Struggle for Recognition* offers an explanation for this as he writes about how social conflict can be manifested as an agonistic struggle over morality.[34] Underlying the relationship between Clerks and MPs is the possibility of co-operation or conflict. When advising Members Clerks are sometimes perceived by MPs as obstructing their aims even if their intention is the opposite. In short, Clerks cannot please all the Members all the time in their advice on the rules, and MPs have conflicting political aims themselves. Since all MPs are under pressure to appear modernising, their frustration with the embodiment of their own failure—that is, with those protecting the rules and due process—can be ferocious. MPs can thus misrecognise their own failures and conflicts as clerkly conservatism and risk-avoidance. Clerks are no more mandarins than they are priests, because unlike civil servants they are not involved in developing or implementing government policies or services. They are custodians and reformers of the rules that ensure a fair contest between conflicting ideas.

Like most of the people and cultures within Parliament the work of Clerks is undervalued in part because it looks quite different on the surface from what goes on beyond the public gaze. So the risk of ill-informed intervention looms on the horizon. Despite the appearance of being priest-like and MPs' assumptions that they may be mandarins, Clerks are neither. They are in danger of being pressurised into following external organisational norms and becoming bureaucrats, who could lose the detailed knowledge of the rules that is required for flexibility and innovation. Clerkly distinction deserves plenty of room for innovation and risk and that only comes with recognition of what it means to be a Clerk.

---

[33] ibid 88.

[34] Axel Honneth, *The Struggle for Recognition: The Moral Grammar of Social Conflicts* (Cambridge, Polity, 1995).

Part II

The Book

4

Persuading the House

The Use of the Commons Journals as a Source of Precedent

MARTYN ATKINS

> In case the question of *la clôture* should come under consideration, we are able to offer—what will be much more persuasive with the House of Commons than any argument—a precedent.
>
> Thomas Erskine May, 1854[1]

INTRODUCTION

THE PRESENT PROCEDURE of the House of Commons derives from four principal sources: the acknowledged custom and practice of the House; its resolutions and standing orders; rulings from the Chair; and procedures laid down in statute passed by the House.[2] Of these, the least tangible is the first class: what is said to be the 'ancient usage' of the House, modified by 'practice', for which no written authority exists. Custom and precedent, not standing orders, determine the number of readings a Bill shall have before passing; similarly, they determine the basic procedure followed in the House—the moving of a motion, the proposition of a question, the ensuing debate on the question, the putting of the question to the House for decision, and the ensuing adoption of an order or resolution of the House.[3] Although many aspects of the ancient usage of the House have been modified or restricted, this essential, uncodified, form of procedure still governs the House's deliberations.

Setting out, in 1854, a critique of the House's approach to legislative business, Thomas Erskine May, well on his way to appointment as Clerk Assistant, made the following observation about the House's relationship with precedent:

> The antiquity of our Parliamentary forms, and the almost unvarying steadiness with which they have been observed for at least three centuries, is a remarkable feature of our Constitution. Precedents for most of the proceedings of the House may be found in the very first volumes of their

---

[1] Thomas Erskine May, 'The Machinery of Parliamentary Legislation', *Edinburgh Review*, January 1854, reprinted with a letter from the author, London, 1881.

[2] R Blackburn and A Kennon (eds), *Griffiths and Ryle on Parliament: Functions, Practice and Procedures*, 2nd edn, (London, Sweet & Maxwell, 2003) 252–56.

[3] ibid, 252.

journals, recorded in a language now quaint and obsolete; but outliving, by the mere force of usage, our written laws, and passing unscathed through civil wars and revolutions. There is a dignity as well as merit in this force of ancient custom, which secures a more willing and reverential obedience than any modern rules or byelaws.[4]

Lest it be thought that May was an advocate of conservatism, he further observed that:

[T]his reverence for custom is not without its evils. ... And thus it has been with our Parliamentary customs, which are part of the Constitution. ... the true faith has not been unmixed with idolatry; and to discontinue an old form was to cast down an idol. ... In matters of form the Commons had almost exposed themselves to Napoleon's sarcasm upon the Bourbons: *Ils n'ont rien appris—ils n'ont rien oublié.*[5]

May had a good deal of sport with the prevailing practices of the House in the 1850s— the difficulty of securing any kind of precedence for government business, the varieties of motion Members sought to have debated, and the utter uselessness of supply procedure— and, as we see in chapter 9, made a case for the reform of legislative business. As the epigraph to this chapter suggests, he argued that precedent could even be found for that procedural device which was anathema to contemporary parliamentarians—the closure.

This chapter sketches the recording of proceedings and precedents in the journals of the House from 1547 and the daily votes from 1680.[6] It examines how the recording of proceedings was constrained out of concern that records of proceedings could be used against the House and individual Members, and examines how the demand for access to precedent drove the later development of the House's information management. It concludes with an assessment of the present value of the House of Commons Journal and the use of alternative sources of information by those seeking authority for procedural continuity and procedural change.

THE 'CLERK'S BOOK' AND THE BEGINNINGS OF THE COMMONS JOURNAL

Since the year of commencement of the first extant Commons journal coincides with the year of the suppression of the College of St Stephen and the gift of its chapel to the House of Commons as a permanent meeting place, it is tempting to imagine the eponymous scribe of the 'booke called Seimour'—John Seymour, chosen MP for Great Bedwyn in 1545, and appointed Under-Clerk of the Parliaments in 1547—sitting in the new House as its Members assembled in November 1547, with a fresh quill, a blank sheet before him and a determination to provide a true record of the House's proceedings.

But JE Neale demonstrated, almost a century ago, that the initial entries in 'Seymour' were in fact John Seymour's fair copies of the jottings of his predecessor at the Table, Robert Ormeston.[7] The first pages of the Journal we attribute to Seymour merely list the readings

[4] May (n 1) 4.
[5] ibid.
[6] The author is indebted to Mark Egan for comments on an earlier draft of this chapter, and to Sir William McKay for assistance in locating the source of the epigraph to this chapter, quoted in the introduction to *Erskine May's Treatise on the Law, Privileges, Proceedings and Usage of Parliament*, 23rd edn (London, LexisNexis, 2004) 5.
[7] JE Neale, 'The Commons' Journals of the Tudor Period' (1920) 4th series, iii *Transactions of the Royal Historical Society* 136.

of bills in the House each day, in a fashion not dissimilar to previous records of proceedings made in the earlier Tudor Parliament Rolls and their Plantagenet predecessors. The preparation, under what seems to have been private initiative, of a record of proceedings by the Commons Clerk, separate from the increasingly cursory record of proceedings made by the Clerk of the Crown in the Parliament Roll, represents a significant step in the development by the Commons of its own separate institutional memory.[8]

According to Neale, Ormeston was in fact the first Clerk in the new House which met in 1547, succeeded by Seymour only in 1548. Even if that is so, he was by no means the first Clerk to attempt to record the House's proceedings from day to day: from at least 1515 records of the House's business are to be found in sources other than the Parliament Rolls,[9] and while there are quibbles over whether these documents can properly be considered a record in the manner of Seymour's book, it is apparent that from the first half of the sixteenth century the Clerks appointed by the Crown to attend upon the Commons appreciated the value of a contemporary record of what had been done in the House. The practice was already established in the House of Lords, the Journal of which dates from 1510.

The journal kept by Seymour's successor, Fulk Onslow, is believed throughout to be a fair copy of notes written at the Table—though by the end of Elizabeth's reign Onslow's frequent absences through illness meant that these notes were increasingly prepared by under-clerks.[10] These records of proceedings are silent on the matter of their own status, and we must take for granted the diligence of Seymour and Onslow in their record-keeping and in their assessment of the merit in this activity.

Thus the Journal was not conceived, from its inception, as a complete procedural record. What AF Pollard described as 'private enterprises on the part of the clerks', later written up into the Journal, developed piecemeal from a list of readings of bills into a more substantial record of proceedings, the content of which must have been dependent on at least two factors: the conscientiousness and consistency of the recording official, and the desire of the House itself to keep a record of its decisions for future reference. For the first three decades of the record, there is scant evidence that it is being used as a reference source or as an authority to demonstrate former usage.

The first evidence of a record made in the Journal at the direction of the House itself occurred in May 1572—a report of an order from the Privy Council for a Member to travel to Stamford, in Lincolnshire, on the Queen's service, directed by the Speaker 'to be set down, and noted accordingly', presumably by the Clerk.[11] The first recorded instance of the Clerk's notes made for the Journal being cited as precedent occurs at the opening of the session in January 1581 when the House appeared unsure how to proceed, Speaker Bell having

---

[8] See AF Pollard, 'The Clerk of the Crown' (1942) 57 *English Historical Review* 312, 329–30.

[9] Neale (n 7) 140.

[10] ibid, 145–46; Sheila Lambert, 'Procedure in the House of Commons in the Early Stuart Period' (1980) 95 *English Historical Review* 753, 771–72.

[11] Commons Journal (hereafter CJ) i (1547–1628) 96, cited in D Menhennet, 'The Journal of the House of Commons: A Bibliographical and Historical Guide', House of Commons Library Paper No 7 (London, 1971) p. 15. The Member in question was Francis Harington, one of the members for Stamford returned in May 1572. The Burghley estate, property of William Cecil, Baron Burghley, Secretary of State until July 1572 and Lord High Treasurer thereafter until his death in 1598, lay just to the south of Stamford. Burghley had served as an MP for Stamford in 1547: his eldest son Thomas Cecil was returned as an MP for Stamford in 1562/3, 1571 and (alongside Harington) in 1572.

died during Prorogation. The choice of Speaker in the Elizabethan Commons was generally a foregone conclusion, though form dictated that the Commons should appear to have a free choice.[12] Francis Knollys, Treasurer of the Household, set proceedings in motion by offering his view on what the nearest precedent should be. He suggested that an analogous situation had occurred in 1566 before the choice of Richard Onslow to succeed Thomas Williams, and cast around for justification:

> But because Fulk Onslowe Gentleman, Brother of the said Mr Onslowe, being the Clerk to attend upon this House, was then present, and sitting in his Place, as Clerk; and had there his original Book of Notes, out of the which the said Copy was taken; he was commanded to read the said Precedent, as it was set down and entered in his said Book; which he did accordingly.

It is notable not only that this appeal to precedent, while eventually conclusive, was disputed, but also that the notebook kept by Onslow at the Table, rather than the Journal subsequently produced from such notes, was the authority upon which Members were said to rely.

If the choice of Speaker on this occasion was indeed stage managed, the episode as recorded in the Journal demonstrates that several participants were either entirely unaware of the artifice or acting the part with a zeal which was not entirely helpful. The Journal entry for the proceeding—a summary by Onslow of the notes he took at the Table— demonstrates the range of recorded opinion in the House over the virtue of relying upon a single precedent:

> Upon the Reading whereof, after divers Motions made, and Speeches delivered, to sundry Ends and Purposes, tending some of them partly to want of sufficient Warrant to deal or treat of that Matter, or any other, among themselves, without a Speaker, and much less of any dealing with the Higher House; and partly to the Singularity of that said Precedent, being the only Precedent, which could be shewed in such Manner of Proceeding, and therefore subject to Peril of Innovation and Inconvenience, rather than warranted upon any good Grounds; Others thinking it to be a Breach of Duty towards her Majesty to enter into that, or any other Consultation, before her Highness's Pleasure first be known touching a Speaker, for want of whom, to take the Voices, and moderate the Consultation, the House had, as yet, no Warrant to resolve of any thing; and that those, which should go on such Message, could have no good Warrant to deliver it in the Name of the House, when as the House could not, as yet, treat of any thing at all; ... It was at last agreed, by the greater Number of the few Voices, that the said Precedent should be followed.[13]

Accordingly a commission of Commons and Lords was appointed to seek the Queen's permission for the Commons to choose a Speaker. A likely candidate, Sir John Popham, one of the Members for Bristol, was at the time assisting in the Lords as Solicitor-General: there was some question as to his eligibility, and accordingly Onslow was obliged to read his notes of 1566 out again to indicate the precedent. Popham was restored to the Commons, made the customary speech seeking to decline the Speakership, and was hauled to the Chair.[14] Not all procedural issues surrounding the election were determined by precedent: in the

---

[12] Andrew Thrush, 'The Officers and Servants of the House' in Andrew Thrush and John P Ferris (eds), The History of Parliament: The House of Commons 1604–1629 (Cambridge, Cambridge University Press, 2010).

[13] CJ i (1547–1628) 116, cited in Menhennet (n 11). None of the motions made, or the names of their movers, are recorded.

[14] CJ i (1547–1628), 116–17.

absence of a Speaker, the question as to whether newly elected Members should be able to vote in the election of Speaker was de facto determined by Knollys, who—with the leave of the House—directed that new Members should forbear from participation until cases relating to their election had been decided. Thus the choice of a favoured Speaker was eventually secured.

The episode above may illustrate the recognition by the late Elizabethan House of the value of recorded precedent, either set down in a Clerk's notebook or journal or—even better—manifest in person in the institutional memory and experience of a long-serving official. Precedent did not automatically trump all other considerations: a single precedent could be a bad one, and acting strictly in accordance with precedent was no sure defence against the ill humour of the sovereign. More to the point, an adherence to precedent which threatened to thwart the designs of the administration could simply be overridden by a decision of the House.

It is beyond the scope of this chapter to provide a detailed exegesis of the relationship between the Journal record, procedural developments and the relative political power of the Commons in the early seventeenth century. It is nevertheless apparent that the record of proceedings in the Journal attracted greater attention, and arguably assumed greater significance, in the Parliaments under James I. In his thorough analysis of the development of the Commons and its procedures, Josef Redlich identified in the Jacobean Journals a number of decisions which sought to determine the order of discussion of matters in the House, indicating a shift from reliance on oral tradition to 'a customary law fixed by reference to the Journals', and beginning to 'create new procedure by express enactment'.[15]

Some care ought to be taken when relying on the form of the Journal record as an indication of procedural development and changes in institutional relationships. For instance, it has been suggested that Wallace Notestein's influential demonstration of the House's greater use of committees in the reign of James I to counter the influence of the King and his privy counsellors may rest in part on a misinterpretation of changes in the method of preparing the Journal.[16] This encapsulates the perennial dilemma inherent in determining the form of entries in the Journal, at least in the modern era, where there is constant pressure to amend settled forms to increase their accessibility and relevance. Since a change in the form of minuting proceedings might be mistaken for a change in their substance, an innate conservatism in minuting style has developed. This has ensured a consistency and continuity in the style of Journal entries to the extent that it is observed—not always kindly—that the proceedings recorded in the modern Journal might be entirely intelligible to a Clerk of the eighteenth century, if not earlier.

The central tenet of Notestein's thesis is undeniably correct. Changes in substance were certainly afoot in the early seventeenth century, and heavily influenced the conditions under which the Journal was prepared. Any autonomy Seymour and Onslow may have enjoyed in recording proceedings was not extended to Onslow's successor, Ralph Ewens, appointed in January 1603. Like Seymour, Ewens had been a Member before his appointment.[17]

---

[15] Josef Redlich, *The Procedure of the House of Commons: A Study of its History and Present Form* (London, Constable, 1908) vol 1, 43–44.

[16] Wallace Notestein, *The Winning of the Initiative by the House of Commons* (London, Oxford University Press, 1924). The misinterpretation of Journal entries is suggested in Lambert (n 10) 772–73.

[17] He was returned for Winchelsea in 1597 and for Beverley in 1601.

His studies at Gray's Inn may not have prepared him sufficiently for the post: an examination of what survives of his rough notes reveals hurried learning on the job, with scribbled *aides-mémoire* on the significance of certain general procedures.[18]

In June 1607 the Committee for Privileges examined the notes made by Ewens 'in his Journal book', and he indicated that he intended to write up his notes into a full Journal for each of the three sessions of the 1604 Parliament. From this point on the Journal was subject to significant editorial control by Members. On 3 July 1607 the House resolved that Ewens should, during the forthcoming prorogation, 'perfect his Journal for these three first Sessions of the 1604 Parliament' and that no matter 'concerning Privilege, Order, or Matter of Message, or Conference, or Resolution of the House, proceeding thereupon' should have force until examined by a similar committee in the forthcoming session and approved by the House.[19] The Committee for Privileges then ordered not only that it should henceforth sit every Saturday afternoon to examine the Clerk's recording of matters of privilege, but also that 'in regard to the great Pains, which the Clerk is to take in perfecting the said Journals, some Course be taken, the next Session, for his better Encouragement'.[20] This was probably less a reflection on Ewens's professional competence—although his record-keeping left much to be desired—than an indication of growing concern in the House about the nature of the record that was being kept and the precedents which were thereby being recorded and established.[21] While the benefit of an independent record to a House gradually asserting its independence from the Crown was clear, the content of the record was capable of being used to the House's detriment, and the clerk, as a Crown appointee, was not necessarily to be trusted. Sheila Lambert suggests that the close attention being paid to 'the Clerk's book' indicated a Commons keen to ensure that unhelpful precedents were not written into the record.[22]

Committees to examine 'the Clerk's book'—that is, the contemporaneous draft of the Journal—were convened regularly in the 1620s, typically meeting on Saturday mornings to examine (and presumably to sanction) the record made by the Clerk. The Journal records the appointment of such committees in 1620, 1621, 1623 and 1628: the committee appointed in 1623 was expressly empowered 'to strike out what they think fit' and ordered 'to examine precedents relating to the manner of the clerk making entries'.[23] The Clerk would take a full note of proceedings at the Table, which, upon agreement with the inspecting committee, would be written up in the Journal as the authorised record. The Clerk could therefore include names of speakers and committee members and the text of contributions in his book, but they would generally not be copied out into the Journal, which, although a valuable repository of sanctioned precedent, was susceptible to seizure and examination.

The method was not absolute proof against interference by the Crown in the House's proceedings. For instance, the notes taken during the 1621–22 Parliament by John Wright,

[18] Lambert (n 10) 771.
[19] CJ i (1547–1628) 390.
[20] See 'EWENS, Ralph (d 1611), of Gray's Inn, London and Southcowton, Yorks' in PW Hasler (ed), *The House of Commons 1558–1603* (London, HMSO, 1981).
[21] For an indication of the process followed by Ewens in the preparation of the Journal from notes—and the deficiencies in his record—see Thrush (n 12).
[22] Lambert (n 12) 771–72, and 'The Clerks and Records of the House of Commons, 1600–1640' (1970) 43 *Bulletin of the Institute of Historical Research* 223.
[23] CJ i, 520, 669, 673, 683 and 734.

appointed Clerk in 1612, fell into the hands of the Privy Council upon Wright's arrest after the end of the 1621 session and were subsequently used in the interrogation of several Members arrested on suspicion of treason in January 1622.[24] Only in 1628, following vociferous complaint from Sir Edward Coke and others, was the practice of recording speeches in the Clerk's book suppressed.[25] It was not to be revived, even after the passage of the Bill of Rights in 1689 with its express protection against the 'impeaching or questioning' of proceedings in Parliament.

Between 1629 and 1640, the period of personal rule when Charles I dispensed with the advice and the supply provided by Parliament, the duties of the Commons Clerk in relation to record-keeping were negligible, and the office fell vacant. When in December 1639 Charles was persuaded of the necessity of summoning Parliament, Henry Elsyng—the younger son of, and sometime assistant to, Henry Elsyng, Clerk of the Parliaments from 1621 to 1635—secured the patent to the Commons clerkship through the good offices of William Laud Archbishop of Canterbury.[26] He was soon called into service, as Charles summoned Parliament to meet in April 1640. Elsyng expressly requested some additional administrative capacity, and John Rushworth was appointed that month as the first recorded Clerk.

The appointment of Rushworth was a shrewd move—both for Elsyng, who no doubt foresaw trouble, and for the House, where Elsyng was assuredly regarded with suspicion in some quarters. Nevertheless, the appointment of an undoubtedly capable man represented a calculated risk. Rushworth was an inveterate scribbler, and had spent, by his own account, much of the period of the Personal Rule from 1629 to 1640 observing, and taking shorthand notes of, 'all occurrences of moment during that interval in the Star Chamber, Court of Honour, and Exchequer Chamber, when all the Judges of England met there upon extraordinary cases; at the Council-table when great cases were heard before the king and council'.[27] His reputation no doubt preceded him, for on his appointment the House expressly ordered—in line with the practice established in 1628 for the Clerk's book—that he 'shall not take any Notes here, without the precedent Directions and Command of this House, but only of the Orders and Reports made in this House'.[28]

Clearly, Rushworth had difficulty complying with the order, since on 1 December 1640 the House further ordered:

> That it be referred to the Committee, that is appointed for the Clerk's Book, to peruse and consider of Mr Rushworth's Notes; and to present to the House what they think fit to be preserved: And, in the meantime, the Clerk, and his Assistant, to be enjoined, that they suffer no Copies to go forth of any Argument or Speech whatsoever: They are likewise to examine, what Copies have heretofore been delivered out, and to whom.[29]

[24] Lambert, 'Clerks and Records' (n 22) 217; Thrush (n 12), and Simon Healy, 'MALLORY, William (1577/8–1646), of Studley Royal, nr Ripon, Yorks' in Thrush and Ferris (n 12).

[25] Lambert (n 12) 772.

[26] Lambert, 'Clerks and Records' (n 22) 218; JC Sainty, 'Elsynge, Henry (bap 1606, d 1656)', *Oxford Dictionary of National Biography* (Oxford, Oxford University Press, 2004).

[27] Joad Raymond, 'Rushworth, John (c 1612–1690)', *Oxford Dictionary of National Biography* (Oxford, Oxford University Press, 2004). Rushworth's surviving observations were later published as *Historical Collections of Private Passages of State* (8 vols, London, 1721).

[28] CJ ii, 12.

[29] CJ ii, 42.

It is a professional requirement of Clerks that they undergo periods of voluntary deafness, and the injunction on Rushworth appears to have had no permanent effect on his noting of proceedings and speeches which, to judge from the published volumes of his works covering the period, continued unabated.[30] Without his disregard for instructions, we would have been deprived of the blow-by-blow account of the incident which occasioned one of the most famous Journal entries.

On 4 January 1642, while at the Table, Rushworth took what he claimed to be a verbatim note of the King's words uttered in the Chamber upon his arrival in an attempt to arrest five Members who Charles considered instrumental not only in inciting the London mob against him but also preparing impeachment proceedings against the Queen for supposed involvement in Catholic plots.[31] The Commons having procrastinated over its response to an order to deliver up the alleged miscreants, Charles arrived in person to seek to arrest them—fruitlessly, as they had fled up on a tip-off. The Journal, apparently in Elsyng's hand, recorded only the King's initial words to the Commons—'Gentlemen, I am sorry to have this occasion to come unto you ...'—alongside the sidenote 'King Charles sits in the Speaker's Chair and speaketh to the Commons': a record of the immediate adjournment of the House on the King's departure followed.[32] By Rushworth's account, later that day Black Rod was sent to bring him to Charles, who had observed his activities and demanded to see the notes. Rushworth pleaded in vain the House's strict injunction, reiterated barely a month earlier, against the reporting of words spoken by Members in the Chamber, to which Charles replied that he wanted only a copy of the words he himself had spoken. Rushworth capitulated and made a fair copy, which Charles immediately had printed and distributed.[33]

Whether or not Rushworth embellished his role in the publication of an account of the incident, the background to the incident demonstrates the sensitivity of the Commons to any record, or publication out of doors, of its activities or of material that might injure its claims of privilege or imperil its Members. Elsyng, in a tricky position, judiciously ignored the substance of the proceeding. Charles no doubt sought to demonstrate the insolence shown by the House to the Sovereign. Instead, the element of the episode which now has greatest resonance is the declaration by Speaker Lenthall—now customarily read as a statement of defiance—that:

> May it please Your Majesty, I Have neither Eyes to see, nor Tongue to speak in this Place, but at the House is pleased to direct me, whose Servant I am here; and humbly beg your Majesty's Pardon, that I cannot give any other Answer than this, to what your Majesty is pleased to demand of me.[34]

A PUBLISHED RECORD OF PROCEEDINGS: THE VOTE

The content of the early Stuart Journals was largely restricted to an account of procedural transactions. The House was nevertheless taking steps to print and distribute certain

---

[30] For his writings for December 1640, see Rushworth, *Historical Collections* (n 27) vol 4, 68–135.

[31] The members concerned were John Hampden, Arthur Haselrig, Denzil Holles, John Pym and William Strode.

[32] CJ ii, 368.

[33] Rushworth, *Historical Collections* (n 27) vol 4, 428.

[34] ibid, 477–78; the account is reproduced in *Cobbett's Parliamentary History of England* (London, 1807) vol 2, cols 1009–11.

accounts of its proceedings, principally for propaganda purposes. In July 1641 the House resolved that two votes—namely a resolution on the Protestation and a resolution that copies be distributed by Members 'to the several places for which they serve'—be attested by the Clerk and printed for distribution, the better to encourage the populace to subscribe to it.[35] In June 1642, as hostilities between Parliament and the Crown escalated, the House appointed a committee

> to consider of the best way of putting the publick Orders and Votes of the House in Execution; and of divulging, dispersing, and publishing the said Orders, Votes, and also the Declarations of the House, through the Kingdom; and of the well and true Printing of them: And have Power to employ Messengers, as they shall see Occasion; and to make them Allowances; and to sit when and where they please.[36]

The Committee ordered the printing and distribution of certain decisions of the House—most notably the Grand Remonstrance of November 1641—but did not order the systematic printing and publication of accounts of its decisions. From May 1649 the Rump Parliament began to publish the weekly newsletter *Severall proceedings in Parliament*, later renamed *General proceedings of state affaires*, edited by the Clerk of the Parliament, Henry Scobell. This cannot, however, be regarded as a complete or reliable procedural record of the proceedings of the House during the Commonwealth.

External access to the full Journal record remained restricted after the restoration of the monarchy in 1660. In October 1666 the House resolved 'That no Persons be permitted to have the Inspection of the Journal Books, but such as are Members of this House', and at the same time gave leave for the introduction of a Bill 'for Punishment of such Members as shall make Misrepresentations abroad of what doth pass in the House'.[37] There was clearly a market for the inside information from the Journal: in 1680 a publication purporting to reproduce manuscript Journal entries for several months in 1678 and 1679 was in profitable circulation.[38]

In October 1680 the House ordered the systematic daily printing and publication of the Vote—a stripped-down account of its proceedings, based on the Journal record but omitting sensitive information such as the numbers voting in divisions and the composition of committees. Although some Members argued for publication of this record out of high principle and the public's right to know, most considered publication to have a more self-serving motivation. It was after all as a means to counter misrepresentation of the actions and decisions of Members opposed to the Court party during the Exclusion Crisis—the period of open hostility between the Crown and Parliament between 1678 and 1681 over legislative attempts to exclude the Roman Catholic heir presumptive, James, Duke of York, from the succession.[39] The order was not revived by the House elected in 1685, and printing of the Votes was recommenced by the Convention Parliament only in October 1689, after two unsuccessful attempts to have printing and publication authorised. At last the House succumbed to the argument that it was impossible 'to keep the Votes out of the Coffee-houses'

---

[35] CJ ii, 230, cited in Betty Kemp, 'Votes and Standing Orders of the House of Commons: The Beginning', House of Commons Library Paper No 8 (London, 1971) 18.

[36] CJ ii, 604.

[37] CJ viii (1660–67) 639, cited in Menhennet (n 11) 17–18.

[38] Menhennet (n 11) 18–19.

[39] Kemp (n 35) 19–21.

and consented to daily publication of an authorised account to counter any false information in circulation.[40]

SUMMONING PRECEDENTS: THE INDEXING OF THE JOURNALS

As recorded in chapter 1, Thomas May's first association with the House of Commons occurred when he was appointed to assist Thomas Vardon, the Librarian.[41] The task of what we would now call information management facing Vardon, and his new assistant, was substantial. Chapters 5 and 6 record some examples of the attempts that were made to collect and categorise precedents taken from the Journals and elsewhere to form manuals of procedure of one kind or another. But these various examples of individual enterprise had a somewhat unofficial (though often respected) nature, and the House began to see the need for more official action.

In 1836 the task of preparing a general index to the House of Commons Journals since 1820 was entrusted to Vardon, and must have taken up a substantial proportion of his time and of the resources of the Library (see chapter 2). The indexing project upon which Vardon embarked was a response to an information management crisis which had its roots several decades earlier, and which itself was symptomatic of the maturing understanding within the Commons of the value of its official records and the uses to which the information they contained might be put.

As described above, the Votes were printed and published regularly and commercially for the first time in 1680, with a hiatus between 1685 and 1689: though initially a means for putting across an authorised account of the proceedings in the House, sanctioned by the Speaker, their form and content settled into a more standard format. They appear to have been in popular demand: in 1701 Daniel Defoe's 'Legion Letter' to the Speaker protested about the high cost of the daily prints of the Votes, which, although they had a cover price of twopence, were apparently being sold for fourpence or more by the printer, who himself had paid £10 for the daily licence to print.[42]

By the end of the seventeenth century the House was therefore keeping two parallel records of its proceedings: the Journal, written up in draft by the Clerk of the House from notes taken at the Table, subsequently checked and rewritten as the definitive, but unpublished, manuscript record;[43] and the Votes, comprising an account of proceedings in the House based on the Clerk's record but on occasion embellished by reports of speeches and other accounts as the Speaker might direct, printed and published as soon as practicable following each sitting day, then bound and indexed at the end of each session.[44]

The manuscript Journals and the printed Votes did not always provide the ready reference for precedents on privilege which Members increasingly sought. The run of Journals

---

[40] ibid, 23.
[41] Vardon was appointed as a Clerk in February 1828 and was appointed Librarian in June 1828: he relinquished his clerkship in September 1831. CC Pond, 'Vardon, Thomas (1799–1867)', *Oxford Dictionary of National Biography* (Oxford, Oxford University Press, 2004).
[42] ibid, 25.
[43] Maurice Bond, *Guide to the Records of Parliament* (London, HMSO, 1971) 205.
[44] From 1680 the practice of printing the Votes in fact greatly assisted in the timely completion of the Journal.

kept by the Clerk was incomplete: upon his appointment as Clerk in 1683, Paul Jodrell had to petition the King for an Order in Council to seize Journal volumes and other records which were 'in several persons' hands', and for a further order for the confiscation of the bootleg Journals referred to above, which were being hawked by unscrupulous Westminster booksellers.[45] From 1689 onwards Jodrell took on a Clerk with the express task of keeping the Journals and other records 'in order and from Confusion', who was required 'to attend constantly whilst the House is sitting, and at all times on Members of the House upon searches'.[46]

Such efforts did not always bear fruit. In 1697 a committee examining a petition undertook a search for precedents for bailing individuals who had been committed to custody by the House. Some precedents had been found, including one from 1680, which in turn drew upon more ancient precedent: a report of those precedents had been made to the House but not entered in the Journal. This in itself was not necessarily surprising. Committee Clerks were issued with their own minute books for the recording of proceedings and for making notes from which committee reports might be prepared, and it was not unusual for manuscript reports of committees to have been be lost or mislaid after they had been read in the Chamber and handed in at the Table.[47] Nevertheless, as a reference source the Journal overall clearly fell short of the standard expected, as the subsequent entry indicates:

> Sir Rowland Gwyn also acquainted the House, That, upon searching for the said Precedents, they found, that many of the Books of the Journals of the House, before the Year One thousand Six hundred and Eighty-five, are much worn, ill written, and without any Indexes.

> Ordered, That all the Journals of this House, until the Year One thousand Six hundred and Eighty-five, be fairly transcribed; and Indexes made, by the Clerk, of the Journals so transcribed, with references to the Folios of the original Books: And that it be recommended to the Lords Commissioners of the Treasury to pay the Charge thereof.[48]

Gwyn's pursuit of precedents was founded less on high principle than on political opportunism, but even if the motivation for seeking out precedents was patently self-serving, the notion that the House's ancient privileges and procedures could be turned to the aid of political projects was a powerful one. The order made by the House thus reflects a concern to preserve—and make more accessible—precedents which were likely to assist Members in their political enterprises.[49] The order that a manuscript copy only be made may also reflect

---

[45] OC Williams, *The Clerical Organisation of the House of Commons* (Oxford, Clarendon Press, 1954) 36–37. It transpired that the Secretary to the Navy, one Samuel Pepys, had borrowed several folios to assist with his attempts to counter allegations of his involvement in the Popish Plot; these were returned promptly upon Jodrell's request.

[46] ibid, 39–40, citing a petition of 1713 of the Clerk and other Officers of the House to Queen Anne for compensation for losses (Appendix II, 291). The first known holder of this post, designated Clerk of the Journals, was the Devon lawyer Zachary Hamlyn (1677–1759): Sheila Lambert, *Bills and Acts: Legislative Procedure in Eighteenth-century England* (Cambridge, Cambridge University Press, 1971) 39–40.

[47] OC Williams, 'The Minute Book of James Courthope' (1953) XX *Camden Miscellany* v–vi. The Courthope minute book—the only one extant—records the proceedings in several committees in 1697 and 1698, though not the proceedings of the committee referred to above.

[48] CJ xii, 256.

[49] Attempts to turn ancient privileges to contemporary political advantage are by no means confined to the seventeenth and eighteenth centuries: see, for example, 'Conduct of the Prime Minister in relation to the war against Iraq', House of Commons Order Paper (Future Business A), 24 November 2004, 9, a notice of motion given on 23 November 2004 inviting the House to appoint a committee to examine the case for impeachment proceedings against the then Prime Minister.

a concern that the Journal and the information it contained should not be made readily available, and certainly not published.[50]

In 1742 a committee was appointed to consider whether the Journals should be printed. The Clerk, Nicholas Hardinge, was ordered to undertake an audit of the present state of the Journals. He found a sizeable lacuna in the record for the later years of Elizabeth I's reign, and several omissions from the record of Parliaments under James I, where the journal consisted often of the Clerk's notes alone without subsequent copying out. Although the record could be made up from other contemporary accounts and from a number of duplicate records, the quality of the hand in which several Journals had been written was poor, and several volumes had been 'impaired, and damaged by Mildew'. The fair copies ordered to be made in 1697 had been prepared, save for the period from 1642 to 1660, but were 'very erroneous', and no index had been compiled.[51] He submitted a further memorandum to the committee, with a detailed business plan for the printing of the Journals, which he concluded with the words: 'It is not doubted, but that the House will effectually restrain the printing or selling of any Edition of the Journals, or any Abridgment thereof, or any Collections therefrom, which shall not be warranted by their own Order.'

The committee inspected the Journals and concurred with Hardinge's opinion.[52] The estimates for the cost of printing, and the business plan, having been examined, the committee recommended printing of the Journal under Hardinge's direction, in thirty volumes, of which 1,000 copies each would be produced, with a preface and index to each volume and a general index to the whole, and further recommended that he be compensated for the loss of income he would sustain for the enterprise. The House assented, allocating £5,000 to the printing project and a further £1,000 compensation to Hardinge. The committee's resolution was amended in only one respect: the House stipulated that the copies of the Journal be printed for the use of Members only.

The order that the Journals should be fully indexed is notable, though it is unsurprising that the order of 1697 that the Journals be indexed was not in fact carried out. Indexing science was in its infancy (see chapter 6) and indexes to publications in English—as opposed to tables of contents—were very rare. In fact, none of the volumes of the Journal printed in 1742 were indexed, and the project of a general index to the Journals was not taken forward. Only in 1766 did a committee recommend that the Speaker take the matter in hand 'instantly', appointing such person or persons as appeared properly qualified to take on the project.[53] Of the proposals to prepare an index put before the Committee, the scheme proposed by Edward Moore was initially preferred, and work put in train.[54] In 1770, however, the plan Moore had devised, and the work he had undertaken, were rejected, and a scheme proposed by Roger Flexman was taken up. The following year this plan was itself superseded by a joint plan drawn up by four indexers—Moore, Flexman, Nathaniel Forster

---

[50] It has since been established that this information loss is most likely to have occurred on the death of the hapless Ralph Ewens in 1612: not only had he failed to complete his task of 'perfecting the Journal', but several of his Commons papers were lost in the dispersal of his estate. See Lambert, 'Clerks and Records' (n 22) 224–25.

[51] CJ xxiv, 262–66, reprinted in Menhennet (n 11) Appendix Two, 58–68.

[52] Menhennet (n 11) 20.

[53] A fuller account of the series of catastrophic decisions which beset the project can be found in chapter 6.

[54] For this passage see Menhennet (n 11) 30–32.

and Timothy Cunningham. But although the scheme had been jointly agreed, the preparation of the general index was then divided chronologically between the four. While it might
have been expected that they would consult as their work advanced, a further committee
set up in 1776 to examine progress on the index found that the four indexes in preparation
diverged so greatly that each ought to be issued separately, prefaced with an explanation by
each indexer. Thus three forms of index were to be produced, Cunningham being ordered
to follow the scheme adopted by Flexman. The indexing project was finally completed by
1785, at a cost estimated in 1911 to have been some £24,490—about £3.5 million in today's
prices.[55] The House had, by then, a general index to the Journals from 1547 to 1774, but
in four parts, under different compilers, and with an inconsistent approach to the subject
matter which meant that researches across the periods covered by the four volumes could
not be undertaken with any consistency or reliability.

Future work on general indexes followed to a great extent the scheme initially proposed
by Moore and largely followed in his section of the index, which was from 1714 to 1774.
In 1818 the Second Clerk Assistant, John Rickman, a vigorous and talented administrator
with a gift for information management, modified Moore's scheme and had the indexes
for 1774–90 and 1790–1800 condensed into one volume. This scheme was followed by the
barrister and man of letters Martin Burney in preparing the indexes for 1801–20.[56] The
task of indexing was then taken in-house. In 1823 a committee on the General Index recommended (on the basis of a memorandum from Rickman, by then Clerk Assistant) that
the sessional index to each Journal volume be incorporated into a running general index,
for ease of consultation. In 1825 Rickman reported to a successor committee that the work
to date had been achieved in a satisfactory manner, with the interim volumes available for
consultation in the Library (a facility for Members established in 1819—see chapter 2).
For the sessions from 1820 until 1829 the sessional aggregation was undertaken by the first
Librarian, Benjamin Spiller, but apparently not continued. Fortunately, Spiller's interim
indexes were saved from the fire which engulfed the original Library, and the rest of the
Palace, in 1834.[57]

It had been anticipated that the eventual general index would be published every twenty
years, but the Standing Committee on the Library recommended in 1835 that the index be
brought up to date for the period 1820–34, and published without delay. Delay there was,
however, and it took a further year for Speaker Abercromby to direct the then Librarian,
Thomas Vardon, to complete the work. The demise of William IV and the accession of
Queen Victoria in 1837 offered a convenient point to break the work on the index and, with
some necessary modifications to the original Moore–Rickman scheme, Vardon completed
the volume in August 1839.

The indexing task must have accounted for a considerable proportion of Vardon's time
and of the Library's resource, of which a principal unit—and perhaps the only other unit
besides Vardon—was the young Thomas May. Vardon did not, in his preface to the Index

[55] Menhennet, ibid, quoting the memorandum of the Librarian of the House of Commons to the Select
Committee on Publications and Debate Reports of 1916, HC (1914–16) 321.
[56] Menhennet, ibid.
[57] Thomas Vardon, Preface to the *General Index to the Journals of the House of Commons, 1820–1837* (London,
1839) v–vii.

for 1820 to 1837, acknowledge any assistance, but the copy of that volume which is presently kept in the House of Commons Journal Office hints at a shared endeavour. On the frontispiece, an unknown hand has inserted in pencil, between the words 'PREPARED BY' and 'Thomas Vardon', the words 'Thomas May &'.

In 1845 the Library Committee examined the indexes and found that the run from 1774 to 1837 was 'precisely uniform', while Moore's index was 'sufficiently uniform' to allow it to sit with the recent indexes. Speaker Shaw-Lefevre nevertheless considered (rightly) that the three earliest volumes in the series, compiled by Cunningham, Flexman and Forster respectively, provided an 'imperfect means of reference' for the Journals from 1547 to 1714, and asked the committee to consider whether a reindexing should be undertaken. The committee readily concurred, having in mind 'the convenience of the House, and the vast importance of the Journals in legal and historical research'.[58] It would not be an easy task: the committee recommended that it be compiled from the seventeen Journal volumes for the period spanning 167 years, which comprised 13,702 pages, and noted that 'the changes which successively arose in the Forms of Proceeding will add to the difficulty of arranging, in a lucid and consistent order, the large mass of Precedents which will be collected'.

Vardon and May took up this task, at the same time as Vardon was compiling the General Index which would run from 1837 to 1852. By the standard of previous indexers, it was compiled in a remarkably short period: the Preface was signed off—this time by both contributors—on 5 April 1852. It has now entirely supplanted its three antecedents as the standard index of the pre-Hanoverian Journals.

The arduous task of arranging precedents which the Library Committee envisaged was in fact completed by Vardon and May with little fanfare. The preface to the new index made no express mention of their work in compiling precedents, or indeed any mention of their significance. Whereas the instances of precedent gathered by Hatsell are set out at length over four volumes, in a style which suggests to the reader the conclusions to be drawn, the Vardon–May index lists a mere sixty-six instances where precedents had expressly been entered in the Journals, over thirty-one categories. A further five Journal entries are indexed as matters which the House has ordered not to be treated as precedent.[59] There are over thirty instances of committees appointed to search the Commons Journals for particular types of proceeding, and forty instances of committees appointed to search expressly for precedents relative to certain matters—such as procedure on elections, the holding of conferences with the Lords, procedure on the passage of bills, privileges of the House and impeachments.[60]

Vardon and May, in the Preface, commended Shaw-Lefevre for 'his enlightened solicitude to improve and simplify the Proceedings of the House, without departing from the principles and spirit of its ancient usage'.[61] In truth, the determinations they made of the precedents to be recognised in the pre-Hanoverian Journals, and the precise fashion in which they dissected the corpus of conflicting and overlapping proceedings and precedents recorded in that period, contributed immeasurably to the demystification of the ancient and immemorial usages invoked as a defence against any modernisation.

---

[58]   Report of the Standing Committee on the Library, HC (1845) 610, 5.

[59]   Thomas Vardon and Thomas Erskine May, *General Index to the Journals of the House of Commons, 1547–1714* (London, 1852) 871–72.

[60]   ibid, 265–66.

[61]   ibid, vi.

THE JOURNALS AFTER MAY'S *TREATISE*

While assisting with the indexing of the Journal for 1820–37 must have occupied a good deal of May's time and energy, he was also, of course, preparing his *Treatise* for publication in 1844, an exercise no doubt well informed by his devilling for Vardon in the Library as well as by the various antecedents to May's *Treatise* described in chapters 5 and 6. His subsequent work on the 1547–1714 index must have influenced the content of the second and third editions, in 1851 and 1855, respectively, and certainly informed the sardonic observation which heads this chapter.

Thomas Vardon concluded his 1857 preface to the General Index to the Journals for 1837–52 with an encomium to May's *Treatise* which seemed almost to suggest that it had eliminated the need for indexes to the Journal. However, he proceeded to compile a further volume—covering the sessions from 1852–53 to 1865—before retiring in 1868, whereupon the task of preparing the General Index was passed to the Clerk of the Journals.

The value of the Journal as an authoritative record and source of precedent continued to be recognised, despite the attempts of those inside and outside the House to rationalise the House's record-keeping. In the early twentieth century the House sought efficiencies through amalgamation and rationalisation of its various printing contracts with commercial printers and with His Majesty's Stationery Office, at the same time as it was seeking efficiencies and rationalisation of its own procedures. A Select Committee on Official Publications, reporting in 1906, after most of the radical reforms of procedure effected in in the early years of the twentieth century had been made, marked a shift from the reverence that earlier committees had shown for the treasure trove of precedent contained in the Journals to an emerging attitude that they were the exclusive preserve of procedural nerds. It observed that while the Journals 'are not much consulted by Members or Government Departments, they are essential to Mr Speaker and Officers of the House in searching for precedents'.[62] A decade later, a grossly impertinent suggestion from the Treasury that the twin publications of the Official Report (*Hansard*) and the Journal be amalgamated received short shrift from Speaker Lowther, even though in the course of his stout defence he too recognised a certain shrinking of the audience for them:

> The Journals in their present form offer a ready instrument in the hands of those whose duty it may be from time to time to search for, and be guided by, the precedents in procedure which they contain.[63]

The Committee, having received a copy of the correspondence, took the hint:

> In view of the strong opinion expressed by the Rt Hon Gentleman, who has a prolonged experience in the Chair and unrivalled knowledge of suddenly arising emergencies or involved points of order, in which the procedure of the House must be guided by precedent, your Committee felt that an annual volume of the nature of the Journal, apart from the Daily Report, must continue to be published.[64]

---

[62] Report from the Select Committee on Official Publications, &c., HC (1906) 209, para 13.

[63] Report from the Select Committee on Publications and Debates Reports, HC (1916) 112, Appendix 2, 68, cited by Menhennet (n 11) 6.

[64] ibid, para 9

Lowther himself would have been bound to acknowledge that by the early years of the twentieth century the Journal was hardly the sole repository of precedent which it had been before the mid-eighteenth century. The increasingly ready availability of reports of debates had undercut the Journal's claim to be the sole record of proceedings in the House: after the absorption of the debate reporting function into the Commons service in 1909, it was less easy to claim that what had by then become the Official Report provided an unreliable procedural record.

In addition, the respect for precedent as the sole guide to the procedures of the House was undoubtedly waning as the importance of other procedural sources grew and as the House recognised its own competence to make orders and resolutions governing ever more of its proceedings. In 1857 the systematic recording and printing—for private use only— of rulings made by the Speaker commenced. Typically rulings made from the Chair have appeared in reports of debates, but rulings given privately have not been published, and it has been the practice to record in the Journal only the most significant rulings *ex cathedra*, such as the explanations given by Speakers on their use of the casting vote. By the time the series, numbering some two dozen volumes, was discontinued in the 1970s, over 2,700 individual rulings had been recorded, very few of which were susceptible to entry in the Journal. Similarly, the House's increasing appetite for restating, revising and overwriting its ancient procedures with the use of standing orders and resolutions has established new precedents but buried ancient ones.

The Journal continues in publication, alongside the Votes and Proceedings—a publication which replaced the old Vote in 1817 and provided a briefer and more systematic daily record of the House's proceedings. The styles of both were adapted in 1967 to enable mutual consistency, so that the Votes and Proceedings are now, in effect, the first draft of the Journal, themselves prepared from what is still a manuscript book kept by the Clerks at the Table, guided in consistency by a formbook issued by the Journal Office.

The 400th anniversary of the first Journal record was marked in November 1947 with an encomium from the then Clerk of the House, Sir Gilbert (later Lord) Campion. Noting the considerable pains taken to ensure the complete accuracy and consistency of the record, he observed that the Journal was admissible in a court of law as evidence of the House's proceedings.[65] The Journal was indeed afforded this status in the Evidence Act 1845, copies being admissible 'without any proof being given that the copies were printed [by printers to the House]'.[66] It remains the case that the use of the Journal as evidence in a court must be preceded by a petition to the House for use of its proceedings, a practice that derives from the 1818 resolution of the House requiring the leave of the House for its servants to give evidence in court proceedings. The practice in respect of the Journals is now almost wholly in abeyance, as a consequence of the House's decision in 1980 to rescind the requirement that leave be sought for reference to be made to the Official Report in court proceedings. The Committee of Privileges in 1978 considered that the House's privilege of freedom of speech was amply protected by the provisions of Article IX of the Bill of Rights and the care then taken by the courts to exclude evidence which might infringe the House's privilege.[67] By resolution, the House thus formally put an end to the abiding concern over the use out

[65] Sir Gilbert Campion, 'The Commons' Journals', *The Times*, 8 November 1947, 5.
[66] 8&9 Vict, cap 113, s 3.
[67] Committee of Privileges, First Report of Session 1978–79, *Reference to Official Report of Debates in Court Proceedings*, HC (1978–79) 102, para 2.

of doors of the records of its debates—a concern that had been such an influential factor in the preparation of the Journal since the early seventeenth century. The decision inadvertently affected the status of the Journal, since the effect of the House's resolution has been that the *Hansard* record has since been admitted in the courts as sufficient evidence of proceedings, without need to petition the House for production of the Journal.[68] Undoubtedly the Journals are now treated with less reverence outside the House than they were in 1905, when a judge threw out evidence submitted by a plaintiff submitted in a civil case because it consisted merely of extracts from the authorised edition of the Parliamentary Debates.[69]

Campion's assessment of the merits of the Journal bears repetition:

> The most intimate record of 400 years of parliamentary evolution, with the stores of precedents which it contains neatly arranged in its indexes, forms an enduring link with the past and remains an indispensable guide to practice. This link, which is characteristic of English institutions, has two outstanding parliamentary merits. It provides a shield for minorities against the abuse of temporary power and, by maintaining consistency with the past, affords some security that order will go hand in hand with progress.

The Journals, which for the first two centuries of their existence were inaccessible to all but Members and officers of the House, are now more accessible than at any point in their history. The provision for consistent indexing has allowed the historian ready and comparative access to an unparalleled primary source. All volumes of, and indexes to, the Journal from 1835 are generally available online, as are the majority of Tudor and Stuart journals.[70] The meticulous care taken in the preparation and indexing of the Journal—together with the researches into recent and distant precedents undertaken daily in the Journal Office—stand as testament to the unique nature of this record and its continued relevance to parliamentary procedure. And yet there is an abiding irony in the fact that, when access to the Journal and the precedents it contains has never been so open, the level of interest in the House and further afield in the basis and origins of the House's procedures has arguably never been so low.

Recent advances in information management provide further potential benefits to be derived from the unique and substantial repository of procedural information contained in forty-six decades of the Journal. The development of indexing science in the eighteenth century—perfected, in its application to the Journal, by Vardon and May in the mid-nineteenth century and sustained thereafter—has provided ready comparative access to the record of precedent in a form immeasurably more accessible than the digest of precedents offered by Hatsell. Large-scale data analysis, when applied to the Journal record, has the potential to offer up insights into procedural practice and development which may be far deeper than those which can be achieved through the use of a purely analogue index. It is therefore possible to envisage a future where the utility in the publication of an index on traditional lines may not merit the time and cost incurred in its production. Yet the continued production of the Journal, to a consistent standard susceptible to modern techniques of information storage and retrieval, is surely vital to a deeper appreciation of the House's operation in the present, and a guide to how procedure may adapt in the future.

---

[68] In fact the last recorded petition to the House for production of the Journal occurred in Session 1964–65.

[69] Cited by the Clerk of the House in his memorandum to the Committee of Privileges, HC (1978–79) 4.

[70] The first twelve volumes of the Journal, from 1547 to 1699, are available online at <www.british-history.ac.uk/search/series/commons-jrnl>; the volumes from 1835 are available at <www.publications.parliament.uk/pa/cm/cmjournal.htm>.

5

Manuals before May

From the Fourteenth to the Seventeenth Century

DAVID NATZLER

BEFORE THOMAS ERSKINE May seized the field in 1844, there had been many attempts to codify, and sometimes explain, the way in which Parliament worked. This chapter considers some precursors of the *Treatise* from the fourteenth to the seventeenth centuries.

MODUS

The mother of all manuals of English (and Irish) parliamentary practice and procedure is a blessedly short Latin tract written around 1320 and known as the *Modus Tenendi Parliamentum*, or How to hold a Parliament: *Modus* for short. It is first referred to around 1400 and became a standard part of lawyers' textbooks in the fifteenth century. It was first printed in 1570 by John Hooker, of whom more below; Tudor and Stuart antiquarians loved it and quarried it for theories of pre-Norman popular sovereignty. The text was carefully copied into the first volume of the House of Lords Journal. There are early translations into French and English. Sadly there has never been an illustrated edition.

The *Modus* has been extensively studied by parliamentary scholars. There is a readily accessible version in English published in 1980 and edited by Nicholas Pronay and John Taylor.[1] It is now accepted that the *Modus* is a genuine attempt by a contemporary lawyer, probably one of the parliamentary Clerks it refers to, to set out the composition, powers and functions of Parliament, inevitably influenced by recent events and controversies, and with some wishful thinking. AF Pollard called it 'the official handbook to Parliaments'.[2] By the time it became better known it had of course ceased to be an accurate description. The editors of the *Modus* even suggest in a footnote that 'it might equally be said that the first edition of Erskine May would be of limited practical help for parliamentary procedure today'.[3] Actually, May's first edition is of considerable help.

---

[1] Nicholas Pronay and John Taylor, *Parliamentary Texts of the Later Middle Ages* (Oxford, Clarendon Press, 1980).

[2] AF Pollard, *The Evolution of Parliament*, 2nd edn (London, Longmans, Green and Co, 1938) 12.

[3] Pronay and Taylor (n 1) 49, n 125.

The twenty-six brief chapters—rarely more than a paragraph in length—cover many subjects, and the format was copied in later centuries, as will be described in this chapter and in Paul Seaward's (chapter 6). There is much missing. It antedates a Speaker in the Commons. There is little idea of the actual procedure followed for petitions or legislation or tax authorisation or the conduct of cases. It gives little clue what actually happened at meetings, for which we have to wait for the account of the Lincoln Parliament of 1316, the first consecutive account of proceedings.

Reading the *Modus* through, it is clear to me at least that it is directed at a future Clerk who is required by the King to call together a Parliament: the sort of file still maintained in the Clerks' offices. Before even mentioning who is to be summoned, chapter I deals with the summons (*Summonitio*):

> *Summonitio Parliamenti precedere debet primum diem Parliamenti per quadraginta dies.* [The summoning of parliament ought to precede the first day of Parliament by forty days.]

One can imagine the harassed senior Chancery Clerk reminding the court and the Council that a Parliament cannot just happen tomorrow, but requires a good forty days to get the writs out, the meeting-place prepared and so on.[4]

As the *Modus* continues, there is much emphasis on administrative tasks. That includes the receipt of documents from those elected or selected, *ad irrotulandum*, to be enrolled; and considerable details on the expenses regime, which depended on Chancery Clerks preparing writs to send to the relevant local authorities setting out the amount which was due to the knights or burgesses, on a carefully constructed scale, to cover coming, staying and going, *veniendo, morando et redeundo*, meaning subsistence and travel. The rates of levying fines for absence without due cause—known as amercements—are set out at length: probably largely theoretical, but in the early fourteenth century there were serious political problems arising from deliberate absences of peers. And in a modern context it is worth remembering that Parliament can meet wherever in the country the monarch wishes: *Parliamentum tenebitur in quo loco regni regi placuerit.*

The *Modus* is infected with the sort of practical detail which a Clerk needed. A sermon is to be preached on one of the first days of a Parliament: but by whom, and who is to decide? The answer is: it is a person selected by the archbishop in whose province the Parliament is being held. When does it meet? Never on Sundays, thank goodness, but plainly on Saturdays: beginning at mid-prime, or at prime on feast days to give time for a service first. Where are people to sit, and how should they speak, sitting or standing? Speak audibly: if obscure or *basse*, repeat it louder or let another speak for them. How is the *kalendarium* of business to be constructed? The basic principle is first come, first served: *qui prime proposuit prius agat*, subject to priority being given to matters of state (war and the Crown), then matters of common concern to the kingdom, and then private business. The inherent priority of government business is disturbingly familiar.

---

[4] The forty-day rule continues to hold sway in some curious places, despite the coming of the stagecoach, railway, motor car and passenger jet. The Canadian *House of Commons Procedure and Practice* (see chapter X) states: 'Members are exempt from appearing as a witness in any court when the House is in session, 40 days before and after a session, and 40 days following a dissolution of Parliament. This includes periods when Parliament is prorogued.' Speaker Fraser reinforced this claim in a May 1989 ruling: '[T]he right of a Member of Parliament to refuse to attend court as a witness during a parliamentary session and during the 40 days preceding and following a parliamentary session is an undoubted and inalienable right supported by a host of precedents. The courts have not always agreed with this viewpoint' (2nd edn, 107).

Even more familiar and useful, and absent from the early Victorian austerity of Thomas Erskine May, the *Modus* notices staff. Early on there is a fulsome description of the recording tasks of the two principal Clerks and the (possibly fictional) five Clerks, and the arrangements for their pay, dependent on whether or not they eat at the King's table. The five *peritos et approbatos* [expert and proven] Clerks *cum eis vacaverit (iuvabunt) clericos principales ad irrotulandum* [when they have time shall assist the principal clerks in enrolling]. Some early demarcation disputes between Clerks may be detected here.

It is hardly surprising that in a tract written by Clerks their tasks should not be understated. What proved to me on my first reading of the *Modus* that it was indeed a handbook for the Clerk are the references to other staff, and in particular to the doorkeepers, or *hostiarii*, who occupy caput XX. The *hostiarius principalis*, or Principal Doorkeeper, guards the door to ensure that nobody enters who should not, and in a description of the task which is true 700 years on

> *oportet quod hostarius ille habeat cognitionem personarum quae ingredi debent ita quod nulli omnino negetur ingressus qui Parliamentum interesse tenetur; et hostiarius ille potest et debet, si necesse sit, habere plures hostiarios sub se.* [it is necessary that this doorkeeper should recognise those who ought to enter so that no one will be denied entry to Parliament who ought to be in Parliament, and the doorkeeper can and ought, if necessary, to have several assistant doorkeepers under him.]

Some distance away the King assigned his *servientes ad arma*, or serjeants, to prevent any demonstration or disturbance.

Parliament also had a *clamator*, or crier, told by the doorkeeper what to cry: possibly the business under consideration, or the names of those to be summoned in to be heard. Doorkeepers in the Commons still shout the title of the business when moving from one item to the next. The modern annunciator screen is a largely silent *clamator*.

For 250 years we have no significant follower in the footsteps of the *Modus*, so that the vigorous parliamentary life of the fifteenth century is conveyed only by the records of its decisions and occasional diary fragments. Even the early Tudor parliaments do not seem to have spawned a describer.

HOOKER

In 1572 John Hooker, also known as John Vowel, published a slim volume entitled *The Order and Usage of the Keeping of a Parliement in England* (hereinafter *Order and Usage*) in two marginally different versions: one dedicated to the mayor and 'Senators' of his native city of Exeter, and the other, of which only one full copy survives, dedicated to Sir William Fitzwilliam, Lord Deputy of Ireland. It was reprinted as part of the 1587 edition of Holinshed's *Chronicles* of which Hooker was the editor. In 1977 it was reprinted together with a very full introduction and contextual essay by Vernon F Snow, under the title of *Parliament in Elizabethan England*.[5]

Hooker was an Exeter civil lawyer, antiquary and city leader, who served briefly as the Member for the Connaught pocket borough of Athenry in the Irish Parliament of 1569,

---

[5] Vernon F Snow, *Parliament in Elizabethan England: John Hooker's Order and Usage* (New Haven, Yale University Press, 1977).

and as one of the two Members for his native city of Exeter in the 1571 and 1586 English Parliaments. Hooker was an early parliamentary diarist. He appended an account of the 1569 Irish Parliament to his edition of Holinshed. He also kept a diary of the 1571 English Parliament, published in 1879,[6] and drew on this for *Order and Usage*. He was not a political player of any significance in either Westminster or Dublin. He is barely recorded as having spoken or been on committees. He seems from his diaries and later career to have been broadly attached to the Edwardian Protestant tradition, founded in part on his years of exile in Strasbourg. As an Exeter notable, he seems to have been close to Miles Coverdale, Bishop of Exeter from 1551 to 1553 and translator of the Psalms. His fame, such as it is, rests on his treatise on Parliament.

Snow suggests that Hooker's tractate 'served the interests of those trained in the Inns of Court'.[7] The evidence is that it was directed not primarily at an English readership or at the circle of lawyers and antiquaries interested in parliamentary processes, but at those responsible for holding parliaments in Ireland. Hooker had experienced, as a carpetbagger in 1569, the disorganisation of an Irish parliament and the hostility of resident Members. Snow records his contacts with a number of Irish officials, including James Stanihurst, Speaker of the Irish House of Commons.[8] Hooker's dedicatory epistle in the Irish edition, to the Lord Deputy Sir William Fitzwilliam, sets out, truthfully or not, that 'as a result of "douts" concerning the orders, usages, rites and directions of a Parlament' being 'left in susepende and not resolved' he had promised 'to procure a perfect instruction of the orders of the Parlements there used'. It was not, as we shall see, the first time that a handbook to procedures at Westminster was developed to meet the needs of other parliaments.

Hooker's *Order and Usage* was in fact used as the basis for the third and last Irish parliament of Elizabeth's reign, in 1585. Attached to a summons list for the parliament there is a list of nine paragraphs of rules to be observed in the Irish House of Commons, plainly taken from Hooker. Evidence that they were in fact relied on comes from what Snow insensitively describes as 'a petty dispute' about fees between the Serjeant in the Lords and the Gentleman Usher appointed to attend the Chancellor: the committee appointed to sort it out appealed to Hooker to resolve the problem.[9] The transfer of the basic rules seems to have worked, save for resistance by the Irish membership to the standards of English dress and in particular Hooker's advocacy of the gown to be worn by members, which to Irish eyes seemed absurd.

What gives *Order and Usage* an additional interest is that it was published together with the earliest known translation into English—and very readable English—of the *Modus*. The translation gives us a glimpse into the House in Hooker's time, including his translation of *portarius* as 'porter', rather than doorkeeper as in the modern idiom. In his own tractate he describes the Serjeant of the lower House as its 'porter', responsible for keeping the door and keeping the place clean. Hooker's Chief Porter is the ancestor of Oxbridge college porters of today, and the contemporary of Shakespeare's drunken porter in Macbeth. Hooker also has a memorable translation of the vital phrase in the *Modus* about setting the agenda: '[H]e who layeth first his bill in shall be first heard.'

---

[6] In *Transactions of the Devonshire Association* (1879) 442–92.
[7] Snow (n 5) 75, n 24.
[8] ibid, 12.
[9] ibid, 92.

HAKEWILL

William Hakewill was a reluctant author. He was above all a legal politician, serving in several Parliaments, ending as the member for Amersham in 1628. He was a vigorous Member, and a learned one; he was Bodley's executor. He died aged 81 in 1655 and is buried in Wendover.

His account of legislative procedure published in 1641, *The Manner how Statutes are enacted in Parliament by Passing of Bills*, only came about, according to his own account, because one of the many manuscript versions of his collection of legislative precedents had been printed earlier that year without his permission, together with an account of the 1640 Parliament and a translation of the *Modus*. There are few differences between his proper version and the earlier pirate edition.[10] Given that there are no precedents quoted later than 1610, it is probably based on work he completed by that year, updated only in manuscript copies.

In Jacobean times, there was no guide to procedure available to Members or Clerks of the House or others. By contrast, the Lords had decided in 1621 to collect their rules and orders and print them, subject each week's business to analysis and, at the end of each session engross (or, in other words, write down systematically) the rules, as Elsynge (see below) had done. They also provided a house for their Clerk where the records could be preserved, rather than, as in the Commons, seeing them vanish with passing Clerks.

Hakewill states in the Preface that he had read the Journals and had 'reduced under apt parliamentary titles' what must be conceived 'to tend to the rule of the House': in other words, to seek and record good precedents for what was in his view a proper way to proceed. He had been most 'sedulous' in his chapter on the passing of bills since that was 'the daily and most proper work of that house'.

We have some clue as to what the rest of his chapters were about. In October 1939 Catherine Strateman Sims published Hakewill's tractate held in the British Library *Concerning the Speaker's duty in putting of things to the question*.[11] In 1970 Elizabeth Read Foster published a tractate, which on good grounds she attributed to Hakewill, on *Speaking in the House of Commons*, from a manuscript in the Cathedral Library at Exeter, with some additions from the 1620s in a manuscript version in the British Library.[12] This contains the earliest description of the previous question. And in *Manner* at page 37, dealing with the form of clerkly endorsement, Hakewill notes that 'more ample mention shall be made in the chapter which treateth of the dutie of the Clarke'. Sadly this chapter has not (yet) been discovered.

Hakewill clearly observed practices closely and was of a practical turn of mind. As Elizabeth Read Foster observed, he brought to his essays on procedure 'daily knowledge of the House during three reigns, the skill of a lawyer and the zest of an antiquary'.[13]

---

[10] In her long introduction to the Liverpool Tractate (*The Liverpool Tractate, an Eighteenth Century Manual on the Procedure of the House of commons* (New York, Columbia University Press, 1937)) to which I am much indebted for the contents of this chapter, Catherine Strateman (later Strateman Sims) says they are 'substantially identical' (xlii).

[11] (1939) XLV *American Historical Review* 90–95.

[12] (1970) XLIII *Bulletin of the Institute of Historical Research* 35–55.

[13] ibid, 43.

For example, he observes that the Clerk writes down the names of members proposed as committees 'leastwise of such whose names (in that confusion) he can distinctly hear'. When it comes to the Clerk reading the amendments made by the committees (twice, which must have been wearing), he notes that the Member who has made the report may stand by him to help where the text is difficult to read 'which falleth out very often by reason of interlineing or ill writing'. He notes that bills on presentation should be 'faire written in paper, with wide lines', obviously to help the 'interlineing'.

Hakewill also gives a commendably full account of the process of amending bills by alteration or addition. It is striking to read of an account of the amendment of a Bill at Third Reading, where the Clerk who ingrossed (that is to say, wrote out) the Bill has to enter the Chamber and make the amendment standing at the Table by the Clerk, unless it be 'but of a few words' in which case it is done by the Clerk himself, 'writing of a faire hand'. Section 6 on Provisoes and Schedules and amendments (what we would call new clauses) sets out the rules on whether they should be offered in paper or parchment, and more importantly explains how new matter introduced should be endorsed and what questions should be put upon it at each stage. It is striking to a modern reader how many readings were required for Lords Amendments to be passed, and how familiar are the conventions on what can and cannot be done by way of amendment as a Bill progresses.

That makes it the more frustrating that not all his parliamentary essays have been found. The chapter on the Speaker includes one practice not hitherto known to me, that the tellers declare the results 'first naming the least number and then the greatest', leaving it to the Speaker to declare to the House the actual outcome, as he still does. By Scobell's time the current practice of reading first the 'ayes' and then the 'noes' had prevailed. The chapter on Speaking is a fund of good advice, notably on the length of speeches:

> [H]e that speaketh if he be observant shall easily perceive (even while he is speaking) how far he may presume upon the patience of the House in that regard, for if they be well pleased with the speech there will be a great silence and attention; if otherwise, they will talk one with the other, which will cause a murmuring noise and sometime they will hawk and hem or make some noise by scraping with their feet.

It may yet be that diligent research in Exeter Cathedral Library, or among the manuscripts in Exeter College Oxford, where some of his papers lie, will turn up other such treasures.

LAMBARDE

William Lambarde would have been surprised to have found himself in this company. Briefly an MP in Elizabeth's Parliaments of the 1560s, he was primarily an antiquary, and from 1597 to 1601 Keeper of the Records at the Rolls Chapel and then the Tower. He wrote the first English county history, a *Perambulation of Kent*; compiled Anglo-Saxon laws as *Archaionomia*; wrote on JPs in *Eirenarcha*; on the High Courts in *Archeion*; and at some point he compiled '*Order[s], Proceedings, Punishments and Priviledges* …',[14] principally a

---

[14] The title *Some certaine notes of the Order, Proceedings, Punishments, and Priviledges of the Lower house of Parliament Gathered by W Lambert* generally given to the treatise is really the title of the whole collection in BL, Additional MS 5123 of which the treatise is only one item.

mass of precedents gathered from the Journals and medieval Parliament rolls. He concentrated almost entirely on the Commons, and there is no precedent later than 1586. The
compilation was first printed in 1641, patently influenced by the troubles of the time. It is
not a book to be read by the unwary, but it has flashes of the unexpected: notably the suggestion that on second reading of a Bill the Speaker could decide that after hearing three
speeches on each side of the question he could bring debate to an end. Its last chapter is,
mysteriously, on the attendance of the Warden of the Fleet.

ELSYNGE

The Clerks of the House of Lords have often been on the scholarly and antiquarian side,
archival scholars above all. The most distinguished was probably Henry Elsynge. He succeeded William Lambarde as Keeper of the Rolls at the Rolls Chapel and then the Tower.
From around 1614 he assisted his uncle by marriage Robert Bowyer, who was Clerk of the
Parliaments from 1609 to 1621, who had also been Keeper of the Rolls. From 1621 to his
death in 1636 he was Clerk of the Parliaments. His son, Henry Elsynge the younger, was
Clerk of the House of Commons from 1639 to 1649. By the end of 1625 Elsynge the elder
had compiled the first volume of what he planned as a two-volume work on *The Manner
of Holding Parliaments in England*, obviously an echo of the *Modus*. The eight chapters covered, in his words, 'ye forme and all things incident thereunto'. It remained in manuscript
until printed in 1660, and was reprinted in 1768, edited by the equally scholarly Clerk of
the House of Commons, Thomas Tyrwhitt. The manuscript plan of the second volume
shows that it would have covered in at least eight chapters 'matters handled in parlement'.
One chapter of this planned volume was printed in 1685, on *The Manner of Passing Bills in
Parliament*, dealing entirely with the House of Lords; another entitled *Expedicio Billarum
Antiquitus*, was published in 1937 in an edition by Catherine Strateman Sims from a 1632
manuscript.[15] Sadly there is no trace of a chapter listed but crossed out in the plan for the
second volume to be entitled *Errata in parlamentis, & by whom committed. My owne especially*. In a marginal note on the list of planned contents of his second volume he wrote
'begun, but god knows when I shall finish this booke: Sept: 1625'.
    You could not hold a parliament based on Elsynge. The issues which concerned him
were historical, including the historical development of the Speaker; how the system of
the presentation of petitions and bills in and by the Commons to the Council or Lords
developed into the Tudor and Stuart legislative system we still have; and how ordinance differed from statute. He is the authoritative source, therefore, for those who looked into the
role of receivers and triers of petitions—with much contemporary resonance now—and
those concerned in the balance between primary (statute) and secondary or prerogative
legislation (ordinance). But what Catherine Strateman Sims has described as 'his loving
and diligent search for medieval precedent'[16] can be rather wearing for a Clerk or Member
seeking enlightenment on current practice at the time he wrote, let alone insight into the
development of procedure.

---

[15]   (1937) XLII *American Historical Review* 225–43.
[16]   Strateman (n 10) 4.

SCOBELL

Henry Scobell was the first Clerk to produce treatises not only on the passage of legislation through both Houses—the *Memorials of the Method and Manner of Proceedings of Parliament in Passing Bills*, or *Memorials*—but also on the practices and procedures of the Lords—*Remembrances of some Methods, Orders and Proceedings of the House of Lords*, or *Remembrances*. On 6 January 1649 he replaced Henry Elsynge the younger as Clerk of the House of Commons; in 1653 he was reappointed in the Barebone's Parliament; and in 1658 he was made Clerk of the Parliaments, meaning of the new second Chamber. He was also secretary to the Cromwellian privy council and a leading Congregationalist. He died in 1660 in bad odour with the restored Rump Parliament, not least for having recorded in the Journal the 1653 expulsion of the Rump as a 'dissolution' rather than the later term of 'interruption'.

Scobell's *Memorials* were published in 1656 and the *Remembrances* in 1657. The *Memorials* were reissued in 1658 as well as in 1670 and in Dublin in 1692. They constitute the clearest statement of the practices and procedures of the House, including legislative procedures, yet to hand, organised in sixteen chapters, without an excess of precedent, and plainly informed by practical experience of dealing with real issues. It is the closest to a manual to which a Clerk or procedurally minded member could turn. It starts with the choice of Speaker. Chapter VII on the rules of debate brings together a very full account of practice for which any Speaker would be grateful. Chapter IX provides some clarity on what actually happened when a Bill was reported from a committee with amendments, at a time when the report stage required the House to endorse or not the amendments made in committee, and on how new clauses and 'provisos' were added. Chapter IV on the Committee of Privileges bears the hallmark of one who had served it. Chapter XIII on Calling the House reveals that calling over was done in the order of the *Book of Names*, presumably compiled in a random order from returns as they were received. And only a Clerk would include as an afterthought a chapter (admittedly a short one) on how an error in a return is to be corrected.

There is scattered through the work matter which I for one do not recognise from other sources, in particular in Chapter IX on procedure in bill committees; the need to procure a resolution amending or repealing an act prior to bringing in a bill with that effect, which presumably acted as a constraint on constant amendment of the existing law; and the description of the Member reporting a bill from a committee as the Reporter, which means we can drop the nasty continentalism of Rapporteur with good authority. And there is a chapter entitled 'Decorum to be Observed in the House', which is an early use of a word still used to try and define how Members should conduct themselves, for example in the use of electronic devices.

All this may sound a trifle dry, as does the barrowload of privilege cases in the last chapter. Even these have local colour, such as Valentine Syre's case of 1606 concerning the arrest of the Clerk of the House's bag-bearer, sadly a post that has withered away; and I was not aware of Holcroft's case of 1607 dealing with the very modern issue of whether a Member could waive privilege and consent to be sued. There is reference to the passage of what seems to be a sunset clause added at third reading to the June 1604 Bill 'to restrain the Haunting of Ale-Houses'. We learn that, in the same month, debate on Third Reading of the Bill for Restraint of the excessive wearing of Cloth of Gold and Silver, Gold and Silver lace etc lasted over two days: what a debate that must have been! And Scobell reaches back to Tudor precedents, to the appearance at the bar of the House of the Abbot of Westminster together with his counsel, making his claim to the continued right to maintain the privilege of Sanctuary at Westminster in 1557.

If Erskine May's *Treatise* has a true seventeenth-century forebear, it is Henry Scobell's *Memorials*.

PETYT

It would be wrong to leave a discussion of the seventeenth-century manuals without at least a brief mention of George Petyt, who in 1690 published a slim volume evidently designed to fit in a pocket, and usefully called *Lex Parliamentaria*. Its modest foreword disclaimed any degree of originality, recognising that carping critics would point out that there was nothing in it that could not be found in Hakewill or Scobell. But that is the point of a compendium. It seems to have functioned for around a century as a very useful resort for those wanting quick answers to quick questions. It was organised in twenty-two chapters on faintly rational lines and written in plain English. There is even an alphabetical list of authors he cites. Petyt was the closest thing to the Handbooks, Manuals and Companions officially produced in more recent times. Notably, Jefferson (see chapter 9) cites it frequently.

6

Parliamentary Law in the Eighteenth Century

From Commonplace to Treatise

PAUL SEAWARD

UNINTELLIGIBLE AND CONFUSED STUFF

John Hatsell wrote in 1811 to Sir John Sinclair, who was passing on his seat at Caithness to his eldest son:

> I am sorry that I can give you no more satisfactory answer to your questions, respecting the rules for passing public and private bills, than what are to be collected from the printed orders of the House of Commons, respecting the latter; and with regard to the former, from attending to the practice of what passes in the House on that subject: and from the votes, which are printed every day; and from the study of the journals. These are the sources, (the only ones), from whence any knowledge can be derived on these subjects; and I should suppose, that you (an experienced member of Parliament, and who have been concerned in passing so many public acts) are fully competent to instruct your son on this head.[1]

Hatsell may have intended some gentle irony in the last sentence, for Sinclair was regarded as a self-important, if harmless, busybody; the venerable Clerk also self-deprecatingly omitted to mention his own *Precedents of Proceedings*. His letter, nonetheless, was an accurate reflection of the way in which knowledge of parliamentary procedure was generally acquired.[2]

The lack of suitable written guidance was a problem familiar to students of the law in general, who had long found it extraordinarily difficult to navigate through the minefield of a common law based on maxims, practice and precedent, a matter of historical development, rather than logical construction, the work of centuries of argument and experience, recorded in a variety of sources.[3] The great eighteenth-century Speaker, Arthur Onslow, himself remarked on the difficulty of studying the law as a 'bundle of unintelligible, and

---

[1] *The Correspondence of The Right Honourable Sir John Sinclair, Bart* (2 vols, London 1831) i, 178.

[2] For Sinclair, see RG Thorne, *The House of Commons, 1790–1820* (London, Secker & Warburg, 1986).

[3] See Michael Lobban, *The Common Law and English Jurisprudence 1760–1850* (Oxford, Clarendon Press, 1991) 47–115.

confus'd stuff': '[Y]ou may as well give a Boy of ten years old Aristotole's metaphysicks to study, as my Lord Coke's commentary upon Littleton to several people who first come to the Law.'[4] The publication of Blackstone's *Commentaries* was hailed as the first systematic guide to the law for students—its first textbook—though it still left much to be desired, and for some, it risked seriously misrepresenting a law that could not be easily reduced to system.[5]

COMMONPLACE BOOKS

Parliament operated similarly on the basis of ancient practice and precedent, though tempered by the fact that the House was perfectly entitled, if it so wished, to overturn completely any rule. Procedural guides were available: William Lambarde's *The Orders, Proceedings, Punishments and Privileges of the Commons House of Parliament in England*; Henry Elsynge's *The Manner of Holding Parliaments in England*; William Hakewill's *The Manner How Statutes are Enacted in Parliament by Passing Bills*; Henry Scobell's *Memorials of the Method and Manner of Proceedings in Parliament in Passing Bills*; and George Petyt's *Lex Parliamentaria* (which was largely a compilation of the others).[6] All of them, however, were far too general and unsophisticated and way out of date by the early eighteenth century. A handful of much briefer procedural briefing papers from the seventeenth century were more helpful to those attempting to achieve something in the House of Commons, but they were prepared for very specific audiences, and none were published.[7] As with the common law more generally, for those who wished to gain a reasonable understanding of parliamentary procedure, there were was no real alternative to hard graft. Firstly, they needed to sit in the chamber, listening and watching.[8] Many novice parliamentarians took careful notes in their early days in the chamber, not just for the purpose of recording the speeches and debates for posterity (though that was, for some, a motive) but also as part of a process of assimilating the procedure and practice of the House.[9]

On top of this, the aspiring 'Parliament-man' needed to obtain a deep acquaintance with precedent. The works listed above all engaged with precedent, but the most authoritative

---

[4] Parliamentary Archives, ONS/3.

[5] See Lobban (n 3) 47–49, 57–59.

[6] These manuals are listed and discussed in Catherine Strateman, *The Liverpool Tractate: An Eighteenth Century Manual on the Procedure of the House of Commons* (New York, Columbia University Press, 1937) lxxiii–lxxxvii.

[7] See the various works edited by Catherine Strateman-Sims: '"Policies in Parliaments": An early Seventeenth-Century Tractate on House of Commons Procedure' (1951) 15 *Huntingdon Library Quarterly* 45–58; 'The Modern Forme of the Parliaments of England' (1948) 53 *American Historical Review* 288–305; and 'The Speaker of the House of Commons' (1939) 45 *American Historical Review* 90–95.

[8] See W Prest, 'The Legal Education of the Gentry at the Inns of Court, 1560–1640' (1967) 38 *Past and Present* 20–39, esp 30–31; David Lemmings, 'Blackstone and Law Reform by Education: Preparation for the Bar and Lawyerly Culture in Eighteenth-Century England' (1998) 16 *Law and History Review* 211–55; Lobban (n 3). For the slightly different case of notes taken by practitioners as a working resource, see James Oldham, 'The Indispensability of Manuscript Case Notes to Eighteenth-Century Barristers and Judges' in Anthony Musson and Chantal Stebbings (eds), *Making Legal History: Approaches and Methodologies* (Cambridge, Cambridge University Press, 2012) 30–52.

[9] There is an extensive literature on the sixteenth- and seventeenth-century parliamentary diaries. On this point, see the remarks of Chris Kyle, *Theater of State: Parliament and Political Culture in Early Stuart England* (Stanford, CA, Stanford University Press, 2012) 74–75.

guide was the book known as *Observations, Rules and Orders*, a collection of key precedents, much circulated in manuscript, and printed in 1707 and 1717. The text appears to have been originally compiled right at the beginning of the seventeenth century, constantly added to, until it eventually become frozen at the reign of James II, its last entry 1685. As its editor, WR McKay, has argued, it is closely associated with the Clerks, and was perhaps, in origin at least, an office record of key precedents.[10] Several senior members are known to have possessed copies, among them the two Speakers William Bromley and Robert Harley, and the key Whig Members John Somers, William Sacheverell and perhaps Sir John Lowther.[11] But even this was a fairly summary guide, and neither it, nor any of the published guides, provided much help with the considerable changes in parliamentary procedure (notably financial procedure, and the handling of election petitions) that had occurred since 1689. For those who aspired to become masters of parliamentary procedure, a deeper acquaintance with the past decisions of the House was essential. They did so by a process familiar from the training of generations of lawyers: creating commonplace books.

Creating commonplace books had been a standard practice for serious readers of all kinds of texts since the Renaissance, recommended by educational theorists and taught in grammar schools: the process of extracting key passages and pithy sayings was both instructive in itself and provided the extractor with a store of useful examples and passages which he or she could return to and embed in writing, speeches or conversation. Commonplace books would be read and re-read, in order to furnish their creators' minds with the ammunition needed in both public and private life. Many scholars and teachers, from Erasmus to Francis Bacon to John Locke, provided extensive advice on how to retrieve this information most effectively for later use—how to index and cross-index one's commonplaces—in order to recognise the fact that some commonplaces could be useful in different ways under more than one heading.[12] One of the problems with commonplace books was effective indexing, particularly where a book was used over a long period, and entries under a particular head might exceed the space initially allotted to them in alphabetical order. Several systems were devised to overcome the problem, one of the most famous being that of John Locke, published in 1706.[13]

As for any other branch of learning, learning the law naturally involved commonplacing: indeed, for a profession in which there was very little formal teaching available, it was a crucial means of acquainting oneself with a huge volume of reports and a poorly navigable collection of confusing and unsystematic guides. John Evelyn characterised the standard practice of common lawyers in 1699 as 'precedents, customs and common-places'.[14] Guides

---

[10] WR McKay, *Observations, Rules and Orders of the House of Commons: An Early Procedural Collection* (London, HMSO, 1989) xliii–xliv.

[11] ibid, xliv–xlvi.

[12] Ann Moss, *Printed Commonplace Books and the Structuring of Renaissance Thought* (Oxford, Clarendon Press, 1996); David Allan, *Commonplace Books and Reading in Georgian England* (Cambridge, Cambridge University Press, 2010); Kevin Sharpe, *Reading Revolutions: The Politics of Reading in Early Modern England* (New Haven and London, Yale University Press, 2000) 277–81.

[13] *A New Method of Making Common-Place-Books; Written By the late Learned Mr John Lock* (London, 1706).

[14] Quoted by Lemmings (n 8) 223. For the importance of commonplacing, see ibid, 240–22; Lois Schwoerer 'Roger North and his Notes on Legal Education' (1959) 22 *Huntington Library Quarterly* 339; Julia Rudolph, *Common Law and Enlightenment in England, 1689–1750* (Woodbridge, Boydell Press, 2013) 40–52, 59.

to learning the law would encourage aspirant lawyers to follow a defined regimen of reading, and to try to boil it down in their commonplace books to a set of clear answers to specific questions, classifying them under 'Titles', or separate headings:

> As well for the Students ease, as for preserving and continuing his Memory, it is a profitable course for him under Titles, to digest the Cases of the Law, into which he may transferre such things as he hears or reads. ... Neither hath there been any Learned and Judicial Lawyer, who hath not made a Collection of his own. Therefore we may conclude, that Common Places are mat[t]ers of great use and essence in study, as that which assureth Copy of Invention, and contracteth Judgement to a strength.[15]

Writers on commonplacing would recommend a process of *division*—a process of indexing notes of one's reading under headings and sub-headings. There were several schemes for most effectively commonplacing the law.[16] It was important not to get bogged down in the details, but to extract the essence of the case concerned.

> The most delightful way, and most profitable, is to reduce the whole Case to as short a Proposition, as words can bear, and so to refer it to its proper place, without troubling himself with the circumstances, of the Persons, Time and Place, or any other matter that is not essential to the conclusion drawn therefrom.[17]

Similar cases did not need to be described exhaustively, but could simply be provided with a reference

> by which means one may run over the whole course of the Law in a small volume, which he may with ease carry along with him when occasion requires, without troubling himself with those vast Volumes, only sufficient to contain the Abridgement of all the particular Cases, which is a labour of unspeakable toyle, and wherein he shall never be free from confusion.[18]

Good commonplace books constructed on this basis were valuable resources, often handed down from lawyer to lawyer.[19]

It was natural that those who wished or needed to understand parliamentary law and practice would follow a similar procedure. In 1800 Thomas Jefferson wrote to George Wythe, Williamsburg lawyer, that: 'I had, at an early period of life, read a good deal on the subject [of 'parliamentary law'], and commonplaced what I read. This common-place has been my pillar.'[20] Wythe, who had been clerk of the Virginia House of Burgesses from 1769 to 1775 and one of Jefferson's early mentors, had described his own way of learning the

[15] W[illiam] P[hilips], *Studii Legalis Ratio, or Directions for the Study of the Law* (London, 1662) 155. The passage is in part a precis of William Fulbeck's *Direction or Preparative to the Study of the Law* (London, 1600).

[16] *Studii Legalis Ratio*, 156. For examples of recommended schemes for commonplace books, see *A Brief Method of the Law. Being an Exact Alphabetical Disposition of all the Heads necessary for a Perfect Common-Place. Useful to all Student and Professor so the Law; Much wanted, and earnestly desired* (London, 1680); *A Collection of Heads and Titles Proper for a Common Place-Book in Law and Equity, Interspers'd with many useful Words for the Benefit of References to the Titles. Which renders the Whole a Copious Index to the Law* (London, 1735)

[17] *Studii Legalis Ratio*, 180–81.

[18] *Studii Legalis Ratio*, 181. For the similar comments of Giles Jacob see Rudolph (n 14) 30, 66.

[19] Rudolph (n 14) 46 and n 58.

[20] WS Howell (ed), *Jefferson's Parliamentary Writings: 'Parliamentary Pocket-Book' and A Manual of Parliamentary Practice* (Princeton, NJ, Princeton University Press, 1988) 3.

rules about Parliament to Jefferson three years before: 'I extracted, thirty years ago, from the journals of the British House of Commons, the parliamentary rules of procedure.'[21]

What are often referred to as parliamentary precedent books are probably the result of this process. One example is the precedent book of William Bromley.[22] A scholarly minded Tory grandee who represented Oxford University for more than thirty years up to his death in February 1732, Bromley served as chairman of the Committee of Privileges and Elections in 1702–05, and as Speaker in 1710–13.[23] Bromley's folio book begins with notes on 'the ancient method of parliamentary proceedings' (1–4), and then proceeds with notes based initially on the earliest Journals.[24] To this were subsequently added references to the later Journals, especially to the post-1660 volumes (the omission of any precedents from the 1642–60 Journals in most of such works is striking). References to other works have been subsequently added, in particular to Sir Simonds D'Ewes's collection of material from the Parliaments of the reign of Elizabeth (eg 60).[25] Pages are headed with a topic in alphabetical order, for example: 'Adjourn and prorogue' (5–6); 'Archbishop of Canterbury' (7); 'Bills' (8–14); 'Boroughs' (15–16); 'Clergyman & Clergy' (17); 'Collection' (19–20); 'Committees' (21–22); 'Commons' (23); and so on. Bromley must have written each head as he came across something he wished to note down, and allotted it some space. As he subsequently discovered another topic he would write it on the next page available, putting a note in the place where it alphabetically should have appeared, cross-referring to the correct page: at the top of the first page on 'Bills', for example, there is a reference to 'Ballotting v. p. 157'. There are also cross-references to related topics: at the top of the page on 'Commons' there are references to 'Their Thanks v. p. 155'; 'Clerk of the House v. p. 161'; 'Serjt. & Servants v. p. 177'; 'Acomodating the H. p. 183'. The entry relating to 'Clergyman and Clergy' relates to the specific interests of this high Tory, as do the pages devoted to Oxford University (71–72). The book was in use while Bromley was Speaker, for there are references to proceedings in May 1713 (80, 83), and after he ceased to hold the Chair, for there are references to proceedings in the 1720s (83, 87). Indeed, as the book proceeds, there are more and more references to proceedings in the 1720s. A large number of entries concern the Committee for Elections and Returns.

Another collection suggests a slightly different approach to creating a commonplace book for parliamentary procedure. It was originally made by Edward Jefferies, a highly successful and effective barrister who 'might have attained the highest honours in his profession, had not his ambition been restrained by his love of country sports, particularly by the pleasures of the chase'.[26] In a style familiar from many other commonplace

---

[21] ibid, 4. See, incidentally, the remarks on the differing cultures of the English and the American bar in Lemmings (n 8) 216–17.

[22] PA, HL/PO/RO/1/51. Bromley also possessed a copy of 'Observations, Rules and Orders', now BL, Add MS 36854: McKay (n 10) xlv.

[23] For Bromley, see DW Hayton, Eveline Cruickshanks and Stuart Handley (eds), *The House of Commons 1690–1715* (5 vols, London, HMSO, 2002) III, and note his interest in translating Tacitus's Annals.

[24] Bromley's references to 'Liber D' are references to one of the early volumes of the Journal, or possibly to a copy.

[25] Simonds D'Ewes, ed Paul Bowes, *The Journals of All the Parliaments during the Reign of Queen Elizabeth* (London, 1682).

[26] Romney Sedgwick (ed), *The House of Commons 1715–1754* (2 vols, London, HMSO, 1970) II, 173. See also The House of Commons 1690–1715 (n 23) V, 894–95.

books, each page is ruled with a margin, in which a short heading indicates the content of each item, and then in another ruled column each item is numbered sequentially: the number is used in an extensive index at the back. Jefferies' book is chronological, rather than thematic, in construction, a basic difference from Bromley's, but this numbering and indexing system overcomes at least in part the deficiencies of the structure (although the index is unclassified, with entries for 'B', for example, listing 'Back Door', 'Bail vid. Security', 'Baldwin a printer', 'Ballotication [sic] of Members', 'Bill for Disbanding the Army', and so on). The book is headed at the beginning 'Parliament November 1708', which suggests that he began it as soon as he arrived in Parliament after the 1708 election (the new Parliament began that year on 16 November). The book is the product both of his reading and his observation. The first few pages are his observations derived from the proceedings of the first few days of the Parliament's sitting. Within a few pages, however, the book is used for notes from the Journal from 1660 onwards, mostly arranged in chronological order.[27] These are interspersed with notes on statutes relating to elections and the qualifications for election to Parliament (27–38), occasional insertions relating to different periods (including a 'manuscript of bro: Winningtons' relating to August 1689),[28] and some additional material where a subject is pursued (see, for example, 60, no 165, on the privilege of franking). Other sources included Scobell (eg 92, no 270), Petyt, Hakewill, *Lex Parliamentaria* ('LP', 9–101), D'Ewes (eg 92, no 269), Rushworth's *Historical Collections*, Nalson's *An Impartial Collection of the Great Affairs of State*, Hayward Townshend's *Historical Collections*, and Eachard's *History of England* (125).

Jefferies' notes include some, occasionally sharp, comments on what he considered to be procedural solecisms of his own time, such as 'the Speaker with more warmth than became him said "What would Gent Have him to do?"' (102). The remark reflected on the Speaker between 1715 and 1727, Sir Spencer Compton, the predecessor of the legendary Sir Arthur Onslow, Speaker from 1728 to 1761. The copy that survives of Jefferies' notes belonged to Onslow, who borrowed the original volume from Jefferies' nephew, Thomas Winnington, 'by whose favour I took this copy upon my promise to him that no copy shou'd be taken from this'.[29] Onslow added his own notes to Jefferies', one of them defending Compton's conduct in the chair on another occasion: a remark about the Speaker's conduct on a division is responded to by Onslow in the margin with 'This reflection is injurious, I then staid in the House as well as the author of this collection and well remember this whole matter in which I see nothing partial or otherwise unbecoming in the Speaker' (112). Jefferies had been a Tory; Onslow, close to Sir Robert Walpole, was a decided Whig.

---

[27] See p 19 onwards. Some entries out of chronological sequence are probably the result of notes made by Jefferies in the margin being incorporated into the volume: others are clearly a copyist's mistake—see, for example, no 90 on p 25, where the copyist must have meant 11 May 1660, rather than 11 May 1722, possibly the year in which he was copying the text. It is notable that at this point Jefferies was only taking notes from the Convention Parliament in the month before the return to England of King Charles II. See also p 127 'note this space is left for inserting notes from the 10 Decr 1667 to the 4th Feb: 1672'.

[28] Presumably a reference to material belonging to Jefferies' elder brother Salwey Winnington, though Winnington was not a Member in 1689. Their father, Sir Francis Winnington, had been a Whig Solicitor General in the late 1670s. (Jefferies adopted the surname of his wife's uncle, when she succeeded to his property.) *The House of Commons 1690–1715* (n 23) V, 894–903.

[29] Parliamentary Archives, ONS/2.

Onslow's extensive notes in Jefferies' collection more broadly reflect his remarkable interest in, and knowledge of, the procedure of the Commons, an engagement remarked on warmly by John Hatsell when he compiled his *Precedents of Proceedings*.[30] Onslow, like Bromley, possessed a deep interest in history, particularly contemporary history and the history of Parliament.[31] He was aware, for example, of the manuscript notes covering the debates of 1667–94 taken down by Anchitell Grey and helped to inspire their publication in 1763.[32] Parliament for the Onslows was a family commitment: among them was a Clerk of the House, Fulk Onslow, as well as his brother who deputised for him during his illness in 1587; the Speaker in 1566, Richard Onslow; Arthur Onslow's great-grandfather Sir Richard, a senior figure among the Presbyterians in the 1640s; and his uncle, Sir Richard Onslow, first Baron Onslow, Bromley's predecessor as Speaker in 1708–10. Onslow was enormously proud of his unique parliamentary heritage. His uncle, he wrote

> was esteemed a good Debater and extremely well versed in the Rules and Orders of Parliament, and for the last twenty years of his sitting there, no Business of any importance was transacted but he had a large share in it. … [He was] as much followed in Parliamentary affairs as most men of that age.[33]

No doubt his consciousness of this heritage bolstered the self-regard that some found deeply irritating.[34] Onslow began studying the law comparatively late, after the death of his father placed his family in a position of some financial embarrassment. Although he seems to have practised little, 'my knowledge of the law (as far as it went)', he wrote, 'particularly in the antiquities of it, which I always took great delight in, has been of eminent use to me in my Parliament Business'.[35]

In addition to his copy of Jefferies' commonplace book, Onslow either compiled, or possessed, two other volumes of parliamentary precedents. One of them, originally in the Onslow family collection and now in the Parliamentary Archives, is titled 'Calendar or Abstract of the Journals of the House of Commons from the year 1660 to the year 1710'.[36] A companion volume is titled 'Calendar or Abstract of the Journals of the House of Commons from Edward 6th Anno 1546 to the Year 1642'.[37] Coming from the House of Commons Journal Office, the latter was presumably incorporated into the office procedural collection at an early stage. Both volumes are compiled in the same clerical hand, and both are annotated and added to, sometimes heavily, in Onslow's: whether they were originally put together by Onslow, or were, like Jefferies', borrowed by him from another

---

[30] John Hatsell, *Precedents of Proceedings in the House of Commons with observations* (4 vols, London, 1818) II, vi–vii (Preface to 1st edn, 1781) 232, 234, 237.

[31] See, for example, his annotations on the history of Gilbert Burnet (including a note on Jefferies'/Winnington's father, Sir Francis), incorporated in O Airy's and earlier editions: *Burnet's History of My Own Time* (2 vols, Oxford, Clarendon Press 1897) I, xi–xiv.

[32] See Annabel Patterson, *The Long Parliament of Charles II* (New Haven and London, Yale University Press, 2008) 244–45.

[33] Parliamentary Archives, ONS/3.

[34] Strateman (n 6) lxiii–lxv.

[35] Parliamentary Archives, ONS/3.

[36] Parliamentary Archives, ONS/1.

[37] Parliamentary Archives, HC/CL/JO/12/1.

source, is unknown. Both volumes share their arrangement of topics, suggesting that they were planned together. In the earlier volume, the references are to a range of sources, not only the Commons Journals. They include 'Cotton's Records', which may have been one of the collections of parliamentary records bound together for the library of Sir Robert Cotton which came to Westminster in the 1620s and which were gifted to the nation by his grandson in 1700.[38] There are also references to D'Ewes, Rushworth and Hakewill, but the text is mainly based on the Journals.[39] The text of the second volume is almost exclusively from the Journals, though other documents are bound. Both volumes were clearly in use throughout Onslow's speakership, for his extensive annotations include references to proceedings in the 1740s and 1750s. How closely Onslow worked with the clerks is suggested by his references to 'the minute book of the Clerk of HC of 21 Novr 1746' and 'my copy of Mr Jodrell's notes'.[40]

INDEXES

There were two major difficulties with creating and using commonplace books such as Bromley's and Onslow's. The first was that their books relied on either the original Journals themselves, or a copy of them. This material was in manuscript, and (as was noted in 1698) in none too good a state.[41] A copy of the Journals was ordered in 1698, but neither it, nor any other scribal copy can have been available to any but a very few, and Nicholas Harding, the then Clerk, also remarked in 1742 that all copies made of the early Journals were 'very erroneous', and that the room in which the originals were kept was so small and dark that it was impossible for the Clerk, let alone Members, to consult them satisfactorily.[42] The Speakers of the House must have been among the few who could have had easy access to them, and extracting directly from them to the extent that the Bromley or Onslow or even Jefferies collections do would have been an immense labour.

The project to print the Journals, initiated after an inquiry by a select committee in 1742, made it possible for more people to access the basis of House of Commons procedure. The impetus to print may have come as much from historical, as procedural or legal

[38] HC/CL/JO/12/1, 17. The pagination and contents do not seemingly reflect James Howell (ed), *Cottoni Posthuma: Divers Choice Pieces of that Renowned Antiquary Sir Robert Cotton* (London, 1651); for Cotton's Library, and its political uses, see Colin GC Tite, 'The Cotton Library in the Seventeenth Century and its Manuscript Records of the English Parliament' (1995) 14 *Parliamentary History* 121–38, and Kevin Sharpe, *Sir Robert Cotton 1586–1631: History and Politics in Early Modern England* (Oxford, Oxford University Press, 1978) 48–83.

[39] HC/CL/JO/12/1, 22, 25.

[40] ONS/2, f 202v. See also Shelia Lambert, *Bills and Acts: Legislative Procedure in Eighteenth Century England* (Cambridge, Cambridge University Press, 1971) 23–24, for the similar collections of material made by Nicholas Hardinge, including British Library, Lansdowne MSS 544–49, 5 vols of notes covering 1603–1730. These have not been reviewed for this survey.

[41] CJ, xii, 256.

[42] David Menhennet, *The Journal of the House of Commons: A Bibliographical and Historical Guide* (1971) 61–63. There are some scribal copies of the journals covering specific periods, for example Add 72605 (Sir William Trumbull, 1685–87), and see Sheila Lambert, *Bills and Acts: Legislative Procedure in Eighteenth Century England* (Cambridge, Cambridge University Press, 1971) 23. The fact that neither Bromley's, nor Onslow's, collections cover the period 1642–60 may suggest that they were compiled using the copy made following the House's order of 1698, which omitted 1642–60: see Menhennet, 62.

interest: it came in the same year as the completion of Richard Chandler's project to produce a collection of all of the parliamentary debates from the Restoration to the end of the reign of George II, *The History and Proceedings of the House of Commons*.[43] A committee was appointed on 5 May 1742 to consider printing the Journal, with its first member Sir Watkin Williams Wynne, the great Welsh landowner and the foremost Tory in the Commons, suggesting that it was a project that had heavyweight support. Wynne reported from the committee within the same month, and the House agreed to its proposals, setting off what would be one of the biggest exercises in the editing of English historical documents yet attempted.[44]

Printing the Journal revolutionised access to the bases of parliamentary procedure. The House agreed to print enough copies for each member of the House to be supplied with a set, and the volumes would become ubiquitous items in gentry libraries. But even with a printed journal, it would be a laborious process to read through the lot and extract the answers to specific procedural questions. Commonplacing was effectively a way of producing an index; but works of the depth and sophistication of Bromley's or Onslow's were only likely to have been prepared by a handful of those most deeply concerned with the management of the House, and they would, naturally, be the idiosyncratic products of individual reading. Some more systematic and more generally available guide to the contents of the Journals was necessary. The obvious solution was an index. The House had in 1742 requested that indexes to individual volumes be provided: this was not done for the initial impression, and when they did appear in subsequent ones they were fairly simple subject indexes, done session by session. They were no more than a half-way house to the proper procedural index, for which there was plainly a demand. But finding a scheme which would deal effectively with procedural complexity and make it possible to find past instances of any particular procedural event was far from straightforward.

A full index was proposed in 1765 by Alexander Forrester and Richard Jackson, about three years after the completion of the printing of the Journals up to the previous session.[45] Forrester, a Scot who was an eminent barrister in England, had ambitions to become Speaker, asking the Duke of Bedford to recommend him to the government in 1761.[46] Jackson, also a barrister, was an intellectual and scholar, known for his wide reading, and close to Benjamin Franklin during his time in England in 1757–62; he acted as agent for Connecticut and for Pennsylvania, and was associated with Grenville, who was regarded as probably the foremost procedural expert in the House, with the possible exception of the Speaker.[47] On 15 May 1765 the House ordered that the printing of the Journals be brought up to the current session 'with a proper index thereto', and recommended to the Speaker— by now Onslow's successor, Sir John Cust—that he identify someone to produce a 'General Index to the printed Journals of this House'.[48] On 23 January 1766 the House established a

[43] See Annabel Patterson, *The Long Parliament of Charles II* (New Haven and London, Yale University Press, 2008) 240–44.
[44] For an outline of the project, see Menhennet (n 42) 19–23.
[45] *General Index to, or Digest of, Seventeen Volumes of the Journals of the House of Commons*, vols 18–34 (1714–74) vi and n.
[46] Sir Lewis Namier and John Brooke (eds), *The House of Commons 1754–90* (3 vols, London, HMSO, 1964) II, 451–52.
[47] ibid, II, 669–72.
[48] CJ, v 30, 426.

committee, with Forrester its first member (Jackson was also a member) to 'consider of a proper plan, for making a General Index to the Printed Journals of this House'. It was John Upton, another, less significant, barrister (and former fellow of King's College, Cambridge), who reported from the committee in May that it had received a number of plans: on their recommendation, the House agreed to ask the Speaker to order an index to be carried out under his directions.

The project, committed to three (eventually four) different indexers, would take more than fifteen years, and produced a messy and unsatisfactory result.[49] The difficulty was in trying to construct something that could operate both as a conventional index, and as a guide to precedent and procedure. On the one hand, the Journals are a straightforward record of business done: bills read and passed, petitions presented, resolutions and orders made, and so on. The index provides information such as the title of a bill, the name of the individuals or organisations on whose behalf petitions were presented, the subject of an order or resolution. On the other hand, the Journals contain evidence of the way things were done: both routine and exceptional treatments of specific pieces of business—bills committed to select committees, or committees of the whole House; Lords' amendments to bills agreed to, rejected or accepted with amendments; the censure of individual offenders, including Members; the way the House dealt with challenges to its privileges; and so on.

It is plain that proceduralists approached the question of indexing in the manner of the commonplace books (and indeed in the manner of those dealing with the law more generally).[50] According to Timothy Cunningham, in his introduction to the 1547–1659 index, Speaker Cust had sketched out a list of twenty-six headwords as 'proper heads to be divided, in order to collect Precedents, and singular Instances of Proceedings from them'.[51] Cust's list of headings very much resemble the headwords for Bromley's or Onslow's commonplacing, and could very well have been derived from them, or from some similar volume in Cust's possession. They were mainly types of House business (Accounts, Addresses, Bills, Committees, Conferences, Debates, Impeachments, Messages, Orders, Supply), but also included subjects concerned with the operation of the House (Elections, House, Journals, Privilege, Speaker, Speeches), and a few general subjects (America and

[49] See reports of 13 and 22 May 1776, and 3 March 1778: CJ, xxxv, 786–88, 804–05, xxxvi, 783. The four men concerned were Edward Moore, Timothy Cunningham, Nathaniel Forster and William Flaxman. Timothy Cunningham, described as a barrister at law, and Fellow of the Society of Antiquaries, was author of *An Historical Account of the Rights of Election of the Several Counties, Cities and Boroughs of Great Britain; containing, The Time when each of them was first Represented in Parliament and by What Authority* (London, 1783). For Flexman, a dissenting minister and also a Fellow of the Society of Antiquaries, and his responsibility for the index to Johnson's *Ramblers* (and Johnson's discontent with it), see *Oxford Dictionary of National Biography*. Nathaniel Forster may have been the political economist and friend of Jeremy Bentham: see *Oxford Dictionary of National Biography*. If so, his support for the House of Commons against Wilkes perhaps helped him to obtain the indexing commission. For Edward Moore, see the entry for his brother, Peter Moore, in Thorne (n 2), and Lucy Sutherland, *Politics and Finance in the Eighteenth Century*, ed Aubrey Newman (London, Hambledon Press, 1984) 428. Moore's index appeared in 1778: see n 45 above. Forster's, covering 1697–1714, was published the same year, *A General Index to the Twelfth [to] Seventeenth Volumes of the Journals of the House of Commons*. Flexman's, covering 1660–97, appeared in 1780: *A General Index to the Eighth [to] Eleventh Volumes of the Journals of the House of Commons*. Cunningham's, covering the earliest period, appeared in 1785, *A General index to the first Seven volumes of the Journals of the House of Commons*.
[50] See the comments of Rudolph (n 14) 48.
[51] See also CJ, xxxv, 786–88, especially 786, which makes it apparent that part of the problem may have been the change of Speaker in 1770.

West Indies, Churches and Chapels, Colleges, Corporations and Companies, Courts, King, Queen). Cust's list formed the basis of the initial work of the indexers, who refined the twenty-six headings; their work was approved by Cust's successor, Sir Fletcher Norton.[52]

The distinction between a procedural index and a conventional one may seem reasonably obvious today, but the selected indexers plainly struggled with it. Edward Moore, for example, the indexer of the most recent journals, made a huge and complicated meal of the distinction. Here is his attempt to explain the reasons why a procedural index was necessary:

> By way of explaining the Second, and perhaps the most interesting Object of this Index—which is, '*to select and bring together such distinct Parts of each Case, as may be useful by way of Precedent*,' in order to facilitate the Enquirer's Search—it is obvious, and must be observed, that Precedents for *particular intermediate Determinations*, or Proceedings, cannot be found at once by the fullest State, or most circumstantial Narrative, of each distinct, original Case. It would be necessary, for this Purpose, to examine the *Whole* of *every Case* in which such Precedent can possibly occur: for it might happen that the Precedent sought for might lie in the very last Case of the Class to which such Case belongs: And the Enquirer could never be certain he had collected *all* the Precedents in any particular Instance, till he had examined the very *last* Case.[53]

Moore's formulation seems to struggle to grasp that the function of a procedural index was to classify procedural events and provide examples of normal instances of those events and divergences from them. The indexing project resulted in four different works, which, while they all followed the same basic plan, diverged significantly and unhelpfully. Cunningham's index was deemed unsatisfactory because entries under the major headings were arranged chronologically, rather than classified: '[T]hus Accounts ordered, Bills passed, Committees appointed, and all other proceedings referable to the main heading, follow each other, not according to their respective character, but merely in chronological sequence', as the 1845 Library Committee complained. Cunningham attempted to mitigate this with a subsidiary 'digest' in which Cust's headings were analysed, with subdivisions; this, the 1845 Library Committee pointed out, failed to help much, because the digest merely offered cross-references to the original index, rather than a proper analysis.[54] The most successful was commonly regarded to have been Moore's, covering 1714–74, perhaps because it was closest to the present and therefore no doubt much closer to current procedural practice and understanding.

HATSELL AND BEYOND

Some had hoped that the indexes could be more than a guide to the contents of the Journals, but rather a comprehensive form of instruction in parliamentary procedure, even for the uninitiated. Moore had written in his preface that:

> I flatter myself, a little Acquaintance with my Plan, and the Work digested upon it, will shew, even the youngest members of the House that this General index is a Kind of *Parliamentary Grammar*,

---

[52] Cunningham (n 49) preface, vii.
[53] Moore (n 45) xv.
[54] Report from the Standing Committee on The Library of the House (HC 610 of Session 1845) 4.

where the Rules and Precedents for their proceedings may, in many Instances, be easily learnt. And I hope that *Members of Parliament*, the *Gentlemen of the Long Robe, Solicitors*, and others, will obtain, from this *Digest* of the Journals of the House of Commons, Information and Precedents, both with respect to the *Powers* and *Privileges* of the House, as well as to the *Forms* and *Order of its Proceedings*, which they would neither have Time nor Patience to search for without.[55]

If so, they were sadly disappointed. Forster, rather more practically, had pointed out that:

[T]o give, indeed, a perfectly full, and systematic View of the whole Body of Parliamentary Proceeding, the obvious Method would be: 1st, to lay down the general Rule: and 2dly, to mark the Exceptions to it; with the Reasons for such Exceptions, where any appear. But a Work of this Kind can hardly be brought within the Plan of an Index. From good Indexes such a System or Theory may indeed be collected. But an Index itself admits not of that scientific Form of Arrangement, or of that methodical Deduction, which are essential to systematic Compositions.[56]

An index, in other words, could not provide a comprehensive and reasoned description of parliamentary procedure.

John Hatsell was working on his *Precedents of Proceedings* at the same time as the indexing project was going ahead, but he seems to have regarded his work as a similar exercise, and disavowed any ambition to save the student the hard graft of understanding procedure in the traditional way, from the original sources. He wrote in the preface to the first volume of his *Precedents of Proceedings*, originally published in 1776, four years before Forster's index appeared, that: 'This work ought therefore to be considered only in the light of an Index, or a Chronological Abridgement of the Cases to be found upon this subject.'[57] In the second volume, first published in 1781, he explained that he had hoped that 'some person, of greater leisure than himself, would select certain titles relating to Parliamentary Proceedings, and … would collect from the Journals, and from other Records, such matter as was referable to any of those titles'. No one else having produced any such thing, he offered his second collection, covering 'titles' which 'happened to stand first in a Collection of Precedents, which the Compiler made several years ago for his own use'. He reiterated the point: [T]his work, as well as the former … are to be considered in no other light than as Indexes to refer [the reader] to the Journals at large, and to other Historical Records: from whence alone can be derived a perfect knowledge of the Law and Proceedings of Parliament.[58] More helpful than a bare index because it provided a classification and discussion of the precedents it presented, the use of the word 'titles' underlined its character: Hatsell's work remained, essentially, a commonplace book with commentary, rather than a more comprehensive guide.

It is indeed hard to imagine that either Moore's index or Hatsell's work would have been much use to Sinclair's son (which is perhaps why Hatsell failed to mention either in his letter to the father). Something much more straightforward—and less focused on

[55] Cunningham (n 49), xviii.
[56] Forster (n 49) preface.
[57] John Hatsell, *Precedents of Proceedings in the House of Commons with observations* (4 vols, London, 1818) I, viii.
[58] John Hatsell, *Precedents of Proceedings in the House of Commons under Separate Titles, with Observations* (London, 1781) vii–viii.

precedent—was required to instruct the novice parliamentarian how he might achieve his ends, perhaps something a little like the so-called 'Liverpool tractate', the only new work on the subject known to have been written in the eighteenth century before 1789. Its author has been identified as George Grenville, 'among the very first, if not the best Parliament-man in the House', according to his brother-in-law William Pitt. Grenville had aimed to succeed Onslow in the chair in 1761, though he became instead the government's principal spokesman in the House of Commons in 1761–62, and eventually First Lord of the Treasury in 1763–65.[59] The description of Grenville by Thomas Pitt could refer to many of those who had compiled works describing the business of the House: 'his experience of the forms and practice of the House … his accurate knowledge of the laws and history of his own country' were among the things that made him respected.[60] Grenville seems to have known Onslow well and respected him, and may have asked him to look over part of his 'tractate'.[61] The work, written in the course of 1762–63, was probably an attempt to distil his recent experience of leading the House on behalf of the government, but while full of practical advice for a Member of the front bench, it was too specialised for a more general audience, and it remained a private and unpublished document until 1937.

Forster's remark concerning the limitations of the index as a guide to parliamentary procedure hinted at a very different approach to the precedent maze of conventional legal learning: one in which there were reasonably clear rules straightforwardly set out, rather than, implicitly at least, an argument in each case over which precedent was the better one. What might have been a catalyst towards such a thing was the process going on across the channel. When Samuel Romilly, the radical intellectual, prominent lawyer and aspirant politician, was asked by the Comte de Sarsfield in 1789 for a guide to parliamentary procedure for the use of the impending meeting of the Estates General in France, he found himself perplexed:

> There was no such book, and I could send him nothing that would answer his purpose. Hatsell omits the common rules which are known to everybody, and which are just what the French would stand the most in need of; and he is very minute and very ample in precedents upon points which, to them, could not be of the smallest use. There was nothing to be done but to draw up a statement of the Rules of the House of Commons myself; and I very cheerfully set about it, though it was likely to occupy a good deal of my time.[62]

Romilly's guide (see also chapter 8) was translated into French by Sarsfield together with the Genevan Etienne Dumont, a friend of Romilly and a close associate of both Jeremy

---

[59] Strateman (n 6) xvi–xvii; *The House of Commons 1754–90* (n 46) II, 537–44.

[60] *The House of Commons 1754–90* (n 46) II, 539.

[61] Strateman (n 6) xiv; see also 72.

[62] *Memoirs of the Life of Sir Samuel Romilly, written by himself; with a Selection from his Correspondence, edited by his Sons*, 3rd edn (John Murray, London, 1841) I, 101–03. Guy Claude, Comte de Sarsfield (d 1789) was a French aristocrat and army officer who was well known to the English philosophic radicals and their continental associates. He had also met Benjamin Franklin in London in the 1760s and had considerable dealings with him during Franklin's time in Paris as American envoy in 1776–85. For the context of Sarsfield's request to Romilly, see Rachel Hammersley, *The English Republican Tradition and Eighteenth-Century France: Between the Ancients and the Moderns* (Manchester, Manchester University Press, 2010) 155–56, and André Castaldo, *Les Méthodes de Travail de la Constituante: Les techniques délibératives de l'Assemblée Nationale 1789–1791* (Paris, Presses universitaires de France, 1989) 84–93 (see especially the quotation from Etienne Dumont's *Souvenirs* at 88–89).

Bentham and the French politician the Comte de Mirabeau. It was published in 1789 as *Règlemens observés dans la Chambre des Communes pour débattre les matières et pour voter*.[63] Bentham's own, rather better known, work designed to help the Assemblée formulate its rules of procedure—the text that became known as *Political Tactics*—was, naturally for Bentham, more speculative than descriptive, recommending a set of practices (including his beloved table of motions) some of which were based on the Westminster Parliament, others of which diverged considerably from it.[64]

These works were unusual efforts at describing procedure from the outside, rather than attempting to construct a description from precedents and rulings. Neither had any significant contemporary impact in Britain. Two other contemporary attempts were much more conventional in form. In the same year François Soulés, translator into French of a number of works on British and American history and travel, produced *Le Vade-Mecum Parlementaire, ou The Parliamentary Pocket-Book*, a work with parallel English and French texts. It was very different to Romilly's or Bentham's, combining an anthology of passages from the usual guides and authorities, often quoted verbatim, with some very basic, and occasionally inaccurate, introductory material ('1. The members of the House of Commons are elective; 2. The Commons are composed of Knights, Citizens or Burgesses'; 'The Knights are the great free-holders of Counties; citizens, the inhabitants of cities; and burgesses, the inhabitants of boroughs').[65] Soulés' work appears to have been at least partly copied from notes that Thomas Jefferson (then American minister in France in 1784–89), had lent him. It is not known when Jefferson began extracting the notes that constitute his Parliamentary Pocket-Book, though it is likely that it was begun in the 1760s during his apprenticeship under George Wythe. The notes were presumably those to which he referred as his 'common-place',[66] derived from the usual sources and authorities, particularly George Petyt's *Lex Parliamentaria*. It is evident that Jefferson either had no access to the Journals, or was unable to go through them systematically in the way that Bromley or Onslow had done, though he benefited hugely from Hatsell's *Precedents* in the later part of the volume.

The work of indexing and commonplacing was far from superseded by Hatsell. Charles Abbot, Speaker from 1802 to 1817, put considerable effort into understanding his role, as he did into much else that he undertook. Charles Abbot was stepbrother to Jeremy Bentham with whom, though he did not like Abbot's profession, and while Abbot was of a far more practical than philosophical bent in his reforming zeal than was Bentham, he shared many interests in administrative reform; and for a time he was close to many of Bentham's circle, including Romilly. Like Bromley and Onslow, Abbot possessed a close interest in history and the public records, though Abbot's interests were as much driven by an unlikely passion for sorting out office procedure as for historical writing. His interests in office procedure

[63] Copies of the work published in 1789 are now difficult to trace. It was published in Dumont's first French edition of *Political Tactics* (*Tactique des Assemblées Legislatives, suivie d'un Traité des Sophismes Politiques*, Geneva and Paris, 1816), and in his general edition of Bentham's works: *Oeuvres de Jérémie Bentham, Jurisconsulte Anglais* (Brussels, 1829) 453–69.

[64] *The Collected Works of Jeremy Bentham: Political Tactics*, ed Michael James, Cyprian Blamires and Catherine Pease-Watkin (Oxford, Clarendon Press, 1999). See also chapter 8.

[65] *Le Vade-Mecum Parlementaire, ou The Parliamentary Pocket-Book*, 7.

[66] See above, n 20.

and records were perhaps kindled by his service from 1794 as Clerk of the Rules in the King's Bench, where he arranged for the rules and orders of the plea side of the court since 1731 to be copied into a register and published, with the register kept open for recording future decisions; he also arranged for an index to be made of the rules. In Parliament from 1795, Abbot concerned himself with a number of issues concerning the tidying up of official documents and records, including membership (and possibly initiation) of a committee on expiring laws, and a committee on the publication of a definitive version of the statutes (an enduring preoccupation of parliamentarians, including May and several of his successors, particularly Courtenay Ilbert).[67] His chairmanship of the finance committee from 1797 to 1798 produced searching inquiries into the office procedures of the revenue departments. In 1800 he chaired a committee on the public records, whose inquiry encompassed the records of both Houses.[68]

Abbot's diary gives plenty of evidence of these historical and procedural interests. He was already in 1796 carefully taking notes on procedural matters and the then Speaker's, and Hatsell's, views on them.[69] A couple of precedent books belonging to Abbot survive, though it seems unlikely that they contain his notes of 1796, or that they are the only, or even the main, notes on procedure that he created. Both books are small notebooks in a bound slipcase, with 'THE SPEAKER' stamped on the cover in gold block. One book appears to be a fair copy of the other: the first has the appearance of a working notebook, with additional entries added in on blank facing pages and in the margins. The coverage of the books is not comprehensive: this is evidently a working collection, in which Abbot scribbled notes of relevance to specific proceedings. It is notable that in the fair copy there are also notes in pencil initialled 'C.M.S.', presumably by Charles Manners Sutton, Abbot's successor as Speaker (1817–35): such books (like Jefferies' of decades before) clearly had a long life.[70]

Abbot himself contributed to the further development of the index to the Journals. In his preface to the 1801–20 Journal Index, John Rickman, Clerk Assistant, and previously Abbot's secretary, wrote that Abbot had produced a 'Synthetical Table of all the various Proceedings of the House of Commons in their regular progress from the first Calling of a Parliament to its Dissolution'.[71] Rickman printed Abbot's system as a sort of additional

---

[67] See *The Diary and Correspondence of Charles Abbot, Lord Colchester*, ed Charles, 2nd earl of Colchester (3 vols, London, 1861), i, 32–34 for him pursuing these concerns directly.

[68] For Abbot's activities on the public records in the 1790s, see RB Pugh, 'Charles Abbot and the Public Records: The First Phase' (1966) xxxix *Bulletin of the Institute of Historical Research* 69–85; see also *Rules and Orders on the Plea Side of the Court of King's Bench* (1795) for his work on the procedure of King's Bench. Abbot's diary and papers are in TNA PRO 30/9. Extracts from his diary were published by his son as *The Diary and Correspondence of Charles Abbot*, Colchester correspondence.

[69] eg *Diary and Correspondence of Charles Abbot*, i, 5, 38–39; see also i, 16.

[70] Another volume in the Parliamentary Archives, HC SO/7/1, is described in its catalogue as 'Speaker Addington's book of precedent'. The volume was originally designed for another purpose, and has been turned round the other way and reused twice. On the front cover (which appears, in the way the volume has been used subsequently, to be the back) there is stamped 'ORDERS OF THE DAY / SESSION / AUGUST 1841 / THE SPEAKER'. The stamp is covered with a label, on which is written in MS 'Bill Book'. From this end of the book, there are a few pages with dates at the top, and one or two short entries which do appear to be references to bills. Beginning from the other end of the book are some pages on which precedents are listed. The book must have been in use in the 1840s, well after Addington's time as Speaker (1789–1801), and in part after he was dead. Presumably the catalogue entry is based on the first entry in the precedent section of the book, which says that Addington was Speaker until resigning in 1801 to become Chancellor of the Exchequer. This must be intended as a precedent, rather than as an indication of ownership.

[71] 'Preface' to the *General Index to the Journals of the House of Commons [1801–1820]*, comp Martin Charles Burney (1825).

index to his index. It was indeed based on a form of chronological analysis of a session, with headings for 'Parliament called'; 'House of Commons' (with sub-headings for, among other things, Members, Privilege, Ceremonies); Speaker; Officers of the House; Sessional forms of Proceeding (with sub-headings for 'first day of a first or subsequent session'; complaints made; Addresses; Orders; Accounts and Papers presented; and so on); Bills; Supply and Ways and Means; 'Intercourse with the Lords'; Impeachments; King and Royal Family; Regency—Demise of the Crown—New Reign'.

THE TREATISE ON PARLIAMENTARY PROCEDURE

As with the law more generally, parliamentary procedure would remain dominated well into the nineteenth century by precedent and historical sources. The attack by Jeremy Bentham and his acolytes on a legal system not based on clear principles, and the more widespread critique of the obscurity and unsystematic nature of the common law, did eventually result in some reform of the law in general.[72] But despite the Benthamite engagement with Parliament—Bentham's own *Political Tactics*, the interest of his closest associate on law reform, Romilly, and the work of his stepbrother Abbot—that parliamentary procedure was also crying out for a more logical arrangement seems barely to have been recognised.

Two attempts were made before Erskine May published his work to produce manuals of procedure that might be helpful to ordinary parliamentarians. Both were created not by Members or parliamentary officials, but by lawyers with close acquaintance with Parliament. George Bramwell's *The Manner of Proceeding on Bills in the House of Commons* was probably the first more generally available modern work which described procedure largely in terms of what actually happened in the House, rather than through a discussion of precedent. Bramwell, a parliamentary agent, responsible for the management of private bills on behalf of his clients, wrote in the edition printed in 1823 by Luke Hansard (though it states on its title page 'Not intended for sale') that the book had its origins in 'a short essay written by myself for the use of a Member of the House of Commons who had complained much of the difficulties which young Members experienced in acquiring a knowledge of the forms of proceedings on passing Bills'. It had been first printed in 1809 and circulated privately among Members and a few others; the work was revised in 1816 and 1823.[73] Bramwell pointed out that 'to obtain information from the accumulated masses deposited in the Journals, now occupying eighty-seven folio volumes, is a work of no ordinary labour, requiring a degree of patient perseverance rarely submitted to by men surrounded with the engagements and allurements of active life'.[74] Notably, even Bramwell's more practical guide incorporated a lengthy introduction which reviewed the historical sources of parliamentary law.

---

[72] For the debate on codification of the law, see Lobban (n 3) 185–222.
[73] Bramwell died in 1837.
[74] *The Manner of Proceeding on Bills in the House of Commons*, preface, x.

The most ambitious attempt to produce a general guide before May's work was that of Anthony Hammond, a retired barrister, who produced his *A Summary Treatise on the Practice and Proceedings in Parliament; the passing of Public and Private Bills; and the Law of Elections* in 1825. Hammond (as Romilly had been until his suicide in 1818) was an enthusiast for the consolidation and, more radically, codification of the criminal law, pursuing the subject during the 1820s through a series of publications, evidence to the 1824 select committee on the subject, and an alliance with Sir Robert Peel which came to grief as it became abundantly clear that his codifying ambitions went well beyond Peel's much more modest intentions.[75] Bentham had been a supporter of Hammond's efforts, and JS Mill met Hammond and welcomed his plans for 'a complete codification of the whole law, common & statute: on the subject of which he has very rational ideas'.[76] Hammond's parliamentary treatise did not, on the face of it, fall clearly into these wider concerns. Much of it was an elaborate and highly informed discussion of the law of elections, and a good deal of what he wrote more generally about procedure in Parliament was essentially a summary of Hatsell, without the extensive citation of precedent. Nevertheless, it plainly was an attempt to provide a clear and comprehensible description of how Parliament normally worked, rather than a detailed and undigested discussion of some of its more abstruse elements. Hammond's work in parliamentary procedure may not have quite represented Benthamite codification. But it did represent an important shift in approaches to parliamentary law, which echoed a movement traceable in the law more generally. Hammond's use of the word 'Treatise' is significant, for it was the word increasingly applied from the 1790s onwards for a burgeoning genre of text books which summarised the state of the law in any particular area.[77] The title May chose for his own work, nearly twenty years later, suggests that he had Hammond's to some extent as a model.

In that *Treatise*, May would articulate more clearly than had been done before that parliamentary procedure was the result of processes which had been going on for hundreds of years:

> The proceedings of Parliament are regulated chiefly by ancient usage, or by the settled practice of modern times, apart from distinct orders and rules: but usage has frequently been declared and explained by both houses, and new rules have been established by positive orders and resolutions. Ancient usage, when not otherwise declared, is collected from the Journals, from history and early treatises and from the continued experience of practised members. Modern practice is often undefined in any written form; it is not recorded in the Journals; it is not to be traced in the published debates; nor is it known in any certain manner but by personal experience, and by the daily practice of Parliament in the conduct of its various descriptions of business.[78]

The transmission and interpretation of parliamentary law had for long been in the hands of scholars, historians or lovers of history such as Onslow or Bromley, who were able to interrogate and interpret a range of complex and rebarbative sources. Even May would achieve

---

[75] See KJM Smith, 'Anthony Hammond: "Mr Surface", Peel's Persistent Codifier' (1999) 20 *Journal of Legal History* 24–44. See also the article on Hammond in the *Oxford Dictionary of National Biography*.

[76] Smith, 'Antony Hammond' (n 75) 31–32, 33.

[77] For the growth of the legal treatise at the end of the eighteenth and the beginning of the nineteenth century, see AWB Simpson, 'The Rise and Fall of the Legal Treatise: Legal Principles and the Forms of Legal Literature' (1981) 48 *University of Chicago Law Review* 632–79.

[78] Erskine May, *A Treatise upon the Law, Privileges, Proceedings and Usage of Parliament* (London, 1844) 131.

more contemporary fame as a historian than as a proceduralist, and his *Treatise* would open with a largely historical account of the British constitution, not dissimilar to those accounts of the place of Parliament in the constitution that would often be included at the beginning of the commonplace books.

May's approach to parliamentary law, however, was implicitly less historical than its predecessors:

> [T]he arrangement of the work has been designed with a view to advance from the more general to the particular and distinct proceedings of Parliament, to avoid repetition, and to prevent any confusion of separate classes of proceedings: and each subject has been treated, by itself, so as to present, first, the rules or principles; secondly the authorities, if any be applicable; and thirdly the particular precedents in illustration of the practice.[79]

To describe it as a process, rather than as a set of individual problems, was to set off a new way of looking at procedure as something which was capable of being rethought and rationalised. It was to recognise underlying principles, a basic logic to procedure, rather than a mass of particular responses to individual questions. As with contemporary debates on the common law more generally, there would continue to be deep scepticism and even unease at any attempt to modernise or rationalise parliamentary procedure. May would find that process frustrating; but his *Treatise* provided one of the tools that would at least make the idea of modernisation conceivable.

---

[79] ibid, vi.

7

From Manual to Authority

The Life and Times of the *Treatise*

PAUL EVANS AND ANDREJ NINKOVIC

GENESIS

THREE YEARS AFTER May began his engagement in the House of Commons Library (see chapter 2), the catastrophic fire of 1834 carried off the vast majority of the manuscript records of the Commons. The 1835 report of the public inquiry into the causes and results of the fire indicated that all the records in the office of the Clerk of the Journals had been destroyed, though the manuscript volumes of the Commons Journal were preserved.[1] May could, therefore, begin his attempts to explain the practice and procedure of the House with a relatively clean slate, guided principally by the evidence of the Journals and with little fear of contradiction from other sources that might be presented. He had a systematic approach, which he outlined in his first preface:

> The arrangement of this work has been designed with a view to advance from the more general to the particular and distinct proceedings of Parliament, to avoid repetition, and to prevent any confusion of separate classes of proceedings: and each subject has been treated, by itself, so as to present, first, the rules or principles; secondly, the authorities, if any be applicable; and thirdly, the particular precedents in illustration of the practice.

May's *Treatise* was published in 1844 to great acclaim: *The Times* considered it (controversially to the modern reader) as 'essentially a popular work, and one that will be prized by every gentleman who reads a newspaper, or dabbles in politics and parliamentary debates'.[2] The reviewer (somewhat hyperbolically) considered it 'the first successful attempt to reduce into order in one systematic treatise the chaos of parliamentary precedents', and particularly praised its treatment of the private business Standing Orders of both Houses, 'about which every country solicitor and every shareholder in a railroad hears so much and comprehends so little'. May's explanation of practice on questions and amendments were found to have been treated 'with a skill and precision that will render anyone who reads them

---

[1] Fire report 1835, and Caroline Shenton, *The Day Parliament Burned Down* (Oxford, Oxford University Press, 2012) 183. Shenton considers that the manuscript Journals must have been rescued in an orderly fashion rather than being thrown out of the nearest Palace window in panic.

[2] 'Law, Privileges and Proceedings of Parliament', *The Times*, 8 October 1844, 8.

qualified to act so as to merit the thanks of [a] meeting "for his very proper and dignified conduct in the chair"'.[3]

The second edition of the *Treatise*, published in 1851, was informed by the time spent by May in preparing the General Index to the House of Commons Journals (see chapters 2 and 4) from 1547 to 1714. It improved somewhat on the first, which had been necessarily experimental, and of course benefited from May's deepened knowledge of procedural history. May's toil on this project also bore fruit in his provocative *Edinburgh Review* essay of 1854 advocating reform of legislative procedure (see chapter 9).[4] May argues indirectly and perhaps a little casuistically in the article that precedents for many parliamentary practices can be found through assiduous study of the Journals—even for those practices which conservatives claimed would be wholly unconstitutional.

Aside from the popular acclaim for his work, May also attracted the praise of his peers. After the publication of the third edition, in 1855, Thomas Vardon concluded his 1857 preface to the General Index to the Journals for 1837 to 1852 thus (rather oddly missing the second edition out, which is no great testament to his punctiliousness as an indexer):

> The importance of the General Index to the Journals, as the only source from whence Precedents of Proceedings in the House of Commons could be found (except in Mr Hatsell's Work, the last edition of which was published in 1818,) has been much lessened by the publication of a Treatise on the Law, Privileges, Proceedings and Usage of Parliament by Mr May, Clerk Assistant, first published in 1844 and reprinted in 1855; which Work contains, in a lucid form, the latest Precedents of Parliamentary Proceedings to the end of the Session 1854 ... and while the Index to the Journals presents the facts which happened during the period over which it extends, Mr May's book collects not only the latest Precedents, but explains the progress of the alterations, and the cause of each change which has taken place in the conduct of Parliamentary Business; and offers to all inquirers the best means of arriving at a correct knowledge of the present Practice on all subjects which belong exclusively to the jurisdiction of Parliament. To Members of the House, and officers of public departments who require a correct knowledge of the conduct of Parliamentary Business in a form more inviting, and less tedious than searching for Precedents in the Index to the Journals, this Work is of the greatest importance; and the present opportunity is gladly seized by the Compiler of this Index to notice its accuracy, and his obligations to its contents.

WISDOM

After becoming Clerk Assistant in 1856, May produced three further editions of the *Treatise* (1859, 1863 and 1867). The last of these represents a more radical reworking of the text than the others—in his 'Advertisement' May reports that 'the work has been greatly extended by successive additions illustrative of the history and proceedings of Parliament'. He had perhaps had more time to give to his revisions after completing his work *The Constitutional History of England since the Accession of George III, 1760–1860* (later revised to 1870), the second volume of which was published in 1863. He became Clerk of the House in 1870, and produced three more editions of the *Treatise* (in 1873, 1879 and 1883), the ninth being the last to be edited by him. These early editions were much preoccupied by the questions of powers and privileges which were the matters that principally concerned the Members of

---

[3] We are indebted for the material underlying these opening paragraphs to Martyn Atkins.
[4] *Edinburgh Review*, January 1854, 244–82; HC 1854 212.

the seventeenth and eighteenth centuries—a preoccupation which has returned to the foreground in more recent editions as Parliament has had to come to terms with the growth of administrative law, judicial review and what is sometimes characterised as a resurgence of judicial 'assertiveness'. The other preoccupation which seems peculiar to the modern reader was the highly specialised area of private business, an area which was, as May wrote in the first edition of the *Treatise* 'marked by much peculiarity'.

Private business—legislation affecting specific interests and persons rather than applying generally—was a grey area which was treated in a semi-judicial way, with counsel heard on the bill, and objections to it discussed and sometimes taken into consideration in forging a compromise. As May noted, 'to discriminate between the conflicting interests of different parties, involves the exercise of judicial inquiry and determination'; the proceedings were conducted with 'all the formalities of a court of justice'. (It might be added that another reason for the greater procedural definition in respect of private legislation was the fact that the Clerks and the Speaker were allowed to take fees from those individuals promoting the bills.) By the early nineteenth century the House possessed a reasonably comprehensive rulebook for private business in a set of standing orders, the first of which was passed in 1685. The Private Business Standing Orders were routinely, and eventually almost annually, reviewed. The committee established in 1837 to review the Standing Orders on Private Business was under the chairmanship of Charles Shaw Lefevre, who would become Speaker the following year and who was regarded by Erskine May as a committed reformer.

May's last edition was the ninth, in 1883. His preface to that last edition marked a shift that was to define the character of all future editions; for the first time May explicitly acknowledged the assistance of his colleagues—Reginald Palgrave (Clerk Assistant), Archibald Milman (Second Clerk Assistant), John Bull (Clerk of the Journals) and Alfred Bonham-Carter (Private Bills). The *Treatise* had already become the expression of the collective wisdom of the Clerk's Department rather than solely of its editor, and this was to set the pattern for the next century and beyond. It had also grown from 460 pages in his first to 903 pages in his last edition. The struggle between comprehensiveness and comprehensibility was to dog the editors of every subsequent edition.

CHRONICLES

Ten years elapsed until the tenth edition in 1893, edited by Reginald Palgrave, May's successor as Clerk of the House in 1886. There is some evidence that Palgrave was at least as committed to spreading an understanding of parliamentary procedure as May had been. He produced thirteen editions of his *Chairman's Handbook* (subtitled *Suggestions and Rules for the Conduct of Chairmen of Public and Other Meetings, Based upon the Procedure and Practice of Parliament*) between 1870 and 1900. He clearly stands in the tradition of Clerks who sought to explain and simplify the obscurities of procedure through popular (more or less) works (including his *The House of Commons: Illustrations of Its History and Practice* of 1869). His Preface to the tenth edition is also one of the more digressive and interesting examples of this aspect of the *Treatise*. He noted:

> The first edition of this book was in preparation exactly fifty years ago, during those halcyon days of parliamentary existence when the standing orders of the House of Commons, now 97 in number, were only 14; when no rule or order prescribed that previous notice should be given of a motion, however important; and when a motion might be met by any form of amendment,

however grotesquely irrelevant. Excluding the standing orders which require the recommendation of the Crown to motions involving a money charge, and which regulate the presentation of petitions, the parliamentary procedure of 1844 was essentially the procedure on which the House of Commons conducted its business during the Long Parliament [1640–60].

He went on to note how (after the turmoil of Irish obstruction) the Commons had

simplified their method of procedure so that the consideration of a bill, from the second reading stage until its third reading, proceeds automatically, freed, as far as possible, from opportunities for delay; and in other ways … have done their best to abate loquacity, and to hinder waste of time.

He also remarked on the modern development of 'the custom of putting questions to Ministers at the outset of each day's sitting' which had 'reached such a formidable dimension, provoking an almost equally formidable crop of rulings from the Chair'. He confessed that:

An attempt to engraft into a treatise framed on the easy-going lines of 1844 the complex procedure of 1893, without some alteration of structure, proved, consequently, of no avail.

And so the transformation of May's work into something quite different, and far more of a joint enterprise, began. Palgrave's list of acknowledgements is far more extensive than May's; alongside the Speaker he names fifteen further collaborators, including a number of scholars and officials from outside the Clerk's Department. Alfred Bonham-Carter is credited as co-editor: it would appear he did all the editorial work on private legislation.

Palgrave was succeeded as Clerk of the House by Archibald Milman, who in his two years in office before his death in 1902 did not have time to produce his own edition. Milman was succeeded by Courtenay Ilbert, brought in from outside the House service from his post as First Parliamentary Counsel. Although Ilbert was to remain in post for nineteen years, he also produced no edition bearing his name as editor,[5] delegating the job to Lonsdale Webster, Second Clerk Assistant and then Clerk Assistant from 1918. Webster seems to have been something of a dry stick, and unusually for a future Clerk of the House produced no works of scholarship or entertainment other than three editions of the *Treatise*. Webster edited the eleventh (1906) edition jointly with William Grey, who followed in Bonham-Carter's footsteps as the separate editor of the parts on private legislation. He went on to edit the twelfth (1917) and (after acceding to the post of Clerk of the House in 1921) thirteenth (1924) editions of the *Treatise*. His prefaces are dull, listing mostly procedural changes (of which, especially between 1906 and 1917, there were many of profound significance, not least the passing of the Parliament Act), but the acknowledgements of collaborators grows longer. In the preface to the 1906 edition he expressed his gratitude, perhaps with a hint of vinegar, for 'the suggestions and criticisms kindly made by Sir Courtenay Ilbert, the present Clerk of the House of Commons'. There is a good deal of preoccupation with Private Bill procedure. One suspects that the ranks of customers for the *Treatise* were greatly swelled by agents, promoters, town clerks and others who needed to take a close interest in an area of procedure which has since become profoundly obscure to all but a few. By the time of the thirteenth edition, the volume had swollen to an almost ungovernable size.

---

[5] Although he produced a highly readable slim volume in the Home University Library series entitled *Parliament: Its History, Constitution and Practice* in 1911, which was reprinted several times including, intriguingly, in an edition edited by Sir Cecil Carr and published by the Independent Labour Party in 1956. He also produced a number of works on legislative drafting, and a long and eloquently amusing preface to the 1908 English translation of Redlich's *The Procedure of the House of Commons*.

Webster also died in office, in 1930, and was succeeded by Sir Horace Dawkins, who has left no trace on the *Treatise*, apart from a terse acknowledgement in the list of collaborators in Webster's preface to the 1924 edition, and there was a long silence during which some might have feared that the *Treatise* had expired. In some ways it had, for the fourteenth edition, which appeared twenty-two years after its predecessor in 1946, was a radical break with May's original structure and style. The editor (perhaps more properly author) was Gilbert Campion, who became Clerk of the House in 1937, succeeding Dawkins. He had published one of those 'popular' guides to Parliament in the tradition of earlier Clerks, *An Introduction to the Procedure of the House of Commons*, in 1929.[6] Its first chapter, in which Campion delivers a sweeping historical analysis of the development of procedure, is still worth reading. It shows a highly analytic and systematising mind which he applied to editing the fourteenth edition of the *Treatise*. Essentially, he dismantled much of the scaffolding constructed by May that still held the book up. He tells his readers in his preface that he is 'conscious of the duty' he owes to the original author and successive editors of the *Treatise*, but goes on:

> This duty might have been discharged by retaining as far as possible the arrangement of the work in the shape which it had reached, and inserting only so much new matter as was necessary to bring it up to date. But my real duty, I felt, was to expound a developing system rather than edit a text, however classical, and I convinced myself that the preservation of their *ipsissima dicta* was not even the truest form of piety to the memory of my predecessors. For the results of a century of rapid political change had so altered the balance of procedure, in particular the relation between the old ground-work of practice and the novel accretion of standing orders (with the practice consequent thereon) that the original statement of the rules had become overweighed with qualifications—to the extent, in some places, that the original text was in danger of becoming a historical introduction to the footnotes. A time had come when further piecemeal addition would have reduced the value of the book as a work of reference, and the original intentions of the author would be best fulfilled by a radical and comprehensive revision and re-arrangement.

The theological allusion to *ipsissima dicta*, and the reference to the imputed 'original intentions' of May, hint at the transformation that had already occurred of the original 'essentially … popular work' into the Bible of Parliamentary Procedure. Of course, the troubling fact underlying the project was that there was no unchanging truth, although Campion clearly thought he could perceive the *ipsissimae sententiae* of May, and somehow preserve them. But he was anxious to shake off some of the burden of history:

> In view of the great accumulation of historical information in an accessible form which has taken place since this work was first written, many points of historical detail which were scattered through its pages have been omitted as no longer necessary. But where the historical process has an important constitutional application, or where its results survive in modern parliamentary law and procedure, as in the case of privilege and financial procedure, a summary of the main points in a connected form has been provided.

The House of Commons was losing interest in precedent as a guide to practice, and losing sight of the (perhaps imaginary or purely factitious) founding and eternal principles of the *lex parliamentaria* which were to be discovered from an examination of the Journals, replacing them with a rationalist but impermanent code in the form of standing orders,

---

[6] A second edition was published in 1947 (London, Macmillan).

restlessly revising its own procedures to address the latest transient or sometimes chimerical obstacle to the government getting its own way.

Whatever the verdict of eternity on Campion's revisions, whether he was a second messiah or an enlightenment iconoclast, the fourteenth edition marked a further decisive shift in the *Treatise* away from a guide for Everyman to a legal textbook.[7] And by now, the list of acknowledgements had grown to some twenty collaborators, though it is noticeable that the Speaker is no longer credited with direct input. The book had become a book produced by the Clerks, and possibly mainly used by the Clerks. Campion edited one more edition, the fifteenth, published in 1950, two years after he had retired.[8]

Campion's successor as Clerk, Frederic Metcalfe, did not produce his own edition of the *Treatise.*[9] His successor, Edward Fellowes, who became Clerk in 1954, edited (along with Barnett Cocks and Campion) the sixteenth edition, published in 1957. Fellowes was a scholarly, and sometimes radical Clerk, who was a founding member of the Study of Parliament Group after his retirement.[10] Chapter 11 of this book contains a version of the history of the standing orders on which he had worked before the 1939–45 war. In his preface, Fellowes was anxious to stress the canonical continuity of the *Treatise*, even though he did not undo Campion's radical restructuring:

> The value of a new edition ... though it supersedes the texts of its forerunners, does not diminish their value as repositories of the former practice. Indeed, the earlier editions of May, taken together, form a continuous guide, and are deliberately edited in such a way that a process of procedure can easily be followed from edition to edition down the years.

'Easily' may have been an overstatement.

Fellowes was succeeded by Barnett Cocks, who edited the seventeenth (1964) and eighteenth (1971) editions of the *Treatise.*[11] In his preface to the 1964 edition, Cocks explicitly acknowledges the collective nature of the authorship of the Treatise: '[W]ithout the devoted scholarship and co-operation of many Clerks at Westminster, this work, which now expresses their collective parliamentary learning, would not have maintained its authority'. In the preface to the 1971 edition, Cocks allows himself some philosophy, with a touch once again of theology, which is worth quoting:

> In 1844 [the Treatise] was the latest and most comprehensive of a long series of manuals describing the forms and manners of conducting public affairs in Parliament. In their descriptions, successive authors have had to take into account at once the element in parliamentary practice which is

---

[7] For the first time, it included a Table of Cases and Statutes.

[8] Campion, after retirement, served as the first Clerk of the Consultative Assembly of the Council of Europe at its opening session in Strasbourg in 1949. In 1950 he was made Baron Campion of Bowes in the County of Surrey.

[9] His rather retrogressive contribution to procedure is noted in chapter 14.

[10] He wrote, with John Waller Hills MP, a study of *British Government Finance* (New York, Columbia University Press, 1932). He also provided a Preface to the Irish University Press facsimile reprint of Hatsell's *Precedents*, published in 1971, in which he somewhat acidly remarks: 'The last edition of the *Precedents* was published in 1818 when Hatsell was 85. They show that he must have devoted during his retirement much time and industry to this work, but, like many men of his epoch, he liked to hide that industry behind a veil of detachment. Curiously enough, that *degagé* air endured among the clerks long after Hatsell was only a name. It was probably not until after the First World War that the clerks in the Commons had a wholly professional oulook.' That seems a little unfair on Erskine May himself.

[11] Barnett Cocks will probably be best remembered by posterity for his affectionate but somewhat scathing history of the building of the new Palace of Westminster, *Mid-Victorian Masterpiece* (London, Hutchinson, 1977). He also appears regularly in the second volume of the Crossman diaries, *The Diaries of a Cabinet Minister*, vol 2: *Lord President of the Council and Leader of the House of Commons (1966–1968)* (London, Hutchinson, 1976).

constantly adapting to changing circumstances, and that which is fundamental and unalterable. ... Texts like Erskine May's cannot be scriptural in their authority.

Cocks was succeeded as Clerk by David Lidderdale, who edited the nineteenth edition published in 1976. In his preface Lidderdale notes the accession of the UK to the European Communities and the radical constitutional innovation of the first referendum held in the UK in 1975—which of course confirmed that accession. He noted that: 'The time has long passed ... when the production of a new edition of Erskine May could be the work of any individual working on his own.' Lidderdale was succeeded by Charles Gordon, who edited the twentieth edition, published in 1983.[12] The House of Lords section of was significantly developed in that edition when some fifty-five pages of exclusively Lords material were collated and a separate chapter on the Lords formed,[13] and this area has been expanded in subsequent years. Clerks in the House of Lords are now recognised amongst the editorial team, though the relationship of that House to the *Treatise* is less wholehearted than that of the Commons. The avowedly authoritative text in the Lords is the *Companion to the Standing Orders and Guide to the Proceedings of the House of Lords*, commonly known as the *House of Lords Companion*. That work bears some resemblance to the *Manual of Procedure in Public Business* of the House of Commons, which went through many editions from 1904 to 1987, a work itself developed by Courtenay Ilbert from May's own *Rules, Orders and Forms of Proceedings of the House of Commons relating to Public Business*, first published by order of the House in 1854 and republished each Parliament up to 1896. Gordon also noted in his preface the momentous innovation in 1979 of the departmentally related select committees, and the disappearance (finally) of the notion of Supply Days.

Clifford Boulton, Clerk of the House from 1987 to 1994, edited the twenty-first (1989) edition of the *Treatise*. Like several of his predecessors, he reported heroic attempts to make sense of the chapters on privilege. It was Boulton who decided to discontinue the Manual of Procedure, apparently on the ground, among others, that it risked offering an alternative and potentially conflicting authority to the *Treatise*. Boulton's successor, Donald Limon, jointly edited the twenty-second (1997) edition with William McKay, who went on to himself edit the twenty-third (2004) edition published during the period of office of his successor as Clerk of the House, Roger Sands. The 1997 edition represented the relegation of Private Bill procedure to a more proportionate element of the volume—truly the end of an era so far as Parliament was concerned. In his preface to the 2004 edition, Roger Sands notes the emerging impact of the radical procedural reforms of the 1997and 2001 Labour governments, including dramatic changes to the daily sitting patterns of the House of Commons, driven by their new invention, the Modernisation Committee (see chapter 12). He also remarks on the changing nature of the role of the Clerk of the House, which was beginning to squeeze out the opportunity for profound procedural lucubrations:

> Gradually since 1992, but decisively since 2000 when the title of Chief Executive was added to the traditional title, the Clerk of the House has assumed overall responsibility for an expanding House of Commons Service which currently employs around 1,700 people and costs around £140 million per annum.

---

[12] Gordon's successor, Kenneth Bradshaw, did not produce an edition, though earlier in his career he had pseudonymously co-authored with his colleague David Pring a rather daring Pelican Special (A Hill and A Whichelow, *What's Wrong with Parliament?* (Hardmondsworth, Penguin, 1964)); and also co-wrote with Pring *Parliament and Congress* (London, Quartet Books, 1972).

[13] Letter from Charles Gordon to RS Lankester, 12 May 1983.

McKay's introductory chapter to that edition is well worth reading, as an elegant, potted guide to the history of procedural development. He also recast substantially, to very beneficial effect, the chapters on parliamentary privilege, following the Herculean (if also, ultimately, Sisyphean) labours of the 1998–99 Joint Committee on Parliamentary Privilege (see chapter 16). Malcolm Jack edited the twenty-fourth (2011) edition. In his preface he picks up some now familiar themes:

> The flexibilities inherent in the United Kingdom's constitutional arrangements mean that the relationships between the principal elements … are not immutable, but even so the rate and extent of change, particularly in respect of the relationships between the legislature and the executive and the legislature and the judiciary, over the period covered by this edition has been remarkable.

And, with respect to the changing nature of the role of the Clerk noticed by Sands:

> A new emphasis on financial controls and the effective use of human resources in managing change has recently come to the fore.

It is striking that Jack does not mention another significant development in the period between 2004 and 2011—the growth in resources and attention devoted by the House service to what is described variously as 'outreach', 'engagement' and 'participation', including educational services. A perception of a loss of confidence in the House itself, following the expenses drama of 2008–09, and of a wider disengagement from representative democracy, generated a drive to explain Parliament more clearly to the people it served. That urge to explanation is one of the factors that may, eventually, drive the *Treatise* into obsolescence, as the digital world displaces it. The focus on management came to a dramatic head in 2014, in a very public row over the selection of the new Clerk of the House. So far as the *Treatise* was concerned, it generated a significant issue about reaching out, described below.

REVELATION

The row over the appointment of a new Clerk of the House culminated in September 2014 with a resolution of the House to appoint a select committee to 'consider the governance of the House of Commons, including the future allocation of the responsibilities currently exercised by the Clerk of the House and Chief Executive'. In December 2014 the House of Commons Governance Committee published its report. Tucked away in a section entitled 'An Implementation Team' was a somewhat surprising recommendation. The responsibilities of the proposed implementation team, the Committee asserted, should include a requirement

> [t]o review the arrangements for the publication of *Erskine May*. The Committee believes that this important work, central to our constitution, should have an audience beyond parliamentary experts. Opening the publication to all in Parliament and beyond will demonstrate the determination of the House to make the workings of Parliament understood by a wider range of staff and the public.[14]

---

[14] Report from the House of Commons Governance Committee, *House of Commons Governance*, House of Commons Paper 692, Session 2014–15, para 202(h).

Perhaps ironically, this recommendation would itself have been largely incomprehensible to most readers outside the Palace of Westminster, and quite possibly to a large number of those within. Very few would have known what exactly were 'the arrangements for the publication of *Erskine May*', and what about them needed to be reviewed.

This recommendation perhaps summed up the totemic and possibly misunderstood significance the *Treatise* has acquired in the mythology surrounding Parliament. Copies of the *Treatise* are strategically placed in the Commons ready to be referred to by Members and staff of the House, and it is regarded by some as having the status of holy writ. Like the Bible and the core texts of other religions it is perhaps more often cited than read. Whilst having a titular continuity with the manual for the better instruction of practitioners and spectators that May produced in his lifetime, it has also come to represent for some commentators one of the sources of the unwritten constitution. This duality has come both to define and plague the *Treatise*. A 1976 letter from Robin Maxwell-Hyslop MP to Richard Barlas, then Clerk of the House, illustrates the problem well; in it, the former protests at the 'blurb' on the back of the nineteenth Edition of the *Treatise*, which claimed that the publication is the 'undisputed authority on matters pertaining to the law, privileges and proceedings of Parliament', suggesting it should instead claim that the *Treatise*

> has been a uniquely comprehensive reference work embodying the collective wisdom and memory of the Clerks of both Houses. Though it does not purport to be, and should not be quoted as, an original authority in itself, it is an indispensable guide to the proceedings and practices of Parliament.[15]

Although Maxwell-Hyslop was quite probably correct, the extent to which his advice has been heard is still something of an open question, as the recommendation from the Straw Committee above suggests that some still believe it to be the source of the rules rather than a compendium. Although, since losing its dustjacket and hence the opportunity for bragging, the *Treatise* no longer purports to be the 'undisputed authority', it is often assumed to be just that by those inside and outside Parliament. So it is sometimes contested that the *Treatise* is no more than the collective wisdom of the Clerks at the Table, on other occasions it is recognised as an expression of the settled will of Parliament about how it should conduct its business, and there are those who argue that it is a reflection of some of the fundamental rules of the British constitution. The appropriate response to the Governance Committee's recommendation hinges to a degree to where you stand on this question. There is no wholly persuasive answer, because it is on the rules of parliamentary procedure that the legitimacy of Parliament must rest, when there is no written constitution or underpinning statutory authority for its powers and privileges, and the *Treatise* tells the reader what the most accurate guess at what those rules is, and how they have been arrived at. As Ferdinand Mount has put it, from an avowedly conservative perspective:

> The basic principle of the law of Parliament must be acceptance and observance of the rules of parliamentary procedure as they stand; it is that acceptance and observance which constitutes the continuity of Parliament, this great boasted rolling tradition. ... By contrast, an assembly which sits down the day after its members have been elected or selected ... and makes up a complete fresh set

---

[15] Letter from Robin Maxwell-Hyslop MP to Richard Barlas, 12 October 1976.

of rules *de novo* is not a parliament; it is a constituent assembly, and its calling together is a visible token of the fact that a revolution has taken place.[16]

The *Treatise*, with its slightly accidental history and not wholly scientific development, may seem a fragile bedrock of such fundamental truths, and of course it is not the bedrock. It is an attempt to deduce the shape and position of the bedrock from the superstructure of procedure that Parliament has built for itself upon that bedrock. But it is the curiously unofficial but exalted status of the *Treatise* that to some extent fuels the healthy scepticism of those such as the late Robin Maxwell-Hyslop. Parliament doesn't own the book, but does the book own Parliament?

The relationship between the *Treatise* and Parliament is unorthodox—and certainly without parallel in any other Commonwealth legislature—though not unduly complex. The copyright to the publication is now owned by a privately held trust, the May Memorial Fund, and it has always been published commercially. Although the trust is held quite separate from Parliament, the trustees comprise of the Speaker and three senior Clerks of the House of Commons. In a fashion appropriately similar to the British constitution, this curious institution built up organically after Erskine May (by then Lord Farnborough) died in 1886. If the *Treatise* is the Bible of Parliamentary Procedure, what follows might be seen as its 'begats'.

May's 1874 will left the copyright of the publication to his widow, who died in 1901, leaving it to her adopted daughter. In the meantime, Reginald Palgrave (May's successor as Clerk of the House) and Alfred Bonham-Carter had begun the next edition, to which they claimed the copyright, even though from the beginning, it appears that there was never any question of the Palgrave edition being a different work—it begins:

> The text of the eminent author of this treatise, and his mode of treatment, so far as practicable, are preserved throughout this edition.[17]

In 1906, Arthur William Nicholson, then Clerk Assistant, bought the copyrights of both May's editions and Palgrave's edition for £25 and £6, respectively, with the understanding that the copyrights would thereafter be invested in whoever held the office of Clerk Assistant of the House of Commons.[18] In 1929, the copyright was sold to then Clerk of the House, Lonsdale Webster, before passing to his widow, Esther Webster upon his death in 1930. In possibly the most important move in its history of ownership, Esther Webster sold the copyrights to Gilbert Campion, then Clerk Assistant, in 1931. As we have seen above, Campion went on radically to revise the work, producing the fourteenth edition in 1946, twenty-two years after the thirteenth.

On 1 August 1957 Edward Fellowes, then Clerk of the House, oversaw the creation of the May Memorial Fund,[19] a trust in which the by then enobled Lord Campion[20] vested the

---

[16] Ferdinand Mount, *The British Constitution Now* (London, Heinemann, 1992) 192–93.
[17] Tenth edition, 1893.
[18] The author is particularly grateful to Sir William McKay KCB for this information.
[19] Letter from the Clerk of the House of Commons to RAW Dent, 30 May 1957.
[20] Campion was only the second Clerk of the House to be raised to the peerage. The first was May himself, though he died before he could take his seat in the Lords as Lord Farnborough. Robert Rogers, Clerk of the House from 2011 to 2014, was the third to be raised to the peerage as Lord Lisvane. Rogers did not produce an edition of May, though he was co-author (with Rhodri Walters) in succession to Paul Silk of the popular work *How Parliament Works*, 7th edn (Abingdon, Routledge, 2015).

copyright of the *Treatise* the following day. The trustees were to be, ex officio, the Speaker of the House of Commons, the Clerk of Public Bills, the Clerk of the Journals and the Principal Clerk of Committees.[21] Campion died in 1958, and the fact that the May Memorial Fund operates in much the same way today demonstrates that this final act of his stewardship of the *Treatise* ensured its continuity for the foreseeable future.

Aside from the obvious role of producing subsequent editions of the *Treatise* and keeping it up to date, the original purpose of the trust is expressed most fulsomely in its founding document:

> [T]o encourage the study and the imparting to mankind the results of the study of the growth, history, development, methods, practice and procedure of Parliamentary or Representative Government and Institutions as well in the United Kingdom as in any other parts of the World.[22]

This is undeniably a stirring and grandiose vision of the role of the Fund, though a 1983 memorandum from RS Lankester puts it into context, explaining that there had to date been only two occasions where the trustees had applied the royalties other than to pay the editors' fees in order to 'impart to mankind' knowledge about parliamentary procedure: Barnett Cocks received a grant to deliver lectures in Canada in 1973, whilst David Lidderdale received a grant in 1977 for research into the origins of Indian parliamentary procedure. Lankester continues:

> For the foreseeable future the income of the Trust will comfortably exceed the periodic costs of producing editions of May and we ought to consider the other objects of the Fund.[23]

And indeed, the other objects of the fund now seem to take greater precedence when the Fund is not preparing a new edition. The Charity Commission describes the Fund's role somewhat dryly:

> The Trust provides subsidised copies of May's Parliamentary Practice to support the professional expertise of smaller parliaments of the Commonwealth and oversees the assembling of updated editions of Erskine May at Westminster.[24]

The Fund may own the copyright to the *Treatise*, but in the days when books had to be typeset, printed, bound, marketed, warehoused and sold, it needed a commercial publisher to take it to the public. Currently the trust has licensed LexisNexis Butterworths to do this. This is a relationship of considerable longevity; in its original guise Butterworths was the publisher of the ninth edition, the last to be written by May himself. Palgrave's tenth edition was published by William Clowes and Sons Ltd, a company later themselves acquired by Butterworths, who went on to publish every subsequent edition up until their acquisition by Reed Elsevier (as LexisNexis) prior to the twenty-second edition.[25] The *Treatise* is inherently a niche publication and the publishers, naturally looking to recoup their costs and make a reasonable and legitimate profit, have set a price they feel is appropriate for this level of demand, and one which is broadly comparable to the other legal textbooks they publish. The end result of the *Treatise* being published as a commercial operation is that

---

[21] The May Memorial Fund Declaration of Trust, 1 August 1957, §5(A)
[22] ibid, §3(A).
[23] RS Lankester, To Clerk Trustees—May Memorial Fund, 16 June 1983.
[24] Charity Commission, 'May Memorial Fund', charity no 306057.
[25] The author is grateful to Richard Kelly of the House of Commons Library for this information.

the retail cost of a copy of the current, twenty-fourth edition, stands at £311. The licence for that edition gave the publishers the final decision in what media to publish, and they have opted to publish in the form of the usual hardback book and an e-book. Following the recommendation of the Governance Committee, the trustees successfully negotiated a licence with the publishers to put the book on the parliamentary 'intranet', thereby making it available more easily to those working in Parliament, including Members and their staff. But, perhaps unsurprisingly as e-books are subject to full VAT, the e-book was not significant in terms of sales, leaving the £311 hardback hardcopy the only realistic point of access for interested readers outside the institution of Parliament. It is this high price that seems mainly to have motivated the recommendations of the Governance Committee and later the Digital Democracy Commission.

This leaves the trust rather in the role of the Society for the Propogation of Christian Knowledge with its mission to take the Bible to the heathen, having to fund from its royalties the subsidy to put the book in reach of others. It is a curious historical irony that the Fund, as a trust initially set up to further the dissemination of the *Treatise*, has had to advance its purpose through an arrangement for publication that now renders the book unreachable to the vast majority. This in turn has fuelled attempts at online piracy and even conspiracy theories about the content of the book. The above explanation of how the system evolved largely by an accident of history and through the best of intentions might put such nonsense to rest, but the evidence is there of the potential for reputational damage through a continued lack of ready access.

In January 2015, the Speaker's Commission on Digital Democracy published its report, which recommended that: 'Erskine May, the definitive guide to parliamentary procedure, should be freely available online by the time the next edition is produced.'[26] This was in some ways a more far-reaching proposal than that of the Governance Committee, in that it was not merely suggesting a review but also a specific direction in which to change the publishing arrangements of the *Treatise*—and giving a timescale for so doing. However, there were financial and editorial challenges to be overcome. No Commonwealth Parliament which publishes its own authoritative text reports breaking even whilst so doing. Whilst the Fund has some resources of its own, it is unable to shoulder this burden by itself. Alternative sources of funding were considered (for example, a grant-in-aid to the Fund as currently happens for The History of Parliament Trust) or a more radical alternative was available of winding up the trust and passing the copyright to the House itself. In the event, with goodwill from the publisher and some willingness to be more flexible by the trustees, a hybrid solution appears to have been found. Preparation of the twenty-fifth edition has begun, under the editorship of David Natzler, and the expectation is that the work will be available online to all for free through the House of Commons website but will also be available as a hardback hardcopy only through the publishers. The likely result is that the royalties paid to the trust (already fairly diminished) will begin to dry up. Like all other Parliaments that produce their equivalents of the *Treatise*, its preparation will become a duty of its staff rather than occurring entirely without the internal chain of command.

Assuming that these issues have been resolved and that the *Treatise* could legally be published free online in future editions as the Speaker's Commission on Digital Democracy

---

[26] *Open Up! Report of the Speaker's Commission on Digital Democracy*, 26 January 2015, 69.

recommends, there would be another significant issue that would have to be addressed—the format of the book. Online publication covers many possibilities—it could mean, at its most basic, that a copy of the e-book is put on the parliamentary website as a flat file, making it available to all but pretty impenetrable to most. It could also mean that a comprehensive electronic version is developed, complete with footnotes and hyperlinks that could give the both the amateur and the professional reader some much needed context. The Canadian Parliament, where this type of arrangement exists, found that this had led to calls for their text to be updated on a continuous basis, rather than in editions as the hardcopy had been. This in turn raised questions of the time that should elapse before a change to procedure is enshrined into the text, and raises questions about whether there is ever an authoritative and settled text. It would end the idea set out by Fellowes that 'earlier editions of May, taken together, form a continuous guide, and are deliberately edited in such a way that a process of procedure can easily be followed from edition to edition down the years'. No longer would it be possible to trace the shifts in procedure and changes in interpretation—and it would be harder to detect when and why a wrong turning had been taken. The Canadian Parliament also found that the transition to online publication of their own text was plagued by losses in translation—mistakes that were made in the copying, leading to procedural issues. To combat this, the Canadian Parliament declared that the only authoritative version of their text was the hardcopy book and that the online version was merely a guide. The UK Parliament would presumably have to do something similar in case of discrepancies between the two formats of the book, if book there continues to be. There is also the real possibility that an interactive, hypertext version would require not only the time and resources of the Clerks to develop, but also changes in the layout of the book. Would changes to the hardcopy then follow, and if so, would it still be the same book?

These rather pragmatic considerations raise once again the fundamental existential question of what the *Treatise* is. Is it the treatise of Thomas Erskine May augmented by the collective wisdom of subsequent Clerks of both Houses, as Maxwell-Hyslop suggested? Is it truly part of the constitutional furniture of the UK (and indeed the Commonwealth). There is of course no such thing as an 'undisputed authority' in the Westminster system, where a government that commands a majority in the House of Commons can, in some versions of the doctrine of parliamentary sovereignty, change any rule it likes. As Philip Norton, along with many others, points out, however, even the most reforming of governments finds itself surrounded by a procedural framework within which it has to work,[27] and for better or worse the *Treatise* has come to embody the most authoritative expression of that framework, even if it has done so only fortuitously. But it is indeed a curious feature of our system that a document originally intended as a scholarly examination of the workings of Parliament and a guide for the perplexed could come to be considered a part of the British constitution.[28]

---

[27] Philip Norton, 'Playing by the Rules: The Constraining Hand of Parliamentary Procedure' (2001) 7(3) *Journal of Legislative Studies* 19.

[28] The same effect could be seen to a lesser extent with Bagehot's *The English Constitution*, where a text is considered comprehensive to the extent that it becomes authoritative—though unlike the *Treatise*, *The English Constitution* has not been continually revised and updated, and so has become more of a historical artefact than a continued work of authority.

Whether the *Treatise* is a constitutional document or not, the question remains, in the context of 'accessibility': what is its purpose? Most commentators agree that it is not a document for the average reader. With the best will in the world, the most determined amateur would struggle to understand much of it. The argument for making the *Treatise* more widely available, online or otherwise, cannot be rooted in turning the work into one with mass appeal. Indeed, if someone were to read the book in an attempt to understand the work of Parliament, they would be likely to come away both confused and disappointed. There are many excellent texts seeking to explain to the interested reader how Parliament works. There would be little point in turning the *Treatise* into a competitor in this crowded field. As one former Clerk of the House has opined, any attempt to do so 'would leave the Houses without an institutional memory'.

So whatever new form emerges in the twenty-fifth edition (and there are plenty of opportunities for greater clarity of expression, better structure and some effort at disambiguation) it is unlikely to turn the *Treatise* back into a popular work of instruction, even if that is to an extent where it started over 170 years ago. But this is not a good enough reason to deny interested outside parties reasonable access to the book. The question could perhaps be expressed in terms of the difference between availability and accessibility. Whilst there appears to be political will to make the *Treatise* more available, any attempts to make it accessible would have to be very cautious of altering the fundamental nature of the publication, lest it lose sight of its present purpose—to explain to Parliament how it has come to bind itself to particular rules and processes and, perhaps, why. Any move to realise the ambitions of the Governance Committee and the Digital Democracy Commission needs to appreciate both what the *Treatise* is and what it is for. But neither can the change in the climate of opinion about access to Parliament be ignored. Whilst the status quo was good enough for the nineteenth and twentieth centuries, it seems likely that even an institution as relatively unknown as the *Treatise* will get swept along in the digital tide eventually. Whether it survives in recognisable form remains to be seen. But if it did not, it would almost certainly need to be reinvented.

8

Controversy at the Antipodes (and Elsewhere)

The International Cousins of the *Treatise*

DAVID NATZLER, DAVID BAGNALL, JEAN-PHILLIPE BROCHU
AND PETER FOWLER

INTRODUCTION[1]

In his preface to the fourth (1859) edition of the *Treatise* May remarked:

> The Author, having received gratifying acknowledgements of the utility of his work in several of the British Colonies, and in the United States of America, has endeavoured to adapt it still more to the requirements of those legislative bodies, in all parts of the world, in which the rules of the British Parliament have been adopted.

By the time of the sixteenth (1957) edition the process of decolonisation was well under way and in his preface, Edward Fellowes, the then Clerk of the House, noted that:

> The creation of new Parliaments within the Commonwealth and the development of others has so stimulated the demand for Erskine May's work on parliamentary practice that for some time the fifteenth edition has been out of print.

Links between Commonwealth Parliaments had always been, and remain, strong. To this day, new procedural and related issues—or old issues under a new guise—arise on which legislatures, at both national and sub-national level, consult each other. Sometimes this is a formal exchange (in 2014, for example, the UK House of Commons Select Committee on House of Commons Governance sought and received evidence from the Parliaments of South Africa, Australia, Canada and New Zealand, in addition to the devolved UK legislatures and a number of non-Commonwealth legislatures).[2] More frequently, there are exchanges between clerks of different Commonwealth Parliaments seeking assistance in the form of opinions or information, whether on immediate issues seeking short-term resolution or to assist with longer-term challenges.

---

[1] This chapter was largely put together by Crispin Poyser, Clerk of the Overseas Office, House of Commons, from 2011 to 2016.

[2] Report from the Select Committee on House of Commons Governance, HC 692, Session 2014–15.

But as the citations from the prefaces above indicate, in earlier days of parliamentary development within the then Empire (when Westminster styled itself the 'Imperial Parliament') the links were perhaps even closer.[3] There was a sense of being one parliamentary community—despite the obstacles of distance and difficulty of communication—although there must also have been inevitable tensions as the colonial and dominion legislatures forged their own solutions to suit their own local political circumstances. It made sense, therefore, for this publication, to ask the lower Chambers in three of the Commonwealth sovereign legislatures with the oldest parliamentary traditions, the House of Representatives in New Zealand, the House of Commons of Canada and the House of Representatives of Australia, for their perspectives of the role of Erskine May's *Treatise* in their own development. These contributions, forming the last three sections of this chapter, look at what use has historically been made of Erskine May in each jurisdiction and how the *Treatise* has been replaced by domestic manuals of procedure and practice.[4]

These contributions reveal, not surprisingly, the extent to which early parliamentary culture and rules drew heavily on those of Westminster (even where none of the members of the legislatures themselves may ever have served at Westminster). Indeed, the Canadian contribution notes that (before the days of May) Hatsell's precedents were even translated into French for the use of the Assembly of Lower Canada. Use of May's 1844 work quickly became part of this picture. The scope and nature of parliamentary privilege, in particular, was a major area for reference and consultation.

As time has moved on, the use of May as a primary reference has rightly diminished and been almost entirely replaced by home-grown works, in particular *Parliamentary Practice in New Zealand* ('McGee'), Canada's *House of Commons Procedure and Practice* and Australia's *House of Representatives Practice*. But the common links remain and, above all, the name of Thomas Erskine May is still held in high regard in professional parliamentary circles throughout the world.

But before turning to May's successors in the Empire and Commonwealth, the next two sections of this chapter first examine some cross-fertilisation from the UK to other new democracies which occurred before Thomas Erskine May had set pen to paper.[5] The international nature of the science of parliamentary procedure goes back at least to the French and American revolutions.

FRANCE: ROMILLY AND BENTHAM

The disturbances in France and the summoning of the States General in 1789 for the first time since 1614 naturally gave rise to a lot of interest into how it should be organised. There

---

[3] As an example of the close attention given to Westminster, Edwin Gordon Blackhouse, Clerk of the Legislative Council and Clerk of the Parliaments of South Australia, and subsequently Clerk of the Australian Federal Convention, 1897–98, edited and published in 1900 *The Decisions of the Rt Hon Arthur Wellesley Peel, Speaker of the House of Commons, from his Election to the Speakership, February 26, 1884 to his Retirement from the Chair, April 9, 1895* (Adelaide, CE Bristow, Govt Printer, 1900).

[4] This limitation of this exercise to lower Houses means that the equivalent guide in the Australian Senate by JR Odgers, *Australian Senate Practice* (Canberra, Govt Printing Office, 1953), and generally referred to in this chapter and elsewhere simply as *Odgers*, is not included.

[5] These two sections are by David Natzler.

was a wealth of experience of provincial assemblies in France set up between 1778 and 1780, and the 1787 and 1788 meetings of the notables had given some idea of the issues that needed to be dealt with. But in the prevalent mood of anglophilia it was natural that there was demand for some explanation of how the British Parliament functioned, as well as drawing on recent experience in revolutionary America. From this came two very different products.

Samuel Romilly was a young and ambitious Londoner of recent French Huguenot descent. Through his connection with the Bowood circle he met Etienne Dumont, a strongly anglophile Swiss radical from Geneva. In July 1788 they visited Paris together and, among others, met Jefferson and Mirabeau. Some months after his return Romilly was asked by the Conte de Sarsfeld to send a book on the rules of the House of Commons so that the forthcoming meeting of the States General could benefit from a full knowledge of the British parliamentary system. Hatsell's first volume (see chapter 6) had appeared in 1781, and was known to some French politicians. But as Romilly in his 1840 memoirs noted:

> Hatsell omits the Commons rules which are known to everybody and are just what the French would stand most in need of; and he is very minute and very ample in precedents upon points which, to them, could not be of the smallest use.[6]

Assisted by barrister George Wilson of the Norfolk circuit, Romilly prepared such an account. Neither he nor Wilson had any evident connection with the House of Commons: they therefore roped in Sir Gilbert Elliot, who showed it to Ley, then Clerk Assistant, to approve the text. This was subsequently translated by Dumont, Sarsfeld having died; it was for political reasons attributed to Mirabeau, and was published in Paris in 1789. Romilly visited Paris in August 1789 and is known to have attended debates of what was by then the Assemblée Constituante. In later life he is said to have lamented that:

> [M]uch of the violence which prevailed in the Assemblée would have been allayed ... if their proceedings had been conducted with order and regularity. ... When I was afterwards present, and witnessed the proceedings, I had often occasion to lament that the trouble I had taken had been of no avail.[7]

In fact, a thorough scholarly study by Andre Castaldo in 1989 showed just how influential Romilly's simple abbreviate of procedure was on the Réglement drawn up in by the Constituante in July 1789.[8] Rule after rule directly reflects the Romilly text. The English manuscript unfortunately missed out the three stages of reading a bill, so that legislative procedure was merely added as an Annex.

Romilly's text has never been found in English or republished in French. It is a very clear statement of the practice of the House of Commons in the 1780s, with only one bizarre claim: that Members sat by county. It is hard to believe that the Clerk Assistant would have let that one through. Maybe it was added by Dumont or Mirabeau as a way of influencing how the 1,200 members of the Constituante would sit.

[6] *Memoirs of the Life of Sir Samuel Romilly, written by himself; with a Selection from his Correspondence, edited by his Sons*, 3rd edn (London, John Murray, 1841) vol 1, 74.

[7] ibid, 75; quoted in Patrick Medd, *Romilly: A Life of Sir Samuel Romilly, Lawyer and Reformer* (London, Collins, 1968) 69.

[8] André Castaldo, *Les méthodes de travail de la Constituante, 1789–1791* (Paris, Presses universitaires de France, 1989).

Jeremy Bentham (1748–1832), the English philosopher, jurist, social reformer and all-round polymath, was willing to seek a practical solution to almost any problem. It is hard to know where to begin with Bentham as a commentator on the House of Commons, let alone as a precursor of Thomas Erskine May. He embarked on his Essay on *Parliamentary Tactics* at more or less the same time as Romilly's tract, and with the same purpose of giving guidance to the French based upon experience of the House of Commons, of which he had no more direct experience than Romilly. Bentham did have access to the proceedings of several provincial French parliaments, and this influenced his approach. In its short form it was published in 1791.[9] His tract was not published in full until 1816, in French and heavily edited by Dumont, who printed it together with the 1816 *Réglement* of the Geneva Assembly which he had authored.[10] It is in no way a description of the practices of the House, but it is the first attempt at a systematic examination of parliamentary practice on an international level; is full of devastating insights and practical observations, as well as curious claims of the four causes of bad decisions and ten inconveniences; and seems to have been influential mainly in the new states of Latin America. There is behind the analysis a clear appreciation of the rules of the House of Commons, which he is not content merely to describe: why do motions need seconders? Why have all this shouting on votes rather than raising a hand or sitting and standing? Why not record abstentions? Alas, his detailed design for a large board—'motion tables'—on which the actual text of a motion under discussion could be displayed for all to see seems never to have been put into practice—unless deep in the Amazonian jungle there is a Bentham board preserved. Josef Redlich noted that, like Hatsell, May was 'a pure empiric',[11] whereas Bentham was the first and almost the last to try and develop a theory of parliamentary practice and procedure.

The idea of conveying British parliamentary rules to a French public, or at least those parts of the rules of which they approved, also occurred to several French writers, including Condorcet and the Abbé Sieyes, whose strong preference for a weak and regularly changing Chair proved decisive. Jacques-Pierre Brissot's *Plan de la municipalité de Paris* included a requirement for written motions, orderly debate and systematic amendments. In 1789 François Soulés published *Le Vade-mecum parlementaire, ou The Parliamentary Pocket-Book*.[12] Paul-Philippe Gudin de La Banellerie published a three-volume *Essai sur l'Histoire des Comtces de Rome, des États-géneraux de la France, et des parléments d'angleterre*, the third volume of which was devoted to Westminster. In many ways these were precursors in the tradition of using the British example to explain democracy to the Continentals, which pretty much ended in the early 1900s with Josef Redlich's magisterial three-volume *Recht und Technik des englischen Parlamentarismus: Die Geschäftsordnung des House of Commons in ihrer geschichtlichen Entwicklung und gegenwärtigen Gestalt*, ostensibly designed

---

[9] *Essay on Political Tactics Containing Six of the Principal Rules proper to be observed by a Political Assembly in the Process of Forming Decisions: with the Reasons on which they are Grounded and a Comparative Application of them to British and French Practice; Being a Fragment of a Larger Work, a Sketch of which is Sub-joined* (London, T Payne, 1791).

[10] A full text in English is available as *The Collected Works of Jeremy Bentham: Political Tactics*, ed Michael James, Cyprian Blamires and Catherine Pease-Watkin (Oxford, Clarendon Press, 1999).

[11] Josef Redlich, *The Procedure of the House of Commons: A Study of its History and present Form*, trans A Ernest Steinthal, with an Introduction and Supplementary Chapter by Sir Courtenay Ilbert, KCSI (London, Archibald Constable & Co Ltd, 1908), vol III, 178.

[12] In French *Statuts, Ordres et Reglements du Parliement d'Angleterre*.

to help the German-speaking peoples get to grips with parliamentarianism,[13] though in fact it proved more useful as a work of reference to the English-speaking peoples in the long run.

JEFFERSON AND THE USA

On 27 February 1801 there was published in Washington DC, as one of the first books produced in the recently occupied capital, *A Manual of Parliamentary Practice: For the use of the Senate of the United States*, by Thomas Jefferson. The next day he stood down as Vice-President and thus presiding officer of the Senate, and days later he was sworn in as the third President of the United States. Jefferson's *Manual* has been reprinted countless times since. A second edition appeared in 1812, drawing on the fourth and final volume of Hatsell; every two years the House of Representatives reprints an edition of it bound together with the House's rules and a vast commentary. It has been translated into many languages, including a French edition in 1814 and a Spanish edition in 1826. Ironically it has been the House of Representatives, of whose practices and procedures Jefferson despaired, and not the Senate over which he presided and at whom the *Manual* was directed, that has kept them alive. And state legislatures in the United States generally rely on *Mason's Manual of Legislative Procedure*, a compilation by a twentieth-century Californian State Senate official, Paul Mason, who published his text first in 1935.

Jefferson had long been interested in parliamentary rules, but then there were few subjects of which that was not true. He had trained as a lawyer with George Wythe, Clerk of the Virginia House of Burgesses from 1769 to 1775, who had his manuscript guide based on extracts from the Journals of the House of Commons, now lost; thirty years later Jefferson turned to Wythe for help with his *Manual*, describing him as 'the only spark of Parliamentary science now remaining to us'.[14] Fortunately Jefferson did not follow the clerkly suggestion to describe the proposed book as an Enchiridion. Jefferson himself was a member of the House of Burgesses, and as a member of the Continental Congress in 1776 had a significant hand in drawing up its short rules. Thereafter he was devoted to politics and statesmanship for twenty years, rather than the niceties of procedure. But he continued to purchase books on procedure, notably the first three volumes of Hatsell purchased while he was on diplomatic duties in France, and he was tireless in compiling his pocketbook of parliamentary precedents. On his election as Vice-President in 1797 it was on the pocketbook that he relied in determining points of controversy in presiding over the Senate. He decided to rely on parliamentary precedent, as being well known and respected, and not on that of the old pre-federation Congress. His idea was to leave a manuscript *Manual* for his successor, but he was persuaded that it would be useful to have it printed.

Jefferson's *Manual* is a remarkable testimony to the basic rules of parliamentary procedure in the late eighteenth century in Great Britain and in the United States, including so far as is known in the colonial and postcolonial state legislatures. Unlike its English predecessors,

---

[13] See n 11 above.
[14] *Jefferson's Parliamentary Writings*, ed Wilbur Samuel Howell (Princeton, NJ, Princeton University Press, 1988) quoted at 18.

the *Manual* is arranged on logical lines and includes basic rules on the place and manner of speaking often omitted from other accounts. Jefferson is tireless in his citations; his principal sources were plainly Hatsell, Hakewill, Scobell and Petyt (see chapters 5 and 6). He may also have had help from John Beckley, Clerk of the House of Representatives during the first four Congresses, and again in the seventh, eighth and ninth. The *Manual* was undoubtedly an influence on May when he came to compile his *Treatise*, just as some of the works described below have in their turn influenced the shape, structure and approach taken in later editions of the *Treatise*.

NEW ZEALAND HOUSE OF REPRESENTATIVES[15]

Thomas Erskine May's *Treatise* was the most significant parliamentary textbook in New Zealand until David McGee published the first edition of *Parliamentary Practice in New Zealand* in 1985, and continues to be a relevant point of reference. However, May's influence went beyond this; his work, expertise and reputation were ever-present in the early development of New Zealand's parliamentary practice. Even though he never ventured around the globe, his pre-eminence there was not simply a matter of cultural cringe,[16] but was also a practical consequence of the wholesale importation of parliamentary tradition and procedure from Britain at the time when he was active.

Fast Pace of Constitutional Developments

When May was born on 8 February 1815, no organised European settlement had occurred in New Zealand. Only a few weeks earlier, on Christmas Day 1814, the Revd Samuel Marsden had held the first Christian missionary church service on a beach in the Bay of Islands, but systematic colonisation did not take place until the founding of Wellington in January 1840. The gathering of signatures on New Zealand's primary founding document, the Treaty of Waitangi, began a couple of weeks later, almost on May's twenty-fifth birthday. Yet representative democracy was up and running in New Zealand by the time he turned forty, with the first meeting of the General Assembly taking place in Auckland in May 1854.

New Zealand's constitutional framework thus was established within a very short period. Much of this process was directed from the Colonial Office in London, half a world away. A Constitution Act was passed at Westminster in 1846 that sought to create a bicameral parliament with two separate provincial legislatures, but this structure was not fully

---

[15] Office of the Clerk: prepared by David Bagnall, Principal Clerk (Procedure), in consultation with Mary Harris, then Clerk of the House, who are grateful to David McGee, QC, former Clerk of the House, for his assistance, and also to staff of the Parliamentary Library for advice and research, especially Alex MacBean, Mary Tinsley and Dr John Martin (former Parliamentary Historian).

[16] In Australia, Harry Evans has argued that Erskine May's status as the innovator of parliamentary procedure textbooks is overstated, and that the acceptance of him as the authority on parliamentary matters in Australia was the result of historical and cultural factors; part of a Westminster hegemony that can be ascribed to a cultural phenomenon of 'Empire loyalty' (Harry Evans, 'The Pedigree of the Practices: Parliamentary Manuals and Australian Government', Papers on Parliament No 52, December 2009, 128).

implemented (a suspending bill was passed at Westminster in 1848, which suspended much of the 1846 Act's constitutional arrangements for five years)[17] and the colony remained firmly under the 'despotism' of the Governor, Sir George Grey.[18] Settlements were founded and shaped by the New Zealand Company,[19] and this occurred independently—and sometimes in defiance—of the British government and the Colonial Office. There was considerable agitation amongst settlers for constitutional arrangements, and particularly for elected representation. These arrangements were actively debated, with Constitutional Associations holding meetings in a number of settlements and communicating various models directly to the Colonial Office as it wrestled with the development of further legislation.[20] When the New Zealand Constitution Act 1852 was passed, it established a bicameral General Assembly for the whole colony, along with a number of unicameral provincial legislatures (there were six provinces at first, with others added prior to the abolition of the provinces in 1876). Occasional inter-tribal gatherings of Māori took place as expressions of *kotahitanga* (solidarity) in the face of burgeoning European settlement, and some of these gatherings were reported as incorporating parliamentary forms.[21]

With so many legislatures suddenly springing into existence, and with widespread contemplation of constitutional matters, there was a general need for—and interest in—the development of parliamentary procedures.

General Adoption of House of Commons Procedures

New Zealand's legislatures were modelled on Westminster, and most early European settlers were from England and Scotland. Ties with the colonies in Australia were very strong, with a close watch kept on their parliamentary developments and controversies,[22] but for many years the United Kingdom was referred to simply as 'Home'—dispatches received from Britain were faithfully reproduced by several newspapers under the heading 'News from Home', or similar. The first elected members were comfortable with English parliamentary traditions, though there is no record that any had previously been members themselves.[23]

---

[17] AH McLintock, *Crown Colony Government in New Zealand* (Wellington, Government Printer, 1958) 291–293.

[18] For a detailed history of the constitutional tussles among the colonists, see McLintock (ibid). Note that Governor Grey should not be confused with Earl Grey, who as Colonial Secretary from 1846 to 1852 was prominent in the passage of the legislation for New Zealand's constitutional arrangements; nor with Rt Hon Sir George Grey, Bt, who was another prominent British politician as Home Secretary during the 1840s and 1850s and then also as Colonial Secretary: see AH McLintock and GA Wood, *The Upper House in Colonial New Zealand: A Study of the Legislative Council of New Zealand in the Period 1854–1887* (Wellington, Government Printer, 1987) 16.

[19] Firstly in Wellington, Nelson and Whanganui, and then in Otago; the company was also involved in the founding of New Plymouth and Canterbury.

[20] McLintock (n 17) ch 14; see also Sir Geoffrey Palmer, QC, 'The Strong New Zealand Democratic Tradition and the "Great Public Meeting" of 1850 in Nelson', 4 VUWLRP 31/2014.

[21] For example, the Kohimārama Conference, held near Auckland in 1860, followed British rules of engagement, although this would largely have been on account of its presiding officer being a government minister (Donald McLean, Native Secretary); Dr Lachlan Paterson, 'The Kohimārama Conference of 1860: A Contextual Reading' (2011) NS 12 *Journal of New Zealand Studies* 34. A tribal assembly met at Pakowhai in Hawke's Bay, in June 1872, with an upper and lower house and formal parliamentary procedures; *Evening Mail, Nelson*, vol VII, issue 163, 10 July 1872, 2.

[22] McLintock and Wood (n 18) 52–53.

[23] ibid, 51, n 62.

In this context it was natural for Westminster procedures to be adopted and adapted in large measure.[24]

The first Standing Orders of the House of Representatives, the General Assembly's lower house, were adopted in 1854. The House of Commons had just published its collated Standing Orders relating to public business for the first time that same year,[25] but this appears coincidental as the two sets of Standing Orders bear little resemblance. However, House of Commons practice was the basis for procedure in the new lower House, whose Standing Order 1 stipulated: 'That in all cases not hereinafter provided for, the Speaker shall decide, taking for his guide the rules, forms and usages of the House of Commons, so far as the same can be applied to the proceedings of this House.'[26] Conveniently, the Speaker could take for his guide a manual of the *Rules, Orders, and Forms of Proceeding of the House of Commons, relating to Public Business* that was also published in 1854. This compilation was prepared by May, who was by then well known for his *Treatise on the Law, Privileges, Proceedings and Usage of Parliament*, as its first edition had been published in 1844. Through these two works, May's influence on New Zealand's early procedures was profound.

In 1865, the House of Representatives adopted an entirely revised set of Standing Orders. Draft copies of the new volume were circulated to Members with a covering letter from the Speaker, who professed that much of the text of the new Standing Orders had been lifted from May's manual:

> The Rules, generally speaking, have been copied (in many instances *verbatim*) from the Manual in use in the House of Commons, which was prepared, in 1854, by Mr Erskine May, under the direction of the then Speaker, Mr Shaw Lefevre. It has been necessary, of course, to make many alterations to adapt it to our own Institutions of Government. But I have endeavoured to follow it as closely as possible.[27]

'Controversy at the Antipodes'

May was consulted in writing by presiding officers, Members, officials and other correspondents from around the Empire and from several other countries.[28] Many such communications were from New Zealand and related to uncertainties or disputes that had arisen in its General Assembly. Some correspondence was of a practical nature, for example the provision of advice about the design of a mace,[29] or the supply of a set of Journals of the House of Commons.[30] But May's advice was also sought on a number of occasions when an

---

[24] For a thorough survey of the development of New Zealand's early Standing Orders and procedures, and particularly the 'aping' of Westminster, see Dr John E Martin, 'From Talking Shop to Party Government: Procedural Change in the New Zealand Parliament, 1854–1894' (2011) 26 *Australasian Parliamentary Review* 64–81, esp 65.

[25] T Erskine May, CB, *A Treatise on the Law, Privileges, Proceedings, and Usage of Parliament*, 5th edn (London Butterworths, 1863) 181.

[26] *Standing Rules and Orders of the House of Representatives* (Auckland, Williamson and Wilson, 1854).

[27] Speaker David Monro, circular to Members dated 20 May 1865, attached to the Alexander Turnbull Library copy of *Standing Orders and Forms of Proceeding of the House of Representatives, Relating to Public Business*.

[28] Catalogue of papers of Thomas Erskine May, UK Parliamentary Archives, ERM/6, <www.parliament.uk>.

[29] Letter from John Morrison, Agent for the New Zealand Government, dated 31 March 1866, Papers of Thomas Erskine May; Correspondence: Colonial and Foreign Parliaments, UK Parliamentary Archives, ERM/6/30, <www.parliament.uk>; *Otago Daily Times*, Issue 1495, 12 October 1866, 5. The Mace was destroyed when fire gutted the Parliament buildings in 1907.

[30] Correspondence as to Arrangements for the Meeting of the Legislature, [1868] AJHR D.2, 5.

impasse had been reached between the upper and lower Houses. This correspondence was reported in newspapers and sometimes even ordered to be published by the lower House.

From the time the General Assembly was established, there had been disagreement about the ability of its upper house, the Legislative Council,[31] to amend bills or provisions dealing with taxation or spending. In 1887 the Premier, Hon Sir Robert Stout, presented to both houses a memorandum that catalogued the incessant wrangling since 1854 and appended relevant correspondence.[32] May's name appeared several times. In one notable case, the House of Representatives took such exception to an amendment made to a bill by the Legislative Council that it resolved that a breach of privilege had occurred,[33] and the Legislative Council appointed a committee to consider the matter. On its recommendation an opinion was sought from the Law Officers of the Crown in England, who opined that the Council had acted within its rights in making the amendment. May had already expressed an opinion in favour of the House, and when supplied with the contrary view of the Law Officers saw no reason to change his mind.[34] His answer was diplomatic and succinct, but resolute:

My Dear Sir,—

I have no desire to be engaged in a controversy at the antipodes, but I have no objection to state, without entering into any arguments, that I adhere to the opinion stated last year—that, if such an amendment ... had been made by the House of Lords to a Bill sent up to them by the Commons, the latter would not have assented to it, in accordance with their own privileges and the usage which is maintained between the two Houses.

I have, &c,
T Erskine May.[35]

The House ordered that this reply be published in its Journals,[36] which seems to have been the last word on the matter.

This saga had dragged on from 1862 to 1864, partly because of the aeons it took for the mail to be shipped around the globe. However, once New Zealand was connected with the world by telegraph (lines reached from Great Britain to the east coast of Australia in 1872, and crossed the Tasman Sea in 1876) it became far easier to consult the oracle. Another significant controversy between the Houses was settled in 1882 by his pronouncements,[37] to the detriment of the Legislative Council. He was careful to 'offer no opinion' about the arguments or actions of one side or the other, but confined himself to stating the practice of the Imperial Parliament, and let that speak for itself. The parliamentary record showed

[31] The Legislative Council was abolished with effect from 1 January 1951, at which point the General Assembly became unicameral. The General Assembly became known as the Parliament of New Zealand on the enactment of the Constitution Act 1986.

[32] Hon Sir Robert Stout, KCMG, Premier, Powers of the Legislative Council and the House of Representatives, [1887] AJHR A.8.

[33] [1862] JHR 179. Interestingly, though, the House still accepted the Council's amendment despite this umbrage, with a further compromise subsequently brokered by the Governor (see McLintock and Wood (n 18) 57–58).

[34] Stout, [1887] AJHR A.8 (n 32), 3–4, in relation to the Native Lands Bill. The Law officers considered that the amendment did not directly impose a tax.

[35] ibid, App 3, 15.

[36] ibid, 4.

[37] Correspondence Relative to the New Zealand Pensions Bill, 1881, [1882] AJHR A.9. In this correspondence, Erskine May also referred to recent communications about a railways bill.

that he 'upheld' the view of the Speaker of the lower house;[38] his status as the arbiter was not questioned. Newspaper reports concurred that May's intervention was conclusive.[39] In gratitude, New Zealand's Agent General in London, Sir Francis Dillon Bell, wrote personally to May that 'Your answer will save what threatened to be a nasty fight in our House.'[40] Bell was himself a former Speaker of the House of Representatives.

Difficulties resolved by taking May's counsel were not confined to the struggle between the Houses. In 1878, his considered view on whether a Governor should accept advice to dissolve Parliament without provision first being made for the public service was published in full among the news columns on the front page of the *New Zealand Herald*.[41] In 1880, the Clerk of the House of Representatives received confirmation from May that the Speaker had no authority to vary an appropriation of money for the legislature.[42] And in 1882, after the result in an election was contested through an electoral petition, there was uncertainty surrounding the swearing in of the (provisional) victor. Anxieties were soothed when, at the opening of Parliament, it was 'understood that Sir Erskine May has been cabled to for advice'.[43]

Like many legislatures during the nineteenth century, New Zealand was afflicted by tactics to delay the passage of legislation, mostly taking advantage of unfettered speaking times or procedural manoeuvres. One solution was proposed in 1881 by a newspaper editor, who cited evidence given by May to a House of Commons select committee in 1878 about the virtues of a system of Grand Committees (see chapter 9). It was also noted that May's views on the idea had been aired as early as 1854, in an article in the *Edinburgh Review*.[44] However, the suggestion was not taken up despite its pedigree. The subsequent 1881 session was one of the worst ever for stonewalling.[45]

On May's retirement, tributes made by Viscount Peel, Speaker of the House of Commons, and by Lord Gladstone were duly reported in New Zealand newspapers, which noted their remarks about the esteem in which he was held in colonial legislatures. Foreign countries looked to him as 'the great classic of Parliamentary lore and learning', and his *Treatise* was 'the mould on which have been formed the practice and proceedings of all our Colonial Legislatures'.[46] Shortly afterwards, May's death was transmitted to New Zealand by cablegram on 19 May 1886 and announced to the House of Representatives by the Speaker, who described him as 'the highest and soundest authority upon parliamentary practice'.[47]

---

[38] Stout, [1887] AJHR A.8, 6.
[39] *New Zealand Herald*, issue 6413, 7 June 1882, 5; *Hawke's Bay Herald*, vol XXI, issue 6270, 7 June 1882, 3; *Wanganui Herald*, vol XVI, issue 4688, 7 June 1882, 2; *The Colonist* (Nelson), vol XXVI, issue 3483, 16 June 1882, 3.
[40] Letter dated 12 May 1882, Papers of Thomas Erskine May; Correspondence: Colonial and Foreign Parliaments, ERM/6/42, <www.parliament.uk>.
[41] *New Zealand Herald*, vol XV, issue 5074, 20 February 1878, 2.
[42] Letter from Erskine May to Major FE Campbell, dated 24 February 1880, reproduced in the appendix to the Report of the Legislative Expenditure Committee (August 1886), AJHR I.10, 19 at para 449.
[43] *Taranaki Herald*, vol XXX, issue 4045, 18 May 1882, 2; *Evening Post* (Wellington), vol XXIII, issue 116, 19 May 1882, 3.
[44] *Hawke's Bay Herald*, vol XXI, issue 5962, 3 May 1881, 2.
[45] Martin (n 24) 9.
[46] HC Deb, 15 April 1886, vol 304 cc 1632–33 and cc 1775–76.
[47] [1886] 54 NZPD 32.

His passing was reported in newspapers around the country,[48] and a round-up of notable persons who had died in 1886 described him as 'the fountain-head of all authority on British Parliamentary procedure and precedent'.[49]

Laid Down in 'M'

May's *Treatise* was the essential companion volume for New Zealand Members of Parliament. The accepted formula was to intone that a practice was 'laid down in May', thus putting an end to any procedural dispute. It was not unusual for Speakers to seek to defuse situations by reading lengthy passages from the book, word-for-word.[50]

The high regard in which May was held during his lifetime meant that his *Treatise* was venerated with almost biblical solemnity thereafter. In the early 1890s, Hon Sir WJ Steward, Speaker of the House of Representatives, compiled a source book of parliamentary procedure. It included rulings from various Speakers (mostly from the House of Commons rather than New Zealand precedents) and rules from the Standing Orders, and a great many excerpts from the book cited simply as 'M'.

The work continues to be referred to as *Erskine May* in preference to its more formal title. During the 1990s it was consulted regularly to inform the intricacies of committee of the whole House procedures. For example, guidance was sought on motions to transfer or divide clauses, which were separately debatable. More recently, with the shift away from clause-by-clause consideration of bills to more generic debates during the committee stage, procedures are now generally less convoluted. But *Erskine May* still assists with more esoteric conundrums about the admissibility of amendments. In 2009, when a determined Opposition filibuster occasioned the lodging of more than 30,000 amendments to a bill,[51] most were ruled out of order, but well over 900 votes were in prospect. *Erskine May* guided the approach to the grouping and selection of the remaining amendments, as these were new procedural concepts in New Zealand. Other rarely encountered procedural tactics, such as the moving of a reasoned amendment to the motion for the second reading of a bill, also prompt Clerks to refer to *Erskine May* when preparing advice.

One area of parliamentary law and procedure in which *Erskine May* has had particular relevance in New Zealand is in the area of parliamentary privilege. An 1864 decision of the Privy Council held that a colonial legislature could confer on itself privileges equivalent to those held by the House of Commons.[52] In New Zealand, the General Assembly accordingly passed the Parliamentary Privileges Act 1865, in which it adopted for itself all of the powers and privileges held, enjoyed and exercised by the House of Commons as at 1 January 1865.[53] The Act followed the precedent of the legislature of the colony of Victoria, in Australia.

---

[48] For example, in the *Grey River Argus* (vol XXXII, issue 5497, 19 May 1886, 2); a full obituary was printed in the *New Zealand Herald* (vol XXIII, issue 7656, 5 June 1886, 2).

[49] *The Star* (Canterbury), 31 December 1886, issue 5814, 3.

[50] For example, [1877] 24 NZPD 539.

[51] Local Government (Auckland Reorganisation) Bill.

[52] Privileges Committee, Question of Privilege Concerning the Defamation Action *Attorney-General and Gow v Leigh*, (June 2013) [2011–14] AJHR I.17A, 13.

[53] Parliamentary Privileges Act 1865, ss 4, 5.

During the second reading of the bill for the 1865 Act, Hugh Carleton, the Chairman of Committees (equivalent to Deputy Speaker), decried this vague means of determining the House's privileges, preferring the more explicit model used in Queensland, South Australia and Tasmania. He observed that it would become necessary to consider what the privileges of the House of Commons really were, and that 'possibly there were honourable members present who did not know what rights they were assuming'. He then regaled the House with examples of punishments reportedly meted out by the House of Commons, and ventured into absurdity by citing the case of Edward Floyde, who was severely punished after the House of Commons dubiously claimed jurisdiction in a libel case in 1621.[54] In his speech, Carleton was quoting extensively from May's *Treatise*, though he did not attribute his source.

Carleton had a point. The relevant provision of the Parliamentary Privileges Act 1865 has recently been re-enacted.[55] In theory, at least, demarcating the privileges enjoyed by the New Zealand House of Representatives continues to involve discerning the privileges of the House of Commons as at 1 January 1865, subject to the passage of statutes and the development of common law since that time. New Zealand courts are enjoined to consult the Journals of the House of Commons for this purpose,[56] but in practical terms judges are inclined to turn to *Erskine May*, in combination with New Zealand authorities.[57]

A Home-Grown Treatise

David McGee, who at the time was the Deputy Clerk of the House,[58] published the first edition of *Parliamentary Practice in New Zealand* in 1985.[59] He prepared for the task of writing this textbook by reading May's *Treatise* from cover to cover. He regarded the latter as a 'primary source', alongside the Standing Orders of the House of Representatives and records of the House's proceedings in *Hansard*, the Journals, and the Appendices to the Journals.[60] This was partly because the provision in the Standing Orders defaulting to House of Commons procedure was still intact at the time—it was retained almost untouched (though renumbered as Standing Order 2) until finally being removed in 1996—but that provision was rarely resorted to because New Zealand's practices had by then become highly developed and distinctive.

When planning his New Zealand textbook, McGee accorded prominence to *Erskine May* mainly because he regarded the *Treatise* as a fundamental element of the 'common law' of parliamentary procedure, the base upon which interpretation was constructed. May's

---

[54] [1864–66] NZPD 318–19.

[55] Parliamentary Privilege Act 2014, s 8; in the meantime, for more than a century, the provision had been incorporated in the Legislature Act 1908, s 242.

[56] Parliamentary Privilege Act 2014, s 8(4).

[57] For example: *Peters v Collinge* [1993] 2 NZLR 554 at 573; *Television New Zealand Ltd v Prebble* [1993] 3 NZLR 513 at 527–528. *Buchanan v Jennings* (CA 106/01) [2002] 3 NZLR 145 at 25, 32, 149.

[58] McGee was appointed as Clerk of the House that same year.

[59] David McGee, *Parliamentary Practice in New Zealand* (Wellington, Government Printer, 1985).

[60] The Appendices include reports of select committees and papers relating to Parliament. In 1985 the Appendices also incorporated parliamentary papers, the vast array of government accountability documents, which are now published in a separate series.

work had long been recognised in New Zealand as having provided the background to procedural thought and the approach to procedural questions.[61] The then current edition of the *Treatise* also provided a model for how to structure the new work. There was some reordering: parliamentary privilege was placed towards the end of McGee's book, though it was a major component.

A complete overhaul of New Zealand's Standing Orders was undertaken in 1995, in anticipation of the newly adopted proportional representation electoral system. When drafting the new Standing Orders, McGee (by then the Clerk of the House) structured them in the same sequence as the subject-matter had been dealt with in his book. The current structure of the Standing Orders thus was ultimately derived from the structure of *Erskine May*. A number of rules were recast in 1995 and some, such as the procedure for urgent debates and the sub judice rules, were also rewritten to reflect principles set out in *Erskine May*.

Like *Erskine May* and *Odgers*, David McGee's work has come to be referred to using eponymous shorthand: members invoke *McGee* much as they had appealed to *Erskine May* with regularity over more than a century prior to 1985. Further editions of *Parliamentary Practice in New Zealand* were published in 1994 and 2005,[62] with the third edition also then being electronically published for free access on the Parliament website in 2010.[63]

Erskine May, as the editor tells us in his introduction, soon made the transition from being the authoritative work of an individual to become the focus of an institutional effort. This has enabled its longevity and continued relevance as a work, and is pertinent to New Zealand because *McGee* has undergone a similar transition. A fourth edition has just been published in 2017, and it is the first edition that has not been prepared by David McGee himself. Like May, responsibility for updating different parts of the work was allocated to staff around the Office of the Clerk, with the Clerk of the House giving final approval. Now that the fourth edition has been published, it is expected that further updates and editions will be more frequent.

Over time, considerable divergence has emerged between New Zealand's parliamentary practice and the practice of the House of Commons from which it originally was derived. Members and staff will not necessarily be aware of these differences in context, which means that there is some peril that direct citation of *Erskine May* could lead to the misrepresentation of New Zealand's home-grown procedures. However, *Erskine May* continues to be an important source. A recent edition of *Erskine May* can still be found within easy reach of the Clerk at the Table in New Zealand's House of Representatives. It sits on the shelf, right next to *McGee*.

---

[61] Other pioneering parliamentary writers had been influential—Alpheus Todd's Parliamentary Government, Bourke's Precedents, and Bramwell, and famous Speakers of the House of Commons: Denison, Brand, Lefevre and Peel; but none was renowned in New Zealand in the same way as Erskine May. Thomas Jefferson, whose legacy is championed by Harry Evans (see n 16 above), was never a significant direct source for New Zealand procedure.

[62] 2nd edn, Wellington, GP Publications, 1994; and 3rd edn, Wellington, Dunmore Publishing, 2005.

[63] <www.parliament.nz/en-nz/about-parliament/how-parliament-works/ppnz>.

THE CANADIAN HOUSE OF COMMONS[64]

Alongside the works of May and Hatsell, a number of books on parliamentary procedure or privilege were published in Canada in the nineteenth, twentieth and twenty-first centuries, including those by Alpheus Todd, John George Bourinot, Arthur Beauchesne, William Dawson and Joseph Maingot.[65] Since the publication of the first edition of the *Treatise*, May has remained an author often referred to by Canadian procedural experts. The influence his book has had is unequivocal, Canadian works of reference on parliamentary procedure having evolved in consequence of or in conjunction with his.

May's Influence on Canadian Parliamentary Procedure

Unlike the cases of New Zealand and the Australian Commonwealth, much of Canada's parliamentary tradition pre-dates the first edition of the *Treatise* in 1844.[66] Nonetheless, May's influence on the development of procedural texts specific to Canada's Parliament was without a doubt significant. Those rules were later incorporated directly in the Constitution and the law, particularly those that establish a legislative foundation for parliamentary privilege.[67] The current edition of *House of Commons Procedure and Practice* states:

> The *Constitution Act* provides that 'the privileges, immunities, and powers to be held, enjoyed and exercised' by the House and its Members are to be 'defined by Act of the Parliament of Canada', with the proviso that such privileges, immunities and powers may not exceed those enjoyed by the British House of Commons and its Members.[68]

The Standing Orders and traditions of the Canadian House of Commons are largely inspired by those of the Legislative Assembly of the Province of Canada (1840–67). At the first session of the newly constituted House of Commons in November 1867, a motion was adopted to continue using the Standing Orders that had been in use in the previous Assembly.

Going back further still, the Standing Orders of the Legislative Assembly of the Province of Canada[69] were themselves inspired by the rules of the House of Assembly of Lower Canada (1791–1840).[70] They originated from one of the first decisions taken by that House on 22 December 1792, when Members decided to adopt rules similar to those in use in the Westminster Parliament.[71] As a consequence, principal authorities on

---

[64] Prepared by Mr Jean-Philippe Brochu, Deputy Principal Clerk, in consultation with Mrs Beverley Isles, Clerk Assistant, who are grateful to Mrs Erica Pereira, Procedural Clerk, for participating in research.

[65] Audrey O'Brien and Marc Bosc (eds), *House of Commons Procedure and Practice*, 2nd edn (Ottawa, House of Commons, 2009) 264–65.

[66] Although the New South Wales Legislative Assembly did not assume a recognisable democratic form until 1856, it did have precursors going as far back as 1824.

[67] *Procedure and Practice* (n 65), 251–52.

[68] ibid, 252.

[69] Gary O'Brien, 'Parliamentary Tradition and the Legacy of 1812' (2012) 35(3) *Canadian Parliamentary Review* 12–13. See also *Journals of the Legislative Assembly of the Province of Canada*, 15 June 1841, 14.

[70] *Procedure and Practice* (n 65), 254. (See also G. O'Brien, *Pre-Confederation Parliamentary Procedure: The Evolution of Legislative Practice in the Lower Houses of Central Canada, 1792–1866* (PhD thesis, Carleton University, 1988) 255–56.)

[71] *Journals of the House of Assembly of Lower-Canada*, 22 December 1792, 48.

parliamentary procedure and practice were also imported from England and even translated into French:[72]

> *Resolved*, That Mr Speaker do cause to be translated into French, the four Volumes of Precedents of proceedings in the House of Commons by John Hatsell, Edition of 1796, and have two hundred copies thereof printed, for the use of the Members of this House. Provided that the expense of translating and printing the same, do not exceed the sum of Seven Hundred Pounds Money of this Province.[73]

At the same time, references were made directly to foreign jurisprudence to decide on unprecedented matters. *House of Commons Procedure and Practice* records that:

> The first representative assemblies on Canadian soil were inspired mainly by British parliamentary tradition, and to a lesser degree by American practice. Until recently, the British influence was explicitly recognized by the House in its Standing Orders and, to this day, in instances where internal precedents do not provide the necessary guidance, the Speaker is given full authority to go beyond the House's jurisprudence 'in cases not provided for hereinafter'. The Speaker may thus turn to provincial or foreign precedents, typically those of Commonwealth legislative bodies, 'so far as they may be applicable to the House'.[74]

On 19 June 1841, the first rules adopted by the Legislative Assembly of the then newly created Province of Canada stated explicitly, under Rule 34, that: '[I]n all unprovided cases, resort shall be had to the Rules, Usages and Forms of [the United Kingdom] Parliament, which shall be followed, until this House shall think fit to make a Rule applicable to such unprovided cases'.[75] An almost identical rule had existed in the House of Assembly of Lower Canada since 1794.[76] In 1867, Rule 116 of the *Rules, Orders and Forms of Proceedings of the House of Commons of Canada* also stated that: '[I]n all cases not provided for in the rules of the Canadian House of Commons, the rules, usages and forms of the House of Commons of the United Kingdom of Great Britain and Ireland were to be followed.'[77] On this basis, after 1844 May's *Treatise* quickly became accepted as an authoritative work of reference within Canada's Parliament.

Early on in Canadian House of Commons debates, references to the *Treatise* can be found which illustrate the influence of May's interpretation of the practice of the UK House of Commons. For example, the First Speaker of the Canadian House of Commons, James Cockburn (1867–73) stated in a ruling on 20 March 1871:

> The question generally whether private Members may introduce and proceed upon measures relating to taxation, which was discussed in the course of the argument, is one of very grave importance, and, though not needful, to the decision of the present objections, I think it proper to say a few words upon it to the House. Instances may undoubtedly be found in the journals of the English House of Commons, of Bills and motions by private Members to increase taxation, some of which have passed unchallenged, whilst in other cases the indirect assent of a Minister has been deemed

---

[72] Henri Brun, *La formation des institutions parlementaires québécoises, 1791–1838* (Québec, Les Presses de l'Université Laval, 1970) 134–35.

[73] *Journals of the House of Assembly of Lower-Canada*, 18 March 1805, 469.

[74] *Procedure and Practice* (n 65) 263.

[75] *Journals of the Legislative Assembly of the Province of Canada*, 19 June 1841, 48.

[76] *Journals of the House of Assembly of Lower-Canada*, 20 January 1794, 120.

[77] *Rules, Orders and Forms of Proceedings of the House of Commons of Canada* (1868) 82.

sufficient. Recently, however, (in 1869) a high authority, Sir Thomas Erskine May, stated before a Joint Committee of the two Houses of Parliament, that 'no private Member is permitted to propose an Imperial tax upon the people; it must proceed from a Minister of the Crown, or be in some other form declared to be necessary for the public service'.[78]

Over the years that followed and into the early twentieth century, citations from the *Treatise* appeared in Canadian Speakers' rulings.[79] On 20 May 1874, Speaker Anglin ruled on the acceptability of a motion to concur in a committee report, referring directly to the authority of May: 'My attention has been directed to this subject, and I have come to the conclusion that the Motion is decidedly out of order. It is laid down distinctly by May.'[80]

Among the procedural topics for which successive Speakers turned to May's treatise for clarification were the admissibility of an amendment (23 May 1917 and 28 February 1929), the need for a notice of motion (26 March 1928), the need to receive royal recommendation (16 February 1923) and sub judice (17 April 1923).

However, what is most noteworthy is that, in the years following the publication of *Treatise*, it became an essential tool for understanding the foundational concepts of parliamentary law. The first of these, and undoubtedly the most important, was the concept of parliamentary privilege. In some cases, the *Treatise* served as an authority to understand the historical background and the context of the privileges of the House.[81] The definition of parliamentary privilege given in May is quoted word for word in *House of Commons Procedure and Practice*.[82] It is also quoted in other Canadian publications, including Beauchesne's *Rules and Forms of the House of Commons of Canada* (sixth edition), *Parliamentary Privilege in Canada* (second edition) and *The House of Commons at Work*.[83]

May was also used to provide a better understanding of breach of privilege and contempt of parliament,[84] freedom of speech and 'proceedings in parliament',[85] the various freedoms Members enjoy in the performance of their duties and the collective rights of the House held in common. However, as is the case with other aspects of parliamentary procedure, the concept of parliamentary privilege as applied today in Canada and the United Kingdom has evolved into relatively distinct bodies of law.[86] In Canada, courts have redefined the framework of parliamentary privilege.[87]

---

[78] See the *Journals of the House of Commons*, 20 March 1871.

[79] For other examples, see *Debates of the House of Commons*, 13 January 1910; 24 February 1915; 28 and 29 March 1916; 10 May 1916; 16 May 1916; 16 May 1917; 23 May 1917; 23 June 1920; 16 February 1923; 17 April 1923; 28 April 1924; 26 March 1928; 28 February 1929; 20 October 1932; 2 November 1932; 10 March 1933.

[80] *Journals of the House of Commons*, 20 May 1874, 282.

[81] See, for example, *Debates of the House of Commons*, 27 April 2010, 2043; 17 September 2012, 10005.

[82] *Procedure and Practice* (n 65) 60.

[83] A Beauchesne, *Rules and Forms of the House of Commons of Canada*, 6th edn, ed A Fraser, WF Dawson and JA Holtby (Toronto, Carswell, 1989) 11; JA Fraser, *The House of Commons at Work* (Montréal, Les Éditions de la Chenelière,. 1993) 151–52; JPJ Maingot, *Parliamentary Privilege in Canada*, 2nd edn (Montréal, House of Commons and McGill-Queen's University Press, 1997) 12.

[84] *Procedure and Practice* (n 65) 82.

[85] ibid, 89–91.

[86] ibid, 67. See also House of Commons, 'Parliamentary Privilege: Current issues', Briefing Paper SN/PC/06390, <www.parliament.uk/briefing-papers/SN06390/parliamentary-privilege-current-issues> accessed 26 November 2014.

[87] See *House of Commons and the Honourable Gilbert Parent v Satnam Vaid and the Canadian Human Rights Commission (Vaid)*, for example.

But it was Gilbert Campion's fourteenth edition of the *Treatise*, published in 1946, that seems to have established the basis for discussion of Canadian concepts of privilege.[88] In Canada, this edition had a direct impact, for example, on how a question of privilege is raised in the House, reflected in an important change in the fourth (1958) edition of Beauchesne's *Rules and Forms of the House of Commons of Canada*, which empowered the Speaker to play a more active role with respect to questions of privilege,[89] that is, in particular, that the question of privilege being raised must meet the prima facie condition and be raised as soon as it could have been.[90]

Today, the *Treatise* remains essential to understanding the historical context of certain Westminster rules and practices that are still in force in Canada. For example, it explains obscure points such as the oath of abjuration, allegiance and supremacy in use in the early eighteenth century.[91] It also provides background on the evolution of parliamentary procedure[92] and practices still in use, such as the rule that strangers are not permitted on the floor of the House.[93] The traditional powers and duties of the Speaker, which can also trace their roots to the Westminster Parliament, to a great extent derive from May's analysis.[94]

Basic procedural concepts and practices codified by May, such as motions being called for debate, the question being put or the process for amending a bill, were described very clearly by Bourinot in the late nineteenth century. Nowadays, precedence is given to Bourinot over May, as it provides examples from Canadian practice. However, May can still be relied on to clarify more complex procedural rules, such as the need for a ways and means motion[95] or the rule of anticipation.[96]

The development and codification of many usages and precedents through many Speakers' rulings also played a crucial role in creating a procedural corpus that is distinctly Canadian. Over time, Speakers have made a point of supporting their analyses using many references and precedents, citing different books, including but not limited to May's *Treatise*.

The Development of Canadian References

When the first edition of the *Treatise* was published, several colonies in British North America had already held parliamentary proceedings and, at least one local book, *The Practice and Privilege of the Two Houses of Parliament*, published in 1840 by Alpheus Todd, preceded the publication of May's renowned book.

Todd, who lived from 1821 to 1884, was a contemporary of May who began his career in a legislative library, in Upper Canada in 1835, four years after May began his own career as an assistant librarian in the UK House of Commons library.[97] After the unification of Upper Canada and Lower Canada, Todd was hired by the new legislative assembly, and

---

[88] *Procedure and Practice* (n 65) 67.
[89] ibid, 73.
[90] ibid, 73.
[91] ibid, 201.
[92] ibid, 250–51.
[93] ibid, 285.
[94] *Debates of the House of Commons*, 28 January 2014, 2204.
[95] *Debates of the House of Commons*, 18 October 2011, 2171; 4 November 2011, 2985.
[96] *Procedure and Practice* (n 65) 560.
[97] Paul Silk, 'Erskine May', *The House Magazine*, 1 July 1983, 6.

his book was used as a reference by the Members.[98] Todd, like May, was interested in the political and constitutional history of England and published *On Parliamentary Government in England* in 1867–69,[99] soon after May himself published *A Constitutional History of England since the Accession of George III*, in 1861. Bruce W Hodgins asserted that:

> As an authority on the operation of British Parliament, Todd's only contemporary rival was the British writer, Sir Thomas Erskine May. The importance to Canada of his work on the British colonies, however, was soon to be overshadowed by the constitutional writings of Sir John George Bourinot.[100]

Sir John George Bourinot occupies a special place in the study of Canadian parliamentary procedure. He based the first edition of *Parliamentary Procedure and Practice*, published in 1884, on the structure and basic concepts of parliamentary procedure that May had used. Like the *Treatise*, Bourinot's work survived to be cited 130 years later. Like Todd before him, Bourinot had much in common with May. He spent thirty-three years serving federal parliamentarians, holding the position of Clerk of the House for twenty-two years. Gary Levy confirmed that: 'Bourinot, Clerk for more than two decades in the last century, was a great admirer of the British authority, Erskine May, and was instrumental in developing procedures for the new Canadian legislature along well established British patterns.'[101]

Bourinot's manual follows the traditional pattern of seeking to elicit general principles from particular examples, and describes parliamentary procedure by reference to numerous precedents, some of which are taken from Westminster. He also quotes May extensively. Two of his stated objectives in publishing his book were to provide detailed references to the work of experts such as May and Hatsell, and to provide a comparative perspective.[102]

Like May, he addressed the procedures used in both Houses of Parliament. Already at that time, Bourinot believed that, while the procedures and practices in use in Canada were derived from Westminster, they had evolved sufficiently to merit the publication of a work that addressed Canadian parliamentary procedure and practice specifically.[103] However, unlike the *Treatise*, Bourinot's work was reissued only twice after his death, in 1903 and 1916. It has not been reissued since.

Another long-serving Clerk, Arthur Beauchesne, also wrote an authoritative Canadian manual of procedure, supplanting Bourinot. In total, six editions of Beauchesne's *Rules and Forms of the House of Commons of Canada* were published, the last of these in 1989. Unlike Bourinot, who adopted a descriptive, even educational approach, Beauchesne's text is first and foremost a collection of rules with annotations, comments and precedents.[104] In his fourth edition, Beauchesne acknowledges the contributions of May, as well as Bourinot, stating in his preface:

---

[98] Bruce W Hodgins, 'Todd, Alpheus', *Dictionary of Canadian Biography*, vol XI (1881–90), <http://biographi.ca> accessed 15 July 2014.
[99] ibid.
[100] ibid.
[101] Gary Levy, (1989) 12(2) *Canadian Parliamentary Review*, <www.revparl.ca/english/index.asp?param=113> accessed 17 September 2014.
[102] JG Bourinot, Preface to first edition, reproduced in *Parliamentary Procedure and Practice in the Dominion of Canada*, 2nd edn rev and enlarged (Montreal, Dawson Brothers Publishers, 1892) vii.
[103] Robert Marleau and Camille Montpetit (eds), *House of Commons Procedure and Practice*, 1st edn (Ottawa, House of Commons, 2000) v.
[104] Beauchesne (n 83) iii. See also Preface to *House of Commons Procedure and Practice*, 1st edn (2000).

The priceless work of Sir Erskine May brought up to date by eminent Clerks of the United Kingdom House, Sir T Lonsdale Webster and Lord Campion, is regarded, except for local circumstances, as an authority upon all matters respecting procedure. I have relied on it as well as on Sir John Bourinot's *Parliamentary Procedure* which has guided many a Speaker since its first appearance in 1884 and is still a safe guide on Canadian parliamentary practice. The fourth edition edited in 1914 [*sic*] by Dr Thomas B Flint, Clerk of the House, carries great authority in our Parliament.[105]

More recently, the Canadian House of Commons has benefited from the result of years of hard work under the inspiration and direction of successive Clerks of the House. The *House of Commons Procedure and Practice*, first published in 2000, is an in-depth study of Canada's parliamentary precedents. The stated purpose of the book was to provide 'a distinctly Canadian reference work on the procedure and practice of the House of Commons'.[106]

Work on this began in the early 1980s. It was agreed that a complete, up-to-date and authoritative reference was required as there was no other authoritative text at the time in Canada that brought together all procedural sources, such as the Standing Orders, constitutional laws, statutes, Speakers' rulings and contemporary practice. In addition, Bourinot's book had not been updated since 1916, and Beauchesne's book was more narrowly focused on rules rather than context and interpretation. May's works continued to inspire Canadian practice but British and Canadian parliamentary procedure had evolved to a point when it was time for a procedural authority that was uniquely Canadian.

The need for a modern, comprehensive text was precipitated by the work of two special committees on reform of the House of Commons. The scope of changes recommended to the rules and practices of the House by those two committees was impressive. In 1982, the Lefebvre Committee recommended changes to the scrutiny of government expenditure, the annual calendar of the House, the scheduling of votes and length of time for debate, for example. The McGrath Committee, which published its third and most important report in June 1985, rendered obsolete the procedural authorities in use at the time, in particular Beauchesne, which was in its fifth edition. The McGrath Committee suggested extensive changes to the committee system, scrutiny of Order-in-Council appointments, Private Members' Business, report stage of bills, petitions, written questions, the Order of Business, meeting times of the House, the prayer, and emergency debates, to name but a few.

A number of options were considered by the House Administration, including publishing a fifth edition of Bourinot. In 1983, representatives of the House of Commons consulted their British and Australian counterparts on how May's and Odgers' treatises were updated.[107]

After creating a detailed database of procedural precedents that was known as the Bourinot Project, a milestone was reached in 1989 when a first edition of the *Annotated Standing Orders of the House of Commons* was published. This text presented each Standing Order in effect at the time, along with a description and historical background. Each Standing Order was accompanied by many references taken from examples that had been recorded over time, including from the Bourinot Project. The *Annotated Standing Orders* were instrumental in implementing the next phase of the vision.

---

[105] Arthur Beauchesne, *Rules and Forms of the House of Commons of Canada*, 4th edn (Toronto, Carswell, 1958) vii.

[106] *Procedure and Practice* (n 103) vi.

[107] Internal notes indicate that Dr Arthur Koester, while Clerk of the day, raised the matter with Australian Clerks during a visit that same year. An exhaustive questionnaire on the editing process for May was also sent to the UK Table Clerks.

The drafting of *House of Commons Procedure and Practice* began in earnest in 1991, ultimately taking nine years to complete. The final book numbered more than 1,000 pages for each English and French volume and had thousands of references, including numerous ones to May. Special attention was paid to providing all the relevant contextual information, using appendices, tables and illustrations. An effort was also made to include historical information, providing valuable details on the evolution of procedure, at the beginning of each chapter. It was also decided to use modern publishing methods, and the House quickly made an electronic version available online at no cost to the user. On 9 February 2000, the first edition of *House of Commons Procedure and Practice*, under the direction of Robert Marleau, Clerk of the House, and Camille Montpetit, former Deputy Clerk, was tabled simultaneously in French and English in the House of Commons.

The second edition, published on 18 November 2009, encompassed major procedural changes introduced in the early 2000s after the work of the Special Committee on Modernization and Improvement of the Procedure of the House of Commons, and legislative changes such as a new Canada Elections Act in 2000 or amendments to the Parliament of Canada Act in 2004 to create an Ethics Commissioner.[108]

House of Commons Procedure and Practice started at the point which May's *Treatise* had reached: it made no claim to be the work of a single author but was a collective effort by a group of procedural employees driven by an objective of professional excellence. Its objectivity and level of detail have made it an indispensable and essential tool for parliamentarians, the public, academics, parliamentary staff, and anyone with an interest in parliamentary procedure. Copies of *House of Commons Procedure and Practice*, first and second editions, sit prominently on the Table of the Canadian House of Commons, just next to copies of past *Selected Speakers Decisions*, late editions of Beauchesne and Bourinot and, of course, the most recent edition of May's *Treatise*.

THE AUSTRALIAN HOUSE OF REPRESENTATIVES[109]

The procedures of the Australian colonial parliaments prior to Federation were derived from United Kingdom practice, and May's *Treatise* was always the essential source of reference.

In 1843 the New South Wales Legislative Council became the first Australian legislature to have elected representatives, and welcomed with some relief, one imagines, the publication the following year of the first edition of the *Treatise*. The Council's Speaker was to write to the author in 1851: 'It is quite impossible … to overrate the advantages which have resulted from the employment of your work in the colonial legislatures.'[110] As other Australian colonies achieved elected representation and then self-government, their Councils and Assemblies naturally turned to the *Treatise* for guidance. May's personal papers in the Parliamentary Archives show that they also wrote directly to May himself, seeking advice on procedural issues. One such correspondent from the South Australian

---

[108] *Procedure and Practice*(n 65) v–vi.

[109] Prepared by Peter Fowler, Chamber Research Office, in consultation with David Elder, Clerk of the House and Catherine Cornish, Clerk Assistant–Table.

[110] Sir Charles Nicholson, UK Parliamentary Archives, ERM/6/1.

Parliament was to become Clerk of the Australasian Federal Convention that drafted the Australian Constitution and later the first Clerk of the Australian Senate.[111]

Section 50 of the Australian Constitution provides that:

Each House of the Parliament may make rules and orders with respect to—

i.   The mode in which its powers, privileges, and immunities may be exercised and upheld.
ii. The order and conduct of its business and proceedings either separately or jointly with the other House.

When the first Parliament of the Commonwealth of Australia opened in 1901 the Senate and the House of Representatives were faced with the urgent business necessary for establishing a new nation, and the settling of their own rules and orders was not an immediate priority. As temporary measures the House adopted a set of standing orders prepared by the new Clerk of the Senate (the Acting Clerk of the House having been allotted the task of overseeing the ceremonial opening and celebrations), and the Senate adopted the standing orders of the South Australian House of Assembly (rejecting the set prepared by its Clerk). Both sets of temporary standing orders were representative of the standing orders of the former Australian colonial, now state, parliaments. This was naturally what many Members and Senators, and parliamentary staff, who had previously served in colonial parliaments, were used to and expected.

The course of events in the two Houses diverged. The Senate took only two years to achieve its permanent rules, and in doing so decisively rejected a proposed formal connection to United Kingdom procedure. When the future Clerk of the Senate, JR Odgers, published *Australian Senate Practice* (subsequently referred to as *Odgers*) in 1953, he cited the *Treatise* only in relation to parliamentary privilege.[112]

In contrast, the House's 'temporary' standing orders, which were to be in force for fifty years, contained in pride of place as standing order number 1 the requirement that, unless other provision was made, the House of Representatives should follow House of Commons procedures:

CHAPTER 1

GENERAL RULE FOR CONDUCT OF BUSINESS

Usages of House of Commons to be observed, unless other provision is made

1. In all cases not provided for hereinafter, or by Sessional or other Orders, resort shall be had to the rules, forms and practice of the Commons House of the Imperial Parliament of Great Britain and Ireland in force at time of the adoption of these Orders, which shall be followed as far as they can be applied to the proceedings of the House of Representatives.

When permanent standing orders were adopted in 1950, the General Rule was amended so that the House could follow current rather than 1901 House of Commons procedures:

1. In all cases not provided for hereinafter, or by Sessional or other Orders or practice of the House, resort shall be had to the practice of the Commons House of the United Kingdom of

---

[111] EG Blackmore, UK Parliamentary Archives, ERM/6/20.
[112] Recent editions of *Odgers* make no reference to *Erskine May*.

Great Britain and Northern Ireland in force for the time being, which shall be followed as far as it can be applied.

The amended General Rule was to survive untouched in the revised standing orders adopted in 1963 following a comprehensive review, one of the goals of which had been 'the omission of obsolete provisions long since discarded by the [UK] House of Commons', and was to remain in the standing orders until 2004. This meant that for over a hundred years Members and officers of the House of Representatives relied on the *Treatise* as the standard reference text when the orders and practice of the House were silent on a particular matter.

There appears to have been initially a heavy reliance on House of Commons practice, and thus on May, during the early years of the Parliament.[113] However, as the House's corporate memory expanded over the years and its own (unpublished) records of rulings and precedents accumulated, there was progressively less need to resort to Commons practice. As noted in the preface of the first edition of *House of Representatives Practice*, the House of Representatives had gradually developed its own practice and procedure, precedent and case history and by the mid-1970s the stage had been reached when reference to the *Treatise* was infrequent, except in relation to matters of privilege.

During the early 1970s there appears to have been an increasing interest among Members in the operation of the House and procedural matters, and in 1975 the Standing Orders Committee, prompted by Members' comments to the effect that it was about time the House stopped relying on May, recognised the need for a text embodying the practice of the House and recommended the preparation of a publication which it anticipated would fulfil a comparable role.

In the following period successive Clerks devoted significant departmental resources to the project,[114] and the resulting text was published as *House of Representatives Practice* in 1981. The publication was from the first a corporate effort, rather than starting as a work of a single individual as had been the case with *Erskine May*, *Odgers* or *McGee*.

Among the guidelines set down for the preparation of *House of Representatives Practice* was one covering the use of *Erskine May*. Writers were directed that '*Erskine May's Parliamentary Practice* is a useful reference document only where there is no House of Representatives practice. It is stressed that [*House of Representatives Practice*] is about current and, where relevant, past House of Representatives practice and procedure, and Commons precedents should be used with discretion'. Despite such exhortation there were to be 150 references to the *Treatise* in the first edition.

The General Rule, the theoretical requirement to resort to Commons practice, was of course still extant in 1981, and was to remain for the second (1989), third (1997) and fourth (2001) editions. By this time, however, with the continued development of the House's own body of practice, and its documentation in *House of Representatives Practice*, resort to House of Commons practice had, in reality, not occurred for many years, and the provision

---

[113] One of the earliest committee inquiries was into 'the improper removal from the Chamber of Mr Speaker's copy of May's *Parliamentary Practice*, with Mr Speaker's notes in connection therewith'. The book was later found in a coal scuttle but, although a detective was engaged, the Speaker's notes were not retrieved and no culprit was identified. See Interim Report from the Select Committee on Irregular Conduct and Interference, June 1914.

[114] NJ Parkes and JA Pettifer.

was omitted, without comment or debate, from the revised standing orders adopted in 2004. It was replaced with standing order 3(e) in the following terms:

> The Speaker (or other Member presiding) is responsible for ruling whenever any question arises as to the interpretation or application of a standing order and for deciding cases not otherwise provided for. In all cases the Speaker shall have regard to previous rulings of Speakers of the House and to established practices of the House.

While the fifth edition (2005), necessitated by the greatly revised and renumbered standing orders, and the recently published sixth edition (2012) were not consciously 'de-Mayed', when the exercise undertaken for the purpose of this chapter commenced it was automatically assumed that the number of citations of the *Treatise* in the text would be far fewer than they used to be. It was somewhat of a surprise to find that there had been only a 10 per cent reduction in citations between the first and sixth editions. Further investigation revealed that while a larger proportion had in fact been dropped, new references to the *Treatise* had been added, even after the demise of Standing Order 1.

The reason for the continuing references to May lies in the purpose and nature of *House of Representatives Practice*. While the core function of the publication was to provide a procedural manual for Members and Clerks, it was also conceived of as having a wider educative role. It covers the nature of Australia's system of government more generally, and provides some information on the history and derivation of Australian practices and procedures. In this wider context the *Treatise* remains relevant. New references to May have been included not to bestow authority but to note interesting differences between the House of Commons and the House of Representatives—for example, the Federation Chamber is compared with Westminster Hall. Similarly, to place the House of Representatives in the wider context there are references to Senate practice and citations of *Odgers*.

For a long time the House had to have copies of May readily available, even though in later years it was decreasingly referred to. A copy was kept in the Chamber. Every senior clerk was issued a personal copy, and copies were provided to office holders. In contrast, the current situation is that the *Treatise* has been almost entirely supplanted by *House of Representatives Practice*. All staff and all Members have a copy of this publication within easy reach, whereas *Erskine May* is not as accessible. Copies of May are held in the Clerk's Office and in the departmental library. There is no longer a copy in the Chamber. The *Treatise* is used, from time to time, as a source of reference to discover House of Commons practice on various procedural matters. This is not in order to determine what the House of Representatives might do, but to gain insight on what the United Kingdom does, in the same way that *McGee* and *House of Commons Procedure and Practice* are consulted to investigate comparable New Zealand and Canadian practice. Such information is periodically pulled together for Procedure Committee briefs. Reference is also made to *Erskine May* in some of the more obscure areas of the financial initiative where the House has fewer precedents to draw on than the UK House of Commons.

An example of the recent use of the *Treatise* as a reference source is the following: an inquiry was received asking about procedures in Australia for the signification of the Queen's consent on matters touching the personal interests or prerogatives of the sovereign (as distinct from Queen's [royal] assent). To answer (and initially to understand) the question, resort was had to *Erskine May*. In the next edition of *House of Representatives Practice* there is likely to be a reference to the relevant pages of *Erskine May* (and also to

Canadian practice) with a note that there is no equivalent requirement or process in the Australian Parliament.

In summary, in procedural matters *House of Representatives Practice* has virtually completely replaced May's *Treatise* as the authoritative reference source. It has the status in relation to the House of Representatives that May has in relation to the House of Commons. Because of its direct relevance and also no doubt because of its ready availability, it is frequently used by Members and quoted in the Chamber, far more than the *Treatise* ever was.

May and Parliamentary Privilege in Australia

The Australian Commonwealth Parliament derives its privilege powers from section 49 of the Australian Constitution, which provides that:

> The powers, privileges, and immunities of the Senate and of the House of Representatives, and of the members and the committees of each House, shall be such as are declared by the Parliament, and until declared shall be those of the Commons House of Parliament of the United Kingdom, and of its members and committees, at the establishment of the Commonwealth.

The *Treatise* was obviously in 1901 the essential reference source on the powers, privileges, and immunities of the UK House of Commons, and consequently of the Australian Houses. This continued to be the situation for a long time, even after the publication of the Senate's and the House's own works of reference, for it was not until many years later that the Australian Parliament actually declared its powers in aspects of this area.

As the first edition of *House of Representatives Practice* stated in 1981, under the heading 'Adherence to House of Commons practice':

> *May* is recognised as the most authoritative and comprehensive work on matters pertaining to the law, privileges, proceedings and usage of a Parliament operating in the Westminster tradition … and it is to *May* that the House usually turns for precedents and guidance when questions of privilege arise.

In 1987 the Parliamentary Privileges Act was enacted under the head of power constituted by section 49 of the Constitution, and from that time the Act itself, along with the corresponding text in later editions of *House of Representatives Practice* and *Odgers*, became the first point of reference, rather than May.

However, the Parliamentary Privileges Act 1987 was not intended to be a complete declaration, in itself, of the privilege powers of the Australian Parliament. The central purpose of the Act had been to maintain, in response to adverse court judgments, the traditional interpretation of Article 9 of the Bill of Rights, 'That the freedom of speech and debates or proceedings in Parliament ought not to be impeached or questioned in any court or place out of Parliament'. Other matters were covered, notably a threshold definition of contempt, but matters not addressed in the Act were declared to be as they had previously been. Section 5 of the Act provides that:

> Except to the extent that this Act expressly provides otherwise, the powers, privileges and immunities of each House, and of the Members and the committees of each House, as in force under section 49 immediately before the commencement of this Act, continue in force.

Because of this, the *Treatise* (and particularly the tenth edition of 1893) has on occasion been consulted to try to ascertain the precise extent of the powers inherited from the Commons in 1901.

In the latest editions of *House of Representatives Practice*, now under the less compelling heading 'Reference to House of Commons practice', the text now merely notes that 'in the area of parliamentary privilege the practice and precedents of the UK House of Commons are of continuing interest'. That is to say, just as an Australian or English court might have regard to judgments from other jurisdictions that share the common law tradition, in privilege matters the Australian Parliament is interested in and may be influenced by precedents from the United Kingdom Parliament when similar issues have been dealt with. In such cases Thomas Erskine May's *Treatise* continues to be an important work of reference.

Part III

Procedural Development

9

The Principle of Progress

May and Procedural Reform

WILLIAM McKAY

INTRODUCTION

A S WE WILL see from the next chapter, after the Great Reform Act, and at a pace accelerating from the mid-nineteenth century, sweeping procedural changes were introduced into the House of Commons. As Palgrave said in his introduction to the 1893 edition of May's *Treatise*, the procedure of 1844 was essentially that of the Long Parliament. Political and social change in Victorian England could not, however, be shaped by seventeenth-century rules tweaked by the eighteenth century, a period more interested in form than progress. Consequently, reforms were designed to sweep away the elaborate forms and manifold opportunities for debate, and replace them with well-oiled, efficient procedural vehicles. It was in the details of reconciling old practice with new needs and proposals while avoiding unnecessary injury to the rights of backbenchers that Clerks had a part to play.

Perhaps 'reconciling' is not the right word. May's work began the process that has dominated procedural development ever since, the superseding of unwritten practice by progressively elaborate codification in standing orders. Even in 1908, when ninety-three of the ninety-six standing orders had been made since 1832,[1] practice remained a significant part of the authority for the House's conduct of business, but it was becoming increasingly unable to bear the weight put on it. For example, when the Clerk of the House Sir Courtenay Ilbert came to give evidence to a select committee on anticipatory motions in 1907, he claimed that the earliest reference to the practice he could find was in *Little Dorrit*,[2] based no doubt on Dickens' experience as a reporter. Even if Ilbert was right—which he probably was not—Dickens and half a century of settled practice were now too slender a basis for the governance of the House's business.[3] Members were persuaded to sacrifice flexibility

---

[1] CP Ilbert in J Redlich, *The Procedure of the House of Commons: A Study of its History and Present Form* (London, Constable, 1908) vol I, xxii.

[2] Select Committee on Procedure (Anticipatory Motions), House of Commons Paper 264 of Session 1907.

[3] Ilbert seems to have been trying—in what seems to be a rather doubtful party-political interest—to obscure the antiquity of the rule.

for certainty: a standing order (now No 28) was made. By 2015, the House of Commons Procedure Committee had recommended its repeal.[4]

THE 1847–48 COMMITTEE ON PUBLIC BUSINESS AND MAY'S 1849 PAMPHLET

May's connection with post-Reform Act procedural change began well before he became a Clerk. Neither John Henry Ley nor any of his colleagues gave evidence to committees on procedure in 1837 or 1848.[5] Even before he appeared himself as a witness, May had a hand in the evidence given in 1848 by Mr Speaker Shaw Lefevre to a committee on the business of the House.[6] What appears to have happened is that May made a series of suggestions to his 'dear old friend' the Speaker. Shaw Lefevre did not put them all to the committee; some the committee rejected; and some the House did not take up. In order to keep the impetus of reform going, May brought out the whole set in his pamphlet *Remarks and suggestions with a view to facilitate the dispatch of public business in Parliament.* That at any rate is a reasonable conclusion from the fact that the pamphlet does not cross the Speaker's evidence at any point, but rather advocates its being taken further and adds cognate points to it.

May's procedural views were securely founded on experience. By 1849 he had served the House for nineteen years as an assistant librarian, indexing the Journal, and for two years he had been examiner of petitions for private bills and taxing master. Above all, five years earlier he had published the first edition of the *Treatise.* In procedure, as in his sometimes all-too-visible politics, May was a Whig. Although many of his proposals were (at least in his earlier years) quite thoroughgoing, in general he believed in partial amendment to remove obvious abuses, and was reluctant to abandon old principles. Reform was necessary, but should be implemented only with the utmost caution. The 1849 pamphlet identified the contemporary malady as 'personal disputes and altercations concerning matters wholly foreign to legislation or any other business, the number [of which] is unhappily very great and is apparently increasing'. As he was to write in another essay on procedure in 1853, 'an obsolete form is rarely without mischief'.

At the same time, government demands on the House's time were becoming insistent. The nub of the difficulty was—much as it still is—to devise a procedure that would on the one hand ensure a fair and sensitive distribution of time between the several matters demanding discussion, while on the other guaranteeing as much certainty and regularity in the despatch of business as possible.[7] The 1849 pamphlet represents May's manifesto, parts of which he was to bring forward at various dates until his retirement. It is therefore worth looking at in more detail.

The Speaker had proposed, and the 1847–48 committee and the House had in part accepted, that the number of questions necessary to be put on a public bill in the course of its career through the House should be reduced. May agreed, believing that the then current (and by today's standards barely imaginable) eighteen led to 'undue frequency of debates'. Similarly, the Speaker had argued forcefully before the committee in 1848 that dilatory and semi-irregular adjournment motions represented a significant interruption to orderly

---

[4] Sixth Report from the Procedure Committee, *Revision of Standing Orders*, House of Commons Paper 654 of Session 2014–15.

[5] JH Ley did, however, give evidence to two select committees on oaths of Members in 1848 and 1850.

[6] Select Committee on Public Business, House of Commons Paper 644 of Session 1847–48.

[7] Select Committee on Business of the House, House of Commons Paper 137 of Session 1871, Q4.

progress of the House's business. As one debate after another was adjourned, business fell into confusion. In the opinion of the Speaker, such motions should be decided without debate; the adjournment should not be allowed to be moved on the same question within an hour after it had previously been moved; no division should be permitted unless twenty-one Members rose in their places; and there should be a procedure with a built-in closure to prevent an adjourned motion from being further adjourned. The Committee took fright at this radicalism, and even such changes as they were prepared to recommend were carried only on the casting vote.

May's pamphlet demonstrated what advantages could be won by courage. Questions for the adjournment had recently been perverted: there was no reason not to adopt the American practice (on which the committee had taken evidence) of declaring such motions incapable of debate. May then took further the Speaker's suggestion that twenty-one Members should be required for a valid division in the direction of what was to become the division-unnecessarily-claimed procedure, in order, as he said, 'to restrain the abuse of divisions'.

The Speaker's proposals had contained the germ of a closure procedure which, after hearing substantial evidence, the committee found too strong meat. They decisively turned down two proposed resolutions of Joseph Hume's to limit all speeches. (It was a suggestion of remarkable self-denial, given Hume's notorious prolixity.) May conceded partial defeat. He would, however, introduce, on an experimental basis, a one-hour speech limit on the short private Members' Wednesdays and in Committee of the whole House, and he would extend the Speaker's proposals so as to block motions for the adjournment of any debate 'for which one night is sufficient'.

Again taking up proposals made by the Speaker, May suggested limiting the number of questions put on opposed second readings and suppressing a question on the committal of Bills. The Speaker had pressed on the 1848 committee means of preventing debate of a Bill in toto on the motion to go into committee on every day on which such a motion was before the House. The committee had watered this sensible proposal down, and May deplored their pusillanimity. The point was, he said, that the Order Paper should indicate clearly what the business was likely to be. The House ought to return to the older and better practice of treating the Orders of the Day as orders. It was an eminently sensible proposal, which unfortunately took very long to realise.

In other areas, May spoke for himself, going further perhaps than the Speaker was prepared to. The most important of these—which again was to have a long history—was that committees of the whole House should be and should appear more independent of the House itself, like the almost extinct Grand Committees dating from the seventeenth century. At the very least, committees of the whole House ought to be able to sit while the House was adjourned, to adjourn from time to time, and to report only when their task was completed. From this—a quarter of a century later—standing committees were born.

A further proposal which was to have a long life was that the rule of relevancy ought to be applied to amendments moved on going into the Committee of Supply. The process of permitting the House to debate anything under the sun on the reading of these orders was, May believed, seriously inconvenient.[8] The substantial issue should come before the House just

---

[8] Despite its seeming close relationship with the principle of redress before Supply, the practice of moving amendments on any topic on going into Supply dated only from 1811, and did not become a nuisance until 1837, as May told a committee in 1871. It appears to have been the House's reaction to the appropriation of certain days of the week to Orders of the Day in preference to Notices of Motions.

as would a case in court, without obstruction or delay. In 1849 he believed—rightly, though he was to resile from the belief later—that the objectionable practice bore no relation to the principle of redress before supply. That being so, the normal rule that amendments should be relevant to the motion to be amended should apply. Once more, years were to pass before the House saw the sense of the proposal.

The 1849 pamphlet proposed that 'in order to encourage talents for practical legislation and to facilitate the passing of useful measures'—a formula which succinctly encompasses the whole of May's suggestions—Members should no longer be required to ask for leave to introduce their Bills. A Member who found four colleagues to back him might simply launch his Bill by depositing it in the Public Bill Office.[9] Not only would this reduce the number of debates on a Bill but it would put an end to the charade of abstract propositions pretending to be Bills. At the same time, motions which could have effect only if turned into statute should be damned as disorderly. Subsequent agreed changes delivered May's ends, though not always by his means.

In 1849, government orders of the day had precedence only on Mondays and Fridays which, when combined with the laxity of the rule of relevance, could readily lead to congestion at the end of the session. Here was a test of where the House wished the balance between progress and debate to come to rest. May was moderately for progress. So much was always expected from the government that they had a proper expectation that facilities for carrying on the public business would be provided. Therefore, there should be no debate on orders for the second reading of private Members' bills after the start of May in any year. After March, orders of the day should have precedence over notices of motion on Thursdays, and after May that priority should be accorded only to government orders of the day. The practice of giving precedence to post-committee stages should be extended from private bills to public bills, thus expediting those proposals which had already commended themselves to the House. Once again May's suggestions were to be adopted—though in the long run and with some alterations.

Finally and somewhat prophetically, May hinted at the need for extra disciplinary powers for the Chair, primarily in defence of relevancy in debate. For the time being, he was prepared to rely on 'the good sense of individual Members, controlled by the critical judgment or impatience of the House', but in principle he believed the disciplinary authority of the Chair needed to be increased and defined.

This, then, was May's 1849 manifesto, and it was a remarkably broad and perceptive one. Although it went beyond the Speaker's submission to the committee, Shaw Lefevre seems to have approved of the examiner's proposals, since in 1850 he attempted—in vain, as it turned out—to secure for May a place at the table of the House.

THE *EDINBURGH REVIEW* 1854

The modest proposals of the 1848–49 committee were not adopted until 1853, which prompted May to return to the field. In an anonymous piece in the January 1854 issue of the *Edinburgh Review* he restated many of his concerns. Organisation, he wrote, 'was not

---

[9] Five was the standard quorum of a select committee.

less essential in a senate than in a factory'.[10] He quoted with approval a view expressed on the floor of the Commons that the House had outgrown its forms—though he added with typical Whig caution that there was always a need to recall the dignity and true merit of ancient custom. He quoted as an example of that approach evidence he had recently given to a select committee on the appointment of a Deputy Speaker.[11] The committee was ultra-cautious, determined to recommend the least possible change. May was fortified by his work on indexing the Journals, and more trenchant than he had been in front of previous committees. He recommended the appointment of a Deputy Speaker whenever the Speaker was 'unavoidably absent and business required attention'. He went further, offering Members both the draft of a standing order permitting the Chairman of Ways and Means to take the Chair, and a Bill to clothe the Chairman with the necessary authority. The committee accepted that the natural Deputy Speaker was the Chairman of Ways and Means, but overcautiously put the arrangement on a day-to-day basis, devolving to the Chairman only the Speaker's duties when in the Chair.[12] In the end, May's solution was adopted in the Deputy Speaker Act 1855 and what is now Standing Order No 3.

For the rest, May's 1854 analysis was much as it had been in 1848–49—too much work on the floor of the House, too many committees ranging over an excessively large number of subjects, and too much aimless debate. Questions were often asked of ministers 'merely to satisfy curiosity or to attract personal notice … fitter for the club window than the senate'. A major government debate could be interrupted by trivial or minor debates bearing no conceivable relationship to it; supply and legislation were delayed and the whole was compounded by late-night sittings. His prescription was also the same: prohibit over-numerous and irrelevant interruptions to the business of the day, and abandon the vehicles that delivered such obstruction. May was for strong governments with plenty of legislation. In the House, as elsewhere, he wrote that idleness—being the root of all evil—set loose every tongue and encouraged unprofitable if not mischievous discussion.

As he became older, however—May was now forty—the edge of his radicalism became less keen. He no longer argued that the principle of redress before supply was irrelevant to the issue of amendments on going into Supply, and he withdrew his 1849 suggestion for limiting time for debate in certain cases because 'latterly there has been less cause for alarm. … The wholesale correction of public opinion has restrained our representatives from such excesses as would have rendered more imperative restrictions unavoidable.'

Nevertheless, he had not quite lost his appetite for change. He brought forward a more or less modern form of closure motion, characteristically fortifying it with a precedent from the parliament of 1604 which he ironically believed would be more persuasive to Members

---

[10] The essay was reprinted a quarter of a century later, shortly before May's retirement and death, as a pamphlet under the author's name as *The Machinery of Parliamentary Legislation* (London, Longmans, Green & Co, 1881).

[11] Select Committee on the Office of Speaker House of Commons Paper 478 of Session 1852–53. It is a measure of May's personal standing that, though not a Clerk, still less Clerk of the House, he and the Speaker were the only witnesses. In defence of the establishment it may, however, be added that Denis Le Marchant had only recently been appointed Clerk of the House, and that a certain amount of statistical evidence was supplied by James Gudge, Clerk of the Journals.

[12] Commons Journal (1852–53) 766. A minority of the committee followed May's more thoroughgoing reform. The solution of 1853 was soon found wanting, when Fitzroy, sitting as Deputy Speaker, was required to swear a new Member, which by statute could be done only by the Speaker in the Chair. An Indemnity Act was the only way to put things right.

than any argument. He repeated his suggestions for experimental limits on certain speeches. There were also new arguments, notably a variation on his earlier committee suggestions. The idea of developing committees of the whole House was dropped, to be replaced by a body halfway between a select committee and a committee of the whole House. The first he concluded was too small to reflect party balance, while the second would do nothing to tackle the issue that the House did everything and committees nothing. May suggested six Grand Committees,[13] using the term in a sense new to the House. They were to have 110 members each, to whom would be added fifteen or twenty ministers and others, in order to reflect the party balance in the House and the several interests affected. A preponderance of each such committee would be Members conversant with the particular type of business, and Bills would be committed to the Grand Committee most appropriate to their subject-matter. Time and Members would become available for the new arrangements by replacing Private Bill Committees by a non-parliamentary judicial body—a proposal which (in the wake of the experience of the HS2 Bill) is still brought up and still to be implemented.

SELECT COMMITTEE ON THE BUSINESS OF THE HOUSE 1854

When May appeared before the 1854 committee,[14] he was well stocked with opinions. Again, however, his arguments failed to carry sufficient conviction. He succeeded in persuading only a minority of the committee to accept his recommendations—though the minority included the chairman—and even then he had to water down his committee proposals, retreating to something not far from his 1849 ideas. Gone were the Grand Committees with their own areas of concern. Instead, it was suggested that there should be Committees of the whole House sitting on two mornings a week and able to adjourn as they saw fit (a system not unlike the 'Grand' committees used today by the Lords). Bills committed to these bodies would be grouped by subjects. For example, on one morning Treasury legislation would be considered, and on another Home Office bills. These committees would have a reduced quorum of twenty-five, and May supposed that in reality only Members with a relevant interest were likely to attend.[15]

It is relevant in passing that Redlich attributes to May the suggestion that bills should not as a general rule be sent to select committees (another idea still regularly ventilated by parliamentary reformers), and suggests that May was 'opposed on principle to committees of the whole House'. In fact, May's evidence on select committees was a good deal less positive. He said that in his opinion no automatic recommittal to a committee of the whole House was necessary when a bill had been reported by a select committee, but he did not think the House would be satisfied with the committal of bills of any importance to a select committee.[16] Such a procedure had had a tendency to cause the postponement of the remaining stages of bills until late in the session, something he always deplored.

---

[13] The Grand Committees originally envisaged were Religion; Law and Courts; Trade, Shipping and Manufacture; Local Taxation and Administration; Colonies and India; and Education and General. In May's 1878 proposals, the last two were omitted.

[14] Select Committee on the Business of the House, House of Commons Paper 212 of Session 1854.

[15] Redlich (n 1) I, 90.

[16] See n 14, Q279.

The issue of the number of questions to be put on bills during their career through the House resurfaced, and this time May proposed a further reduction from fourteen to ten. He would abandon preparatory questions on the introduction of certain bills, and those on the committal of all bills.[17] He repeated the Speaker's suggestion of 1848–49 for the reduction of the number of questions put on or in connection with second reading, and the virtual abolition of instructions.[18] The number of questions necessary to add a new clause to a bill on report should be reduced from four to one; and no question should be required to be put for the passing of a bill. Motions on going into or coming out of committee should be drastically pruned and the original 1848–49 suggestion for a rule of progress adopted, by which on every occasion on which the House resolved itself into committee the Speaker would leave the Chair without putting any question. It was suggested a similar rule should apply on all days but the first, when the House went into Committee of Supply on certain classes of Estimates. May again denounced the current practice in this matter as responsible for prolonging the session more than any other cause, and again he suggested accelerating the progress of government business by according orders of the day precedence over motions towards the end of the session. Another improvement in that area would be the introduction of more bills into the Lords, and its corollary a more relaxed attitude by the Commons to breaches of their financial privileges.

As he did in the matter of committee structure, May retreated somewhat from his earlier radicalism with regard to speeches and debate. Days on which notices of motions rather than orders of the day had precedence should be subject to a fixed adjournment hour, though orders would not be affected. A Member moving a dilatory motion for the adjournment of the House or of the debate would be permitted to explain his reasons, but further discussion would not be admissible.

The centuries-old practice that messages from the Lords were brought by Masters in Chancery had to be changed in view of the impending abolition of that office. Previously, in the absence of a Master, communications from their lordships would arrive by hand of the upper House's Clerk Assistant, a procedure regarded by the Commons as informal and routinely deplored in a standard entry in the Commons Journal.[19] May suggested (and the Speaker agreed) that in future messages should pass by Clerks. The proposal was made at the end of February 1854, and its implementation was—unlike every other proposal for change—swift. By mid-May both Houses had agreed the change and a message was first carried to the Lords by a Commons Clerk on 25 May 1854.[20]

When the committee came to consider their conclusions, Sir John Pakington, the Conservative chairman, put forward thirty-six draft resolutions embodying May's proposals. He found very little support. Although there was a Conservative majority on the committee, it was decided to proceed on the basis of a set of resolutions in the name of Sir George Grey, a Liberal, in preference to the Chairman's drafts. The extreme timidity of what emerged must have been a great discouragement to May. Instead of changing the rules of

---

[17] This was to be avoided by the making of a standing order to the effect that unless the House otherwise ordered, all bills should stand committed to a committee of the whole House.

[18] This was to be done by empowering any committee to which a bill had been sent to make amendments which were relevant to the subject-matter.

[19] Messages *to* the Lords were carried by four (previously eight) Members.

[20] Commons Journal (1854) 248, 263, 255.

debate as suggested, the committee preferred to rely on 'the good sense and right feeling of the House', and the hope that the salutary influence of the evidence would lead to a more general determination on the part of Members to contribute to the efficient and satisfactory despatch of business. To do the committee justice, a few suggestions were picked up. The power of committees to amend bills was to be extended, as May and the Speaker had recommended, in order to avoid frequent debates on instructions. The opportunity was taken to reduce the number of questions which had to be put on a bill, but the tentative nature of the recommendations may be judged by the fact that the principal change was to allow more than one bill to be considered in committee on any day without the Chairman leaving the chair at the conclusion of each. This inconsiderable package was almost completely accepted by the House.[21]

SELECT COMMITTEE ON THE BUSINESS OF THE HOUSE 1861

It was not long before it became generally recognised that half-hearted tinkering along the lines of 1854 was wholly unsatisfactory, and in 1861 another committee was appointed to look into necessary changes in procedure.[22] By this time Denison—who had been a member of the 1854 committee—was Speaker and May was Clerk Assistant. Either his election to the Chair had changed Denison's mind or May had convinced him of the error of his earlier ways. The new Speaker came out strongly against uncertainty in the progress of business which derived from the ability of any Member to raise any matter on going into Supply on every occasion. He suggested a modified version of the rule of progress similar to May's proposal of 1854. Most of May's evidence related to this aspect of procedure, but he also talked about a recommendation made by the 1854 committee (withdrawn after only a brief debate in the House) to adjourn from Friday to Monday by standing order rather than by ad hoc motions, which were too often the vehicle for irregular questions and debates. He was not asked (though the Speaker was) about the role of committees in legislation.

As on previous occasions, the committee's report began from entrenched and extremely cautious principles. The maintenance of old rules, they asserted, was preferable to new but speculative amendments. In consequence, while they accepted that the multiplication of motions on going into Committee of Supply was a serious obstacle to that certainty which two Speakers as well as May had argued for (not to mention the cause of much delay), they could not bring themselves to recommend adoption of the rule of progress. Equally, though they recognised the defects of the irregular debates which arose on the weekend adjournment motion, they declined (by a majority of two) to accept that the debate should be cut off at a particular hour. What they did suggest went no way at all towards solving the problem: desultory debate could continue under the guise of discussion of grievances in Supply on Fridays.[23] All that May got from the 1861 committee was some recognition

---

[21] ibid, 284, 413.

[22] Select Committee on the Business of the House, House of Commons Paper 173 of Session 1861.

[23] May had an opportunity to condemn this proposal in 1878 while giving evidence before a subsequent committee. The matters raised in such debates were rarely grievances, and the debates were incomplete. Nor had the number of irregular questions asked been diminished thereby (Select Committee on Public Business, House of Commons Paper 208 of Session 1878, Q75–76).

that more time was necessary for orders of the day—particularly government orders—as opposed to motions. The committee accepted the principle that all bills committed to a select committee did not need to be recommitted to a committee of the whole House—but the House did not.

JOINT COMMITTEE ON THE DESPATCH OF BUSINESS 1869

The 1860s were a decade of very little procedural innovation. One can only assume that May was being blandly ironic to the point of insolence when he told the joint committee on the despatch of business in 1869 that so many committees had sat since 1850 that the subject of improved procedure was very nearly exhausted. Almost every conceivable improvement had been adopted, and there was scarcely any field for further suggestions.[24] The accusation of irony is supported by the fact that the Member to whom May addressed this absurd proposition was Sir George Grey who had been responsible for the mouse of a report in 1854. Nor did May himself believe that procedural perfection had been achieved. He resurrected the 1854 *Edinburgh Review* proposal for an intermediate committee between the Committee of the whole House and select committees, this time with a quorum of twenty and giving voices to all Members who attended.

SELECT COMMITTEE ON THE BUSINESS OF THE HOUSE 1871

The 1870s, by contrast, were May's golden decade. In 1871, the year in which he became Clerk of the House, he appeared before another select committee and laid out his analysis of parliamentary shortcomings.[25] It was much the same as it had ever been—the increasing pressure of business in what May called 'an age of discussion', leading to the interruption of scheduled debate by a multiplicity of adjourned discussions; Bills abandoned, because they were sent to the Lords too late in the session or were badly drafted; and Supply unreasonably delayed by irrelevant and pointless debates.

Although his belief in the need to apply the rule of progress to Supply had not wavered, in view of repeated rejections May rather grandly declined to advocate its merits again. Nor did he canvass the virtues of applying the rule of relevance to debates on going into Supply, which he considered 'the proper view of the case as expressed by high authorities'. Instead— and probably after some informal contacts in advance—he backed a scheme suggested by Denison and Lowe, the Chairman of Ways and Means, that at least one day a week the Speaker should leave the Chair on going into Supply without putting any question.

The 1871 committee allowed May to reiterate some proposals he had not made for seventeen years. While he deplored late sittings, he had never been keen on hard and fast rules about ending sittings, so that he believed the solution lay in a general improvement in the conduct of business and a simple determination not to sit late.[26] On the abuse of

---

[24] House of Commons Paper 386 of Session 1869, Q144.
[25] House of Commons Paper 137 of Session 1871.
[26] Redlich (n 1) I, 106 gives the impression that May favoured a fixed hour of adjournment. That this is not the case can be seen from the evidence May gave to this committee, especially at Q33–34.

adjournment debates in order to delay the House, May took up the same stance as he had in 1849, with a little variation. He had been doubtful then about limiting the length of speeches, and in 1871 he abandoned the idea as impracticable and unnecessary, and he was prepared to allow debate on adjournment motions, provided there was a kind of closure on the third such motion in succession. In general, May did not favour the artificial shortening of the House's business, believing that by 'judicious regulation' it would be possible to get business through without interfering with Members' rights.

Other old favourites that made a reappearance were an attempt to appropriate notice days late in the session for bills, and a division-unnecessarily-claimed procedure. Although on other matters his feelings were less strong, at Sir John Pakington's suggestion he repeated the 1854 proposal for a simplified means of introducing bills, and select committee membership reduced to eleven in appropriate cases (though with the demise of election committees and the resultant drop in demands on Members' time he regarded that suggestion as less critical than it had been).

Perhaps of greatest importance to May himself was his resurrection of the Grand Committee idea. This time the committees might sit simultaneously; they would consider bills of secondary importance or less controversy; their debates would be more formal than those of select committees; and they would sit in public. There would be six, each of 110 Members.

This committee delivered on some of May's suggestions which its predecessors had turned down. It accepted the principle of progress in Supply, and the following year so did the House. It went further than May did in recommending a rule to prohibit the opening of new opposed business after half-past midnight, and in 1873 the House agreed. It did not, however, buy into the Grand Committee proposal and though it liked May's scheme for the unopposed introduction of bills, the House took no action.

Thereafter, progress stalled and indeed by the time May gave evidence to his last procedure committee in 1878 the impetus for reform had temporarily gone into reverse.[27] The principle of progress and the need for the relevancy of amendments were not taken up by the Disraeli government in 1874, and when in 1876 the topic was considered again, only the first survived—and it was not renewed in 1877.

SELECT COMMITTEE ON PUBLIC BUSINESS 1878

May expressed himself strongly before the 1878 committee. Opportunities for discussion on going into Supply were 'a great evil … which requires to be corrected vigorously'. His proposal, however, was less thoroughgoing than before. He did not believe that the House would accept the radical solution that on all government nights when Supply was first order the Speaker should leave the Chair without giving some opportunity for preliminary debate. If such a procedure were possible on only one night a week, however, there would be some improvement.[28] It was in effect a reiteration of his 1871 proposal—not wholly satisfactory but the best that could be obtained.

The vexed issue of private Members' bills surfaced again, with complaints that would be familiar to today's Procedure Committee. May had made several suggestions for clearing

[27] Select Committee on Public Business, House of Commons Paper 268 of Session 1878.
[28] In stating that May argued for such a rule on both government days, Redlich (n 1) I, 112 has misread May's evidence.

the Order Book of bills that stood a steadily diminishing chance of making progress as the session proceeded. This time he suggested that bills unlikely to be reached on any private Members' order days should be entered into a ballot to determine the sequence in which the Members in charge should be able to name a day for further proceeding. After a particular date in the session, orders should have more time than motions. The House should exercise more freely its power to reject motions for leave to bring in bills. After a certain date, private Members' bills which had not received a second reading should drop. Finally—with becoming modesty—he admitted original authorship of a proposal made by Sir Charles Dilke that on later private Members' bill days post-committee stages should have preference. Most of these proposals reflect modern practice on private Members' bills.

May's views were also sought on topics with which he must by 1878 have been very weary—principally a division-unnecessarily-claimed procedure and the need (or otherwise) to recommit to the whole House bills reported by select committees. He moderated earlier views in the first of those areas by suggesting that the procedure should apply only to dilatory motions for the adjournment.

Finally, the committee asked May about his committee proposals. These emerged significantly different from their last manifestation. May stipulated, as he had previously, that he envisaged only bills of secondary importance coming before these bodies, a category which he believed would encompass three-quarters of all public bills. He reduced the scope of the scheme: there were now to be only four committees, not six, and each would have only twenty permanent members with a further ten added for each bill. What in effect he did was to retreat from scaled-down Grand Committees to what looked rather like—and were in four years to be—standing committees, the predecessor of today's public bill committees. Members should be chosen more with regard to their special acquaintanceship with a subject than their politics, though both would have a part to play.

In many ways, the 1878 committee was the most satisfactory of May's official career. His *pis aller* of one Supply day a week without irrelevant preliminary debate was recommended, though without the flexibility he thought it needed, and further weakened by the House's insistence on restricting the rule to the Main Estimates. May would no doubt have been correspondingly pleased when in 1882 the rule was extended to all days on which Supply stood as first order. In some areas—notably private Members' bills and divisions—the committee recommended what May had argued for, if sometimes by different means.

DISCIPLINARY RULES 1877–78

It was strange that May was never publicly asked for his views on how the disciplinary powers of the Chair could be deployed against the obstruction which became a trouble in 1877. In private, of course he was deeply involved. When on 2 July 1877 the Irish party kept the House sitting for seventeen continuous hours by use of repeated dilatory motions, so that despite as many divisions the House failed to grant the supply sought by the government, Mr Speaker Brand said that he found Members in general anxious to review the House's rules and practice relating to 'similar scandals'.[29] When May was asked to prepare material for some sort of response, he no doubt happily resurrected some of his more radical

---

[29] Brand's Diary in the Parliamentary Archives, 3 July 1877.

nostrums of earlier years. They included: no debate at all to be permitted on dilatory motions; a Member called to order more than once in the same debate to be barred from speaking again to that question; a closure automatically granted on the main question when fewer than a fifth of the Members participating in a division voted for a dilatory motion; and the reintroduction of a practice declaring a Member who wilfully and persistently obstructed business guilty of contempt, and thus liable to censure or suspension.

Stafford Northcote, the Leader of the House, was inclined to accept at least the first two of May's suggestions, but the Speaker doubted whether Northcote had the determination or the votes to carry these propositions, especially since the Liberals favoured sending the matter to a committee for advice before taking action. Brand and May both believed that the House's rules and orders should be revised 'with a bold hand', and in September 1877 Brand wrote to his old friend Sir George Grey that he and the Clerk agreed that suspension could be the only remedy.[30] Northcote remained paralysed, so that by the time the next crisis broke in July 1878 no remedy had been prepared. After Parnell, the leader of the Irish party, had forced twenty-one divisions on the South Africa Bill, the Speaker, Northcote, and Forster, the opposition spokesman, met to decide how to handle the emergency. May did not attend: he could not be spared from the Table.[31]

Much to the Speaker's relief, no immediate action was required, but on a complaint being made about a phrase used in debate by Parnell which gave particular offence, the Speaker used May's last suggestion not as a proposed rule but as an established practice of the House.[32] The government tabled a motion on lines suggested by May for silencing an unruly Member—though the official draft added a requirement for action by the House as a whole in addition to the Speaker. The government also watered down May's suggestion that dilatory motions should be undebatable, preferring to limit the times a Member could move or speak to such a motion.

The problem rumbled on through the late summer of 1877. An increasingly pain-ridden Clerk of the House had to wrestle with the difficult issues surrounding the right of a majority to abridge that of a minority, and the procedural consequences which would flow from accepting such a principle. These were not of course wholly new. As he told Mr Speaker Brand in October 1877,[33] the moving of the adjournment of the House as a dilatory motion had become a grave abuse, and one which he feared could no longer be controlled by existing measures. Even if debate were blocked, the House could still be 'vexed' by a number of 'unseemly' divisions. The government would inevitably be drawn, May believed, to closure in one form or another, though for his part the Clerk of the House would restrict the right to move closure to dilatory motions where a previous such motion had been negatived by a majority of three-quarters of the Members present. The Speaker developed this notion in a memorandum to Northcote in preparation for a Procedure Committee which was to look into the whole matter.[34] The government remained very fearful, and the Speaker told Sir George Grey that the House was not in earnest in wanting to facilitate the progress of business, nor was the government prepared to tread on any toes.

[30]   ibid, 4 September 1877.
[31]   He was in any case on the brink of a serious illness.
[32]   Parl Deb 1877 vol 235, c 1814.
[33]   May to Mr Speaker Brand, 8 October 1877 (Parliamentary Archives, Brand letters).
[34]   Memorandum to the Chancellor, October 1877 (Parliamentary Archives, Brand letters).

May was scathing about the government's attitude, describing Northcote's performance as 'how not to do it'.[35] He had no fear of the tyranny of the majority: '[I]f timid counsels are to prevail, the House must submit to the impertinent domination of a few of its Members and sacrifice its own dignity and the interests of the country.'

Not long after delivering this fusillade, May was invited to Downing Street. What he then heard must have driven him to despair. The government anticipated a trebling of the obstructionists in 1878. They had determined to respond by appointing a Procedure Committee, and—if that was not feeble enough—not to put any concrete proposals to it. That Committee's report, as noted above, contained the resolution relating to progress in Supply which was the only one of its nine recommendations to be adopted by the House. Three of the proposed resolutions related to overcoming obstruction, crucially including enforcement powers for the Chair (the forerunner of the provisions for 'naming' disorderly Members). In the event, after prolonged debates on 17, 21 and 24 February 1879, Gladstone gave up the struggle against the Irish, and the debate was never resumed. It was left to Speaker Brand to take dramatic action on his own initiative on the famous occasion of 1 February 1881, when the closure was used for the first time.

MAY AND THE DEVELOPMENT OF STATUTE LAW

It is not hard to understand how May, who was a barrister—he was called in 1838—became involved in the codification, consolidation and indexing of the statute law, which was so much discussed in the first half of the nineteenth century.

His concern began, appropriately enough, with electoral law and disqualification. In 1850 he wrote to the *Law Magazine* that his research had disclosed nearly 250 Acts in force in this area, some spent, some superseded but unrepealed, and many obscure, overlapping or inconsistent. Election Committees in the House had to struggle with a particularly complex and unclear area of law. In the *Edinburgh Review* article of 1854, he wrote:

> Is it fitting that the Legislature of an old country, with long-established institutions and defined principles of law, should be engaged, year after year, in deliberating upon new laws, as if it were the Constituent Assembly of a Model Republic, having institutions and laws to create out of political chaos?[36]

Not only the process of legislating but the character of the product needed improvement. 'Next to an epic poem, an Act of Parliament was the most difficult of all compositions.'[37]

Although May agreed that the parliamentary process was too apt to destroy the original unity of a drafted bill, exposing it thereby to unexpected interpretations, he naturally could not accept the radical solutions which would limit parliamentary powers over the draft text or add a non-parliamentary revising instrument to law-making. May's solution was to attach a drafting sub-committee to each of his Grand Committees.[38] When giving evidence in 1857 to a select committee he rejected non-elected interference in law-making,[39]

---

[35] May to Mr Speaker Brand, 2 November 1877 (Parliamentary Archives, Brand letters).
[36] See n 10, 10.
[37] ibid, 39.
[38] ibid, 41.
[39] Select Committee on the Statute Law Commission, House of Commons Paper 99 of Session 1857.

in favour of more communication between those engaged in drafting bills, the preparation of model bills (examples of which in the area of private bills lasted until the 1960s) and an Interpretation Act, which had been found useful in New York. The draftsman should append to every bill an explanation of the legal framework against which the bill should be seen, and Mr Speaker's Counsel or a similar officer of the House should scrutinise bills, explanatory notes, and amendments in the interests of uniformity and consistency, reporting thereafter to one of May's Grand Committees. In addition, May agreed with some other witnesses that there should be a small select committee attended by Speaker's Counsel and the draftsman with the responsibility of revising bills from a technical point of view. This should be achieved 'without interfering more than was absolutely necessary with their progress through Parliament, acting through the voluntary agreement of the Members in charge of Bills and amendments'.

Even to mid-Victorian eyes, this must have seemed far removed from the reality of parliamentary law-making, and indeed May admitted to the sceptical select committee that the scheme would cause delay and impair ministerial responsibility. He fell back to the position that it would apply principally to private Members' bills. Nothing was done, and the only outcome was that May found himself on Lord Westbury's Royal Commission to inquire into the expediency and means of making a digest of the law. When that too ran into the sand, May became a member of its successor body, the Statute Law Revision Committee, of which he eventually became president and thus technically responsible under the Lord Chancellor for the first edition of the Statutes Revised.[40]

By 1875, when May next gave evidence before a select committee on statutory issues,[41] he explained that matters had greatly improved. Parliamentary Counsel's Office had been founded (Courtenay Ilbert, the second holder of the office of First Parliamentary Counsel, was to become Clerk of the House in 1902); statute law reform was almost up to date; consolidation—particularly of the criminal law—had made great strides; and the Statutes Revised, together with a chronological index, were satisfactorily under way. He was less radical than he had been in 1857. He did not push the revising officer solution very hard, and while he thought there ought to be some limitation on the scope of debate on bills which were pure consolidation, he could see no way achieving that end. He elaborated these thoughts before the 1878 committee by proposing a sessional committee on consolidation bills. Although such a committee was appointed in 1894, it did not become a regular parliamentary feature until 1911. And the problem of legislation made in haste and revised, if at all, at leisure, continues to vex reformers. Pre-legislative scrutiny has been attempted as a solution, granting evidence-taking powers to public bill committees was offered as a mitigation, and post-legislative scrutiny employed as an occasional remedy. Perhaps curiously, the least enthusiastic partner in all these endeavours seems to have been successive governments, in whom the urge to legislate and do it quickly has, if anything, intensified in the twenty-first century. May's service on the committees dedicated to reform of the statute law can be seen as an early attempt to bridge the gap between Parliament, the government and the courts in refining the legislative process.

---

[40] The moving spirit in the creation of the committee was not May but Sir John Shaw Lefevre, Clerk of the Parliaments: see Courtenay Ilbert, *Legislative Methods and Forms* (Oxford, Clarendon Press, 1901) 64–66.

[41] Select Committee on Acts of Parliament, House of Commons Paper 280 of Session 1875.

10

May on Money

Supply Proceedings and the Functions
of a Legislature

COLIN LEE

INTRODUCTION

A CCORDING TO THOMAS Erskine May, 'No constitutional change has been more important in securing popular control over the executive government than the voting of supplies by the House of Commons.'[1] In the period when May was working for and writing about the House of Commons, Supply proceedings—the method by which that House makes provision for the statutory authorisation of public expenditure subject to annual control—were at the heart of vigorous debates on the priority the House should accord to its various functions, the time taken in pursuit of them, and its effectiveness in the performance of them. These were debates in which May and his fellow Clerks at the Table, Reginald Palgrave and Archibald Milman, participated, albeit in the latter cases anonymously.[2] The debate over Supply procedure reflects some of the themes found elsewhere in this book including the tensions between the efficient conduct of business and Members' conceptions of effectiveness, between ministers and backbenchers and between the needs of the executive and the duties of representation. This chapter traces the development of Supply proceedings from the 1840s to the early 1880s and concludes with reflections on May's immediate legacy in this area and on the extent to which the debates on financial procedure in the Victorian era have more recent echoes.

IRRESPONSIBLE EAGERNESS: SUPPLY VERSUS REPRESENTATION

In the late 1840s, May began a campaign for the rationalisation of the way in which the House conducted its financial and legislative business, reflecting his views that organisation

---

[1] TE May, *Constitutional History of England since the Accession of George the Third* (London, Longmans, Green and Co, 1912, 2 vols) I, 155–56.

[2] The authorship of the articles cited below written by Palgrave and Milman is only known following publication of *The Wellesley Index to Victorian Periodicals* between 1965 and 1988. May's article in the *Edinburgh Review* was also anonymous, but his authorship was acknowledged in his lifetime: see W McCullagh Torrens, *Reform of Procedure in Parliament to Clear the Block of Public Business* (London, 1881) 115, 121; HC Deb, 8 November 1882, col 1071.

was 'not less essential in a Senate than in a factory'.[3] His aim, as expressed in the title of his 1849 leaflet, was 'to facilitate the dispatch of public business in Parliament'.[4] This emphasis on certain categories of business was to place May in conflict with Members who asserted the priority of other parliamentary functions. Throughout his career, May seemed reluctant to accept that the changing franchise and the constituency representation role should have a major impact on the conduct of business and the use of time.[5] As late as 1881, in a survey of the period since the 1832 Reform Act, he contended that: '[T]he irresponsible eagerness of Members to press forward their own views, and the interests of their constituents, on every practicable occasion, was a serious obstacle to the regular and orderly dispatch of public business.'[6]

May always considered that transacting the business of Supply had priority over the representative function. He argued in 1844 that: '[T]he most important power vested in any branch of the legislature is the right of imposing taxes upon the people, and of voting money for the exigencies of the public service.'[7] In his interpretive approach, May followed in the footsteps of John Hatsell, who had seen in the assertion of the role of the Commons in the control of money 'the seeds and origin of those principles of political freedom' which lay at the heart of 'the present most excellent constitution of this country'.[8] In May's view, the control of the Commons over supplies and taxes had been 'the means of extorting concessions from the Crown and advancing the liberties of the people',[9] liberties which were 'bought ... with hard cash'.[10] It flowed from May's perception of the constitutional role of financial control that the Supply proceedings were to be viewed as 'one of the most important functions of the House of Commons'.[11]

May was therefore dismayed at the delaying and distorting effect on the conduct of Supply arising from amendments to the question "That the Speaker do leave the Chair", preceding the Committee of Supply. The use of such amendments had first been devised, by the Whig Thomas Creevey, in 1811 as a direct response to measures by Prime Minister Spencer Perceval to give orders of the day, including orders for Committee of Supply, precedence over notices of motions on certain days of the week. Perceval's intention was to secure priority of government business, but Creevey realised that it could be frustrated by amendments allowing for debate before the substantive business of Supply could be embarked upon. In doing so, he emphasised that he was asserting 'his undoubted right as a member of parliament, of saying or moving any thing upon the subject of Grievances, whenever the question of Supply was before the House', a right previously available through

---

[3] TE May, 'The Machinery of Parliamentary Legislation' (1854) 99 *Edinburgh Review* 244–82 (hereafter 'Machinery') 244.

[4] TE May, *Remarks and Suggestions with a View to Facilitate the Dispatch of Public Business in Parliament* (London, 1849) (hereafter *Remarks*).

[5] Report from the Select Committee on Business of the House, HC (1871) 137, QQ 136–37.

[6] British Library (hereafter BL) Add MS 44194, ff 98–102: Memorandum on Changes of Procedure since 1832, dated 29 November 1881 (also printed in E Hughes, 'Sir Erskine May's Views on Parliamentary Procedure in 1882' (1956) 34 *Public Administration* 419, 419–20 (all subsequent references are to the printed version in the short form 'Views').

[7] TE May, *A Treatise upon the Law, Privileges, Proceedings, and Usage of Parliament*, 1st edn (London, 1844) 39.

[8] J Hatsell, *Precedents of Proceedings in the House of Commons* (London, 1818, 4 vols) III, 106.

[9] May, *Constitutional History* (n 1) I, 374.

[10] May, 'Machinery' (n 3) 262.

[11] Report from the Select Committee on the Business of the House, HC (1854) 212, Q 340.

the priority given to motions.[12] Such amendments were moved infrequently in the decade after their inception, and about twice a year in the 1820s and 1830s, but the number rose substantially thereafter, reflecting the wider contest for control of time between ministers and backbenchers.[13]

In 1839 or 1840, May's predecessor but one as Clerk Assistant, John Rickman, had written of the 'bad effect' of the admissibility of these amendments, which he viewed as 'an abuse' which meant that 'the peculiar function of the House of Commons is now so postponed as to be habitually transacted in a hurry' and the principle that money should be authorised before the start of the financial year in the spring was 'wholly inoperative, and annually made ridiculous by Votes of Supply delayed to the months of July and August'.[14] May took up the baton from Rickman, first in his pamphlet, then in an anonymous article in the *Edinburgh Review* in January 1854 and finally in evidence to select committees.

May felt that the principle of grievances preceding Supply had 'little application to the circumstances of the present time' and he noted that it was rarely pretended that the subjects of such amendments 'have any reference to the redress of grievances properly so called',[15] encompassing 'a medley of chance motions' and creating a situation in which equal weight was given to debates on the government of India and the case of a woman who had called a police officer 'a pig'.[16]

May was also concerned about the effect of such debates on the rational progress of public business. He echoed Rickman in arguing that the business of Supply and Ways and Means, which was 'the peculiar province of the House of Commons', was interrupted and thus 'deferred till a very late period of the Session, when the attendance of Members is comparatively small, and they are discussed with haste and impatience'.[17] It also delayed legislative business so that the Commons often sat late while the Lords waited for its bills (and sometimes sat 'long enough to boil an egg') and 'many Bills are sent up late to the House of Lords, or abandoned altogether'.[18] Above all, it jeopardised the quality of financial scrutiny: '[T]he only result of the present license of debate is, that less vigilance is exercised in controlling public expenditure, than is devoted to the scrutiny of a Private Bill.'[19]

May's preferred solution was to adopt the 'rule of progress', whereby amendments would only be permitted on the first occasion of going into Committee of Supply on each of

[12] P Fraser, 'The Growth of Ministerial Control in the Nineteenth-Century House of Commons' (1960) LXXV *English Historical Review* 444, 446–67; HC Deb, 27 February 1811, cols 106–08; HC Deb, 5 March 1811, cols 244–46; HC Deb, 6 March 1811, cols 246–49; HC (1871) 137, QQ 10, 88–93.

[13] HC (1871) 137, Q 10; GW Cox, *The Efficient Secret: The Cabinet and the Development of Political Parties in Victorian England* (Cambridge, Cambridge University Press, 1987) 48–51.

[14] The Parliamentary Archives (hereafter TPA), HC/CL/PU1/7, Table of Contents for Chapter 6; HC (1854) 212, Q 152. Rickman's Treatise was just over 135 pages in length and dealt with Committee proceedings. The Table of Contents and the first 23 pages survive. The remainder was probably lost or irreparably damaged in the fire of 1941. On the dating, Rickman's paper referred to a decision of 6 February 1839 and he died in August 1840. On his death, his papers on privilege, practice and precedents were bequeathed to the House by his son: HC Deb, 2 February 1841, cols 180–81. I am indebted to Dr Mari Takayanagi, Senior Archivist, TPA, for advice on the likely fate of Rickman's treatise.

[15] May, *Remarks* (n 4) 17.

[16] May, 'Machinery' (n 3) 254. Her sentence of transportation was increased from 7 to 10 years for her mode of address: HC Deb, 8 March 1853, cols 310–12.

[17] May, *Remarks* (n 4) 18.

[18] May, 'Machinery' (n 3) 255, 266–67; HC (1854) 212, Q 340.

[19] May, 'Machinery' (n 3) 262.

the categories of Estimates.[20] This was the case he outlined to a select committee on the despatch of public business in 1854.[21] In his 1854 article, May had recognised that his proposed reforms ought to be 'accompanied by the concession of other facilities for bringing on motions, at more convenient times',[22] but he was not more specific, perhaps because his imagination was never fired as much by enhancing opportunities for private Members as it was by facilitating the more efficient despatch of government or legislative business.

The Chairman's draft report for the 1854 committee fully endorsed the case for change, arguing that the right to raise grievances before Supply was 'now evaded and abused'. It created uncertainty, and 'evenings intended for the discussion of finance are consumed in extraneous, desultory and often unimportant debates'.[23] However, the committee rejected the Chairman's draft and instead agreed to one which argued that any procedural change would deprive Members of the right to raise cases of 'urgent and serious grievance', instead suggesting that the practice of excessive amendments should be 'hereafter discouraged and restrained by the general feeling of the House'.[24] These warm words had predictably little effect, and use of the practice grew. For example, in 1856, the Committee of Supply took place on twenty-one sitting days; on six of these days, an amendment to the motion that the Speaker do now leave the Chair was moved, and on five of those occasions the House sat beyond midnight.[25] In 1857, there were nine such amendments, in 1858, twelve and in 1860, eleven.[26]

In 1861 another select committee returned to the issue. The new Speaker, John Evelyn Denison, supported the application of the rule of progress to the four main classes of Estimates, arguing that this would remedy a great evil without unduly curtailing the legitimate privileges of independent Members.[27] May, in his own evidence, estimated that in 1860 just over fifty hours had been devoted to proceedings preliminary to the Committee of Supply, compared with eighty-four hours on proceedings in the Committee itself, and that thirty hours a Session could be saved by applying the rule of progress.[28] As in 1854, the committee came down against any change, arguing 'that the statement and consideration of grievances before Supply are among the most ancient and important Privileges of the Commons'.[29] The committee indeed sought to entrench the practice by arguing that such amendments should replace the motion for the weekend adjournment as the basis for private Members' debates on Fridays.[30] This change was implemented, and, as May acknowledged in 1871, assisted private Members.[31] Fridays in effect became a private Members' day, a flavour they have retained to this day.[32] However, as May was later to observe, the means used to

[20] ibid, 260–261, 263. On the adoption of the rule of progress for legislation, see J Redlich, *The Procedure of the House of Commons* (London, Constable, 1908, 3 vols) I, 84–85.

[21] HC (1854) 212, QQ 338, 340, 343–44, 346.

[22] May, 'Machinery' (n 3) 263.

[23] HC (1854) 212, xviii.

[24] ibid, xxi–xxvi, v.

[25] CJ (1856) 49, 76, 124, 243, 268, 277.

[26] HC (1871) 137, Q 10.

[27] Report from the Select Committee on the Business of the House, HC (1861) 173, QQ 28–32.

[28] ibid, QQ 251, 262–64.

[29] ibid, para 13.

[30] ibid, paras 16–17.

[31] CJ (1861–62) 185; HC (1871) 137, Q 271.

[32] TE May, *A Treatise upon the Law, Privileges, Proceedings, and Usage of Parliament*, 5th edn (London, Butterworths, 1863) 554–55.

achieve this gave 'a certain sanction' for the very 'evil' which May and Denison had sought to remove.[33]

The pivotal figure in the defeat of May's proposal was the Prime Minister, Palmerston, who argued that it would be 'very inexpedient to gag, as it were, this House, and prevent it from fully expressing the views of the nation on matters as they arose, by the introduction of any regulations which we might imagine would be conducive to the despatch of public business'.[34] It was Palmerston rather than the Chairman of the committee who then moved the motions arising from the committee's report, and he used the occasion to launch a blistering attack on the approach to reform of which May had been in the vanguard since 1849. Palmerston thought that such proposals were 'likely to trench inconveniently and injuriously on that latitude of discussion which it is so important to preserve unimpaired'.[35] For Palmerston, who was more an administrator than a legislator, Parliament was a place to reconcile interests through debate above all.[36] He acknowledged that the House had a legislative function—'We meet here to pass laws'—and that the financial functions of the House were no less important. However, he went on to argue that the House had a third function of equal importance, namely

> that of being the mouthpiece of the nation; the organ by which all opinions, all complaints, all notions of grievances, all hopes and expectations, all wishes and suggestions which may arise among the people at large, may be brought to an expression here, may be discussed, examined, answered, rejected, or redressed.

For Palmerston, May's proposals were probably among many arrangements which he accepted 'might greatly facilitate the discharge of the first two duties, but which would interfere essentially with the full and complete performance of the third'. On these grounds, Palmerston felt it was appropriate to exclude measures which would 'gag the House of Commons, to prevent it from being the free and unfettered organ for the expression of all the feelings and opinions which on any subject, great or small, any part of the nation might wish to have laid before it'.[37]

REPULSIVE LABOUR: THE GLADSTONIAN PARADOX AND THE BUSINESS OF SUPPLY

The prospects for progress of May's vision for Supply within a rationally organised framework of business ought to have been enhanced by the pre-eminence, after Palmerston, of William Gladstone, for whom 'the enforcement of thrift in the public expenditure' was a moral duty.[38] Robert Lowe, Chancellor of the Exchequer for most of Gladstone's first administration, also signalled the greater priority to be accorded to thrift, claiming in 1872 that 'the business of Supply was the core and kernel of the work of the House of Commons'.[39]

---

[33] 'Views' (n 6) 422.
[34] Fraser (n 12) 456; HC (1861) 173, pp xiv, xvii, xxiii–xiv; HC Deb, 11 February 1862, col 160.
[35] HC Deb, 3 May 1861, col 1492.
[36] J Parry, *The Rise and Fall of Liberal Government in Victorian Britain* (London, Yale University Press, 1993) 192–93.
[37] HC Deb, 3 May 1861, col 1492.
[38] HC Deb, 7 April 1864, cols 588–89.
[39] HC Deb, 26 February 1872, col 1060.

However, there was a paradox at the heart of the development of Supply business through Gladstonian reform, a process which strengthened the control of the Treasury and of independent audit, but, in its emphasis on detail, in its growing reach and in its enhanced complexity, distanced that business further from the priorities of Members.

For Gladstone, effective scrutiny relied upon 'the wearying, irksome, and self-denying work of making themselves thoroughly acquainted with a vast mass of details'.[40] Lowe contended that economy could only be achieved through the 'repulsive labour from which men naturally shrink' of 'inquiring into minute matters of detail'.[41] The procedures of the House had been adapted to assist such repulsive labour. In 1856 Estimates could only be debated at the level of a vote, even though they comprised several items. According to May, 'every item comprised in a vote was open to discussion, at the same time, which often occasioned confusion, if not absurdity'.[42] When amendments were proposed to a vote, no record was kept of the item of expenditure to which it related,[43] and the sequencing of amendments was determined by the principle that larger reductions should be considered before smaller reductions, rather than by reference to the logical sequence of items.[44] In 1857, the House agreed changes to enable amendments to be tabled to leave out or reduce each item, which, according to May, 'entirely altered the practice of the committee of supply in dealing with the votes proposed'.[45]

The estimates themselves were also adapted in response to the quest for detail. Until the late 1840s, 'the Votes proposed in the Estimates simply stated certain services with scarcely any detail', on the assumption that any further detail required would be provided by a minister in the Committee of Supply.[46] The main change was the result of the work of a select committee on Miscellaneous Estimates in 1848, after which the civil estimates began to assume recognisably modern form.[47] The extension of appropriation accounts from the 1860s also encouraged the preparation of fuller and more detailed estimates.[48] These two developments together enabled consideration of Estimates in remarkable detail: on one page of an Estimate in 1887 relating to Public Works and Buildings, there were thirty-four separate items that could be subject of a motion for reduction.[49]

The scope of the expenditure subject to annual control through Supply proceedings also expanded enormously. Prior to 1854, the running costs of the Inland Revenue, the Customs Department and the Post Office were deducted from their levies, meaning those costs were not, in May's words, 'within the immediate control of Parliament'.[50] As Chancellor,

[40] HC Deb, 26 February 1866, col 1134.

[41] HC Deb, 4 April 1872, col 765.

[42] TE May, *A Practical Treatise upon the Law, Privileges, Proceedings, and Usage of Parliament*, 4th edn (London, Butterworths, 1859) 527.

[43] ibid, 527–28.

[44] ibid, 526–27; HC Deb, 19 June 1857, col 58.

[45] HC Deb, 19 June 1857, cols 43–64; Report from the Select Committee on Committees of Supply, HC (1857 Sess 2) 261, iii; CJ (1857–59) 42; HC Deb, 9 February 1858, col 1083; May, *Treatise*, 4th edn (n 42) 528.

[46] HC Deb, 19 June 1857, cols 61–62.

[47] B Chubb, *The Control of Public Expenditure: Financial Committees of the House of Commons* (Oxford, Clarendon Press, 1952) 11.

[48] V Cromwell, 'The Problem of Supply in Great Britain in the Nineteenth Century', in *Études sur l'Histoire des Assemblées d'États* (Paris, Presses universitaires de France 1966) 1–12, 6.

[49] Report from the Select Committee on Estimates Procedure (Grants of Supply), HC (1888) 281, Q 255.

[50] TE May, *A Practical Treatise on the Law, Privileges, Proceedings and Usage of Parliament*, 2nd edn (London, Butterworths, 1851) 420.

Gladstone introduced estimates for their expenditure, so that the charges were under 'the supervision and control of Parliament'.[51] In 1844 May had noted that Supply proceedings accounted for only two-fifths of public expenditure; the remaining three-fifths taking the form of payments out of the Consolidated Fund not requiring the annual sanction of Parliament.[52] In 1854 Gladstone sought a 'better classification' of charges between the Consolidated Fund on the one hand and Supply services on the other.[53]

The financial reforms with which Gladstone was most associated were enshrined in the Exchequer and Audit Departments Act 1866 by which he sought to complete the circle of control, which was to be a unified process starting with the presentation of Estimates, passing through the parliamentary process to the Appropriation Act, leading on to the preparation of annual appropriation accounts, to the independent audit of those accounts and then finally their consideration by the Committee of Public Accounts. With this circle complete, he felt that it 'could fairly be said that the office of the House, as the real authoritative steward of public monies, had been discharged'.[54]

Paradoxically, these Gladstonian reforms made the House's job harder from the viewpoint of its Members. Prior to the 1860s, the Treasury was empowered to 'apply any surpluses remaining from any of the Votes of the department to defray any unforeseen and unprovided expenditure connected with that department', enabling departments to retain underspends from one year as a 'nest egg' for use in a subsequent year.[55] The curbing of that arrangement by Gladstone and the introduction of the principle of 'annuality', at the urging of the new Committee of Public Accounts, led to Civil Votes on Accounts (authorising expenditure for the current financial year while approval of the Estimates was awaited) becoming the norm rather than the exception.[56] Similarly, Supplementary Estimates (adjusting expenditure in-year), which an 1848 select committee had characterised as '*very objectionable*' and which Gladstone initially deplored, became an annual necessity, as even Gladstone came to acknowledge.[57] In consequence of these changes, a vastly better system of control over departmental expenditure was undoubtedly achieved. Yet, while characterised as parliamentary control, it was exercised in practice by the Treasury, the Comptroller and Auditor General and the Committee of Public Accounts, often acting in concert, far more than in the House.[58]

The Committee of Supply was undoubtedly busier, May noting that there had been 'a continual increase in the labours' of the Committee of Supply in the 1850s and 1860s.[59] He had earlier observed that the addition of expenditure of the Revenue departments imposed 'a very arduous duty' on the House, which would have the effect of more than

---

[51] A Todd, *On Parliamentary Government in England* (London, 1887, 2 vols) I, 733–36; HC Deb, 2 June 1854, cols 1258–60; HC Deb, 2 February 1854, cols 216–17.

[52] May, *Treatise*, 1st edn (n 7) 327–28.

[53] HC Deb, 2 February 1854, col 217; HC Deb, 2 June 1854, col 1261.

[54] HC Deb, 1 March 1866, col 1373.

[55] Second Report from the Select Committee on Army and Ordnance Expenditure, HC (1849) 499, 1; R Palgrave, 'Parliament and the Public Moneys' (1876) 141 *Quarterly Review* 224, 241, 235–36.

[56] First Report from the Select Committee on Public Accounts, HC (1861) 329, iv; Cromwell (n 48) 7; HC Deb, 13 March 1882, col 852; HC (1888) 281, QQ 2, 630; May, *Treatise*, 2nd edn (n 50) 421; HC (1871) 137, Q 17.

[57] Report on the Navy Estimates from the Select Committee on Navy, Army, and Ordnance Estimates, HC (1847–48) 555, xvi (emphasis in original); HC Deb, 23 July 1866, col 1292; HC Deb, 24 November 1882, col 87.

[58] H Roseveare, *The Treasury: The Evolution of a British Institution* (London, Allen Lane, 1969) 138–42.

[59] HC (1871) 137, Q 16.

doubling the size of the Civil Service Estimates.[60] As the third Earl Grey had warned, the House was in danger of becoming mired in self-defeating detail.[61] In 1857, the Chancellor of the Exchequer, argued that the Estimates were 'now really loaded with an amount of details which almost defeated the purpose which that detailed information was sought for, and prevented hon. Members from reading and studying the Estimates to the extent to which they might attend them if less information were given'.[62] These views were echoed by Disraeli: 'It was perfectly absurd to fill up the Vote with the details of every miserable item, as if the Ministers could not, for example, be charged without the interference of the House with the responsibility of a water-closet'.[63] Reginald Palgrave, who served as Clerk Assistant throughout May's clerkship, thought that 'inherent mischief lurks both in that craving for detail and in its gratification' because it enabled ministers to cede responsibility for that detail to Parliament.[64]

However, that sense of control was illusory. Although the new procedure facilitated more structured debate, it did not translate into direct control, because departments remained free to reassign grants with Treasury approval.[65] May conceded in 1871 that 'the multiplication of items, and other explanations that appear on the face of the votes', intended to reduce the need for debate, 'tend to encourage, rather than to avert discussion, and the consideration of them occupies much time'.[66]

Palgrave believed that the changes had converted 'into a complex system the simple financial procedure of former times'.[67] Between the 1840s and the 1870s, the House moved from the ideal of expenditure requests, to use Palgrave's phrase, being placed before the House 'in one bag' to them being 'in many bags, called by different names, and constructed in different ways'.[68] Palgrave felt that these demands 'treble the financial labour of each session'.[69] He calculated that, in an extreme (and notional) case, it was possible for the same item of expenditure to 'come before the House on 17 different occasions in the same Session'.[70]

It was unsurprising that Palgrave noted a sense of 'dissatisfaction' and 'failure' that surrounded the House's Supply procedures.[71] In 1879, *The Spectator* argued that Supply proceedings were 'a pure farce. The House does not check the votes in any way.'[72] Walter Bagehot reported a very experienced financier as saying: 'If you want to raise a certain cheer in the House of Commons make a general panegyric on economy; if you want to invite a sure defeat, propose a particular saving.'[73] Robert Lowe echoed this view somewhat bitterly

---

[60] HC (1854) 212, Q 340.
[61] Earl Grey, *Parliamentary Government Considered with Reference to Reform* (London, John Murray, 1864) 86–89.
[62] HC Deb, 19 June 1857, col 62 (Sir George Cornewall Lewis).
[63] HC Deb, 19 June 1857, cols 65–66.
[64] Palgrave (n 55) 243.
[65] HC (1888) 281, QQ 622–26, 643, 781. But supervision by the Committee of Public Accounts was exercised at the level of sub-heads: ibid, QQ 653–54.
[66] HC (1871) 137, Q 17.
[67] TE May, *A Treatise on the Law, Privileges, Proceedings, and Usage of Parliament*, 10th edn (London, 1893) viii.
[68] Palgrave (n 55) 246–47.
[69] May, *Treatise*, 10th edn (n 67) ix.
[70] HC (1888) 281, QQ 2, 148–50.
[71] Palgrave (n 55) 224.
[72] *The Spectator*, 15 February 1879, 1.
[73] W Bagehot, *The English Constitution* (London, Kegan Paul, 1878) 136.

on departing from the Chancellorship, writing that: '[E]verybody is in favour of economy in the abstract and most people are in favour of extravagance in the concrete.'[74]

May himself was under no illusions about the balance of power between the Commons as an entity and the executive. In his *Constitutional History*, he noted the apparent paradox that the growth of control by the Commons since 1688 had been favourable to the Crown. When the Commons had had limited knowledge of the needs of the Crown, it had sometimes been willing to reject requests from the executive, but ministerial demands were now seldom disappointed: 'Not a soldier has been struck from the rank and file of the army; not a sailor or ship from the fleet, by any vote of the Commons.'[75] The only instances he could find of reductions to votes were 'so trifling as sometimes to be almost ridiculous', such as the removal of the salary of the travelling agent of the National Gallery.[76]

Palgrave recognised this as a political problem, but one with a procedural dimension. The method identified by Hatsell, and reinforced in the era of May, of pursuing reductions was, argued Palgrave, actually counterproductive and the belief that the aim of Supply proceedings was to cut down the Estimates was harmful. Because these efforts almost invariably failed, 'they have discredited the sacred cause of thrift, retarded the realisation of salutary financial reforms, and obscured the operative action of Parliament upon the estimates', which, in his view, arose from the work of the Committee of Public Accounts.[77]

MAY'S HOLLOW VICTORY

Although the scope of Supply proceedings had expanded enormously in the 1850s and 1860s, the problem of proceedings preliminary to Supply itself remained essentially the same, after the rebuffs of 1854 and 1861. As May later noted, 'the evil … continued unchecked for several years, and for a considerable part of the Session, nearly every Government Supply night was, more or less, appropriated for notices wholly unconnected with the Estimates'.[78] Some partial attempts to curb the opportunities for delay through the moving of amendments to the motion for going into Committee of Supply were made. In 1871 a new select committee was established to look at what May had come to regard as the 'intractable and wearisome subject' of the despatch of public business.[79] The weariness that he confided to his private journal was to some degree apparent in his evidence. Although he argued that the problem had got worse since 1861, he saw no reason again to press his proposal to apply the rule of progress to the Committee of Supply.[80] Instead, he supported a simpler proposition from the Chairman of the Committee, Robert Lowe, and also advocated by the Speaker, that when the Committee of Supply stood as first business on a particular day of the week, the Speaker would leave the Chair without putting any question, thus precluding

---

[74] *The Times*, 5 September 1873, 3, cited in J Maloney, 'Gladstone's Gladstone? The Chancellorship of Robert Lowe, 1868–73' (2006) 79 *Historical Research* 404, 410.

[75] May, *Constitutional History* (n 1) I, 375–76.

[76] ibid.

[77] Palgrave (n 55) 248–49.

[78] 'Views' (n 6) 422.

[79] D Holland and D Menhennet (eds), *Erskine May's Private Journal, 1857–1882: Diary of a Great Parliamentarian* (London, HMSO, 1972) (hereafter *Private Journal*) 25.

[80] HC (1871) 137, QQ 10–14.

the possibility of any amendment.[81] Lowe's initial preference was for such a provision for two days a week, but when an amendment was proposed by Disraeli limiting its application to Mondays only, he accepted this offer, securing a majority in the Committee despite the continued objection of some backbenchers.[82] The motion to give effect to this proposal was tabled in 1871, but, in part as a result of the clear internal divisions within the Committee and in part due to the pressures on the handling of the business, no decision was reached.[83]

In 1872, however, Lowe came forward with a compromise motion; this allowed relevant amendments on the first day set down for the Army, Navy and Civil Service Estimates (a proposal defeated in the Committee only on the Chairman's casting vote), but otherwise provided for the Speaker to leave the chair without putting a question on Mondays.[84] He made it clear that the proposal 'had the full approval of the Speaker and of the able and experienced Clerk at the Table', as well as Disraeli.[85] Lowe told the House that his proposal would help to remedy the problem whereby the government was forced to prioritise legislation over Supply, because the latter was so vulnerable to delaying tactics, and '[t]hus Supply got postponed till the fag-end of the Session, when hon Members were fatigued with their labours, and little disposed to watch the Votes with jealousy'.[86] May later noted that the resolution enshrined 'very considerable alterations of the previous practice'.[87] The 1872 resolution was passed, and adopted again in 1873, with cross-party frontbench support and implied support from May, and was relatively effective.[88] However, it did not become a Standing Order and was not re-adopted by the incoming Conservative administration in 1874.

In 1876, Disraeli admitted that his attempts to proceed without this provision had caused unacceptable uncertainty.[89] The number of amendments moved on motions for Committee of Supply on days other than a Friday had increased to ten in 1874 and 1875.[90] He sought to revive the resolution of 1872 and 1873. He acknowledged that it had 'considerably and beneficially affected the conduct of Business during the remaining years of the last Parliament'. However, in debate he made a significant concession, agreeing a modification of the text so that amendments were permitted on every Monday, subject only to a requirement for relevance which did not apply on Thursdays and Fridays.[91] In May's view, this concession 'seriously impaired' the effect of the resolution: because it enabled amendments on every occasion on which Supply was put down, 'the old rules were almost revived'.[92]

This retreat from reform coincided with the onset of Parnell's pioneering use of systematic delaying tactics. Supply proceedings and their prefatory business were very vulnerable to

[81] ibid, QQ 23, 295.
[82] ibid, iii, v; HC Deb, 26 February 1872, cols 1066–67.
[83] JE Denison, Viscount Ossington, *Notes from my Journal when Speaker of the House of Commons* (London, John Murray, 1899) 264; HC Deb, 8 February 1872, cols 154, 167; *Private Journal* (n 79) 25–26.
[84] CJ (1872) 66; HC (1871) 137, v–vi; 'Views' (n 6) 422.
[85] HC Deb, 26 February 1872, col 1092.
[86] ibid, col 1060.
[87] Report from the Select Committee on Public Business, HC (1878) 268, Q 3.
[88] CJ (1873) 28; HC Deb, 10 February 1873, col 268; HC Deb, 24 November 1882, col 88.
[89] HC Deb, 17 February 1876, cols 469–70.
[90] Return of the number of days on which the House was in Committee of Supply, and Business was transacted, in each Years from 1869 to 1882 inclusive ..., HC (1882) 384, 6–7.
[91] CJ (1876) 48; HC Deb, 17 February 1876, cols 469–74.
[92] HC (1878) 268, Qq 65, 73. See also TE May, *A Treatise on the Law, Privileges, Proceedings and Usage of Parliament*, 8th edn (London, Butterworths, 1879) 613. For a similar verdict, see HC Deb, 24 November 1882, col 88.

the tactics of obstruction. The number of amendments moved other than on a Friday rose to fifteen in 1877 and twenty in 1878, and on seven of the days in 1878 no Supply business was transacted after the amendment was disposed of.[93] Supply provided fertile ground for obstruction, as was noted by Archibald Milman, who as Second Clerk Assistant was the other Clerk at the Table with May and Palgrave throughout the former's clerkship. According to Milman, 'debate upon the supplies for the current year might easily be carried on, without any breach of order, into the middle of the next century'.[94] Supply was disrupted by obstruction in 1877,[95] and the situation worsened in 1878. By 'going into infinitesimal points of detail', a small group of Irish Members was able to ration the progress of business, turning it on and off like a tap.[96] Vast amounts of expenditure were authorised in great haste in August, in conditions termed by one Member 'an utter farce'.[97]

In 1878 another select committee considered the problems of public business in this new environment. Much of its focus was on disciplinary powers, and with regard to Supply it did little more than revisit the arguments of 1871. May made clear his view that 'opportunities for discussion on going into Committee of Supply have become a great evil, and an evil which requires to be corrected, and corrected vigorously, in some form or another'.[98] His first preference, and what he considered 'the rational course', would be to allow the government to proceed directly to Supply on Mondays and Thursdays;[99] failing that, he supported an effective reversion to the proposal of 1871.[100] The Speaker favoured the revival of the resolution of 1872 and 1873.[101] The committee endorsed a resolution similar to that proposed in 1871, simply providing that no question would be put about the Speaker leaving the Chair, thus precluding amendments, on Mondays.[102]

By 1879 May thought that 'the vicious tactics of obstruction had become insufferable',[103] and the motion to give effect to the 1878 Committee's proposal itself fell victim to these tactics. On the third day of an extended debate and faced with a flood of amendments, Northcote accepted certain amendments 'in order to cut short the protracted discussion'. These had the effect of making the resolution considerably narrower in its effect than the resolutions of 1872 and 1873, by applying it only to the Army, Navy and Civil Service Main Estimates and by permitting amendments on the first day on each.[104] It at least 'had a marked effect of allowing the House to get into Committee of Supply without resistance or impediment'.[105]

---

[93] HC (1882) 384, pp 9–10.

[94] A Milman, 'The Block in the House of Commons' (1878) 146 *Quarterly Review* 185. On Milman and his analysis of obstruction, see C Lee, 'Archibald Milman and the Procedural Response to Obstruction' (2015) 83 *The Table: The Journal of the the Society of Clerks-at-the-Table in Commonwealth Parliaments* 22–44.

[95] A Milman, 'The House of Commons and the Obstructive Party' (1878) 144 *Quarterly Review* 231, 239–40; Redlich (n 20) I, 143.

[96] HC (1878) 268, Q 1104; Milman (n 94) 188–89.

[97] HC Deb, 7 August 1878, col 1445.

[98] HC (1878) 268, Q 7.

[99] ibid, Q 71.

[100] ibid, Q 28.

[101] ibid, Q 367.

[102] ibid, para 7(1).

[103] *Private Journal* (n 79) 52.

[104] CJ (1878–79) 42, 53–54, 58–60; HC Deb, 24 February 1879, col 1664.

[105] HC Deb, 24 November 1882, col 88.

Gladstone's second administration faced much worse problems than its predecessor. Not only were the Irish tactics of obstruction becoming, in May's view, 'more intolerable', but the government also faced the storm over Bradlaugh and the parliamentary oath, and the guerrilla tactics of the so-called Fourth Party led by Lord Randolph Churchill.[106] The resolution of 1879, dubbed by Gladstone 'the Monday rule', was agreed to again in 1880 without debate,[107] but provided only limited defence against obstruction. This reached its apogee on Thursday 26 August, when consideration of the constabulary vote on the Irish estimates was the subject of nine separate delaying divisions and the House sat from 3.45 pm until 12.50 pm the following day.[108] The business of Supply was not completed until 31 August.[109]

The problems in 1880 were dwarfed by those in 1881, which proved in May's words 'to be wholly unexampled' and, in Redlich's words, constituted 'one of the severest trials of endurance that the House of Commons had ever undergone'.[110] In view of the pressure of Irish business, the government did not attempt to bring forward even the Monday rule.[111] In early February, the Speaker brought debate on the question for leave to introduce the Protection of Person and Property in Ireland Bill to a conclusion through the first use of the closure, citing the 'crisis' which was facing the House.[112] This was then followed by the introduction of the Urgency Rules which had been prepared together by Gladstone, May and Speaker Brand, before the Session began.[113] These gave the government and the Speaker exceptional powers to curtail debate on the most pressing public business.[114] The initial proposals were supplemented in March by provisions to enable the Committee of Supply to proceed with the Speaker leaving the Chair without a question put, to apply the rules of the House rather than the more complex rules of Committee to Supply proceedings, and to apply the closure in the Committee of Supply.[115] However, the government was unsuccessful in seeking the necessary Conservative support to apply the new urgency rules for Supply, in part because Gladstone was hoist by his own petard of contending that Irish business should take precedence over all other business.[116] Northcote was later to contend that Supply proceeded 'perfectly well without Urgency', although the business of Supply was not completed until 22 August, and amendments on going into Supply were moved on seventeen days other than Fridays.[117]

---

[106] *Private Journal* (n 79) 52.
[107] CJ (1880) 152; HC Deb, 20 February 1882, col 1135.
[108] CJ (1880) 406–07; *Private Journal* (n 79) 52.
[109] CJ (1880) 420.
[110] *Private Journal* (n 79) 53; Redlich (n 20) I, 167–68 (footnote).
[111] HC Deb, 20 February 1882, cols 1135–36.
[112] CJ (1881) 49–50; *Private Journal* (n 79) 53–54.
[113] E Hughes, 'The Changes in Parliamentary Procedure, 1880–1882', in R Pares and AJP Taylor (eds), *Essays Presented to Sir Lewis Namier* (London, Macmillan 1956) 301–06; RA Vieira, *Time and Politics: Parliament and the Culture of Modernity in Britain and the British World* (Oxford, Oxford University Press, 2015) 105.
[114] TE May, *A Treatise on the Law, Privileges, Proceedings and Usage of Parliament*, 9th edn (London, Butterworths, 1883) 381–82.
[115] CJ (1881) 122–23; reprinted in Redlich (n 20) II, 250.
[116] May, *Treatise*, 9th edn (n 114) 382; CJ (1881) 124–25; HC Deb, 14 March 1881, col 927; TE May, *A Treatise on the Law, Privileges, Proceedings and Usage of Parliament*, 13th edn (London, Butterworth, 1924) 333 footnote; *Private Journal* (n 79) 53; *The Annual Register 1881* (London, 1882) 67–68; HC Deb, 20 February 1882, col 1159.
[117] HC Deb, 20 February 1882, col 1159; HC (1882) 384, p 13; CJ (1881) 483.

With the Session complete, Gladstone pursued with Brand and May options for more enduring procedural reform. May prepared papers for the Cabinet on proposed reforms and then on the development of procedure since 1832.[118] May and Brand attended several meetings of the Cabinet to discuss the proposals.[119] While the main focus of May's proposals was on the establishment of Grand Committees and the strengthening of the disciplinary powers of the Chair, he made his most radical suggestions yet on Supply proceedings. In 1878, Milman had raised the possibility of early sittings of the Committee of the whole House, between 12 noon and 4.00 pm, separate from those of the House and with an independent power to adjourn from time to time, for legislative business.[120] In his first paper for the Cabinet, May revived this idea, but went further in proposing that it extend to the Committee of Supply. This would at once 'put an end to the inconvenient and objectionable practice of moving Amendments on going into Committee of Supply'. When the Committee of Supply was held in the course of actual sittings of the House, the Speaker would at once leave the Chair, precluding all preliminary debate.[121] May also saw a case for considering the proposition that had been advanced by the Chairman of Ways and Means in 1878 that Members other than ministers should only be able to speak once on the same question in Committee of Supply.[122]

May's proposal to give the Committee of Supply an identity separate from the House was radical indeed, in some ways foreshadowing the creation in 1999 of 'sittings in Westminster Hall'. Gladstone wrote privately to May conceding that the measure would 'relieve the House if not of the whole by far the greater part of the Grants in Aid', but nevertheless confiding that 'I do not feel very sure about the morning Committees of the whole House for Estimates.'[123] The Cabinet evidently shared Gladstone's doubts, although May sought to revive the idea in January 1882, submitting a proposal to the Cabinet that would enable any Committee of the whole House to sit independently of the House.[124]

The Cabinet was clearly too focused on the revolutionary proposals for the closure to entertain radical notions with regard to Supply. In mid-January, May prepared draft proposals for the Cabinet including a motion which would go further than the resolution of 1879, applying its provisions to all Government Order days except Friday.[125] Even this proposal was adjudged too much by the Cabinet at its pre-Session meeting on 30 January, which retreated to the terms of the resolution of 1879, limiting motions on leaving the Chair to Mondays alone, which had been agreed without debate in 1880.[126] On that day, the Cabinet did not even commit to tabling the motion as part of its wider procedural package, although it did do so at the opening of the Session.[127]

[118] BL Add MS 44154, ff 79–85: Memorandum from May dated 2 November 1881, printed for the Cabinet on 8 November 1881 (also available as The National Archives [TNA], CAB 37/6/29); 'Views' (n 6) passim.

[119] *Private Journal* (n 79) 55.

[120] Milman (n 95) 253–54.

[121] BL Add MS 44154, ff 82v–83v (TNA, CAB 37/6/29, pp 8–10).

[122] BL Add MS 44154, f 83v (TNA, CAB 37/6/29, p 10); HC (1878) 268, Q 1209.

[123] TPA, ERM 1/31–33, Gladstone to May, 7 November 1881.

[124] BL Add MS 44154, ff 112–15, additional rules for consideration, 18 January 1882, f 114.

[125] ibid, f 113.

[126] ibid, f 134.

[127] ibid; *Annual Register 1882* (London, 1883) 27–28.

However, events were to change the government's attitude considerably as the Session wore on. First, the failure to make significant progress on the proposal for the closure during debates in February, March and May made it clear that progress on procedural reform would require a separate meeting of the House in the autumn.[128] More importantly, the Supply proceedings proved tortured in the extreme. The Committee of Supply sat on twenty-seven days; on twenty-six of those days, the House sat after midnight, and on twenty-two until after 2.00 am. The Appropriation Act did not receive the Royal Assent until 18 August. Amendments to the question on leaving the Chair were debated on twelve days other than Fridays.[129] The rate of progress in Committee of Supply was extraordinarily slow, with between 170 and 180 votes outstanding on 24 July.[130] The remainder were passed in the closing days in a state of exhaustion, with the House sitting on Saturdays in August to complete legislative business.[131] As May said: '[T]he Session of 1882 clearly proved the necessity of further regulations for the improvement of the business of the House.'[132]

In the light of this experience, May made one more attempt to revive his radical proposal for the Committee of Supply to meet separately from the House. He prepared resolutions which converted the Committee of Supply into a Committee open to all Members, with the power of adjournment and a standard sitting time between 12 noon and 3.45 pm on Tuesdays and Fridays.[133] This proposal was still unacceptable to the Cabinet, but it was willing to contemplate a more sweeping measure than envisaged at the start of the Session. The motion eventually tabled in the autumn went further in several ways and was akin to the rule of progress as first envisaged for Supply proceedings by May over thirty years earlier: it limited amendments to the first day of debate on each Estimate; it required all amendments to be relevant to the Estimate in question; and it applied the prohibition on subsequent amendments to any day other than Fridays on which Orders had precedence.[134] This motion was agreed to, Gladstone having conceded that it would apply only on Mondays and Thursdays, which were anyway the only days on which Orders had precedence in the normal course of events. The measure for which May had campaigned for over thirty years thus became enshrined as a Standing Order.[135]

The reforms of Supply which May was instrumental in securing in 1882 failed completely in their aims. In March 1884, the House had to sit until 7.00 am on a Sunday to agree the Votes on Account before the start of the financial year.[136] The number of days in Committee of Supply on the Estimates rose from twenty-five in 1882 to twenty-six in 1884 and to thirty-eight in 1887.[137] This was in part due to the problem of displacement, whereby the debates which had taken place on motions or amendments relating to the Speaker leaving the Chair instead took place in the Committee of Supply itself. May had noted this

---

[128] ibid, 29, 36–40.
[129] CJ (1882) 63–469; HC (1882) 384, 14.
[130] HC Deb, 24 July 1882, col 1549.
[131] CJ (1882) 399–472.
[132] *Private Journal* (n 79) 55.
[133] BL Add MS 44154, ff 143–143v, May to Gladstone, 20 October 1882, and ff 145–46, draft resolutions of same date.
[134] CJ (1882) 516.
[135] CJ (1882) 517; HC Deb, 24 November 1882, cols 62–93.
[136] HC (1888) 281, Q 3.
[137] ibid, 65.

displacement effect with regard to all efforts to secure a greater priority for Government business, because 'the removal of one abuse has generally aggravated another'.[138] He also acknowledged that 'it is vain ... to expect that discussions, repressed in one form, will not break out in other directions'.[139] A select committee examining Supply procedure in 1888 noted how the Committee of Supply had itself become the repository of debate on 'subjects of interest which might otherwise escape the attention of the House', including 'much irrelevant and unimportant matter'.[140] In 1902, a veteran Member, Sir John Gorst, contended:

> Since successive Governments took to restricting, or endeavouring to restrict, the opportunities and powers of Members for discussing their policy, and made Committee of Supply the only place where it could be discussed, discussion in Committee of Supply has extended out in the way it has done now. You spend night after night in Committee of Supply when you are really not discussing matters of Supply at all.[141]

Although May had discerned motions and amendments preliminary to the Committee of Supply as, in Redlich's words, 'the real centre of the problem of procedure' in the mid-Victorian period, the nature of the problem had changed radically by the time the solution was adopted.[142] This was in part because of the growing demand for general debates. It was also because the principal challenge to the conduct of the government's business now lay not in the urge of backbenchers to fulfil their representative function, but in the determined use of delay and obstruction as a political strategy, initially by Parnell and his party, and subsequently by others.

CONCLUSIONS

The development of Supply practice and procedure in May's time shows both the strengths and the weaknesses of his approach. The first strength on display was the quality of his analysis: he was the essential synthesiser of the 'unique and intricate network of rules and arrangements' that constituted financial procedure.[143] He combined this with an astute capacity to discern purpose in those procedures. He never lost sight of the underlying role of Supply procedure, including its place in the balance of power between the executive and the House.

Another strength lay in his willingness to act as a procedural innovator. His proposals on moving directly to the Committee of Supply were radical within the context of the 1850s and 1860s, and proved unacceptable to a procedurally conservative House. In the face of the crisis of obstruction, Supply proceedings were not exempt from his willingness to propose radical ideas: his support for the Committee of the whole House to meet before the House sat in 1881, and the subsequent proposal for Supply to be committed to a Committee composed of all Members of the House, placed him once again well beyond the procedural mainstream.

---

[138] 'Views' (n 6) 423.
[139] ibid, 424.
[140] HC (1888) 281, iii. See also ibid, Q 380.
[141] Report from the Select Committee on National Expenditure, HC (1902) 387, Q 2487.
[142] Redlich (n 20) I, 98.
[143] ibid, III, 113.

He was also willing to act as a campaigner and an agitator for reform. He used a variety of campaigning tools. On the back of the celebrity status engendered by the publication of the *Treatise*, he published a strongly worded pamphlet. He became even more forthright under the veil of anonymity in the *Edinburgh Review*. He was accepted as a pivotal witness to select committees on procedure even before he became Clerk Assistant, and over time he became a more influential one. Frontbenchers and backbenchers alike were keen to cite him as an authority and a supporter.[144]

May also demonstrated, above all in the face of the crisis of obstruction in 1881 and 1882, what could be achieved through profound influence on, and close working with, both the Speaker of the House and the government of the day. This working partnership was integral to the introduction of the closure and the urgency rules in February 1881, later dubbed by Milman 'the Gettysburg of the parliamentary rebellion'.[145] In developing the procedural reforms of 1882, May provided secretariat services to the Cabinet, and drew upon the strong relationships he had forged with members of the Cabinet and above all Gladstone himself.

Yet it is important to recognise the limitations and weaknesses in May's approach. The closeness of his relationship with Gladstone was sometimes reflected, both in public and in private, in a cloying admiration.[146] It is notable that he seemed unable to forge the same relationship of trust with Conservatives, which may have contributed in a small way to the vigorous opposition they mounted to procedural reforms even in the face of obstruction. The sense that the Speakership was always vacated during Liberal administrations, and became for a long time a Liberal monopoly, also meant that May's loyalty to successive Speakers was seen through a political prism. Lord Randolph Churchill found May 'very grumpy' when he sought procedural advice on the possibility of contesting the Speaker's re-election in 1886.[147]

In the context of the particular developments examined in this chapter, May's greatest weakness lay in his underestimation of the importance of the representative function and of policy debates not giving rise to decisions, which he revealingly termed 'irregular debates'.[148] He was keen for non-government days to be used for 'the discussion of grievances and other "burning questions"' so that they did not impinge on the transaction of Government business'.[149] While he did see the need for additional opportunities for debate on grievances and policy, including possibly through a standing committee of grievances with a power to examine witnesses,[150] he did not bring to such proposals the same zeal as he did to reforms designed to secure what he saw as 'the proper dispatch of business'.[151]

---

[144] HC Deb, 23 May 1861, cols 50–51; HC Deb, 26 February 1872, col 1092; HC Deb, 10 February 1873, col 268. On his celebrity, see Redlich (n 20) I, 88–89 (footnote).

[145] A Milman, 'The Peril of Parliament' (1894) 178 *Quarterly Review* 263, 275.

[146] See, for example, 'Machinery' (n 3) 261 and BL Add MSS 44154, ff 33–34, May to Gladstone, 3 February 1871: 'I must be permitted to add that I hope it will long be my pleasure to witness, from my seat at the Table, your continued triumphs, as Leader of the House of Commons.'

[147] Lord Randolph Churchill to Lord Salisbury, 29 November 1885, cited in W S Churchill, *Lord Randolph Churchill* (London, 1907), p 430.

[148] 'Views' (n 6) 423.

[149] ibid, 424.

[150] ibid.

[151] ibid, 423.

The efforts to reform financial procedure from the 1840s to the early 1880s were marked by several linked characteristics which have also been apparent in the subsequent reform—or lack of it—of financial procedure. First among these has been a tendency to nostalgia, a constant harking back to an earlier, supposedly golden age of proper financial scrutiny and a matching reluctance to acknowledge the strengths of current arrangements. In the 1870s, Palgrave recalled the 1840s and 1850 as the era when Supply debates had been 'the chief fighting occasions' in the House.[152] In 1881, one Liberal Member looked to the years after the Napoleonic War as the time when 'one of the chief preoccupations of the House of Commons consisted in auditing, carefully and minutely, the public expenditure of the year'.[153] In 1885, Gladstone mourned the passing amongst Members of 'political *thrift*—of a sense of economy which used to be a sort of "religion"'.[154]

Second, there has been a reluctance to consider how far the original constitutional and procedural rationale for procedures reflected contemporary needs. Hatsell saw 'great wisdom' in a multi-stage process to give 'every opportunity for free and frequent discussions' so that the Commons 'may not, by sudden and hasty votes, incur expenses, or be induced to approve of measures, which might entail heavy and lengthy burthens upon themselves and their posterity'.[155] May similarly valued the procedural protections for the public purse 'against hasty and inconsiderate resolutions' which he viewed as necessary because there were 'no checks upon the liberality of the Commons, but such as they impose upon themselves'.[156] Reverence for a multi-stage process has continued long after it represented a meaningful check of this kind. And, of course, 'thrift' may no longer capture the ideological range of the House's preoccupations. For many backbenchers from all parts of the House it is involvement in the planning of public expenditure for the relief of social evils or for the advance of innovation, education or wider social goals that lights their fire. 'Control' of expenditure often fails to capture those concerns.

Third, the complexity of financial procedures which gathered pace in May's lifetime has continued to baffle and defeat Members and others wishing to see reform. In 1876 Palgrave posed the question: 'What chance had a new Member of comprehending, even to a partial degree, the financial operation of his first Session?'[157] It is a question that could still be posed today.

Fourth, and partly in consequence of these characteristics, it has remained accepted that financial procedures formally concerned with serving as the basis for authorisation of expenditure can best be used for another purpose—the raising of grievances in the nineteenth century, debates at the behest of Opposition parties for much of the twentieth and debates on select committee reports since 1982. This ignores one of the main lessons from May's time: that in seeking to combine the function of scrutinising and authorising public expenditure with that of debating policy and grievances, the House of Commons guaranteed dissatisfaction with the performance of both.

[152] Palgrave (n 55) 224.
[153] McCullagh Torrens (n 2) 8–9.
[154] DWR Bahlmann, *The Diary of Sir Edward Walter Hamilton 1885–1906* (Hull, University of Hull Press, 1993) 6.
[155] Hatsell (n 8) III, 176.
[156] May, *Constitutional History* (n 1) I, 378.
[157] Palgrave (n 55) 246.

11

A History of the Standing Orders

SIMON PATRICK[1]

INTRODUCTION

THE FIRST RECOGNISED digest of the Standing Orders of the House of Commons published for general consumption (perhaps in an attempt to exploit the potential purchasers amongst new MPs elected in the Whig landslide of that year) is generally believed to be the *Orders, Standing Orders, and Resolutions of the Honourable House of Commons, relating to Their Forms of Proceeding, Privileges, &c &c*, 'Printed for A Steward, in Flower-de-luce-court, Fleet Street' in 1747. 'A Steward' is thought to be either Nicholas Hardinge or his successor as Clerk of the House of Commons from 1748, Jeremy Dyson. Clerkly involvement in the composition of the volume is probably confirmed by the entry on page 117 collected from the Journal for Monday 6 April 1700:

> The Clerk of the House, Serjeant at Arms, Clerk Assistant, and other Clerks and Officers of this House, having served with great Diligence and Fidelity, and being but slenderly provided for;
>
> *Resolved*, That the said Clerk of the House, Serjeant at Arms, Clerk Assistant, and other Clerks and Officers be humbly recommended to his Majesty, that they may have competent Salaries, answerable to their Trust and Services, settled upon them.

As its title page makes clear, however, the volume was an unofficial attempt to gather precedents 'collected out of the Journals and Digested under their several Heads' rather than an authorised collection of standing orders, and although its form is not unlike the present standing orders, its content is more akin to that of the various manuals and commonplace books described earlier by David Natzler and Paul Seaward.[2] Its Preface though, is eloquent, and deserves to be quoted in full:

> If it is reasonable to wonder, that this Manual was never published before, it will be of much the less necessary to apologise for publishing it now: and, surely, it if appear, that not only all who have Seats in Parliament, or who are in a Capacity to sit, or who have Business to transact there, but the whole People in general, are interested in the Rules and Orders of their Representatives, it will not be dispute, that they ought to be acquainted with them; and the Person will rather deserve their Thanks than Censure, who put it in their Power to be so.
>
> Now, barely to read them, is to be convinced of this; for they will be found to reach almost all Order of Men, either mediately or immediately, from the Judge to the Bailiff's Follower, and from the

---

[1] Based on the work of the late Sir Edward Fellowes.
[2] See chapters 5 and 6.

Petitioner at the Bar to the Footman of the Stairs, and the Vagrant in the Street: and it is fit for those without Doors to reflect, with a due Mixture of Reverence and Attention, that the word Privilege is become as sacred as the Word Law; and that Ignorance may be held as insufficient a Plea, in a case of an Offence, against the one as the other.

Then for those within, if we may presume to speak of them at all, it can scarce be said, that they are qualified for the Trust reposed in them, till they are acquainted, in some Degree, with the Methods in which it is to be discharged: And this is a known Truth, that Men of very slender Parts, by rendering themselves thorough Masters of the Forms of the House, have made themselves considerable, have fancied themselves to be so; and, by the mere Dint of calling to Order, and quoting Journals and Precedents, have sometimes defeated Arguments they could answer, and triumphed over Talents and Abilities that infinitely transcended their own; which is all that need to be said to recommend a Study, hitherto, perhaps, too much neglected; and to justify a Publication, that could never be more reasonable, than when so many new Members are just entering into the Service of their County.

In the first edition of the *Treatise* May contrasts the diligence of the Lords in maintaining their 'Roll of Standing Orders' with the carelessness displayed by the Commons:

In the House of Commons no such care is taken; for when an order or resolution has been agreed to be made a standing order, it appears in that form in the Journals; but there is no authorized collection of the standing orders, except in relation to private bills.[3]

By the time of the fourth edition (1859) of the *Treatise*, May is able to note that: 'Until 1854, no authorised collection of the standing orders of the House of Commons had ever been compiled.' He added (in a modest footnote) that:

In 1854, a manual of 'Rules, Orders and Forms of Proceedings of the House of Commons, relating to Public Business' was drawn up by the author of this work, under the direction of the Speaker; and was printed by order of the house in 1854 and again in 1857.[4]

However, that manual, which continued to be published in each Parliament up until 1896, had more in common in some ways with the digests of precedents and (looking forward) the *Manual of Procedure in Public Business* (derived in 1904 from May's manual by Courtenay Ilbert, Clerk of the House from 1902 to 1921)[5] than with the explicitly endorsed collections of standing orders as bare rules without interpretative commentary of modern times.[6] Palgrave, in his tenth (1893) edition of the *Treatise*, asserts that 'standing orders of the House of Commons were first printed in collected form by order of the House during the session of 1810',[7] but it was not until the edition so ordered of 1882 that the public business standing orders were brought to the forefront and the private business standing orders relegated to the back end of the volume, and two years later the public business standing

---

[3] *Treatise*, 1st edn (1844) 132. May appears to have discounted the 1810 publication mentioned by Palgrave in 1893 (see below). This list (and one of 1830) do not appear to have been comprehensive as regards the small number of public business standing orders listed at the back: see Betty Kemp, *Votes and Standing Orders of the House of Commons: The Beginning*, House of Commons Library Document No 8 (London, HMSO, 1971) particularly 12.

[4] *Treatise*, 4th edn (1859), 181.

[5] *Treatise*, 11th edn (1906) 148.

[6] Though editions of the Manual of Procedure for some time contained the Standing Orders relating to Public Business as an Appendix.

[7] *Treatise*, 10th edn (1893) 145.

orders were, for the first time, numbered. By the time Campion did his great reordering of the *Treatise* in 1948, the existence of a regularly approved set of numbered standing orders seems to have become hardly worth explaining. In 1959 the Private Business Standing Orders were hived-off into a separate volume, where they have largely stagnated since.

Sir Edward Abdy Fellowes KCB CMG MC (1895–1970) was Clerk of the House of Commons from 1954 to 1961. Much earlier in his career, in the 1930s, he investigated the history of the Public Business Standing Orders: Sir David Lidderdale (a later Clerk of the House) refers to this work in his entry for Fellowes in the *Oxford Dictionary of National Biography*, and says that he left unpublished papers. These papers were found in a desk in the Journal Office of the House of Commons in 2001, some in typescript and some in manuscript, and the author of this chapter set about editing them into a complete document. Fellowes, possibly with some assistance from colleagues, had examined in detail the several dozen select committee reports on procedural matters that had been published in the century following the Reform Act of 1832, the debates on procedural matters contained in *Hansard* and the records of decisions in the Journals of the House of Commons. Fellowes analysed all this material, dividing it into chapters relating to different periods and within each chapter by subject-matter, for example sittings of the House, procedure on bills, committees, etc. The chapter headings are reproduced as the section headings in this summary.

What is a standing order? The decisions of the House are minuted either as orders (where the House takes a decision on matters within its control, such as to give a bill a second reading) or resolutions (where the House expresses an opinion, or decides what it should itself do, such as adjourn). Those orders that are not of their nature superseded by events are usually considered to be temporary, remaining in force only until the end of the session in which they are passed; so those considered of lasting value have either been passed at the beginning of each subsequent session, or either immediately or later converted into *standing* orders, which remain in force until amended or repealed (except in rare cases where they are expressed as expiring at a particular point such as the end of a Parliament). The distinction between orders and resolutions has not always been clear cut (depending to some extent at least on the choices of the Clerks as to how to record particular decisions of the House), and some standing orders (such as those on the hours of sitting of the House) were originally passed as resolutions.

The standing orders are, and have been since at least the early nineteenth century, divided into those relating to public and private business. Private business relates mainly to private bills, which do not originate from the government or private (backbench) Members (these are termed *public* bills) but from petitions by local authorities or other organisations or people seeking amendments to the law in their area or in their particular interests. Until the nineteenth century private legislation formed by far the bulk of the law made by Parliament, and until the mid-20th century, private bills related largely to powers for railway companies to acquire land to build railways and for local authorities on such matters as police and public health. The private business standing orders pre-date 1832 and have developed almost entirely separately, and Fellowes did not cover them in his work.[8] By contrast, although there have been standing orders relating to public business since at

---

[8] For the private business standing orders, see OC Williams, *The Historical Development of Private Bill Procedure and Standing Orders in the House of Commons* (London, HMSO, 1948–49).

least 1678, they initially governed only a very small part of parliamentary procedure, and in 1832 there were only eight of them (compared to over 100 private business standing orders).

Unfortunately, Fellowes did not find time to prepare his work for publication or to update it beyond about 1936, but the occasional conclusions that he drew give a valuable insight into the mind-set of the House in the late nineteenth and early twentieth century. He contributed a more general description of the growth of the standing orders up to the 1960s to a book written by members of the Study of Parliament Group, of which he was the first Chairman.[9]

Fellowes's unpublished work contains full texts of most of the new standing orders and of significant amendments to them, but this chapter concentrates on the main themes of parliamentary procedural reform and attempts to preserve the flavour of his conclusions.[10]

THE HOUSE OF COMMONS IN 1832

There were three areas of work which took up a considerable amount of MPs' time in 1832 but are much less significant today. The first was private bills, where the need for numerous committees to meet simultaneously gave rise to the large number of committee rooms built as part of the new Palace following the fire of 1834. Second, the House spent a large amount of its time considering petitions (public petitions, unrelated to private bills), and third, the Estimates of government expenditure had to be considered by the House sitting as the Committee of Supply, and then be endorsed by the House itself, before they could be authorised by Act of Parliament and result in any actual expenditure. (Taxation was dealt with in another Committee of the whole House, the Committee of Ways and Means, but did not take up as much time.) Public bills, then as now, took up considerable time: for several hundred years, they had been subject to a complicated procedure involving a large number of questions to be decided by the House, designed mainly to avoid MPs being taken by surprise. Committee stages of bills were taken in Committee of the whole House (even bills sent to select committees were recommitted to the Committee of the whole House afterwards). The government had precedence for its business on Mondays and Fridays only by convention, and the powers of the Chair (at this time, only the Speaker could chair the House) were so weak that any MP could bring about a debate on any subject at almost any time by moving an amendment (which did not have to relate to the motion being amended). A debate continued until no more MPs wished to speak, but an MP who had the floor could move to adjourn the debate (or the House), and this motion in turn could be debated for as long as desired. Business which had been started but not concluded was set down for a future day as an 'Order of the Day' (either an adjourned debate or the next stage of a bill). The House was, however, under no obligation to go through the orders as set out on the Order Paper: when an order on the paper was reached, the question would be proposed that it be read, and an MP could move, without notice, to amend this question

---

[9] Sir Edward Fellowes, 'Standing Orders' in AH Hanson and Bernard Crick (eds), *The Commons in Transition* (London, Fontana/Collins, 1970) 26–40.
[10] Quotations attributed to Fellowes refer to this unpublished work rather than his chapter in the 1970 book.

and consider some other business instead. The House set up select committees from time to time, but very few records appear to have been made of their decisions, and their reports were often merely a set of resolutions reported to the House and printed in the Journals. Divisions were taken by requiring MPs on one side of the question to go out into the lobby and be counted as they returned to the House; those remaining in the House were counted at the same time. Any lists of those voting were unofficial and usually very inaccurate.

The procedural rules, such as they were, were almost entirely based on precedent and occasional resolutions of the House. For example, there has never been a standing order providing that a bill requires three readings before it is treated as having been passed by the House: standing orders made since 1832 do mention first, second or third readings when modifying the previous procedure. Six of the eight standing orders in force in 1832 related to public money (including one relating to the financial privileges of the House of Commons in relation to the House of Lords).

The system worked at all only because MPs were willing to make it work by avoiding excessively obstructive tactics and eventually letting the House approve the Estimates and pass legislation.

CLEARING THE GROUND (1833–55)

Most changes in procedure have been preceded by select committee inquiries, and although the committees which were appointed up until 1880 proceeded very cautiously, their reports carried considerable weight. (Later committees' reports were either strongly influenced by the government or unsupported by the front benches and therefore often not implemented.) The enthusiasm of MPs following the Reform Act to take part in debates caused considerable congestion of business, and the early committees were principally concerned with eliminating unnecessary opportunities for debate, caused by the large number of successive questions that were required to be decided, as mentioned above. As we have seen in Bill McKay's chapter 9 on May as a reformer, May took a key part in influencing the deliberations of these committees on the later part of this era. In this period the following changes were made:

Sitting hours: The House was unwilling to fix a time of rising on most days of the week: an MP would usually move the adjournment of the House at around midnight, and the House would usually agree. On Wednesdays, however, the House decided to sit at 12 noon and rise at 6 pm.

Petitions: After various experiments, the House agreed to abolish immediate debates on petitions, which were to be presented with a short statement only. A Public Petitions Committee (which lasted until 1974) was appointed with very narrow terms of reference: it was to classify and summarise petitions, and state the numbers of signatures appended to them.

Notices of Motions: The range of future dates for which motions could be tabled was restricted and a ballot (which was not mentioned in the standing orders until 1933) was introduced to decide which motions should have priority. ('Ballot' is a term used in the House not to denote a vote of some kind, but something more akin to a draw or raffle in normal terms.)

Orders of the Day: The House would no longer debate, when each order was reached, whether it should be read or whether some other business should be taken. The Speaker would instruct the Clerk to read the Orders of the Day and they would then be dealt with in the order in which they appeared on the paper, although the government could arrange its orders on the paper as it saw fit. (Government orders related mainly to stages of government bills or Supply business.)

Bills: A bill was presented either after financial resolutions from a committee had been agreed to or after the House had given an MP leave to present it. In either case the House would no longer subsequently debate or decide whether the bill should be read the first time or whether it should be printed. At committee stage, except on the first day, the House would resolve itself into a committee without debating the motion that the Speaker should leave the chair. In committee, any amendment could be made which was relevant to the subject-matter of the bill (previously any amendment not covered by the title of the Bill could be considered only on an instruction from the House), and material printed in italics would be treated as part of the text rather than needing to be inserted (italics, which are now used solely to indicate material involving charges which need authorisation by a money or ways and means resolution, were at that time also used to suggest commencement dates, etc, which the committee used to insert as it came to them). The addition of new clauses was simplified. At report stage the House would consider the bill in its amended state rather than having first to ratify each amendment made in committee. More bills with financial provisions could be brought from the House of Lords rather than having to begin in the Commons.

Divisions: Clerks were appointed to list the names of MPs voting, and the new Chamber was equipped with two separate division lobbies through which MPs passed to be counted by the tellers. MPs had two minutes to reach the Chamber (in practice longer, as the doors were not locked while other MPs were still seen to be approaching): the question was then put again and those in the House were obliged to vote.

Speaker: Although any MP could preside over a Committee of the whole House, only the Speaker could chair the House itself, which meant that the House could not sit on the rare occasions when the Speaker was ill. In 1853 the Chairman of Ways and Means (the MP who normally chaired the Committee of Ways and Means) was empowered to take the Chair as Deputy Speaker when the unavoidable absence of the Speaker was announced by the Clerk.

Select committees: Rules were introduced requiring notice of the names of MPs to be nominated to select committees, that the minutes of evidence should show which MP asked each question, and that minutes of proceedings should be kept showing the attendance of MPs and which way they voted in any division. If no quorum was present, the Clerk was to alert the chairman, who had to suspend the sitting until a quorum was again present, or adjourn it.

Members of the public ('strangers'): Orders which had been passed at the start of each session banning the public from sittings of the House (which had in any case been regularly disregarded) were modified to prevent disorder by strangers, but the right of any MP to clear the galleries of strangers by saying 'I spy strangers' was maintained.

THE GOVERNMENT VERSUS PRIVATE MEMBERS (1856–80)

The reforms of the previous twenty years had been mainly consensual, but difficulties remained because of the uncertainty of sitting times and the way in which the subject of debate could be diverted by any MP moving a motion to adjourn the debate. The next period revealed tensions between those on the two front benches and the remaining MPs.

Sittings of the House: The House usually sat (except on Wednesdays) at 4 pm, but it could decide to sit at 12 noon or 2 pm, in which case there was a break between 7 and 9 pm. The House usually adjourned from Friday until Monday (until 1861 this required a specific, debatable, motion each Friday), but it could still sit on a Saturday if business were put down for that day. From 1872 onwards, the House would rise at 12.30 am unless the business was unopposed or fell into certain exempted categories. Since 1811 Mondays and Fridays had, by an order passed each session, been 'order days' and the government orders had had priority on those days. Wednesday was an order day for private Members' orders from 1832. These provisions became a standing order in 1852. Tuesdays and Thursdays were 'notice days', on which new business (notices of motions) had priority, unless the House agreed to 'pass to the Orders of the Day'. In 1860 the government was given Thursdays instead of Fridays, and in 1861 the government was given both Thursdays and Fridays.

Bills: Bills were no longer subject to amendment at third reading, except for 'merely verbal' amendments, affecting only the wording and not the substance.

Financial procedure: Whenever the House was to consider 'Supply' (expenditure), it first debated whether the Speaker should leave the chair (any matter could be raised on this motion). These motions, says Fellowes, 'were at once a hindrance to that "certainty of business" which was the ideal of procedure committees and also a bar to that full and proper discussion of the Estimates which all Houses of Commons are convinced has been achieved in the past but which never seems capable of being repeated in the present'. The House eventually agreed that there should be no debate on whether the Speaker should leave the Chair on Mondays, except if the business before the Committee of Supply was the first consideration in that session of the Army, Navy or Civil Estimates. A Committee of Public Accounts was established in 1861 to examine the accounts of the sums granted by Parliament to meet the public expenditure.

Disorder by MPs: The Speaker (or Chairman, in Committee of the whole House) was empowered to 'name' an MP for disregarding the chair's authority or abusing the rules of the House, at which point the House could decide, without debate, to suspend him.

Oaths: All MPs had to swear an oath of allegiance before they sat or voted in the House of Commons (except during the election of a Speaker at the beginning of a Parliament). Although Quakers and Moravians had been allowed, since 1833, to affirm instead of swearing an oath of allegiance (as in the courts), the rules prevented Jews taking an oath (as the oath ended with the words 'on the true faith of a Christian') or atheists affirming. Following the experience with Mr Bradlaugh being refused permission to affirm, and then not being allowed even to take the oath, the House agreed to a form of oath that did not mention Christianity and decided that any person who could make an affirmation in a court of law should be allowed to do so in the House.

Select Committees: Standing orders were passed to give select committees power to sit when the House was sitting and to report without special leave to do so. Legislation was passed to allow the House itself or select committees to administer an oath (or affirmation) to witnesses. In practice evidence was very seldom taken on oath except by witnesses before committees on private bills.

Members of the public: The right of any MP to require the galleries to be cleared was abolished, but instead an MP could spy strangers and the House or Committee would vote without debate on whether 'Strangers be ordered to withdraw'.

COLLAPSE OF THE OLD PROCEDURE AND FOUNDATION OF THE NEW (1881–88)

The House had so far failed to deal properly with adjournment motions and the increasing pressure of business. In time, a solution might have been found, but obstruction by Irish nationalists soon brought affairs to a crisis, and drastic measures were needed. Irish MPs used all their opportunities for debate to hinder the transaction of business, and the new powers to name individual MPs and suspend them proved to be insufficient to deal with this.

In 1881 the Liberal government proposed repressive measures for Ireland, and following a protracted debate on the Queen's Speech it obtained an order of the House to give the Protection of Person and Property (Ireland) Bill (usually referred to as the Coercion Bill) priority over all other business, and then moved for leave to bring in the bill. Following several days' debate, proceedings were resumed on a Monday and the House was still sitting on Wednesday morning (in what became the longest ever sitting of the Commons at 41½ hours). At 9 am the Speaker took the Chair, replacing the Deputy Speaker, and declared that he would call no further MPs to speak but would put the question. He said that he did this because 'the dignity, credit and authority of the House were seriously threatened and could only be vindicated by a new and exceptional course of proceeding'.

The Speaker had, before acting in this way, obtained an undertaking from the government that it would confer more authority to control proceedings on either the House or the Chair, and at the same sitting the government outlined the 'urgency procedure' which it very soon brought in, whereby the Speaker could introduce new rules to be used whenever the House agreed that the state of public business was urgent. The Speaker introduced rules allowing the Speaker or Chairman to order an MP engaging in continued irrelevance or tedious repetition to resume his seat, and to refuse to accept a motion for adjourning the House or the debate, or to put the question on it without debate (and if a debate were allowed it would have to be confined to the matter of the motion). These and several other rules were used extensively in 1881 and for a brief time in 1882, and most of them were subsequently converted into standing orders.

The main changes made during this period were as follows:

Sitting hours: From 1888 the House sat (except on Wednesdays) at 3 pm instead of 4 pm and most business would be interrupted at midnight. If a sitting beginning at 2 pm were arranged, there would be a break between 7 and 9 pm and the sitting would end no later than 1 am.

Questions: The number of questions per day had increased enormously in the previous few years, but considerable time was saved from 1881 onwards as MPs were no longer required to read out the text of their questions; and from 1886 questions were tabled in writing rather than notice being given orally in the House. There was nevertheless no limit to the time that questions could take in the House each day.

Government business: On the days (Mondays, Thursdays and Fridays) on which government business had priority, both motions and orders could be taken, and the government could arrange them on the paper in the desired order.

Bills: The 'ten-minute rule' procedure was invented whereby MPs could obtain leave to present a bill after only two brief speeches (one for and one against) rather than a full debate. At report stage the House would consider the new clauses and amendments without first debating the motion 'that the bill be now considered', and amendments were not acceptable if they would have required an instruction in committee. After Whitsun, private Members' bills which had made the most progress would take priority over the others. (At that time the typical session lasted from February to August.) The first government bills were guillotined under the Speaker's urgency rules in 1881 and another bill was the subject of a guillotine motion in 1888. (Guillotines, officially called 'allocation of time motions', continued to be used for a minority of Bills, but were not catered for in the standing orders until 1947. From 2000 onwards they were largely replaced by programme motions, which are now almost universal for government bills.)

Disorder by MPs: As a less drastic alternative to naming an MP, the Speaker was given power to send a disorderly MP out for the remainder of the day without any vote by the House, and the urgency rule empowering the Speaker to make a tedious or repetitive MP resume his seat was made a standing order.

Divisions: The Speaker was given power to declare that a division was frivolously or vexatiously claimed and decide the question by calling upon the MPs on each side to stand in turn. (The names of those in the minority were recorded until 1919.)

Closure: One of the urgency rules allowed the Speaker to announce that the 'general sense of the House' was that the question being debated should be put and that if a motion was then moved to that effect it would be put forthwith and carried if supported by a majority of 3:1. In 1882, after numerous days' debate, this rule was converted into a standing order, where the required majority was 200 in favour, or 100 in favour and fewer than 40 against. In 1887 the closure system was altered to provide that an MP rather than the Speaker should initiate the procedure by interrupting the MP who had the floor and claiming to move that 'the Question be now put'; that the Speaker could refuse to accept the closure if he considered that the motion was an abuse of the rules of the House or an infringement of the rights of the minority; that if the closure was on an amendment the main question could be put immediately afterwards without any further closure motion; and that an MP could also move that the question that certain words of a clause stand part of that clause, or that a clause stand part of the bill, be now put. (This final provision was popularly called the 'kangaroo closure', as it involved leaping over some of the amendments to a point in the bill beyond where those amendments could be moved: it was largely replaced by the later power for the Speaker to select amendments and was abolished in 1986.) In 1888 the number of MPs required to support a closure, if divided on, was reduced to its current figure, 100.

The Chair: The Deputy Speaker was empowered to replace the Speaker in the chair without the latter's unavoidable absence being announced, and a small group of MPs was appointed to take the chair temporarily in Committee of the whole House (the previous practice being that any MP could be asked to do so). Temporary chairmen did not have the power to accept a closure motion.

Adjournment motions: Adjournment motions could be moved by private Members to discuss a matter of urgent public importance only with the support of forty MPs (or of the House on a division). (The procedure remains available, except that since 2007 the 'urgent debate' has taken place on a motion that the House has considered the matter rather than for the adjournment.) Motions to adjourn the debate (or the House) moved during a debate could be refused by the Chair or decided without debate.

Committee of the whole House: The House would resolve itself into a Committee of the whole House, when reaching an order of the day to do so, without having to debate whether the Speaker should leave the chair. (This provision did not at this stage apply to the Committee of Ways and Means and did not apply on three occasions per session to the Committee of Supply.)

Standing committees: Two standing committees, one on law and one on trade, were set up to consider some Bills (instead of the Committee of the whole House). Each committee consisted of between sixty and eighty MPs (later reduced to between forty and sixty) with up to fifty extra MPs appointed in relation to a particular Bill. The object of standing committees, which had been advocated by May in evidence before procedure committees for some years, was to save the time of the House by allowing the committee stage to be taken elsewhere by a reasonably representative group of MPs.

THE GOVERNMENT GAIN CONTROL OF THE TIME OF THE HOUSE (1889–1919)

After the revolutionary changes in 1882 and 1888, there was a period of quiet before further reforms in 1902, 1906 and 1919. Meanwhile the government often wanted to take over private Members' days (Tuesdays and Wednesdays), particularly towards the end of each session, but this required a debate and justification on each occasion. The making in 1902 of a new standing order stating that government business had priority at every sitting, and then listing the exceptions, was the final step in a gradual process rather than a revolution, as is sometimes claimed.

Sittings: In 1891 the provisions for sittings which began at 2 pm (which were somewhat misleadingly called 'morning sittings') were aligned with the others, with a moment of interruption at midnight. In 1902 the short day, finishing at 6 pm, was moved from Wednesday to Friday, and on the other days the House sat at 2 pm instead of 3 pm and had an adjournment for dinner between 7.30 and 9 pm. (Previously the House had often suspended for half an hour for dinner, an arrangement called the 'Speaker's chop'.) These arrangements were changed again in 1906: the sitting hour was put back to 2.45 pm, the dinner adjournment was abolished, and the moment of interruption was set at 11 pm, with the House usually rising no later than 11.30 pm. Friday sittings would finish at 5.30 pm. In 1919, the consideration of reports from Committee of the whole House was included in exempted business (business which could continue after the moment of interruption, even if opposed), except for bills and reports from the Committee of Supply.

Questions: A fixed length of time was allotted for questions (forty minutes in 1902, changed in 1906 to one hour less the time taken by prayers and private business): questions not reached would receive a written answer (and, for the first time, questions could also be tabled for written answer).

Priority for government business: From 1902 government business was given precedence at every sitting except Tuesday and Wednesday evenings (when private Members' motions would have precedence) and Fridays (when private Members' bills would have precedence), but the government would have Tuesday evenings after Easter and Wednesday evenings after Whitsun, and all but two Fridays after Whitsun (until Michaelmas, 29 September). Opposed private business was taken at evening sittings instead of delaying questions and government business. In 1906, as the break between afternoon and evening sittings was abolished, private Members' business or opposed private business was taken at 8.15 pm.

Bills: From 1902 an MP could give notice to present a bill rather than having to obtain the leave of the House after a debate. In practice, important government bills were still introduced on a motion for leave until 1918. Private Members continued to present bills under the 'ten-minute rule' as well as taking advantage of the new procedure. The 'ten-minute rule' (two short speeches, one for and one against) was extended to motions to recommit bills to a committee. A (third) standing committee to consider Scottish bills was set up in 1894, and in 1901 the House decided that all bills reported from a standing committee should have a report stage, whether amended or not, but the question 'that the Bill be now considered' should no longer be debated first. (Bills considered in Committee of the whole House do not have a report stage unless they have been amended.) In 1906 the number of standing committees (other than for Scottish bills) was increased to four (with government bills having priority in all but one of them) and it was provided that all bills (other than Finance and Consolidated Fund Bills) should be committed to standing committees unless the House otherwise ordered. The closure rule was extended to standing committees. In 1919 the number of standing committees was again raised (to six).

Finance: In 1896 the House limited the number of days to be spent in Committee of Supply (approving Estimates of public expenditure) to twenty per session; on the nineteenth day the Committee of Supply would decide on all remaining unapproved Estimates and the House would do the same on the twentieth day. Various modifications were made over the next few years, including voting the remaining Estimates as a lump sum rather than potentially dozens of individual questions, and the procedure was converted into a standing order in 1902. In 1919 the government experimented with referring nearly all the Estimates to standing committees, but this was not successful: 'again and again the House had to take back into its own hands Estimates which had been referred to a standing committee but which had never got reported' (Fellowes). The experiment was not repeated. In 1901 the motion that the Speaker leave the Chair before going into Committee of Ways and Means was abolished (it was still used on four supply days in each session).

Disorder by MPs: In 1902 the procedure for naming MPs was modified (if an MP had been named in Committee both the Committee and the House had had to vote to suspend the MP: now just the House would). The existing periods of suspension were left out of the standing order but the House did not agree what the replacements should be, so the House was left with a standing order with the deleted words printed with a line through them until 1926, and the House had to decide when to end each suspension (which would otherwise have lasted until the end of the session). The Speaker was also given power to suspend or adjourn the House if 'grave disorder' arose.

Divisions: In 1906, the procedure for divisions was changed: the question was still put a second time, but this was now after exactly two minutes, and MPs had six minutes to reach the House and were no longer obliged to vote if they had heard the question put, or prohibited from doing so if they had not. In 1919, the Speaker's power to dispense with a division was extended to all those unnecessarily claimed (rather than just those 'frivolously or vexatiously' claimed).

Count of the House: If an MP drew attention to the lack of forty MPs in the House at any time after 4 pm, the bells were rung and if forty MPs did not appear the sitting was ended. In 1902 it was provided that this procedure could no longer be used between 9 and 10 pm, and in 1906 this period was changed to 8.15–9.15 pm. Counting the House continued to be possible under a variety of restrictions until 1971, when the now mysterious paragraph (2) of Standing Order No 41 was made: 'The House shall not be counted at any time.'

Selection of amendments: In 1909 the closure rule was extended to allow an MP to move that the Chair should be empowered to select which amendments could be moved to the words, clauses or schedules defined in the motion. In 1919 this was converted into a permanent power to allow the Speaker (in the House) and the Chairman of Ways and Means and Deputy Chairman (in Committee of the whole House) to select amendments to Bills or motions without any individual decision. (The power was not extended to the chairmen of standing committees until 1934.) This represented a fundamental change in the balance of power in the House, and vastly increased the ability of the Chair to control debate. It remained critical to a Bill's ability to make progress until the introduction of programming in 2000.

Chair: A Deputy Chairman of Ways and Means was appointed in 1902 and was given powers to accept closure in Committee in 1906. He could also act as a second Deputy Speaker. (A Second Deputy Chairman of Ways and Means was appointed in 1971.)

The anticipation rule: The rule (which appeared to have been formulated some time before 1860 and received an early mention in chapter 34 of Charles Dickens' *Little Dorrit*) forbade the House from debating a subject if the same subject was already set down for a later date, unless the earlier debate was on a more effective form of proceeding (such as a bill if the later debate was due to be held on a motion). An MP could therefore table an early day motion to prevent a matter being raised in a question or on an adjournment motion. Following a select committee report in 1907, the House (in 1914) gave the Speaker the power to consider, when applying the rule, the likelihood of the debate, if not anticipated, taking place within a reasonable time.

TIDYING UP (1920–35)

Between 1920 and 1935 the House's procedures were not reformed to the same extent as in the previous decades, but there were several Procedure Committees and numerous minor amendments to the standing orders, including some resulting from an informal Speaker's Committee in 1933 which undertook the same type of tidying-up for which Standing Orders (Revision) Committees were appointed in the mid-nineteenth and late twentieth centuries. Not all the Procedure Committees' recommendations were implemented during the period, although some were taken up again decades later, such as the suspension of public bills from one session to the next (as had been done with private bills since the mid-nineteenth century, and had been discussed intermittently by Procedure Committees for public bills ever since), and the introduction of a 'priority' category of questions for written answer.

Sitting hours: In 1921, Friday sittings were changed from 11 am to 4 pm instead of 12 noon to 5 pm (the first time for centuries that 'morning sittings' had actually begun in the morning).

Arrangement of business: In 1927 it was decided that private Members' motions should be moved from Tuesday and Wednesday evenings to all day on Wednesdays (with two motions being taken at each sitting) with minor changes as to which Wednesdays and Fridays would be taken by the government. In 1929, following the decision to begin sessions in November instead of February, the standing order was adapted to apply to the new dates. From 1927 opposed private business and urgent adjournment debates were taken at 7.30 pm instead of 8.15 pm.

Bills: Fellowes records: 'The hopes that an increase in the number of standing committees would relieve the House of a great deal of the work involved in the detailed consideration of legislation was never realised.' The number of committees was reduced in 1926 from six to five, with fewer members (30–50 with 10–35 added for each Bill). In 1934 the Chairmen were given the power to select amendments, and the power of appointing the Chairman for each bill was transferred from the Chairmen's Panel itself to the Speaker. At the same time the Speaker (rather than the Committee of Selection) was made responsible for appointing the Panel, which became the same as the panel of temporary chairman for the Committee of the whole House.

CONCLUSION IN 1935

The Public Business Standing Orders increased in number from eight in 1835 to ninety-seven in 1935, with the procedure changing from a somewhat ramshackle set of precedents and a chaotic approach to the business to be transacted on any particular day to a fairly constrained body of rules about timings and the questions to be put. However, in 1935 much of the procedure was still based on pre-1835 precedents, notably parts of public bill procedure and financial procedure; individual select committees (other than the Committee of Public Accounts) were reappointed each session even if (such as the Select Committee on Estimates) they were in effect permanent. Restrictions on lengths of speeches (other than under the ten-minute rule) and use of standing committees for business other than the committee stage of Bills were to come much later. Unlike in many other legislatures, no attempt was made to codify the procedural rules as a whole, although the previously mentioned guides for MPs such as *Rules, Orders and Forms of Procedure* (first written by May in 1854 and later called *Manual of Procedure in the Public Business*, last issued in 1987) to some extent filled the gap.

CHANGES SINCE 1935

The number of Public Business Standing Orders continued to increase: to 113 in 1948, 122 in 1971, 163 in 1997, and 216 in 2016 (including an extra 15, containing something over 5,000 words, about the circumstances in which MPs representing particular parts of the United Kingdom are entitled to vote separately on certain proposals—'English Votes for English Laws'). Amendments have been made so often that the volume usually has to be reprinted at least once a year. The following is a brief summary of significant changes since 1935. Some of these are mentioned in greater detail in chapter 12.

Wartime: During the Second World War there were hardly any changes to the standing orders, but the House changed its sitting hours by sessional orders and abolished private Members' bills and motions. In 1944 the Speaker introduced balloting arrangements for the adjournment debates at the end of each sitting; these debates gained a protected half-hour in 1947. (Private Members' bills and motions were not restored until 1948–49 and 1950, respectively.)

Chair: The method of electing the Speaker was changed in 1972: the proceedings were to be chaired by the Father of the House (instead of the Clerk of the House) and second and subsequent proposals of candidates were to be moved as amendments to the first motion rather than as independent motions to be considered if previous motions had been negatived. The system was changed again in 2001 to a secret, exhaustive ballot, except that a former Speaker seeking re-election was subject to this process only if the House were to negative a motion to reappoint him or her. The three Deputy Speakers have been elected by secret ballot since 2010.

Sittings: The post-war sitting pattern of a 2.30 pm start on Mondays to Thursdays and an 11 am start on Fridays largely persisted until 1980, when Friday sittings were moved 1½ hours earlier; changes to sitting times on other days (except Mondays) were made in 2002, 2005 and 2012. In 1966 the House experimented with morning sittings on Mondays and Wednesdays, and then changed this into a provision for suspending a late sitting until the following morning, but abandoned the practice shortly after the provisions were made into a Standing Order in 1968. A series of adjournment debates for private Members was instituted on Wednesday mornings in 1994, and these were transferred to 'Westminster Hall sittings' (actually taking place in a committee room off Westminster Hall) in 1999: some of these debates are on subjects selected by the Liaison Committee or the Backbench Business Committee. Since 1994 the House has not sat on all Fridays in sitting weeks, and since 2002 the House has sat on Fridays only to consider private Members' bills. Following a number of sessional orders since 1920 allowing the Speaker to recall the House for emergency sittings (originally after consulting the government, but since 1932 only at the request of the government), the provisions were made permanent in 1947. Until the early 1990s the House regularly sat for long periods beyond 10 pm, in particular for the Report Stage of bills and for debates on Statutory Instruments. The programming of bills and the transfer of most debates on Statutory Instruments to standing (later 'general') committees (see below) greatly reduced the number of late sittings. Recess dates were fixed by order of the House (normally moved very near to the recess concerned); these became the vehicle for debate on matters needing to be discussed before the recess. In 1982 these debates were limited to three hours, and in 1995 the question was to be decided without debate, and the previous debates were usually held instead on the last sitting day before the recess (recently as backbench business—see below).

Private Members' and backbench business: When private Members' motions and bills were reinstated in 1948, they were taken on Fridays. From the late 1950s motions were also taken until 7 pm on four other days in each session (originally Wednesdays, later Mondays). In 1994, private Members' motions were abolished (having been replaced by the Wednesday morning adjournment debates mentioned above). A Backbench Business Committee was set up in 2010 to allocate time for debates (but not bills) on allotted Backbench Business Days in the House and also for some of the debates in Westminster Hall.

Supply, Ways and Means and opposition business: The business which could be taken on a Supply Day was widened to include motions that the Speaker leave the Chair (thus allowing for debate on matters unrelated to Supply, which came to be used for items which the opposition wished to raise). The Committees of Supply and Ways and Means were abolished in 1966–67 and the relevant business was taken in the House itself, and Supply business was to include 'any substantive motion' (again, with the understanding that the opposition would usually table the motion concerned). In 1982 the fact that very little Supply business was actually about supply was recognised, and the time concerned was replaced by nineteen (later twenty) opposition days per session (three of which were reserved for the second largest opposition party) and three Estimates Days, for the consideration of Estimates chosen by the Liaison Committee (generally on the basis of relevant select committee reports). Debate on the Consolidated Fund Bills giving statutory authority for the Estimates was often allowed to continue all night; in 1982 the proceedings on the bills were to be without any debate, but the time lost was replaced by an all-night debate on an adjournment motion (in turn abolished in 1995).

Deferred divisions: Since 2001, divisions which would otherwise have occurred after the moment of interruption have been deferred and dealt with by a written process the following sitting Wednesday. There are, however, numerous exceptions to this procedure, including all proceedings on bills.

Questions: Although not provided for in the Standing Orders, in 1975 a formal random shuffle was introduced to establish priority for questions for oral answer, and from the 1900s onwards there has been some sort of rota governing which departments are due to answer each day. A provision for 'priority' (later 'named day') questions for written answer was introduced in 1972, which required an answer on the day for which they were put down (although the reply might just be a 'holding answer'). A provision for the government to make written statements (rather than reply to an 'inspired' written question from a friendly backbencher) was introduced in 2002.

Debate: Following experiments in 1979, 1984 and 1986, the Speaker was given power in 1988 to impose time-limits on backbench speeches (originally an eight-minute limit, but now more flexible), with the possibility of time-limits on front-benchers added in 2007 (but very little used). This reform has meant that any Member who has notified the Speaker in advance can usually rely on being called, if only for a very short speech.

Public bills: In 1947 the procedure in committee was slightly changed: the chairman was empowered to put the question on a clause (or schedule) standing part of the bill without debate if its principle had been adequately discussed in the course of debate on amendments proposed to it. In 1967 a third reading was to be taken without debate unless six Members gave notice requiring a debate (they nearly always did, so the provision was repealed in 1986). Also in the mid-1960s the House experimented with taking the second reading debate on a bill in a standing committee, a practice which has continued fairly rarely ever since, and also made a standing order allowing the report stage to be taken in a standing committee as well, which was used only once. From 1980 the House experimented sporadically with standing committees which could take evidence (called 'special standing committees'); this procedure became the norm only in 2006, when they were renamed 'public bill committees'. In the 1990s abbreviated procedures were introduced for consolidation bills, and Law Commission bills were to be sent to a second reading committee unless the House decided otherwise. In 2000, the House agreed on a series of orders programming the time allowed for bills: the procedures were very similar to the existing allocation of time motions ('guillotines'), but passed for most government bills immediately after second reading rather than being imposed only when it became clear that progress on a bill was taking much longer than expected. In 2002 the House agreed to procedures for carrying over public bills from one session to the next (something which had been possible for private Bills since the mid-nineteenth century). In 2003 provision was made for bills and Lords amendments received from the Lords to be printed even if the House was not sitting. In 2015 the House agreed to a procedure allowing MPs representing England and Wales (or England only) to have a separate vote on provisions of bills affecting only those territories.

Standing committees: With the exception of the 1919 experiment with referring the Estimates to standing committees, they were used only for the committee stage of bills until 1948. After that the House experimented with committees (which were eventually designated 'Grand Committees') for Scotland, Wales and Northern Ireland, and allowed them to hold the second reading debate on bills, to consider other matters, and eventually (in the 1990s) to operate as mini-chambers with the possibility of oral questions, statements and adjournment debates, often with the sittings taking place away from Westminster. With the progress of devolution, Grand Committees have met less frequently. In 1960, the House abolished the distinction between the 'nucleus' of a standing committee (the permanent membership) and those MPs added for a particular matter. Since 1973, statutory instruments and European documents have been able to be debated in standing committees, which has removed a considerable amount of late-night business from the floor of the House. With the abolition of the 'nucleus', the term 'standing committee' (except for the

Grand Committees) had become a misnomer: this fact was eventually recognised in 2006 and they were called 'general committees' instead.

Select committees: The only select committees regularly appointed until the 1950s were the Committee of Public Accounts (appointed by standing order) and the Estimates Committee (appointed session by session). A Committee of Privileges was also appointed whenever there was a case to consider. In 1951 the House appointed a Select Committee on Nationalised Industries, which came to have a semi-permanent existence until 1979, and from the 1960s the House experimented with committees to examine individual government departments (notably Agriculture and Scotland) and increased the number of other committees appointed. In 1971 the Estimates Committee became the Expenditure Committee, with wider terms of reference, which was itself replaced in 1979 with a set of select committees to examine the expenditure, administration and policy of each major government department. In 1980 a Liaison Committee (which had existed for some years informally) was appointed consisting of the chairmen (later 'chairs') of the other select committees, to consider matters affecting select committees and (since 2002) to take oral evidence from the Prime Minister. Since 2010 the chairs of most select committees have been elected by the House, after a sharing of the posts between the parties has been proposed and approved. The remaining committee members are elected within their parties before being proposed to the House by a member of the Committee of Selection.

CONCLUSION

May was able to declare in 1844 that:

> The proceedings of Parliament are regulated chiefly by ancient usage, or by the settled practice of modern times, apart from distinct orders and rules: but usage has frequently been declared and explained by both Houses, and new rules have been established by positive orders and resolutions. Ancient usage, when not otherwise declared, is collected from the Journals, from history and early treatises, and from the continued experience of practised members. Modern practice is often undefined in any written form; it is not recorded in the Journals; it is not to be traced in the published debates; nor is it known in any certain manner but by personal experience, and by the daily practice of Parliament in the conduct of its various descriptions of business.[11]

In the intervening 170-odd years, modern practice has become more and more defined in written form by positive orders and resolutions, and distinct orders and rules of increasing complexity have come to dominate over ancient usage. The House of Commons is less interested in precedent, and the *Treatise* has accordingly become more a guide to the interpretation of the rules than a source of them. But an understanding of the historical development of procedure as well as the daily practice of Parliament is still essential to making sense of the standing orders as a set of practical rules for the solving of political problems, and May's *Treatise* represents the continuing efforts of Clerks to capture and explain that context. As such, it is still an essential guide to what the standing orders really mean.

---

[11] *Treatise*, 1st edn (1844) 131.

12

Pursuing the Efficient Despatch of Business

The Role of Committees in Procedural Reform since 1900

MARK EGAN

INTRODUCTION

THROUGHOUT THE TIME since Erskine May's death committees on procedural matters have been a common, if often obscure, feature of the Westminster landscape. This chapter provides an overview of committees on procedure since 1900, discussing why they were established, who sat on them and how they operated. It looks in more detail at some of the procedural conundrums such committees have attempted to solve, on sitting hours and legislation, financial scrutiny, questions, select committees and the method of taking divisions. There are common themes running throughout the period which are identified at the end of the chapter as well as some significant changes which shed light on the role of select committees in initiating, influencing and holding back procedural change.

It is first necessary to define terms. Some committees on procedural matters are easily identifiable, not least the Procedure Committee established on a permanent basis under Standing Order No 147, which was made in 1997.[1] However, there have also been select committees on sitting hours, on what was termed Unofficial Members' Business (now described as private Members' Business), various committees on specific aspects of public business and the Select Committee on the Modernisation of the House of Commons which, from 1997 to 2008, operated in parallel to the Procedure Committee but occupied the same turf and dominated the field.[2] Private and hybrid legislative business operates under separate standing orders and on the rare occasions when procedural change in this

---

[1] A select committee on procedure had been set up for a Parliament at a time since 1983.

[2] A sessional Procedure Committee, appointed to consider 'any matters which may be referred to them by the House in relation to the procedure of the House', coexisted with a Procedure Committee appointed to consider 'the practice and procedure of the House in relation to public business and to make recommendations for the more effective performance of its functions' from 1976 to 1978. The latter committee's report, published in July 1978, was wide-ranging and recommended the introduction of select committees to shadow government departments, later implemented by the incoming Conservative government elected the following year.

area has been discussed, separate committees have been established for that purpose,[3] and they are not taken into account in this chapter. Committees on matters with a procedural dimension, such as those on privilege and standards matters, and departmental, domestic or other forms of committee which have from time to time commented on the House's procedures are also excluded.[4]

Until the mid-1950s procedure committees were appointed relatively infrequently. In the latter decades of the nineteenth century the activities of the Irish Parliamentary Party and their use of obstruction as a political weapon precipitated a procedural crisis. However, Gladstone's reforms of 1882 did not resolve the problem. After the 1906 Liberal landslide, the obstruction started to come from the official opposition, working in cahoots with 'Mr Balfour's poodle',[5] the House of Lords. A reforming and radical government found itself stymied by Parliament, and turned again to reform. The 1906 committee, which published two significant reports, was the first to consider public business since the 1890 committee on 'abridged procedure on partly considered bills'. With the passing of the 1910–11 constitutional crisis, the Great War and the resolution of the Irish question by violent means, procedure was again out of focus until the late 1920s when committees were appointed on Unofficial Members' Business and sitting hours. The 1931 Procedure Committee, and its successor in 1932, which published a report based on the evidence taken by its predecessor, conducted a wide-ranging inquiry on procedural and constitutional matters but famine again followed feast until the 1945 Procedure Committee set to work.

From the mid-1950s until the late-1970s committees on procedure were appointed in most sessions and often produced more than one report: the 1966–67 committee published six. The pace of procedural scrutiny slackened in the 1980s but picked up again with the appointment of the permanent Procedure Committee in its modern-day form, the 1991–92 Jopling Committee on sitting hours, the 1997–2008 Modernisation Committee and the 2009 Wright Committee on the Reform of the Commons. Even so, the attention paid by the House's committees to procedural reform can vary markedly from one session to the next.[6]

Procedure committees have typically had wide terms of reference:

— to consider the question of procedure in the House of Commons, and to report as to the amendment of the existing rules and upon any new rules which they may consider desirable for the efficient despatch of business (1906);

---

[3] Exceptions to this rule included, Select Committee on House of Commons (Procedure), First Report, Session 1906, HC 89, which included recommendations on the timing of private business and Select Committee on Procedure, Session 1958–59 Report, HC 92 (hereafter 1959 Procedure Committee) paras 21–23, which dealt with the presentation of private bills and arrangements for unopposed private business.

[4] Discussion of the House's procedures can arise in almost any committee context. For example, questioning of Sir Frederic Metcalfe, the then Clerk of the House by the 1953 committee on House of Commons accommodation, moved swiftly from whether it was necessary for the clerks to retain a bathroom to why the House had two separately compiled records of its proceedings, the daily Votes and Proceedings and sessional Journal. When asked to choose which was most important, Sir Frederic said he would 'fight to my last gasp' for the Journal. Select Committee on House of Commons Accommodation, &c, Report, Session 1952–53, HC 309, Q145.

[5] The expression is Lloyd George's. See Roy Jenkins, *Mr Balfour's Poodle: Peers v People* (London, Heinemann, 1954).

[6] For example, there were seven reports from the Procedure Committee in 2012–13 but just one report from that committee in 2007–08.

— to consider the procedure in the public business of the House and to report what alterations, if any, are desirable for the more efficient despatch of such business (1945, 1958, 1964, 1966);
— to consider the practice and procedure in relation to questions and question time in the House and to recommend what changes might be desirable (1972);
— to examine the House's financial procedures and to make recommendations (1982);
— to consider how the practices and procedures of the House should be modernised, and to make recommendations thereon (1997);
— to consider the practice and procedure of the House in the conduct of public business, and to make recommendations (Standing Order No 147).

These have occasionally been supplemented by formal instructions to consider specific matters.[7] The 2009 Wright Committee on reform of the Commons was tasked with looking at four areas: the appointment of members and chairs of select committees; the appointment of the Chairman and Deputy Chairmen of Ways and Means; scheduling business in the House; and enabling the public to initiate debates and proceedings in the House.

As we will see, much of the work by procedure committees during the period under discussion was initiated by the government. Some of the most significant procedure committees, such as those of 1906 and 1945 as well as the post-1997 Modernisation Committee, were explicitly set up by the government of the day to implement reform proposals designed to facilitate the enactment of ambitious programmes of legislation. The procedure committees of the mid-1960s were a product of the Labour government's parliamentary reform agenda, spearheaded by Richard Crossman.[8] Procedure committees initiated by backbenchers have been unusual.[9]

There is a clear pattern through much of the period for the membership of procedure committees to be inclined towards senior Members, in terms of both political stature and length of service. The 1906 committee included Labour leader Keir Hardie; a future Speaker, JH Whitley; Sir Joseph Leese, who first stood for Parliament in 1868; Aretas Akers-Douglas and Sir Henry Fowler, both first elected in 1880; and William Redmond, brother of the Irish nationalist leader. The nine Members of the 1932 committee had amassed 166 years' experience of sitting in the Commons, the baby of the group being Ernest Brown who had sat since 1923. The 1945 committee included Earl Winterton, first elected in 1904, as well as the Liberal leader, Clement Davies, the future Labour leader, Hugh Gaitskell, and a future Labour Leader of the House, Richard Crossman. The 1966–67 committee included a future Speaker, Selwyn Lloyd; stalwarts such as Sir Hugh Munro-Lucas-Tooth, first elected in 1924, and Dame Irene Ward, who was elected in 1931; the academic John Mackintosh; future Liberal leader David Steel; as well as the likes of Paul Channon, Eric Heffer and Roy Hattersley, who would also rise to senior positions in their parties.

---

[7] For example, the Select Committee on Procedure appointed in 1945 was instructed to 'report as soon as possible upon any scheme for the acceleration of proceedings on Public Bills which may be submitted to them on behalf of His Majesty's Government'. CJ (1945–46) 33 (24 August 1945).

[8] See R Crossman, *The Diaries of a Cabinet Minister*, vol 1: *Minister of Housing 1964–66* (London, Hamish Hamilton and Jonathan Cape, 1975) 549 (entry for 23 June 1966).

[9] For examples of committees initiated by backbenchers, see 1959 Procedure Committee (n 3) esp para 1, and House of Commons Reform Committee, First Report, Session 2008–09, Rebuilding the House, HC 1117.

In recent years it has become more common for newer Members to be appointed to procedure committees. The 1997 Modernisation Committee included three Members elected for the first time in that year's general election.[10] Six of the fifteen Members of the Procedure Committee appointed in 2015 were first elected in that year. Attendance has also sometimes been problematic during this time. Average attendance at Procedure Committee meetings was consistently below 60 per cent during the 2005 Parliament, although attendance has improved since then.

LEGISLATION AND SITTING HOURS

Throughout the period covered by this chapter procedure committees grappled with the question of how to ensure that the Commons passed legislation more efficiently. As time went on there was an increasing focus on the related matter of reducing the frequency of sittings of the House beyond midnight and, in recent decades, on achieving 'family-friendly' sitting hours.

As we have seen, May had long advocated a rationalisation of the process for passing legislation,[11] which Walkland described as 'traditionally obstructive'.[12] A significant step had been taken in 1882 with the creation of standing committees to consider certain bills, but it remained the norm for bills to be considered by the Committee of the whole House.[13] The 1906 procedure committee was invited by the government to recommend that most bills be considered in standing committee and duly obliged, thereby creating a system which, with modifications, persisted throughout the century. This change was strongly supported by the then Clerk of the House, Sir Courtenay Ilbert, who described (echoing May from twenty-odd years earlier) the changes as 'a line on which one is bound to proceed if one is to take any efficient step to facilitate the course of legislative procedure'. 'I do not think anyone defends the existing system', he went on, 'no reasonable person in his sober senses would sit down and deliberately suggest such a method of procedure'.[14]

However, the change was not without controversy, given that it arose from the Liberal government's desire to make progress with a host of contentious bills. Efficient scrutiny was about ensuring the government got its legislative programme through broadly intact and without undue delay. The increasing prominence of the concept of efficiency as a persuasive force perhaps demonstrated the growing power of the executive and of party government. The Commons was becoming, perhaps had become, a means by which the executive governed rather than the central institution of resistance to government. Sensing this, the 1906 committee narrowly voted down an alternative draft report which would

---

[10] Helen Jackson, Phyllis Starkey and Andrew Stunell.

[11] See chapter 13.

[12] SA Walkland (ed), *The House of Commons in the Twentieth Century* (Oxford, Oxford University Press, 1979) 248.

[13] ibid, 252–53 and Select Committee on House of Commons (Procedure), Second Report, Session 1906, HC 181 (hereafter 1906 Second Report) QQ 243–77 (Sir Courtney Ilbert).

[14] 1906 Second Report, ibid, Q278. It is, perhaps, worth recalling that Ilbert was an 'outsider', having been brought in as Clerk of the House after a career as the government draftsman, owing to a perceived lack of management talent amongst the then Clerks. His view of procedure was coloured as much by the executive perspective as by the parliamentary one.

have declined to reach a view on standing committee changes until the government had laid before the committee 'a complete scheme of the Reform of Procedure which they have in mind'.[15] Unionist members moved numerous amendments to exempt certain classes of bills, including those relating to the franchise, parliamentary reform or 'bills which contain general controversial matter or arouse acute religious sensibilities' from automatic referral to a standing committee. They also proposed the establishment of a business committee, chaired by the Speaker, which would decide on the appropriate process for committee consideration of each bill, an idea that was to recur in various guises in future years.[16]

The wide-ranging 1931–32 procedure committees were also concerned with the efficiency of legislative scrutiny, recommending that all committee chairs be given the power to select amendments for debates.[17] The 1932 committee concluded that if governments increasingly used guillotine motions to ensure bills made progress through the Commons 'a more scientific method must be devised for giving ample time for every point of substance to be discussed' and that this should be organised by 'a small expert committee'.[18] Acknowledging the connection between efficient scrutiny and sitting periods, the committee noted that 'the complete allocation of time throughout the session' was the only way of shortening sessions, as was widely considered to be desirable.[19]

Further legislative efficiency was sought when Labour gained power in 1945 with a radical manifesto of sweeping economic reform and, like the Liberals forty years before, was determined to enact legislation to which the official opposition and the House of Lords were fundamentally opposed. The procedure committee set up in that year endorsed proposals for standing committees to sit longer hours. It also agreed that, where a guillotine motion was necessary, this would specify a date for the bill to be reported from the committee and that a business sub-committee (appointed by the Speaker) would allocate sittings to parts of the bill. However, the provision for the appointment of business sub-committees was rarely used and, in practice, was superseded by more effective whipping of government Members.[20]

The pursuit of efficiency continued to drive proposals for procedural reform in the 1950s and 1960s. The 1959 committee aimed at 'removing as much [legislative] detail as is practicable from the floor of the House' and making procedure 'more modern and business like'.[21] Its conclusions were relatively minor, for example ruling out taking some report stages in committee. However, it did recommend committing parts of the annual Finance Bill to a standing committee, arguing that the time saved on the floor could be given to private members, in response to demands for Wednesday morning sittings for that purpose.[22] Provision for second reading and report stage debates to be taken in specially constituted committees was introduced in 1967 but these have been rarely used.[23]

---

[15] ibid, vii.
[16] ibid.
[17] Select Committee on Procedure, Report, Session 1931–32, HC 129 (hereafter 1932 Committee) para 11.
[18] ibid, para 12.
[19] ibid, para 7 (c)(i).
[20] Business sub-committees were appointed in respect of two bills in 1946–47 (CJ 121) and one bill in 1948–49 (CJ 46). Also see Walkland (n 12) 272–74.
[21] 1959 Procedure Committee (n 3) para 2.
[22] ibid, para 9.
[23] M Jack (ed), *Erskine May's Treatise on the Law, Privileges, Proceedings and Usage of Parliament*, 24th edn (London, LexisNexis, 2011) 551–53 and 591.

The enthusiasm for efficiency peaked in 1967 with a proposal from the Study of Parliament Group (founded in 1964 and made up of academics and parliamentary officials) for legislation to be drafted differently, so that the House authorised broad principles in much shorter bills and left all of the detail to ministers.[24] This was too much for the Procedure Committee, which was not convinced that time would be saved by leaving detailed matters for secondary legislation and which considered that it was 'normally desirable … that the details of legislation should be subject to full scrutiny and possible amendment'.[25] By the 1970s there was growing dissatisfaction with heavily whipped, formulaic debates in committee on bills, which very rarely seemed to influence government policy. The concept of effective scrutiny, which aimed to achieve better law, not necessarily to the government's preferred timetable, was now beginning to assert itself.[26] The 1977–78 procedure committee, known for proposing the introduction of departmental select committees, also recommended the introduction of public bill committees in which oral hearings on a bill would precede formal line-by-line scrutiny. This recommendation was eventually implemented in 1980 but special standing committees, as they were called, were appointed for just nine bills in twenty years.[27] A 2005–06 modernisation committee report finally led to the routine referral of public bills to committees which start by taking oral evidence, both to help inform debate and to engage the public in law-making.[28] Whether or not these have enhanced the efficacy of legislative scrutiny remains an open question.[29]

By the 1960s, attention had turned to ways of enabling the House not to sit so late. The first report of the 1966–67 procedure committee addressed this matter on the basis of an instruction by the House. It found that from 21 April to 8 July 1966 the House sat on average until 11.42 pm on days excluding Fridays and that, when the Finance Bill was considered in committee, the average time of rising was, exhaustingly, 3.44 am.[30] Legislation exempted from the automatic interruption of business at 10 pm was largely to blame. The committee ran through various reforms which had been proposed but not implemented, from use of second reading committees to split committal of the Finance Bill between the floor of the House and committee and concluded that 'the House should come to accept timetabling of bills as a regular pattern' including for bills not supported by both parties.[31]

The committee also recommended experimental sittings on Wednesday and Thursday mornings to consider ten-minute rule motions, statutory instruments and proceedings

---

[24] Select Committee on Procedure, Sixth Report, Session 1966–67, Public Bill Procedure, etc, HC 539, Appendix 4, Ev 96–99. The memorandum was originally submitted to the 1964–65 Procedure Committee.

[25] ibid, para 22.

[26] My attention was drawn to the distinction between the efficiency and effectiveness of parliamentary procedures by Alexandra Kelso in her book *Parliamentary Reform at Westminster* (Manchester, Manchester University Press, 2009).

[27] Select Committee on Procedure, First Report, Session 1977–78, HC 588 (hereafter 1978 Procedure Committee) para 2.18; Select Committee on Procedure, Second Report, Session 1984–85, Public Bill Procedure, HC 49 (hereafter 1984–85 Public Bill Procedure) para 11; and Select Committee on the Modernisation of the House of Commons, First Report, Session 2005–06, The Legislative Process, HC 1097 (hereafter Modernisation Committee, Legislative Process) paras 58–60.

[28] See Modernisation Committee, Legislative Process (n 27) paras 53–55.

[29] See Louise Thompson, *Making British Law: Committees in Action* (Basingstoke, Palgrave, 2015).

[30] Select Committee on Procedure, First Report, Session 1966–67, The Times and Sittings of the House, HC 153, para 2.

[31] ibid, para 5.

on uncontroversial public bills 'to provide some immediate relief from late sittings'.[32] The proposal had been emphatically opposed by the then Speaker, Dr Horace King, who spent several minutes at the beginning of his oral evidence spelling out his view of why such sittings were impractical.[33] The committee divided eight to seven in favour of this proposal, with opponents including future Speaker Selwyn Lloyd.[34] It is unsurprising that when morning sittings (on Mondays and Wednesdays) were introduced they lasted for just a few months.[35]

A decade on, the same issues were again under consideration by a procedure committee. The incoming Labour government in 1974 brimmed with ideas to achieve early finish times, including interrupting main business at 8 pm, reducing debate on the Budget and on the Queen's Speech and moving more types of business into committee.[36] In its third report of 1974–75 the procedure committee rejected the suggestion from the Leader of the House that report stages could be moved into committee.[37] Significantly, time savings could only be achieved by taking contentious report stages off the floor of the House, denying the whole House the opportunity to debate and amend the legislation.[38] In other words, efficient legislating which risked being less effective.

The Labour landslide of 1997 can be compared in procedural terms, as it has so often been in political terms, to the victories of the radicals of 1906 and 1945. It established a new vehicle for driving the government's reform agenda forward and it included in its title one of New Labour's totemic words: modernisation.[39] The first report from the Modernisation Committee, as it became known, referred to the need to enhance Members' effectiveness, both in terms of their activity in Parliament and their constituency work. There was also reference to ensuring 'parents of young children [can] combine a representative role with family duty'.[40] Thursday sittings were brought forward to start at 11.30 am and have since advanced a further two hours. The Wednesday start time changed to 11.30 am in 2002. Earlier Tuesday sittings were agreed, reversed and then restored in 2012, following an important procedure committee report on sitting times. September sittings, also introduced at the instigation of the Modernisation Committee on the grounds that good government required more constant vigilance by Parliament, are also now an established part of the parliamentary landscape.[41]

Probably the most profound and enduring legacy of 'ModCom' was the 'programming' of all government legislative business. In its first report of 1997–98 and second report

---

[32] ibid, paras 12–15.
[33] ibid, Q60.
[34] ibid, xxxi.
[35] Walkland (n 12) 510.
[36] Select Committee on Procedure, Third Report, Session 1974–75, Late Sittings, HC 491, para 5.
[37] ibid, 1 and Q2.
[38] ibid, para 21.
[39] The rationale for the establishment of the Modernisation Committee is exemplified by the following exchange on the Business Question in the Commons in 2005: 'Mr McLoughlin: Can the Leader of the House tell us what the Modernisation Committee can do that the Procedure Committee could not do? Mr Hoon: I think that the short answer is probably "deliver".' HC Deb, 13 July 2005, c848.
[40] Select Committee on Modernisation of the House of Commons, First Report, Session 1997–98, The Legislative Process, HC 190 (hereafter Modernisation Committee, First Report 97–98) para 9.
[41] R Kelly, 'Sitting Hours', House of Commons Library Briefing Paper 6380, 5 November 2015.

of 1999–2000 it proposed the most far-reaching reform of the way in which time was allocated to legislation, in a package that would have shocked even the most ardent proponents of efficiency at the start of the century. The details are discussed by Jacqy Sharpe in chapter 13 on the history of the legislative process. The other enduring legacy of this committee was the establishment in 1999 of the parallel chamber known as 'the House sitting in Westminster Hall', or just Westminster Hall for short, into which most non-legislative backbench business was shifted, to clear space in the main Chamber, including the Wednesday morning sittings which had been briefly introduced by the 1991–92 Jopling Committee on sitting hours.

In 2012 the House narrowly decided to retain private Member's business on Fridays rather than to move it to Tuesday nights, a change proposed with the intention of improving attendance and making it easier for bill supporters to claim the closure and stop bills from being talked out.[42] The procedure committee rejected this reform in 2013 but made numerous recommendations to make the procedures applying to private Members' bills more transparent and less helpful to obstructionists. This debate again links the efficiency of the House's legislative procedures—whether, in the words of the procedure committee, the House is 'a mere sausage machine, churning out endless bills introduced, timetabled, amended and whipped through by the Executive'[43]—with the effectiveness of scrutiny and the implications of the balance struck between those concepts for the hours the House sits. As far back as 1927 a committee was appointed to improve procedure applying to private Members' bills. It attempted to find a distinction between controversial and uncontroversial bills, with a view to making it easier for backbenchers to pilot uncontentious measures onto the statute book. The committee's chairman dissented even from the modest recommendations agreed by his colleagues, illustrating the difficulties of squaring this particular circle, which comes round again and again in discussions of backbench-initiated legislation.[44] In the latest exchanges between the procedure committee and the government, inertia justified as protecting minority rights has kept private Members' bill procedure, in the words of the committee, 'resting on procedural practices and assumptions which would be familiar to Members of a century, if not two centuries, ago'. The committee went on to add: 'There are arguments to be made for tradition, but they are unconvincing when adherence to past rituals makes the House look ridiculous, puny and ineffectual.'[45]

QUESTIONS

Parliamentary questions can be an effective way of holding the executive to account but, from the executive's perspective, are an inefficient use of time because they involve discussion of issues without there being an opportunity to make decisions.

---

[42] ibid, s 2.3 (the debate took place on 11 July 2012).

[43] Procedure Committee, Second Report, Session 2013–14, private Members' Bills, HC 188, summary.

[44] Select Committee on Procedure (Unofficial Members' Business), Report, Session 1927, HC 102, esp para 12. For the most recent iteration see Procedure Committee, Third Report, Session 2015–16, private Members' Bills, HC 684.

[45] Select Committee on Procedure, Second Report, 2016–17, HC 684, private Members' Bills: Observations on the Government Response, para 37.

Committees on procedure have largely driven reform of procedure on questions since 1945. However, the issues relating to questions have changed during the period. At first the main problem related to the imbalance between the number of oral questions being tabled and the time available to answer them. The 1945 procedure committee, which acknowledged the problem but made no recommendations to address it, appealed to Members to be sparing in their use of questions. It asserted that 'Questions, especially Oral Questions, should only be put down when other and less formal methods have failed to produce a satisfactory result, or when some information or action is urgently desired' and suggested that, at the start of each session, the Speaker should exhort Members to act with discretion in tabling questions.[46] It need hardly be said that the expression of this sentiment proved utterly ineffective.

A succession of procedure committees in the 1950s, 1960s and 1970s dealt with the same problem and gradually introduced the framework for the current system of oral questions, whereby departments answer on a rota and Members may only table one question for answer by each department. One matter of particular concern was how to order the questions submitted for oral answer, particularly when questions low down on the list were likely not to be reached and would instead receive a written answer. Questions were not processed chronologically. All questions tabled before 4 pm on the first day on which questions for a particular department could be tabled were reordered by the printer, who tipped out the relevant 'pouches' sent over by the Table Office and drew out questions, apparently at random. In 1975 a more systematic paper shuffle was introduced, which Members could observe if they wished.[47] The 1975–76 sessional committee on procedure conducted an inquiry into the method of ordering oral questions and considered the practicalities of using a tombola drum to mix up question papers, or a system for drawing counters from a box, akin to an FA Cup draw. Out of this emerged the present-day computerised shuffle.

Fixed times at which the Prime Minister would answer oral questions—on Tuesdays and Thursdays at 3.15 pm—was a recommendation of the 1959 procedure committee, implemented in 1961.[48] Procedure committees have regularly reviewed the operation of Prime Minister's Questions. In 1972 a committee on parliamentary questions deplored the increasing use of questions which gave no indication of the subject of a Member's supplementary, for example a question on when the Prime Minister would visit a specific constituency, as a 'surrender to the tendency to trivialise' the question time.[49] James Callaghan later accepted a procedure committee recommendation not to transfer questions on specific subjects to other ministers, but the practice of tabling questions which can enable a supplementary question on any subject to be asked has continued and, indeed, in 2007 time for completely open 'topical' questions to the main departments was introduced.[50] In 1997 incoming Prime Minister Tony Blair amalgamated the two Prime Minister's Question times

[46] Select Committee on Procedure, Second Report, 1945–46, HC 58 (hereafter 1945 Committee, Second Report) paragraph 3.

[47] Select Committee on Procedure (Sessional Committee), First Report, 1975–76, The Procedure for Establishing the Order of Oral Questions, HC 618, para 5.

[48] 1959 Procedure Committee (n 3) para 42 and Walkland (n 12) 487.

[49] Select Committee on Parliamentary Questions, Report, Session 1971–72, HC 393 (hereafter 1972 Questions Committee) para 23.

[50] M Sandford, 'Parliamentary Questions: Recent Issues', House of Commons Library Briefing Paper 4148, 6 May 2015.

into one 30-minute slot on Wednesdays. The procedure committee subsequently noted that this idea had been raised in evidence it had received, although it had not been recommended by the committee.[51] The procedure committee has been successful in reducing the notice period for questions to the Prime Minister and other ministers, ensuring that oral questions are now more topical than was possible before.[52]

The rules on the content of questions have developed piecemeal over time, mostly as a result of rulings from the Chair.[53] In 1972 a procedure committee came close to recommending the abolition of such rules as 'an unnecessary restriction of the freedom of a Member', with the Chairman of the committee casting his vote against the proposition.[54] The rules of order were again considered and largely upheld in 1991.[55] Since then the *sub judice* rule, applying to questions and other forms of proceedings, has been subject to thorough review.[56] However, procedure committees have increasingly focused on the process for tabling questions rather than the rules relating to them. In 1976 the sessional committee on procedure sought to prohibit Members' staff from entering the Table Office and to stop Members handing in batches of oral questions by requiring each question to be handed in by the Member wishing to table it, or sent (with a signature) in the post.[57] Neither proposal was in tune with changes in Members' working practices but such detailed matters were again to the fore in 2002 when the procedure committee agreed to the introduction of the electronic tabling of questions.[58] So considerable has been the contribution made by procedure committees, over some 60 years, to determining procedure and practice relating to questions it is now expected that even minor changes require the procedure committee's approval.

The committee's interest has now moved on again, to the monitoring of the quality of written answers. Members can now appeal to the committee to intervene with a minister where a question has not been answered, either fully or in part.[59] This is a new and potentially significant way of holding the government to account which has the potential to strengthen the effectiveness of parliamentary questions.

FINANCIAL PROCEDURE

Reform of financial procedure, often discussed by procedure committees, especially in the twenty-five years from 1945, can be dealt with succinctly. Elsewhere in this volume Colin Lee has described how reform of supply procedure in the nineteenth century had

---

[51] Procedure Committee, Third Report, Session 2001–02, Parliamentary Questions, HC 622 (hereafter 2002 Questions Report) para 54.

[52] ibid.

[53] For example, in relation to the prohibition on questions which seek an interpretation of the law, see HC Deb, 5 July 1955, cc 960–64.

[54] 1972 Questions Committee (n 49) xxi.

[55] Select Committee on Procedure, Third Report, Session 1990–91, Parliamentary Questions, HC 178.

[56] For example, Procedure Committee, First Report, Session 2004–05, The Sub Judice Rule of the House of Commons, HC 125.

[57] Select Committee on Procedure (Sessional Committee), Third Report, Session 1975–76, HC 719.

[58] 2002 Questions Report (n 51).

[59] Procedure Committee, Seventh Report, Session 2014–15, Matters for the Procedure Committee in the 2015 Parliament, HC 1121, paras 4–10.

to face up to the House's increasing inability or unwillingness to use the elaborate tools at its disposal to control the supply of funds to the executive. Opportunities to debate supply were increasingly used for general debates on topical or specialist matters with little reference to the estimate formally under consideration (or to the provisions of a consolidated fund bill). Ryle has described how this system gradually evolved into the modern system of Opposition Days, now entirely divorced from consideration of the estimates.[60] Apparently dramatic procedural innovations, such as a procedure committee recommendation in 1966 to abolish the use of a Committee of the whole House to consider supply,[61] were in fact belated recognition that long-established forms of supply procedure bore little relation to the realities of mid-twentieth-century politics. 'Little short of farcical' was the Clerk Assistant's view in 1966 of the procedural devices necessary for Opposition Day debates to be linked to supply;[62] a welcome reduction in 'mumbo-jumbo' was another reaction.[63]

In 1982 responsibility for choosing the subjects for debate when the estimates were under consideration was transferred to the Liaison Committee, a move described by that Committee three years later as 'a significant shift in the balance between Parliament and the Executive'.[64] 'For the first time in at least half a century', said the Committee, 'the House is carrying out its historic function of examining and debating details of government expenditure on a systematic basis.'[65] If this was an accurate reflection of the vitality of financial scrutiny in the mid-1980s, it certainly did not reflect the situation in the 1990s and beyond. The formal processes continue to be obscure and little understood; debates on estimates tend to focus on questions of policy with references to spending which are superficial at best, inspiring the procedure committee to open another inquiry into the subject in 2016. The evidence received did not appear to confirm the optimistic views expressed in the 1980s.

The problem for financial scrutiny is that government has long moved on from annual budgeting to setting expenditure plans over longer timescales. As Michael Ryle put it in 1979:

> [T]he House has found it less easy to develop methods of matching the vital political decisions of Ministers regarding the balance of expenditures within an agreed over-all total (where, in other words, to cut or where to increase) with equally important occasions for Parliamentary debate of these same political discussions.[66]

More than thirty-five years later the same problem is evident. The government's periodic spending reviews, which are of far more significance than the annual estimates, are simply announced in the form of an oral statement, followed by a couple of hours of questioning. There is no specific parliamentary approval for such plans, no line-by-line scrutiny, no opportunity to move amendments. Seeking the chimera of effective scrutiny of the estimates, parliamentary reformers have so far failed to get to grips with finding ways of scrutinising the government's medium-term financial plans. The solution to this apparently

---

[60] *Walkland* (n 12) 385–86 and 398–402.
[61] Select Committee on Procedure, Report, Session 1965–66, HC 122, paragraph 6.
[62] Select Committee on Procedure, Fourth Report, Session 1964–65, HC 303 (hereafter 1964–65 Fourth Report) Q63.
[63] Walkland (n 12) 411.
[64] Liaison Committee, The Select Committee System, First Report, Session 1984–85, HC 363, para 2.
[65] ibid, para 13.
[66] Walkland (n 12) 423.

irreversible abdication of responsibility by the House, put forward by outside reformers (notably the Study of Parliament Group) has been the revivification of the select committee system.

THE DEVELOPMENT OF SCRUTINY

'Scrutiny' was a term largely unknown to political science before the 1960s. Until the late 1950s select committees were rarely a focus of the attention of procedure committees. When changes were mooted these concerned the use of committees to strengthen financial scrutiny, in recognition of the increasing complexity of government expenditure and the obvious defects of the Committee of Supply as a tool for controlling the estimates. Thus the 1906 procedure committee made no reference to select committees. The report of the 1932 committee referred to the role of select committees only in relation to financial scrutiny, recommending closer working between the Estimates Committee and the Committee of Public Accounts to achieve better control by the House over public spending.[67] The committee also recommended that the Estimates Committee should be allowed to consider matters of policy, apparently reflecting evidence from the Committee's chairman, Sir Vivian Henderson, that it already did so.[68] The committee also mentioned proposals for the House's control over 'expenditure and action, if not the policy, of the Departments' to be devolved to 'numerous small Standing Committees' but did not comment on the merits of the proposal.[69]

In its work, this procedure committee faithfully reflected the orthodoxy of the time that the Commons exerted control over the government using various mechanisms, all of which were operated on the floor of the House. Delegation to committees was relatively limited and regarded by some as constitutionally improper. The distinction between policy—solely the preserve of the Chamber—and expenditure and administration—detailed, technical matters which committees could usefully examine—was zealously maintained for decades, despite the difficulties in practice of separating them.

Select committees played no part in the Labour Party's procedural reforms of 1945 and the attempt by Sir Gilbert Campion (then Clerk of the House) to persuade that year's procedure committee to rationalise procedure upheld the orthodox position on the role of such committees. He delineated several means by which the House controlled policy, all of which involved Chamber proceedings. As with the 1932 committee, his only contribution to the reform of select committees was to call for the Estimates Committee and the Committee of Public Accounts to be strengthened.[70]

Things began to change in the 1950s. A select committee on nationalised industries was established in 1951, due to Conservative concerns with the accountability of nationalised bodies. There was no suggestion that this would or could control nationalised industries and one commentator said its main success was to improve public knowledge of those industries.[71] However, it laid some of the foundations for reforms to come.[72] Then came a

---

[67] 1932 Committee (n 17) paras 9–10.
[68] ibid, para 10 and QQ53–54.
[69] ibid, para 7(a).
[70] 1945 Committee, Second Report (n 46) Appendix, xxviii.
[71] Walkland (n 12) 453.
[72] See, for example, D Coombes, *The Member of Parliament and the Administration: The Case of the Select Committee on the Nationalized Industries* (London, Allen & Unwin, 1966).

proposal in 1958 from the Clerk of the House, Sir Edward Fellowes, for the establishment of a joint committee on colonial affairs and a defence committee as well as ad hoc committees on specific estimates.[73] Strikingly, the committee justified its rejection of the idea in terms of not wishing for committees to take executive power over areas of government activity.[74]

Thinking on this subject continued to develop. In 1964, two young and radical House of Commons clerks (David Pring and Kenneth Bradshaw) pseudonymously published a 'Pelican Special' daringly entitled *What's Wrong with Parliament?*,[75] which again advanced the increasingly fashionable technocratic argument that the House's deficit in expertise by which to understand and hold government to account could best be remedied through the establishment of specialist committees. In 1964–65 the procedure committee, influenced by a memorandum from the Study of Parliament Group, presented by the now-retired Fellowes, recommended the replacement of the Estimates Committee with an Expenditure Committee with a broader remit and power to appoint more specialised sub-committees.[76] This recommendation was largely repeated by the procedure committee appointed in 1968–69 before being accepted by the incoming Conservative government in 1970.[77] However, during this period the Labour government introduced six subject committees at the instigation of Richard Crossman, a reforming Leader of the House, several of which continued after 1970.[78] Committees on agriculture, education and science and overseas aid shadowed departments; those on science and technology, race relations and Scottish Affairs had remits that cut across Whitehall fiefdoms. The leap had been made from seeing committees as a means of controlling government activity to scrutiny of that activity, a subtle but far-reaching change which opened the way later in the 1970s for the procedure committee to recommend the establishment of scrutiny committees for each government department and the subsequent implementation of that recommendation by the incoming Conservative government in 1979.[79]

Although select committees continue to innovate, for example by using social media to ask the public for questions to put to ministers in oral hearings, their formal procedures, as discussed by Mark Hutton in chapter 14, have changed little since the modern system was established in 1979. This may have to change as committees seek to acquire, develop and publish videos, infographics and other material that does not fit the conventional evidence-and-report format.

DIVISIONS

Following a change in practice in 1906 aimed at permitting Members who had not been present in the Chamber when a question was put to take part in divisions, voting took around ten minutes to complete. More time was needed immediately after general elections when the clerks recording Members' names were unfamiliar with some of the people

---

[73] Walkland (n 12) 459.
[74] ibid, 459 and 1959 Procedure Committee (n 3) para 47.
[75] A Hill and A Whichelow, *What's Wrong with Parliament?* (Harmondsworth, Penguin, 1964).
[76] Walkland (n 12) 463.
[77] Select Committees of the House of Commons, Cmnd 4507, October 1970.
[78] ibid.
[79] 1978 Procedure Committee (n 27) ch 5.

voting. This had the potential to inconvenience Members, especially when several divisions took place consecutively. By 1945 requiring Members to vote by queuing to be ticked off by clerks perched on high stools looked distinctly old fashioned, particularly to the influx of new Members at that year's election.

The 1945 procedure committee decided to look at schemes for reducing the time spent on divisions and invited evidence from Public Bill Office Clerks. They suggested that, in the absence of a designated seat in the Chamber for each Member, only a mechanical means of counting votes would save time. Their suggestion, based on a scheme in operation at Manchester City Council, was to install two paper strips along the length of each side of each division lobby, divided into panels which would accommodate name plates and voting buttons for five Members. During divisions Members would find their names, sign the paper and press their button to vote. However, the Public Bill Office memorandum to the Committee was hardly encouraging. Mechanical systems could break down, they warned, and 'lead to grave confusion'; 'no system yet devised can entirely eliminate the possibility of abuse by practical joking or, however unlikely, by deliberate interference'; and any changes from a system which had worked well since 1836 'must start surrounded by many imponderable factors'.[80] The scheme failed to convince the committee, with Members expressing concern about the prospect of the paper strips being torn down by 'irate and jostling' Members.[81] Perhaps deliberately, the Clerks had not thought through the practicalities and were content to emphasise how much of a gamble a new system might be. It was also clear that reform should have been discussed when the House was deciding on the reconstruction of the Chamber, a ship which by this time had sailed.[82]

Divisions were discussed again in 1959, when international examples of push-button voting were considered and rejected because Members did not have their own dedicated seats in the Chamber.[83] In 1966 the Ministry of Public Building and Works put forward a new scheme for mechanical voting, the most novel aspect of which was remote 'voting stations' to enable Members on the Committee Corridor or at functions to vote without walking to the lobbies.[84] Annunciators in the form of 'electro-mechanical alpha-numeric flap' indicators, then being introduced at railway stations, would show the results.[85] Although Members could take reassurance that 'we have got nothing as complex as a computer here',[86] the Committee remained unswayed. There would be no time savings, Members voting remotely might not understand what they were voting on, and the cost—£10,000 for a year-long feasibility study and £70,000 to introduce the new system—seemed disproportionate given the modest benefits likely to arise from change.

Thirty years on, divisions were again under scrutiny because of the increased time taken up by voting due to the large influx of new Members and the large numerical disparity between government and opposition Members. A third division desk was quickly installed

---

[80] 1945 Committee, Second Report (n 46) Ev, 50–52.
[81] ibid, Q1725.
[82] ibid, Q1664.
[83] 1959 Procedure Committee (n 3) para 36.
[84] Select Committee on Procedure, Third Report, Session 1966–67, HC 283.
[85] ibid, Memorandum by the Ministry of Public Building and Works, Appendix 1, para 16.
[86] ibid, Q67.

in each lobby, a reform that had been tried for a few years from 1906.[87] Some Members considered that the introduction of electronic voting, in some form, was obviously preferable to a manual system little changed from the 1830s. Others expressed concern that electronic voting from Members' offices or other locations (which would be the only feasible way of saving time) would make it harder to seek out ministers and shadow spokespersons and engage in the informal networking which is at the heart of much parliamentary business. The Modernisation Committee canvassed views and found that 'no one alternative to the present system commands any great support and all of them are regarded as unacceptable by between 46 and 65 per cent of Members who replied'.[88] Detailed recommendations to enable Members to register abstentions and to modernise the method by which Division Clerks marked off names went unimplemented.[89] In the event, the introduction in 2015 of electronic tablets for recording names was necessitated by another procedural reform driven by an incoming government, the requirement to be able to calculate and record both UK-wide and English and/or English and Welsh majorities in certain divisions. Another reform, provision from 2000 for the deferral of certain divisions due to take place after the moment of interruption until lunchtime on the following Wednesday, was also a by-product of other objectives, in this case a wish to reduce the amount of business after that time for which Members would be required to stay in the House.

CONCLUSION

Anyone prepared to cast an eye over reports by committees on Commons procedure dating back for more than a century could be forgiven for concluding that few themes of note spanned the period. Each report was a product of its time and of its authors. Matters of pressing concern to one group of MPs in one year can seem quaint or esoteric when examined years later. However, standing back from the morass of procedural detail it is possible to draw five broad conclusions about the role of committees in procedural reform since the 1880s.

Firstly, most procedural reform has been instigated by the government of the day, irrespective of whether or not a procedure committee has called for change or been invited to scrutinise government proposals. Thus, Balfour's reforms of sitting times and of the allocation of time in the House proceeded without being examined in committee. The 1906 procedure committee was instigated by the incoming Liberal government to develop Balfour's system on the basis of proposals made to the committee's chairman but not more widely disseminated. The 1945 Labour government also used a procedure committee to examine and legitimate its proposals for procedural reform, which were aimed at speeding up the passage of legislation. The introduction of specialist select committees to scrutinise government in the mid-1960s was spearheaded by the Leader of the House, building on ideas discussed but not endorsed by procedure committees. Changes in sitting hours, legislative

---

[87] 1945 Committee, Second Report (n 46) Ev, 51.

[88] Select Committee on the Modernisation of the House of Commons, Sixth Report, Session 1997–98, Voting Methods, HC 779, para 2.

[89] ibid, paras 3–4.

procedure and other matters after 1997 arose from government proposals put to the Select Committee on the Modernisation of the Commons, which was chaired by the Leader of the House.

However, the routine of establishing procedure committees in most sessions since the late 1950s, and more recently as committees set up under standing order with members nominated for the duration of a Parliament, has led to a growing expectation that significant procedural change will be discussed in committee before implementation. It is scarcely conceivable that the changes to the organisation of the House promoted in the late nineteenth century by Balfour would not be scrutinised in committee if something similar were proposed today. For example, in 2015 the incoming Conservative administration attempted to introduce novel and complex procedures for 'English votes for English laws' without committee scrutiny but ended up having to delay implementation, enabling the procedure committee to report.[90]

There have been three significant exceptions to the general rule of government primacy in this field. In relation to parliamentary questions, repeated, detailed scrutiny by successive procedure committees since the mid-1950s has effectively established that the procedure committee has ownership over the detailed rules and practices applying to this aspect of parliamentary life.[91] Nevertheless, in 1997 the government was able to change the format of Prime Minister's Questions without reference to the committee (or even a decision of the House).

Secondly, the modern select committee system is based on the recommendations of a 1978 procedure committee report, which also made far-reaching proposals for the scrutiny of legislation, many of which were later implemented or remain moot. Parliament's scrutiny function was legitimated by that report, which tackled the argument, put forward by ministers, that the Commons' main purpose was to get through the work demanded of it by the government and asserted instead that growing executive power was 'inimical to the proper working of our parliamentary democracy'.[92] Nevertheless, the committee was set up by the government, implementing a Queen's Speech commitment.[93] Its appointment reflected the growing sense of crisis in 1970s Britain that both government and Parliament were unequal to the task of managing the nation's problems.[94] Its recommendations were conservative—'changes in practice of an evolutionary kind'[95]—and built on proposals made by the Study of Parliament Group a decade before.

By far the most striking, perhaps unique, example of backbench assertiveness was the 2009 Wright Committee on reform of the House. This was every inch a backbench initiative, though supported by a Prime Minister panicked by the backwash of the expenses scandal, bringing together reform-minded MPs from all parties including, crucially, Labour

---

[90] Procedure Committee, First Report, Session 2015–16, English Votes for English Laws Standing Orders: Interim Report, HC 410.

[91] For example, Procedure Committee, Third Report, Session 2012–13, E-Tabling of Written Questions, HC 775.

[92] 1978 Procedure Committee (n 27) para 1.5.

[93] CJ (1975–76) 371 and ibid, para 1.1.

[94] As if to illustrate this point, in the week in which the committee was established the Commons sat past 2 am each day except Friday, when it sat past 6 pm, in order to debate legislation on industrial relations, economic development and policing.

[95] 1978 Procedure Committee (n 27) para 1.6.

MPs who were planning to retire or felt they had no prospect of achieving ministerial office. Amongst the far-reaching reforms it pioneered were the election by secret ballot of the whole House of select committee chairs and the establishment of a committee of backbenchers to allocate business on thirty-five days set aside for them to use.[96] For the first time in over a century executive dominance of the House was checked. Undoubtedly a significant development in the relationship between the House and the government, the committee was unable to secure the implementation of an even more dramatic change, the appointment of a House business committee to determine the time allocated for government business.

The Wright Committee stands out because of the boldness of its recommendations, intended to help restore the House's tarnished reputation following the Members' expenses scandal. For the most part procedure committees were timid, eschewing ambitious programmes of reform in favour of tinkering with existing rules and practices. The committees set up in 1931–32 best exemplify this tendency. Appointed in response to 'a large body of criticism of Parliament, both by Members and by representative citizens',[97] they heard evidence from a broad range of perspectives, some wishing to restore Parliament's pre-eminence in the early 1800s, others wanting the Commons to accept that its role was to legitimate decisions taken by the government without undue fuss or delay. Here was the opportunity for a committee to acknowledge that the rapid development of the modern state was rendering obsolescent earlier notions of parliamentary control of the executive and to do something about it. However, the committee ducked the challenge, insisting that its terms of reference precluded consideration of constitutional matters.[98]

What this demonstrates is that rarely has there been a coherent drive for procedural reform in the Commons other than, occasionally, from the government. As a result procedure committees have tended to hold the ring between proponents and opponents of change rather than to develop their own agenda.

A third, related, conclusion is that procedure committees have approached reform piecemeal, rarely stepping back to ask what the House and its Members should be seeking to achieve and how the forms of parliamentary activity could achieve such aims. One consequence of this was the persistence of procedures which had long outlasted their usefulness. Sustained efforts to make outdated procedures for financial control relevant to the concerns and interests of Members are a case in point. With a little more vision tools could have been created for scrutinising the government's medium-term expenditure plans, reflecting the shift within government away from managing finances annually. Another consequence was lack of coherence between different aspects of reform. Proposals for reforming procedure on divisions in the 1940s foundered because they came too late to influence plans to rebuild the Chamber and division lobbies after they had been bombed. Changes to sitting hours have aimed to reduce the frequency of late sittings without properly addressing the knock-on effects, particularly in relation to attendance later in the week, the timing of committee meetings and the effect of different sitting hours on the House's working culture.

---

[96] Standing Order No 14(4). The time may be divided between the Chamber and Westminster Hall, with a minimum of 27 days provided in the Chamber.

[97] 1932 Committee (n 17) para 2.

[98] ibid, para 4.

On occasions when comprehensive schemes were put to procedure committees, they generally received short shrift.[99]

Particularly striking to the modern eye is the insular character of procedure committee deliberations, especially before the late 1950s. In the earlier period committees rarely heard evidence from anyone other than the Speaker, the Clerk of the House and perhaps one or two senior Members. This provides another explanation for the cautious approach such committees tended to take to procedural reform. Although the 1931 procedure committee heard from numerous witnesses, almost all were Members of Parliament. One exception was the academic Ramsay Muir, but he was invited on the basis that he had sat briefly in the House as Liberal MP for Rochdale.

Fresh ground was broken in 1965 when oral evidence was heard from a group of academics, all members of the newly founded Study of Parliament Group, who argued in favour of the introduction of subject specialist committees to scrutinise government departments.[100] It became common from the 1960s onwards to distribute surveys to all Members on issues of general interest, such as sitting hours, and, later, to hear oral evidence from newer Members as well as those with long experience. Nevertheless, recommendations for entirely new procedures, or radical departures from existing practice, have been exceptional. The introduction of debates in Westminster Hall, as a parallel debating arena to the main Chamber, is a rare example of innovation based on overseas, in this case Australian, practice.[101]

The fifth broad theme has been referred to throughout this chapter and throughout this book: the contest between the efficiency and effectiveness of the procedures of the Commons. Nowhere was this better demonstrated than in the evidence given to the procedure committee in 1985. One minister spoke of the importance of evidence-taking in the legislative process and how it had demonstrated defects in a bill which required urgent remedial action, which otherwise would not have happened: another said he was 'agnostic about the special procedure in that it does not seem to save very much time'.[102] For much of the period discussed in this chapter efficiency was the order of the day. Parliamentary procedures were seen as outmoded and too readily capable of being used by minorities intent on obstructing the ambitions of elected governments, especially in respect of legislating. However, by the 1960s the tide turned and it now runs strongly in the direction of procedures that are more effective at holding the government to account. This reflected a little-articulated change in the prevailing consensus about what the House of Commons was for, from controlling the executive to overseeing its activities. This can be observed in the renaissance of select committees, the creation of evidence-taking public bill committees, and the growth of parliamentary questions. Calls for better engagement with the public, in response to lower turnouts in general elections and perceived voter apathy, have intensified demands for Parliament to be more assertive in its relationship with the executive and to throw more light on the workings of the Whitehall machine.

---

[99] For example, 1932 Committee (n 17) esp para 7; Select Committee on Procedure, Third Report, Session 1945–46, HC 189, Appendix, xi–xlix; and 1959 Procedure Committee (n 3) Ev, 1–19 (General Memorandum on Procedure Reform from Sir Edward Fellowes, Clerk of the House).

[100] 1964–65 Fourth Committee, QQ 212–83. The academics included Peter Bromhead, a founding member of the Study of Parliament Group, who had submitted a memorandum to the 1959 Procedure Committee (n 3) although it was not printed.

[101] Modernisation Committee, First Report 97–98 (n 27) paras 90–94.

[102] 1984–85 Public Bill Procedure (n 27) para 12.

However, the recent inroads into executive dominance of Parliament, whether by virtue of the work of the Backbench Business Committee, the election of select committee chairs, the provision of additional time for backbench debates in Westminster Hall, or other recent reforms, have been modest when compared with the position in May's era. It could be countered that this is an inevitability. A modern, democratic state of the size and complexity of the United Kingdom surely requires a parliamentary system capable of delivering stable government which can put in place the legislation necessary to organise a range of socially desirable services, such as health and education, and the financial and regulatory frameworks which support them. However, in reviewing discussion in committees of procedural reform since 1900 it is hard to escape the conclusion that, for much of the period, politicians missed opportunities to make the significant reforms necessary to retain parliamentary influence over government spending and policy. The Commons allowed itself to become a mere sausage machine for government initiatives by focusing on procedural minutiae and failing to see the bigger picture. There can be no better example of this than the procedure committees of 1931–32 which were presented with the evidence that Victorian procedure was no longer capable of controlling the activities of the modern-day state but were not up to the task of producing a credible response. Ironically, reforming Leaders of the House such as Richard Crossman, Norman St John-Stevas and Robin Cook led the way on reforming parliamentary procedure, recognising from within government that the weakness of the legislature weakened the whole political system.

The challenge now, and in the decades to come, is for the Commons to be more assertive in deciding its own procedures; to be braver in ditching procedures whose day has passed and in trying new things; to look outside of Westminster at alternative ways of debating and scrutinising; and to be more nimble at adjusting rules and procedures to suit new political developments. All of this requires leadership, preferably from the backbenches: procedural innovation should not have to rely on the appointment from time to time of a Leader of the House with a penchant for reform. The omens are good, given the changes pioneered by the Wright committee, innovation by select committees, and other factors, such as the increasing use of ministerial statements and urgent questions as tools of scrutiny, but there is much more that could be achieved.

13

Finding Time

Legislative Procedure since May

JACQY SHARPE AND PAUL EVANS

INTRODUCTION

WE HAVE SEEN elsewhere the attempts (not always successful) of Thomas Erskine May to rationalise the processes by which the House of Commons passed legislation.[1] As Mark Egan shows in chapter 12, the search for ever-greater 'efficiency' in the procedures of the House, particularly in the making of legislation, has been a concern of successive governments. This chapter describes some of the substantive changes which were made between 1871 and 2016, many of which are noted in the prefaces to the relevant editions of the *Treatise* from the seventh edition (1873) to the twenty-fourth edition (2011).[2] The main changes fall into seven categories: the method of introducing bills; the treatment of private Members' bills;[3] taking the committee stage of most bills off the floor of the House; enabling legislative committees to take evidence as well as undertake line-by-line consideration of bills; carry-over of bills; programming of government bills; and restricting the powers of the Lords in relation to legislation introduced in the Commons. In addition, many government bills are now published in draft and considered by committees before being formally introduced and the process of legislating has become more transparent and open.

In 1844, when the first edition of May was published, there were few Standing Orders and, as May noted, there was 'no authorised collection of the standing orders, except in relation to private bills'.[4] By 2015, the number of Standing Orders had risen to 204, including over sixty relating directly to legislation.[5] In October 2015 a further fifteen Standing Orders were added to deal exclusively with 'English votes for English laws'.[6] These, together with

---

[1] Chapter 9.

[2] *The History of the Standing Orders of the House of Commons relating to Public Business, 1833–1935*, by Sir Edward Fellowes, Clerk of the House from 1954 to 1961, edited by Simon Patrick (revised 2005–06) provides a historical context for the evolution of the Standing Orders relating to legislation. See also chapter 12.

[3] Bills introduced by individual Members who are not members of the government.

[4] May, *Treatise*, 1971 facsimile of the first edition (Irish University Press, Shannon) 132.

[5] See <www.publications.parliament.uk/pa/cm201516/cmstords/0002/toc.htm>.

[6] See the First Report from the Procedure Committee (Commons) of Session 2015–16, English Votes for English Laws Standing Orders: Interim Report, HC 410; Third Report of Session 2015–16, English Votes for English Laws Standing Orders: Report of the Committee's Technical Evaluation, HC 189; Fifth Report of Session 2014–15 from

consequential amendments, amounted to some thirty extra pages (or around 16 per cent of the pre-existing total). A whole new stage of the legislative process (Legislative Grand Committees) was introduced by these to try and answer the famous 'West Lothian question', that is how to reconcile the existence of legislatures in Northern Ireland, Scotland and Wales with extensive domestic law-making powers with the absence of a separate legislature for England. This change, it is worth noting, was the first deliberately to increase the number of stages through which a bill is required to pass since May began the process of simplification.

Procedurally, primary legislation (the making of Acts of Parliament) has been the central concern of the House. But since time immemorial legislation has been made by ordinance, rule, regulation, order and Order in Council. The first edition of the *Treatise* makes no reference to delegated legislation. By the time of the last edition in his lifetime (the ninth, of 1883) May had taken notice of the

> [n]umerous administrative orders and regulations relating to prisons, education, charities, endowed schools, and other matters, presented to both houses, in pursuance of Acts of Parliament[7]

As Cecil Carr commented in 1921, however: 'The direct legislation of Parliament cannot be treated as something separate and self-contained; the statute book is not only incomplete but even misleading unless it be read with the delegated legislation which amplifies and amends it.'[8] Delegated legislation is considered in the second part of this chapter.

STIRRINGS OF REFORM

When May began his study of procedure, '[t]he passage of a bill was a long and complicated process which in 1832 had altered little from the procedure followed in the Parliaments of Elizabeth I'.[9] A minimum of four questions, and a maximum of over twelve questions, had to be put before a bill could go forward for its second reading. At least five questions were put at second reading with further questions being put if an amendment was moved or the debate on second reading was adjourned. At committee stage, a minimum of nine questions, in addition to any questions on individual amendments and clauses, was required. A bill which had not been amended in committee could go through the report stage with only three questions; a bill which had been amended required at least eight questions, as well as one for each amendment proposed. At least six questions had to be put on third reading.[10]

Over the next fifty years procedures were simplified to enable consideration of a bill to proceed automatically from the second reading stage to its third reading, freed, as far

the Public Administration and Constitutional Affairs Committee, The Future of the Union, Part One: English Votes for English Laws, HC 523; Michael Kenny and Daniel Gover, 'Finding the Good in EVEL: An Evaluation of English Votes for English Laws', Constitution Unit, University College London, November 2016; Sixth Report of Session 2015–16 from the Constitution Committee, English Votes for English Laws, HL Paper 61; and the government's Technical Review of the Standing Orders Related to English Votes for English Laws and the Procedures they Introduced, CM9430, March 2017.

[7] *Treatise*, 9th edn (London, Butterworths, 1883) 630.
[8] Cecil T Carr, *Delegated Legislation* (Cambridge, Cambridge University Press, 1921) 6.
[9] *The History of the Standing Orders* (n 2) 4.
[10] ibid, 4–5.

as possible, from these numerous opportunities for delay.[11] In 1848, the Committee on Public Business made several recommendations to reduce the number of opportunities for debates on bills.[12] At the end of the debate on the Committee's report, the House agreed that for any bill presented in pursuance of an order of the House or brought from the Lords, 'the Questions "That this Bill be now read a first time", and "That this Bill be printed", shall be decided without Amendment or Debate'. It also agreed that, where a bill had been partly considered in committee and the House had been ordered to sit again on a particular day, when the order for committee was read, the Speaker would leave the Chair without putting any question and the House would resolve itself into the committee.[13] The report of a later Committee[14] included a recommendation, subsequently made a Standing Order,[15] that Lords Amendments to public bills should be appointed to be considered on a future day unless the House ordered them to be considered forthwith. Two years later, following the recommendation of a Standing Orders Revision Committee,[16] the House agreed not to permit any amendments, other than verbal amendments, to be made on third reading of a bill.[17] Few verbal amendments have been moved on third reading since that Standing Order was made, the most recent being to the long title of the Control of Smoke Pollution Bill in 1988.[18]

In 1882, four years before May's retirement rapidly followed by his death, the House agreed to a further limitation on debate on bills:

> That when the Order of the Day for the Consideration of a Bill, as amended, in the Committee of the whole House, has been read, the House do proceed to consider the same without Question put, unless the Member in charge thereof shall desire to postpone its consideration or a Motion shall be made to re-commit the Bill.[19]

And by 1919 the House had agreed

> [t]hat, if on an amendment to the Question that the Bill be now read a second time or the third time it is decided that the word 'now' or any words proposed to be left out stand part of the Question, Mr Speaker shall forthwith declare the Question to be read a second or the third time as the case may be.[20]

Following the decision to commit most bills to standing committee (see below), the Standing Orders were amended in 1901 to provide that all bills reported from standing committee be considered on report, instead of only those bills which had been amended in the committee.[21]

In 1871 most public bills, whether proposed by the government or by individual Members, were introduced on a motion for leave to bring in a bill. Following the introduction of

---

[11] See preface to the *Treatise*, 10th edn.
[12] House of Commons Paper 644, Session 1847–48.
[13] Commons Journal (hereinafter CJ) (104) 22.
[14] Despatch of Public Business of House of Commons, House of Commons Paper 212, Session 1854.
[15] CJ (109) 285, 413.
[16] House of Commons Paper 856, Session 1852–53.
[17] CJ (111) 365; HC Deb (1856) 143, c 1103–5.
[18] CJ (245) 297; HC Deb (1989) 150, cc 1158–1207. The verbal amendment was subsequently withdrawn; the title was later amended in the Lords.
[19] CJ (137) 516; HC Deb (1882) 25, cc 57–62.
[20] CJ (174) 38.
[21] CJ (156) 118.

the 12 o'clock rule, which prevented opposed business from being taken after midnight,[22] objections to motions to bring in bills at the moment of interruption increased. In order to counter this practice, the House agreed in 1888 '[t]hat on Tuesdays and Fridays and, if set down by the Government, on Mondays and Thursdays, Motions for leave to bring in Bills ... may be set down for consideration at the commencement of Public Business' and that if the Motions were opposed, the Speaker, after permitting a brief explanatory statement from the Member who moved and the Member who opposed any such Motion, should put the Question forthwith'.[23] This has become time-hallowed as the ten-minute rule, and ten-minute rule bills are still a regular feature of the House of Commons week. If, however, a Member is granted leave, *Today in Parliament* will almost certainly solemnly report that 'the bill has no chance of becoming law'. After the First World War the practice of introducing major government bills on motion was discontinued.

In 1902, the Standing Order relating to the introduction of bills was amended to enable Members to present bills after notice without an order of the House. The bills were deemed to have been read a first time and ordered to be printed.[24] Most government, and many private Members', bills are presented under this Standing Order, currently Standing Order No 57.[25] These are known as 'presentation bills'.

Thus by 1919, the requirement for commencing any given stage of a bill's progress had been pretty much reduced to one question, and the opportunities for delay through procedural chicanery at second or third reading much reduced. The lineaments of the current legislative procedure had been settled. But these simplifications did not withstand the pressures of the twentieth century. Greater speed and simplicity were constantly demanded.

But before turning to later reforms, the next section considers an area of legislative procedure that a House of Commons procedure committee recently described as 'resting on procedural practices and assumptions which would be familiar to Members of a century, if not two centuries, ago'.[26]

PRIVATE MEMBERS' BILLS

In evidence to the Select Committee on Public Business 1878, May suggested that after a certain date private Members' bills which had not received a second reading should drop and that the proposal made originally by Sir Charles Dilke, Member for Chelsea,[27] that on later private Members' bill days, post-committee stages should have preference, should be implemented. The House took no action at that time but, as we learn in chapter 11, in 1888 it agreed that after Whitsuntide the later stages of private Members' bills should have priority in the following order: consideration of Lords amendments, third readings, report stages, bills in progress in Committee of the whole House, bills appointed for committee, and second readings.[28]

---

[22] HC Deb (1888) 323, cc 514–23.
[23] CJ (143) 84.
[24] *The History of the Standing Orders* (n 2) 97.
[25] See, for example, Order of Business, 28 May and 6 July 2015.
[26] Second Report of Session 2016–17 from the Procedure Committee, HC 684, Private Members' Bills: Observations on the Government Response, para 37.
[27] In evidence to the Committee on Despatch of Public Business of House of Commons, House of Commons Paper 268, Session 1878.
[28] CJ (143) 74–75; HC Deb (1888) 322, cc 1774–87.

The precedence accorded to private Members' bills in any session is determined by a ballot conducted under Standing Order No 14(10). The ballot is held on the second Thursday on which the House sits during a session with Members entering their names in the ballot on the preceding Tuesday and Wednesday. Twenty names are drawn out in reverse order[29] and it is these twenty Members who have precedence in introducing a private Members' bill. Notices of presentation, that is the short and long titles of the bills, are set down for the fifth Wednesday the House sits. Standing Order No 14 also specifies which stages of bills have priority on days when private Members' bills are taken. Private Members' bills have precedence over government business on thirteen Fridays in a session. On the first seven of those Fridays, second readings of bills are given priority; on the remaining eight Fridays, with the exception that new report stages have precedence over report stages which have started, bills are taken in the same order as in 1888.[30]

No other private Members' bills may be introduced until the ballot bills have been presented.[31] In order to get other bills as high as possible on the Order Paper, Members often queue overnight to give notice of presentation of bills at the first possible opportunity, namely the fifth Thursday of the session, and may give notice of any number of bills. In 2016, for example, six Members gave notice of eighteen bills. These were presented and given a formal first reading on the following Monday, the next sitting day.

In addition to presenting bills under Standing Order No 57, individual Members, as described above, may also seek leave to introduce a bill under Standing Order No 23 (ten-minute rule bills).[32] Members may also take up private Members' bills brought from the Lords but again cannot do so until the ballot bills have been presented.[33]

Private Members' bills have, in recent years, become a matter of controversy. They have never been a reliable way of achieving legislative change, but the greater assertiveness of backbenchers in the twenty-first century has meant that the practice of talking out or simply blocking the vast majority of such bills has engendered growing dissatisfaction with the existing procedures. In 2016, the Commons Procedure Committee, in its third report since 2013–14 on handling private Members' bills, described the private Members' bill process as it presently operates as bringing 'increasing discredit on the House because of the way it is now largely reduced to an exercise in futility'.[34] The Committee recommended that Standing Orders be amended to provide that the question that the bill be read a second time should be put at the moment of interruption (currently 2.30 pm) if the bill was the first

---

[29] The Speaker determines the number of names to be drawn. Until 2013 the names were drawn in descending order.

[30] SO No. 14(9).

[31] Five bills presented by private Members other than on the first day on which such presentations are allowed for 'balloted' bills (the fifth Wednesday of a Session) have received royal assent in the last twenty years: Leasehold Reform (Amendment) in 2013–14, Holocaust (Return of Cultural Objects) and Driving Instruction (Suspension and Exemption Powers) in 2008–09, and Waste Minimisation and Registered Establishments (Scotland) in 1997–98.

[32] In the last twenty years, six ten-minute rule bills have received royal assent: Driving Instructors (Registration) and House of Commons (Members' Fund) in 2015–16, Specialist Printing Equipment and Materials (Offences) in 2014–15, Divorce (Religious Marriages) and Private Hire Vehicles (Carriage of Guide Dogs etc) in 2001–02, and Animal Health (Amendment) in 1997–98.

[33] SO No 14(11)(c).

[34] Third Report, Private Members' Bills, House of Commons Paper 684, Session 2015–16, para 9. See also Second Report, Private Members' Bills, House of Commons Paper 188, Session 2013–14; Fifth Report, Private Members' Bills: Government Response and Revised Proposals, House of Commons Paper 1171, Session 2013–14.

order of the day on the first seven sitting Fridays in a session (when second readings have precedence) if that business had not already been disposed of.[35] The government did not support that recommendation.[36] The Committee also recommended that the ballot system be supplemented by a scheme under which the Backbench Business Committee would consider bids from backbench members for bills to have their second readings debated in no more than the first four backbench legislative opportunities in each session.[37] The Committee considered 'that a legislative proposition which has support on all sides of the House, backed by support from the public, will be more likely to result in engaged debates on sitting Fridays'.[38] In its response, the government expressed concern that the proposed change might be seen as taking opportunities away from backbench Members and suggested that the Backbench Business Committee might wish to allocate time for a general debate in the House.[39]

The procedure committee published a further report in October 2016 in which it put forward a limited range of proposals for reform.[40] The new system would provide for up to four bills in each session to be given priority for consideration by the House on the recommendation of the Backbench Business Committee, based on an assessment of their preparation, the prior consultation undertaken on them and the support for the proposition across the House; the total number of bills to be given priority on Fridays, whether by the new route or through the ballot, would be reduced from twenty to fourteen; and the House would explicitly authorise the Speaker and his deputies to apply the existing provisions for imposing time limits on backbench and frontbench speeches to proceedings on sitting Fridays. The Committee also stated that:

> If the response to our recommendations is a further period of Government inaction, we believe the House should simply abandon the pretence that there are meaningful opportunities for non-government legislation to be made when that legislation does not have the active support of the Government of the day, no matter what the merits are of the legislation proposed or the level of cross-party support it has.[41]

COMMITTEES ON PUBLIC BILLS

As we saw in chapter 9, in 1854 May argued that the practice of considering all bills in Committee of the whole House should be discontinued and that, instead, bills should be considered in select committees and only discussed on report by the House, subject to a right of recommittal to a Committee of the whole House. In 1869 May had again recommended that bills of secondary importance be referred to select committees and also proposed an

[35] Third Report from Procedure Committee (n 34) para 36.
[36] Private Members' Bills: Government Response to Committee's Third Report of Session 2015–16, House of Commons Paper 383, Session 2016–17.
[37] Third Report from Procedure Committee (n 34), para 41.
[38] ibid, para 46.
[39] Private Members' Bills: Government Response to Committee's Third Report of Session 2015–16, (n 36).
[40] Second Report, Private Members' Bills: Observations on the Government Response to the Committee's Third Report of Session 2015–16, (n 34).
[41] ibid, Summary.

intermediate kind of committee in which bills of secondary importance might be discussed. In 1871 May suggested that committees of less consequence than Committees of the whole House might be constituted to consider public bills. The committees could sit independently of the sittings of the House and at times when the business of the House would not be interfered with. Later, in evidence to the Committee on Despatch of Public Business in 1878, May proposed that: 'Committees upon Public Bills should be specially constituted and have permanent functions not limited to a single bill.'[42] May intended his scheme to apply only to 'Bills of a practical kind, which would not involve party questions'.[43] Although that proposal was not immediately accepted, in 1882 the House agreed to a Standing Order, to be in force until the end of the 1883 session, to provide for bills relating to law and courts of justice and legal procedure, and to trade, shipping and manufactures, to be committed to two standing committees of not fewer than sixty or more than eighty Members, nominated by the Committee of Selection. The Committee of Selection was also given power to add not more than fifteen Members in respect of any bill referred to a standing committee.[44] The order was renewed at the beginning of 1884 for the session but was then dropped until 1888 when the resolutions were revived as Standing Orders with agriculture and fishing being included within the remit of the trade standing committee.[45]

At the turn of the twentieth century there was a more concerted attempt, now explicitly supported by the government, to rationalise legislative procedure and delegate legislative scrutiny from the Chamber to committees. In 1906, the procedure committee recommended that when a bill, other than a bill for imposing taxes or a Consolidated Fund or appropriation bill, or a bill for confirming provisional orders, had been read a second time, it should stand committed to a standing committee unless the House, on motion, otherwise ordered. It also made recommendations about the number and size of, and procedures in, the committees.[46] Following the passage of the implementing Standing Order in 1907, in the face of considerable opposition, the majority of bills were committed to standing committees. The Standing Order also provided for the committal of a bill in respect of some of its provisions to a standing committee and in respect of other provisions to a Committee of the whole House.[47] That provision is nowadays most commonly used in relation to the Finance Bill but has also been utilised for particularly controversial clauses of other sills, such as the Hunting Bill 2000 and the Human Fertilisation and Embryology Bill [*Lords*] 2007.

In 1919, the House agreed that standing committees should have power to sit while the House itself was sitting without having to seek leave each time, a practice which is now universal.[48] In 1934 the power to select amendments was extended to the chairmen of standing committees. The Speaker was given power both to appoint the Chairmen's Panel whose members would chair the standing committees and also constitute the panel of temporary

---

[42] *The History of the Standing Orders* (n 2) 78.
[43] ibid, 79.
[44] CJ (137) 520, 523.
[45] CJ (143) 84.
[46] First Report from the Procedure Committee, House of Commons Paper 181, Session 1906. See also HC Deb (1907) 171, cc 889–936, and subsequent days.
[47] CJ (162) 120.
[48] CJ (174) 34.

chairmen of Committees of the whole House and to appoint the chairmen of individual standing committees.[49] Those provisions still apply.

The traditional role of standing committees was to go through a bill clause by clause and line by line but there was no opportunity for the committees to examine more widely the terms of the legislation. In its report of 1978, the procedure committee proposed that special standing committees be established with power to hold three sessions of oral evidence following committal of a bill.[50] The recommendation was implemented in 1980 by means of, first, a temporary and, later, a permanent Standing Order.[51] The procedure was rarely used, only nine bills being taken in special standing committees between 1980, when the first such committee was established, and 2001.[52]

In 2001 the Modernisation Committee recommended that all bills be committed to 'public bill committees'[53] and the term 'standing committee' was (appropriately) relegated to history. Most bills are committed immediately after second reading to public bill committees. The committees to which bills which start in the Commons are committed under a programme order (see below) have power to send for persons, papers and records, that is, to gather written and oral evidence.[54] Under Standing Order No 63 a committee on a bill which has not been programmed (which will almost invariably mean a private Members' bill) may be given the same power but that provision has not yet been used.

CARRY-OVER

In 1882, Edward Clarke, the Member for Plymouth, proposed that consideration of bills which had passed second reading but not become law should be resumed in the succeeding session of the same Parliament at committee stage.[55] The motion was lost on division. The issue was subsequently considered by various committees including the Business of House of Commons (Abridged Procedure on partly considered Bills) Committee in 1890,[56] the Procedure Committee in 1914,[57] and the Joint Committee on Suspension of Bills in 1928;[58] but no action was taken. That remained the position until 1997 when in its first report the Select Committee on Modernisation of the House of Commons proposed a number of ways in which the House's scrutiny of legislation might be improved.[59] Since these would tend to increase the time bills took to complete their passage through Parliament the Committee recommended that in certain defined circumstances it should be possible to carry a bill over to complete its remaining stages in the next session.[60]

[49] CJ (189) 355.
[50] First Report, House of Commons Paper 588, Session 1977–78, paras 2.19–2.20.
[51] HC Deb (1980) 991, cc 835–37; CJ (242) 207. The standing order was repealed on 1 November 2006 when the new programming standing orders were made.
[52] See First Report from the Modernisation Committee, The Legislative Process, House of Commons Paper 1097, Session 2005–06, para 60.
[53] ibid, para 65.
[54] SO No 84A.
[55] CJ (137) 59; HC Deb (1882) 266, cc 1265–85.
[56] House of Commons Paper 298, Session 1890.
[57] House of Commons Paper 378, Session 1914.
[58] House of Commons Paper 106, Session 1928–29.
[59] First Report, The Legislative Process, House of Commons Paper 190, Session 1997–98.
[60] *Treatise*, 23rd edn 649.

Following the House's agreement to its report,[61] the Committee published a report on the procedural methods that might be used to carry-over government bills. It recommended that bills should be carried over by means of ad hoc motions, that the procedure should be used for bills which had not left the first House, and that the eligibility of bills for carry-over should be settled by agreement.[62] The Financial Services and Markets Bill 1998 was the first public bill to be carried over to the next session.[63] A further report from the Modernisation Committee in 2002 recommended that Standing Orders be amended to allow bills to be carried over by resolution for an experimental period.[64] That recommendation was implemented by a temporary Standing Order effective until the end of the 2001 Parliament.[65] The House later passed a permanent Standing Order to allow for government bills presented in the Commons to be carried over to the next session.[66] Twenty bills were carried over in the three subsequent Parliaments, from 2005 to 2015.[67] A further Standing Order was passed in 2011 to allow bills brought in on ways and means resolutions to be carried over.[68] Three bills were carried over under that Standing Order between 2012 and 2014.[69]

Carry-over was a radical change from the usual practice which had meant that public bills were lost if they were not passed during a session but, despite initial reservations about the introduction of carry-over,[70] it has become an accepted part of Commons procedure and many carry-over motions are agreed without a vote. It is an example of how the slaughtering of sacred cows, even if it takes over a century, can eventually be accommodated to tradition.

ALLOCATION OF TIME AND PROGRAMMING

As we have seen in preceding chapters, in May's time and ever since, the great goal of governments has been to improve the 'efficiency' of the legislative process and remove opportunities for opposition parties and individual Members to delay. Orders for bringing proceedings on stages of certain bills to a close had so increased in number and scope by 1917 that, as the preface to the twelfth edition of the *Treatise* acknowledges, some description of their objects and terms had become necessary. At the end of the sitting on 1 February 1881, Speaker Brand[71] initiated a new procedure when he announced that he would decline to call any more Members to speak on the government's motion seeking leave to introduce the Protection of Person and Property (Ireland) Bill and give it priority over all other business.[72] On 3 February the Prime Minister introduced a motion to require the Speaker

---

[61] HC Deb (1997–98), cc 1061–1129.

[62] Third Report, Carry-over of Public Bills, House of Commons Paper 543, Session 1997–98, para 7.

[63] CJ (255) 518; CJ (256) 8.

[64] Second Report, A Reform Programme, HC (2001–02) 1168-I, paras 35–43.

[65] CJ (258) 781. Five bills were carried over during the experimental period.

[66] SO No 80A, 26 October 2004.

[67] For list of bills and a fuller description of the procedure, see Library Standard Note, SN/PC/03236, 3 June 2016 <http://researchbriefings.files.parliament.uk/documents/SN03236/SN03236.pdf>.

[68] SO No 80B, 14 December 2011.

[69] See Library Standard Note, SN/PC/03236, 3 June 2016 <http://researchbriefings.files.parliament.uk/documents/SN03236/SN03236.pdf>, Appendix B.

[70] HC Deb (425) cc 1308–80.

[71] Speaker of the House of Commons, 1872–84.

[72] CJ (136) 65.

to put the question forthwith if a Minister gave notice that the state of public business was urgent and declared 'that any Bill, Motion or other Question then before the House is urgent and that it is of importance to the public interest that the same should be proceeded with without delay'—the Urgency Procedure.[73] The business which followed was recorded in *Hansard* as proceeding under 'indescribable confusion'.[74] On 9 February 1881 the Speaker laid a code of Rules regulating the conduct of business so long as the state of urgency continued.[75]

The first attempt at putting an end to obstruction was unsuccessful and on 17 February the Speaker laid three further Rules allowing the House to fix a time for the summary conclusion of the proceedings in committee on, or report of, a bill.[76] Sir Edward Fellowes concluded in retrospect that: 'These Rules however proved not to have been well drafted. ... The Speaker thereupon on 18 February promulgated one Rule to take the place of the three Rules.'[77] Under this Rule both the Protection of Person and Property (Ireland) and the Peace Preservation (Ireland) Bills were guillotined. Redlich, somewhat dramatically, described the reforms of 1881 in the following terms:

> The resolution brought in by Mr Gladstone with the object of preventing further Irish obstruction is one of the most remarkable documents in English parliamentary history. Its contents may be characterised in one word. It proclaimed a parliamentary state of siege and introduced *dictatorship* into the House of Commons.[78]

Dictatorship was not a development of which Redlich entirely disapproved, in his pursuit of an efficient Parliament suited to a modern state. But he noted that the dictatorship was one exercised by the Speaker, not the government. Whether this analysis held true over the next century is at least debatable.

A further guillotine was agreed in 1888 for the Members of Parliament (Charges and Allegations) Bill.[79] Although the closure and the guillotine were attacked from all directions as the first step on the road to continental-style tyranny (opponents regularly used the expression 'clôture' rather than 'closure' to emphasise its inherently foreign nature), so began the slow but inexorable journey to the timetabling of legislative scrutiny that is now a seemingly inevitable part of House of Commons procedures.

Guillotines on bills continued to be governed by ad hoc motions,[80] although Standing Orders making provision for Business Committees and sub-committees to divide a guillotined bill into parts and allot to each part as many days or parts of a day as they considered

---

[73] HC Deb (1881) 258, cc 68–156.

[74] HC Deb (1881) 258, c 72.

[75] CJ (136) 65.

[76] CJ (136) 78–79.

[77] *The History of the Standing Orders* (n 2) 63. See also CJ (1881) 83.

[78] Josef Redlich, *The Procedure of the House of Commons: A Study of its History and Present Form*, trans A Ernest Steinthal, with an Introduction and Supplementary Chapter by Sir Courtenay Ilbert, KCSI (London, Archibald Constable, 1908) I, 164.

[79] CJ (1888) 420.

[80] Some ninety-one bills were guillotined between 1946 and 1997, see Second Report from the Select Committee on Modernisation of the House of Commons, Programming of Legislation and Timing of Votes, House of Commons Paper 589, Session 1999–2000, Annex C.

appropriate were made in 1947.[81] Debate on such motions, formally known as allocation of time motions, has been limited by Standing Order since 1967.[82]

The case for routinely regulating the time spent on proceedings on bills in the House of Commons has been examined on several occasions as the Select Committee on Modernisation of the House of Commons acknowledged in its report on the legislative process in 1997. The Committee noted the advantages of applying timetabling provisions to all stages of government bills: 'We have explored the possibility of using arrangements for programming legislation which are more formal than the usual channels but more flexible than the guillotine. We believe that the spirit of these reforms requires co-operation from all sides of the House.'[83] So-called programming provisions were introduced as an experiment in 1998 and incorporated as Standing Orders Nos 83A to 83I in 2004.[84] Under Standing Order No 83A if, before second reading of a bill, notice of a motion providing (a) for committal of the bill and (b) for any proceedings on the bill to be programmed is given by a minister of the Crown the motion may be made immediately after second reading and the question put forthwith.

Virtually all government bills are now programmed,[85] in contrast to the period when allocation of time motions were sought for a minority of government bills and where there was an informal tariff of time to be spent on debate on a bill before an allocation of time motion was tabled. In July 2000 the Modernisation Committee, while acknowledging that there remained deficiencies in the agreed programming procedures used since 1997, concluded that:

> [I]t remains our firm judgement that, whilst voluntary informal agreements will continue to have a role to play, agreed programming of legislation can have a role to play in ensuring a more effective and efficient use of Parliamentary time and improvement in the scrutiny of legislation.[86]

Whether the Committee's second objective—improved scrutiny of legislation—has been achieved remains open to question as the provisions in programme motions for bringing proceedings to a conclusion can mean that there is often little time available to debate in detail amendments tabled for report stage.

POWER OF THE LORDS

Bills may originate in either House but the exclusive right of the Commons to authorise expenditure or impose charges on the people (financial privilege) means that money bills or bills of aids and supply are invariably introduced in the House of Commons. Two of the earliest Standing Orders still surviving in the House of Commons made this settlement crystal clear.

---

[81] SOs Nos 82 and 120.

[82] SO No 83.

[83] First Report, HC (1997–98) 190, para 89. See also Second Report, Programming of legislation and timing of votes, (n 80).

[84] CJ (260) 568.

[85] A programme motion was tabled, but not moved, for the House of Lords Reform Bill 2012, see Order of Business, 10 July 2012 and HC Deb (2012), 548, col 188. The bill was subsequently withdrawn.

[86] Second Report, Programming of Legislation and Timing of Votes, (n 80), para 13.

Until the passing of the Parliament Act 1911, the only effective restrictions on the House of Lords in relation to legislation were those imposed by practice or the Commons' financial privilege.[87] The Commons asserts its sole right to initiate and amend bills of aids and supplies under resolutions of 1671 and 1678, the latter of which states

> that all aids and supplies, and aids to his Majesty in Parliament, are the sole gift of the Commons, and all [such] bills ... ought to begin with the Commons ... which ought not to be changed or altered by the House of Lords.[88]

But the dispute which culminated in the constitutional crisis of 1910/11 had not primarily been about money—it had been as much about Irish Home Rule, Welsh disestablishment, and education. In 1907, in his supplementary chapter to Redlich's work, the then Clerk of the House, Courtenay Ilbert, noted:

> [T]he House of Commons has passed a momentous resolution, the effects of which it is impossible at this moment to forecast. ... On 26th June 1907 the House, on a motion of the Prime Minister, resolved by a majority of 285 (432 to 147) 'That, in order to give effect to the will of the people as expressed by their elected representatives, it is necessary that the power of the other House to alter or reject bills passed by this House should be so restricted by law as to secure that within the limits of a single Parliament the final decision of the Commons shall prevail.'[89]

So although in 1910 the question of the Commons' financial authority was the proximate cause of the crisis, the 1911 Act and the amending 1949 Parliament Act transformed fundamentally the House of Lords' powers in relation to all legislation. With the exception of bills to extend the life of Parliament, the House of Lords no longer had a sustainable veto over primary public legislation originating in the Commons.[90]

The Bill that paved the way to the 1911 Act was originally drafted by Courtenay Ilbert, continuing the close and sometimes clandestine engagement in parliamentary reform of his distinguished predecessor. Under subsection 1(1) of the Parliament Act 1911 if a money bill, having been passed by the House of Commons and sent up to the House of Lords at least one month before the end of the session, is not passed by the House of Lords without amendment within one month after it is so sent up to that House, the bill shall, unless the House of Commons direct to the contrary,[91] be presented for royal assent. To date no money bill has been presented for royal assent under that subsection. The Commons has, however, occasionally directed that a bill not be presented for royal assent after the end

---

[87] For a lucid explanation of the working of financial privilege (and recommendations for reform) see Meg Russell and Daniel Gover, *Demystifying Financial Privilege: Does the Commons' Claim of Financial Primacy on Lords Amendments Need Reform?* (London, Constitution Unit, University College, 2014).

[88] Commons Journals 1667–87, 509.

[89] Redlich (n 78) III, 223.

[90] Two of the most cogent and dramatic accounts of the 1910/11 crisis are Roy Jenkins' *Mr Balfour's Poodle: Peers v People* (London, Heinemann, 1954) and Frank Dilnot's *The Old Order Changeth: The Passing of Power from the House of Lords* (Waterloo, Smith, Elder & Co, 1911).

[91] 'A Money Bill means a Public Bill which, in the opinion of the Speaker of the House of Commons contains only provisions dealing with all or any of the following subjects, namely, the imposition, repeal, remission, alteration, or regulation of taxation; the imposition for the payment of debt or other financial purposes of charges on the Consolidated Fund, or on money provided by Parliament, or the variation or repeal of any such charges; supply; the appropriation, receipt, custody, issue or audit of accounts of public money; the raising or guarantee of any loan or the repayment thereof; or subordinate matters incidental to those subjects or any of them.' Parliament Act 1911, s 1(2).

of the month grace period, thereby enabling the Lords to take more time to consider it.[92] This provision has generally been used to accommodate the Lords' summer adjournments.

The more substantial change made by the Parliament Act 1911, as amended by the Parliament Act 1949, was to provide that if any public bill, other than a money bill or a bill to extend the maximum duration of Parliament, passed by the Commons and

> having been sent up to the House of Lords at least one month before the end of the session, is rejected by the House of Lords in each of those sessions … [it] shall, on its rejection by the House of Lords, unless the House of Commons direct to the contrary, … become an Act of Parliament on the Royal Assent being signified thereto.[93]

At least one year must have elapsed between the date the bill was read a second time in the Commons in the first session and the date it passed the Commons in the second session. A bill is deemed to be the same bill as a former bill sent to the Lords if, when it is sent to the Lords, it is identical or contains only such alterations as are certified by the Speaker of the Commons to be necessary because of the passage of time or to reflect faithfully amendments made by the Lords and agreed to by the Commons.[94] As the two Houses usually succeed in reaching agreement under the pressure of the veto and because the Lords generally accept, in the face of Commons' persistence, the supremacy of the elected House, the provisions of the Parliament Acts have been used only rarely. Seven bills have been presented for Royal Assent under the Parliament Acts: the Government of Ireland Bill 1914, the Welsh Church Bill 1914, the Parliament Bill 1949, the War Crimes Bill 1991, the European Parliamentary Elections Bill 1999, the Sexual Offences (Amendment) Bill 2000 and the Hunting Bill 2004.[95]

Following the general election of 1945, when the Labour Party had a substantial majority in the Commons and the Conservatives an overwhelming majority in the Lords, the Salisbury–Addison Convention was developed as a means of dealing with the relationship between the two Houses. The Convention states 'that the Lords should not seek to prevent the Government from implementing manifesto pledges in legislation'.[96] During the 1990s there was considerable debate about the Convention and in 2006 a Joint Committee was appointed to consider the practicality of codifying the key conventions on the relationship between the two Houses which affect the consideration of legislation.[97] Its report concluded that the Salisbury–Addison Convention had changed since 1945 and that it now differed from the original Convention in two respects: first the agreement that a manifesto bill should be accorded a second reading now applied to bills introduced in either House; and, second, that it was recognised by the whole House. In addition, its provisions were that

---

[92] For example, Ministerial and other Salaries Bill 1997, CJ (254) 201.

[93] Parliament Acts, s 2(1). A bill is deemed to be rejected by the Lords if it is not passed either without amendment or with only such amendments as may be agreed to by both Houses: ibid, s 2(3).

[94] The Acts also provide that the Commons may suggest amendments which shall be considered by the Lords: ibid, s 2(4).

[95] The Trade Union and Labour Relations (Amendment) Bill 1974/76 and the Aircraft and Shipbuilding Industries Bill 1975/77 were certified by the Speaker when sent up to the Lords in the second session but were subsequently passed by the Lords.

[96] See First Report from the Joint Committee on Conventions of the UK Parliament, 2005–06, House of Lords Paper 265-I/House of Commons Paper 1212-I, 24–35.

[97] HL Deb (2005–06) 681, cc 74–95; HC Deb (2005–06) 446, cc 436–74.

a manifesto bill should not be subject to 'wrecking amendments' which changed the government's manifesto intention as proposed in the bill and that the House of Lords should consider government business in reasonable time. The Committee did not recommend any form of codification.[98] The report was approved in general terms by both Houses in January 2007.[99]

With the exception of bills passed under the Parliament Acts, all bills must be agreed by the two Houses with identical wording before they can be presented for Royal Assent. When May produced the first edition of his *Treatise*, either House could demand a conference to offer reasons for disagreeing to amendments made by one House to bills passed by the other. Each House could appoint managers to represent it at the conference whose duty was confined to the delivery and receipt of the resolutions to be communicated, or the bills to be returned, with reasons for disagreeing to the amendments, but by the middle of the nineteenth century the practice had fallen into disuse with the last conference on amendments being held in 1858 on the Oaths Bill.[100]

Messages are now carried between the two Houses by Clerks and the amendments are considered by the respective Houses, usually, for government bills in the Commons, under the provisions of a programme motion. The Lords may propose amendments which infringe the financial privileges of the Commons but if the Commons does not agree to those amendments they are returned to the Lords with the only reason offered being that they would interfere with the public revenue, alter the area of taxation or financial arrangements made by the Commons, or otherwise infringe the privileges of the House and with the suffix 'that the Commons do not offer any further Reason, trusting that this Reason may be deemed sufficient'.[101] Variations on the original amendment may then be offered but it is not the practice of the Lords ultimately to insist on amendments that infringe Commons' financial privilege.[102]

DELEGATED LEGISLATION

A vast corpus of UK law made over the last century and a half, namely that made by way of delegated or secondary legislation (often in the form of statutory instruments), is much less visible procedurally than the primary legislation which grants powers for it to be made. From at least the eighteenth century onwards, rule-making by ordinance developed in a haphazard way to enable administrative decisions of many different kinds to be legislated for without recourse to primary legislation.[103] By the latter half of the nineteenth century, the practice could be reasonably described as endemic. Henry Thring, the first holder of

[98] Joint Committee on Conventions (n 96) 3–5.
[99] HL Deb (2006–07) 688, cc 573–638; HC Deb (2006–07) 455, cc 808–87.
[100] May (n 4) 253–55.
[101] See, for example, Votes and Proceedings, 17 March 2014.
[102] See, for example, the Housing and Planning Bill 2016, <http://services.parliament.uk/bills/2015-16/housingandplanning/stages.html>.
[103] See, for example, CK Allen, *Law and Orders: An Inquiry into the Nature and Scope of Delegated Legislation and Executive Orders in English Law* (London, Stevens & Sons, 1950). The 1953 Report from the Select on Delegated Legislation (HC (1952–53) 310-I) also provides a brisk historical overview in its opening paragraphs. Cecil Carr's *Delegated Legislation* (n 8) gives an excellent historical panorama at 22–26.

the office of First Parliamentary Counsel (the government's draftsman) wrote in an official minute in 1877:

> The adoption of a system of confining the attention of Parliament to material provisions only, and leaving details to be settled departmentally is probably the only mode in which parliamentary government can, as respects its legislative functions, be carried on. The province of Parliament is to decide material questions affecting the public interest; and the more procedure and subordinate matters can be withdrawn from their cognizance, the greater will be the time afforded for consideration of more serious questions involved in legislation.[104]

However, it was often difficult to establish what the law was, never mind how it had come to be made. Some semblance of order was attempted by the Statutory Rules Committee, which in 1892 published an Index to Statutory Rules and Orders. The Rules Publication Act of 1893 sought to ensure that these laws were at least systematically published, printed and made available for sale. This form of statute reached its first peak with the Defence of the Realm Act 1914, which gave vast powers to ministers to legislate by ordinance, and the effect was to produce something of a kickback between the wars, although the continued utility of delegated powers was also widely recognised and acknowledged.[105] The House of Lords, customarily ahead of the game on matters relating to delegated legislation, had first appointed its Special Orders Committee to consider aspects of the use of delegated powers in 1925. Between the Donoughmore Committee's report on the Powers of Ministers in 1932[106] and the 2017 White Paper on the so-called Great Repeal Bill,[107] there has been a constant tension between the ambition of achieving greater efficiency in the making of law by ministers and the fear that the exclusion of Parliament from the process is a harbinger of tyranny.[108] *The Spectator*'s reaction to the publication of the Donoughmore report sums it up quite well:

> Lord Hewart's spirited protest in *The New Despotism* against the tendency of the Government Departments to exercise not merely legislative but also judicial functions, was no doubt partly responsible for the appointment in 1929 of the exceptionally strong Committee on Ministers' Powers. His complaints are substantially confirmed in its Report, which indicates that the powers conferred upon Ministers by Statute should be closely watched and strictly defined. On the legislative side it is doubtless impossible for Parliament, overworked and hampered by its own procedure, not to leave the Departments the power of making rules and regulations concerning endless details. But Parliament could and should adopt at once the Committee's suggestion that a Standing Committee should examine every Government Bill and see that the rule-making function is duly circumscribed. ... The Committee's Report demands not merely close attention but immediate action. Departmental autocracy may have been less evident since the War, but it is still a serious menace to our liberties.[109]

---

[104] Quoted in the Report from the Select Committee on Delegated Legislation, HC (1952–53) 310-I, para 11.

[105] Edward Page, *Governing by Numbers: Delegated Legislation and Everyday Policy Making* (Oxford, Hart Publishing, 2001) 21–22.

[106] Cmd 4060.

[107] Cm 9446; commented on in the Seventh Report of Session 2016–17 from the House of Commons Procedure Committee, Matters for the Procedure Committee in the 2017 Parliament, HC 1091, paras 3–17.

[108] The most thorough recent analysis of the development and current state of delegated legislation is Ruth Fox and Joel Blackwell, *The Devil is in the Detail: Parliament and Delegated Legislation* (London, Hansard Society, 2015).

[109] *The Spectator*, 13 May 1932, 2.

However, in the period after 1932 Parliament was preoccupied with other matters and did not find time to act on the Donoughmore recommendations. The Emergency Powers (Defence) Act 1939 again provided recourse to legislation by ordinance. Today, it is a rare Act of Parliament that does not contain some provision for the making of delegated legislation.

In the second edition of his *Introduction to the Procedure of the House of Commons*, Gilbert Campion, the then Clerk of the House noted:

> Great divergences formerly existed in the periods during which rules, etc, were required to lie before Parliament, the time varying from eight to 100 days.[110]

In 1944 the House of Commons first appointed a Select Committee on Statutory Rules and Orders (later the Select Committee on Statutory Instruments), charged with ensuring that ministers were not exceeding or abusing the powers they had been granted to make delegated legislation. In 1946 a successful attempt was made to codify the use of delegated legislation in the Statutory Instruments Act, implementing more of the Donoughmore recommendations. The Act, which defined by statute and standardised the parliamentary procedures applying to various forms of delegated legislation, is an example of Parliament's willingness to accommodate a statutory codification of its procedures which might, at one time, have seemed slightly unconstitutional.

The schema of the 1946 Act is essentially tripartite, setting out the 'affirmative', 'negative' and (by implication) 'no procedure' processes for the making of law by delegated means. It has been added to in various ways since the early 1990s.

In 1994, the Deregulation and Contracting-out Act introduced for the first time the concept of the 'super-affirmative' process, which was designed to balance the broadening of the scope of delegated powers given to ministers with enhanced parliamentary involvement. In return for ministerial power to amend primary legislation by secondary legislation, where the Act to be amended contained no such explicit power (commonly known as a 'Henry VIII clause'),[111] a committee of each House was given the opportunity (written into statute) to examine and report on the legislative proposals *before* they were presented to Parliament for approval.[112] The failure to ignite the promised 'bonfire of the regulations' led to the 1994 Act being replaced by the Regulatory Reform Act 2001, which in turn was quickly supplanted by the Legislative and Regulatory Reform Act 2006. All used developments of the super-affirmative process, involving dedicated or ad hoc committees of the two Houses, to justify wider and wider ministerial powers to amend and repeal primary legislation. The bill paving the way to the 2006 Act was so widely drawn that it became the subject of a campaign to 'Stop the Abolition of Parliament Bill'. The campaign against the more far-reaching provisions of the bill, outside Parliament and within the two Houses, was

---

[110] Sir Gilbert Campion, *Introduction to the Procedure of the House of Commons*, 2nd edn (London, Macmillan, 1947).

[111] So called after the famous Statute of Proclamations of 1539, which explained in its preamble (thought possibly to have been penned by the King himself) 'that sudden causes and occasions fortune many times which do require speedy remedies and that by abiding for a Parliament in the meantime might happen great prejudice to ensue to the Realm ... it is therefore thought in a manner more than necessary that the King's Highness of this Realm for the time being with the advice of his honourable Council should make and set forth proclamations for the good and public order and governance of this his Realm ... as the cause of necessity should require'.

[112] Deregulation and Contracting-out Act 1994, s 4.

successful in reining-in ministerial powers, but the drafting of the Bill, if deliberate, was a signal of ministerial impatience with even the attenuated primary legislative procedures in the era of programming.[113] Variations on the super-affirmative process have been adopted in several Acts since 1994: for example for the making of remedial orders under the Human Rights Act 1998;[114] for making certain orders under the Public Bodies Act 2011 (heralding the 'bonfire of the quangos');[115] and for the exercise of certain powers under the Localism Act 2011.[116] Variations on this theme were also adopted for achieving joint consideration between Westminster and the UK's devolved legislatures of certain legislative proposals (for example, section 85 of the Northern Ireland Act 1998).[117]

Parliament's attitude to delegated legislation has always been anxious but equivocal. The Commons generally disapproves of its use in principle and largely ignores it in practice. But it has been a continued, if minority, preoccupation. The 1952 Select Committee on Delegated Legislation took a careful look at procedures for consideration of statutory instruments and made some fairly conservative recommendations, though they did suggest that '[t]he Prayer for the annulment of a Statutory Instrument should set out the reasons for such annulment',[118] an idea which has come round again and again since then and never yet been accepted. In 1971 the Commons Procedure Committee appointed to look at the legislative process recommended the establishment of a Joint Committee to look at delegated legislation.[119] That Joint Committee was appointed (it became known as the 'Brooke Committee') and it led to the establishment of the Joint Committee on Statutory Instruments which survives to this day, as well as the system of Standing Committees on Statutory Instruments (now known as Delegated Legislation Committees).[120] In 1978 the Commons Procedure Committee commented on delegated legislation at some length in its review of the effectiveness of procedure across the whole range of public business.[121] It recommended greater but more flexible and effective use of standing committees to consider statutory instruments, and presaged the introduction of the super-affirmative procedure by suggesting the use of 'proposals' for instruments in particularly complex or controversial cases. In 1987 the Procedure Committee returned to the subject in the context of its report on the better use of the House's time, seeking to trade off the greater use of standing committees with more robust powers to enable those committees to require the government to think again.[122] The government accepted the first part of the bargain and declined the reciprocal part—a pattern that has been repeated most often since then.

---

[113] See Peter Davis, 'The Significance of Parliamentary Procedures in Control of the Executive: A Case Study: The Passage of Part 1 of the Legislative and Regulatory Reform Act 2006' (2007) no 4 *Public Law* 677.

[114] Human Rights Act 1998, s 10. See also Standing Order No 152B of the House of Commons and the Seventh Report from the Joint Committee on Human Rights of Session 2001–02, Making of Remedial Orders, HC 473/HL Paper 58.

[115] Public Bodies Act 2011, s 11 and Standing Order No 152K of the House of Commons.

[116] Localism Act 2011, s 19.

[117] See also, for example, Sue Griffiths and Paul Evans 'Constitution by Committee? Legislative Competence Orders under the Government of Wales Act (2007–11)' (2013) 66 *Parliamentary Affairs* 480.

[118] Report from the Select Committee on Delegated Legislation, HC (1952–53) 310-I, para 102.

[119] Second Report of Session 1970–71 from the Procedure Committee, The Process of Legislation, HC 538, para 50.

[120] First Report of Session 1971–72 from the Joint Committee on Delegated Legislation, HC475/HL184.

[121] First Report of Session 1977–78 from the Select Committee on Procedure, HC588-I, paras 3.1–3.24.

[122] Second Report of Session 1986–87 from the Procedure Committee, The Use of Time on the Floor of the House, HC350, paras 11–38.

The Procedure Committee again returned to the subject in 1996, in a wide-ranging review which, as well as expressing by now well-rehearsed anxieties about the growth of legislation, proposed some practical measures to enhance scrutiny of instruments subject only to annulment, where it was feared that a lot more was going on beneath the radar of Parliament.[123] It drew on some of the reforms that had been brought in to enable Deregulation Orders to be permitted, particularly the use of select committees, as well as picking up on the long-standing demand (since at least the Donoughmore Report) for some sort of sifting committee to separate the wheat of delegated legislation from the chaff, so that the attention of the two Houses could be focused on what mattered. It was, as usual, ignored by the government. In 2000, at the behest of the then Chair of the new Modernisation Committee, the Procedure Committee returned to the subject. Its report, essentially, endorsed the 1996 recommendations.[124] In particular, it noted that the recent royal commission on House of Lords reform had backed the establishment of a joint sifting committee.[125] It was again ignored. In March 2003, the Commons committee published a further report, responding to the House of Lords' decision of the previous month to take unilateral action by establishing its own committee on the merits of statutory instruments.[126] Once again the government ignored the Committee which, in a particularly bad-tempered response, castigated ministers for failing to implement any of the reforms proposed in 1996 and 2000.[127]

In the Commons those instruments that do require approval have, since 1995 been automatically referred to delegated legislation committees which give them more or less cursory scrutiny before they return to the House for a vote without any further debate. And, since 2000, most such motions for approval have, if opposed, been subject to the procedure of deferred divisions. The same procedure can be applied, ad hoc, to motions relating to instruments subject to annulment, and often is. The implication of the 1946 Act that a motion to annul a statutory instrument which had already been made would be debated within the forty-day 'praying time' has never really been fully honoured in the observance in the Commons, but since the growth in demand for more civilised sitting hours since the 1990s, the chances of such a motion being debated on the floor of the House have withered almost to nothing.

The procedural response of the two Houses has been to have ever-increasing recourse to the use of select committees to keep a check on ministerial powers. The main formal check is the Joint Committee on Statutory Instruments. It considers all statutory instruments against the tests set out in its standing order, mainly designed to prevent inappropriate or excessive use of any delegated powers.[128] The Lords Committee on the Merits of Statutory Instruments was established in 2003 (thereby finally implementing a key recommendation of the Donoughmore Committee seventy years after it had first been made). It is now the Secondary Legislation Scrutiny Committee. Its terms of reference require it to consider

---

[123] Fourth Report of Session 1995–96 from the Select Committee on Procedure, Delegated Legislation, HC152.

[124] First Report of Session 1999–2000 from the Procedure Committee, Delegated Legislation, HC48.

[125] A House for the Future, Cm 4534.

[126] First Report of Session 2002–03 from the Procedure Committee, Delegated Legislation: Proposals for a Sifting Committee, HC 501.

[127] Second Report of Session 2002–03 from the Procedure Committee, Delegated Legislation: Proposals for a Sifting Committee: The Government's Response to the Committee's First Report, HC 684.

[128] See Standing Order No 151 of the House of Commons.

whether the special attention of the House of Lords should be drawn to a statutory instrument on any of the following grounds: that it is politically or legally important or gives rise to issues of public policy likely to be of interest to the House; that it may be inappropriate in view of changed circumstances since the enactment of the parent Act; that it may inappropriately implement European Union legislation; or that it may imperfectly achieve its policy objectives. The Lords also established a Delegated Powers Committee as far back as 1992 (now the Delegated Powers and Regulatory Reform Committee) whose task is to report whether the provisions of any Bill inappropriately delegate legislative power, or whether they subject the exercise of legislative power to an inappropriate degree of parliamentary scrutiny (again giving effect finally to a recommendation made by the Donoughmore Committee). This Committee therefore exercises a kind ex-ante scrutiny to complement the post-hoc scrutiny of the Joint Committee on Statutory Instruments and the Secondary Legislation Scrutiny Committee, as well as keeping an eye on legislative reform orders. In the Commons, the task of special scrutiny of orders made under the Legislative and Regulatory Reform Act 2006 is delegated to its Regulatory Reform Committee, which meets infrequently, since the flow of such orders from the government has never been great.

Procedures relating to delegated legislation therefore continue to have a very low profile in the Commons, though in recent years they have taken on a higher profile in the Lords, which has self-consciously carved-out something of a niche for itself in this area of law-making. Aggressive use of the powers the two Houses do possess has been rare: the last time the Commons declined to approve an affirmative procedure instrument was in 1978,[129] and the last time it decided (without a vote, and perhaps rather accidentally) to annul a negative procedure instrument was in 1979.[130] However, perhaps unthinkingly, the 1946 Statutory Instruments Act left the Lords with a unilateral power to defeat delegated legislation. It has declined to approve instruments on five occasions,[131] and has annulled one,[132] since the 1946 Act was made. The Joint Committee on Conventions of 2006 had considered whether there was a convention against the Lords exercising its unilateral veto of delegated legislation, and come to a rather uncertain conclusion.[133]

So although the use of delegated powers was viewed with suspicion and much reviewed in the fifty years following the 1946 Act, much of the steam seemed to have gone out of the debate in the last decade. But the last occasion on which the Lords rebelled, in October 2015, was described by the then Chancellor of the Exchequer as precipitating a constitutional crisis (it should be remembered that after the election of 2015 was the first time since the invention of political parties in their modern form that a Conservative government had not enjoyed a natural majority in the House of Lords). The effect of the Lords' decision was to delay or rebuff changes to the tax credits scheme which were claimed by the government

---

[129] The draft Dock Labour Scheme 1978, defeated by 301 votes to 291 on 24 July 1978.

[130] The Paraffin (Maximum Retail Prices) (Revocation) Order 1979 (SI 1979/797) on 24 October 1979.

[131] 18 June 1968, the Southern Rhodesia (United Nations Sanctions) Order 1968; 22 February 2000, the draft Greater London Authority Elections Election (Expenses) Order 2000; 28 March 2007, the draft Gambling (Geographical Distribution of Casino Premises Licences) Order 2007; 3 December 2012, the draft Legal Aid, Sentencing and Punishment of Offenders Act 2012 (Amendment of Schedule 1) Order 2012; 26 October 2015 the draft Tax Credits (Income Thresholds and Determination of Rates) (Amendment) Regulations 2015.

[132] 22 February 2000, the Greater London Authority Elections Rules (SI 2000/208).

[133] See First Report from the Joint Committee on Conventions of the UK Parliament, 2005–06, HL 265-I/HC 1212-I, para 227.

to be worth £4 billion to the Exchequer, so the question of the Lords' exercise of this power engaged the particular issue of the Commons' financial primacy as well as the more general question of the acceptability of the Lords defying the Commons in the making of delegated legislation. The Prime Minister appointed Lord Strathclyde to review the powers of the two Houses. His report was published in December 2015,[134] and identified three approaches to provide the House of Commons with a decisive role on delegated legislation: to remove the House of Lords from the procedure altogether; to retain the present role of the House of Lords and 'revert to a position where the veto is left unused'; or to create a new statutory procedure 'allowing the Lords to invite the Commons to think again when a disagreement exists and insist on its primacy', consciously and avowedly modelled on the Parliament Act arrangements. Lord Strathclyde recommended the third option. A flurry of select committee reports from both Houses suggested that this was an over-reaction.[135] The government responded to the original Strathclyde Review in December 2016, expressing support for the third option, but in a further response to the Lords' Committees in January 2017 indicated that it did not intend to legislate in the foreseeable future.[136]

Since May's time, then, not only has the doctrine of efficiency been applied quite ruthlessly to the primary legislative procedures of the Commons, but vast areas of detailed law have been handed over to ministers using delegated powers with a greater or lesser degree of parliamentary control. This victory for efficiency has always been viewed with mixed feelings by Members of the two Houses and observers of their proceedings: many would argue that it would be better for Parliament to concentrate on the big stuff even more and leave the detail to the technocratic processes of delegated legislation. But committees of both Houses have constantly been haunted by the anxiety that the government may be getting away with murder.

The answer to the latter concern has been twofold: to ramp-up the use of committee scrutiny (supported by substantial professional staffs) and for the Commons to largely sub-contract the boring stuff to the Lords who, seeing their opportunity, have made this kind of detailed technical scrutiny a key activity in justifying their uncertain constitutional role. By and large, the arrangements that have evolved work, although they may appear to leave MPs disengaged from the process. But it looks likely that the debate over how to handle the enormous legislative burden of the UK's exit from the EU may once again bring these arguments to the fore.

---

[134] Secondary Legislation and the Primacy of the House of Commons, Cm 9177.

[135] Ninth Report of Session 2015–16 from the Constitution Committee, Delegated Legislation and Parliament: A Response to the Strathclyde Review, HL Paper 116; Special Report from the Delegated Powers and Regulatory Reform Committee, Response to the Strathclyde Review, HL Paper 119; Thirty-second Report of Session 2015–16 from Secondary Legislation Scrutiny Committee, Response to the Strathclyde Review: Effective Scrutiny of Secondary Legislation, HL Paper 128; Eighth Report of Session 2015–16 from the Public Administration and Constitutional Affairs Committee, The Strathclyde Review: Statutory Instruments and the Power of the House of Lords, HC 752.

[136] Government Response to the Strathclyde Review: Secondary Legislation and the Primacy of the House of Commons and the Related Select Committee Reports, Cm 9363. See also Nineteenth Report of Session 2016–17 from the Secondary Legislation Scrutiny Committee, Joint Response to the Government Response to the Strathclyde Review and Related Select Committee Reports by the Constitution Committee, the Delegated Powers and Regulatory Reform Committee and the Secondary Legislation Scrutiny Committee, HL Paper 90.

MAKING LEGISLATIVE PROCESSES MORE TRANSPARENT

Writing nearly a century ago, a former Lord Chief Justice remarked:

> The obscurity of the language of statutes is a matter for a separate treatise. ... It is not many months since a Judge expressed himself pretty plainly in Court upon the scandal of introducing Bills, or enacting statutes, in the complicated and unintelligible form of many of the statutes referred to in the particular case. If he was bewildered as an expert in that very breach of law, what must be the position of the ordinary tax-payer? The answer given by the Law Officer who was conducting the case for the Crown ... was that it would not be possible to get Bills through the House of Commons in any other form ... [It] appears to be that, if Bills are to be got through ... within a reasonable time, care must be taken that they shall not expose too large a surface for possible attack ... to be intelligible is to be found out, and to be found out is to be defeated.[137]

That separate treatise has been written several times over, and a discussion of how the process of *handling* legislation has been made more transparent over the years could fill a chapter of its own. It includes committee inquiries and the subsequent debates in the House and the broadcasting and, more recently, webcasting of proceedings of the House and its committees. Amendments are increasingly accompanied by explanatory statements,[138] three bills have had a public reading stage, aimed at giving the public more opportunity to engage in the legislative process,[139] and between 1997–98 and 2014–15, over 100 draft bills or parts of bills were published, the majority of which were scrutinised by select or joint committees.[140] In addition, since 2013, the Office of Parliamentary Counsel, which drafts government legislation, has published a number of its pamphlets on various aspects of handling legislation.[141] This increased transparency reflects one of the greatest changes in the legislative process over the last 150 years: a recognition that legislation affects everyone and that accordingly everyone has the right to know more about the legislative process. But the language of statute still remains a bar to scrutiny by both Parliament and the public, and the actual process of making the law seems to fail to engage the imagination of either the modern politician or the modern elector. There remains plenty of room for greater simplification, clarification and explanation.

---

[137] Lord Hewart of Bury, *The New Despotism* (London, Benn, 1929) 77–78.

[138] See, for example, amendments to the Scotland Bill 2015, <www.publications.parliament.uk/pa/bills/cbill/2015-2016/0048/amend/pbc0480911m.1-7.html>.

[139] Protection of Freedoms Bill 2010–12; Small Charitable Donations Bill 2012–13; Children and Families Bill 2012–13, see Library Standard Note, SN06406, 19 March 2014, <http://researchbriefings.parliament.uk/Research-Briefing/Summary/SN06406#fullreport>. In addition the draft Care and Support Bill 2012–13 was subject to an online consultation whilst it was undergoing prelegislative scrutiny.

[140] See Library Standard Note, SN/PC/5859, 13 August 2015 <http://researchbriefings.parliament.uk/ResearchBriefing/Summary/SN05859#fullreport>.

[141] See <www.gov.uk/government/organisations/office-of-the-parliamentary-counsel>.

Part IV

Select Committees

14

Where Did It All Go Right

Developments in Select Committees, 1913–1960

MARK HUTTON

INTRODUCTION

I N THE FIRST edition of the *Treatise*, May devoted two chapters, totalling seventeen
pages, to select committees of the two Houses. The second of these chapters
(chapter 15) is mainly concerned with what are known today as 'PPR'—the powers to
send for 'persons, papers and records' as the standing orders put it (in other words, the powers to obtain evidence). Beyond that arena, procedure in select committees was relatively
underdeveloped, and consequently offered little in the way of law, practice and procedure,
and only scant pickings on privilege. Perhaps because of this flexibility of purpose and
freedom of manoeuvre, in Victorian times select committees were seen as great engines of
social and political reform, before that function was ceded to governments. But for much
of the first half of the twentieth century select committees seemed to have been relegated to
a sideshow of the Commons, and barely functioned at all in the Lords. This chapter takes a
somewhat sidelong look at the functioning of select committees in that period, and draws
some lessons on the role of 'procedure' and 'practice' in empowering or inhibiting their
effectiveness.

THE DOLDRUMS

Orlo Williams retired as Clerk of Committees on 3 May 1948. He had joined the House of
Commons as a Junior Clerk in 1907 and at his retirement party talked of the 'good old days
when grey frock coats and rakish life and no work were the order of the day amongst the
clerks'.[1] Sir Gilbert Campion retired as Clerk of the House in the same year. In the following
years something happened that arguably set back the influence and role of select committees more even than the Marconi scandal had thirty-five years earlier.

The Marconi affair involved allegations of what would now be described as insider dealing by members of the Cabinet. These allegations caused sufficient political fever that the

---

[1] Drennan letter, 29 April 1948.

Government was obliged to agree to the establishment of a select committee to investigate them. That committee divided on party lines. It was not the first to do so, nor was it the last, but its 'highly visible' failure (alongside that of the select committee on British South Africa which inquired into the abortive Jameson raid of 1895–96) has been described as a 'political disaster' for the select committee system, which 'condemned their successors to a very limited role for almost half a century'.[2] What happened in the years following 1948 was by no means highly visible. Whether there was political involvement at all is unclear: the Government and possibly the Whips of both main parties occasionally appear in what may be described as broadly supportive roles, but they do not seem to have been initiators or principal actors.

Select committees stand somewhat out of line with other organs and procedures of the House of Commons. They are characteristically small groups of Members drawn from different political parties conducting their business often behind closed doors. Their formal records—reports, minutes of evidence, minutes of proceedings—can create an impression of orderliness and calm deliberation which does not always reflect the reality. The description given by one of the first women ever to take part in parliamentary proceedings from, as it were, the Members' side of the table of her experience of the 1918 Select Committee on Luxury Duty (of which more later) is a salutary reminder:

> I have no words to describe how loose end are [*sic*] the proceedings of the subcommittees. Acland, the chairman of the main committee, has never called us together; no instructions have been issued by the parent Committee, and no general principles laid down for us to follow. The Sub-Committees are composed of politicians and amateur ladies who are absolutely unfitted to deal with a highly technical matter of this kind. We have been given no officials, no experts to help us. … In all my experience of public work I have never known business conducted in such a slip shod, loose end way as by the Select Committee and sub-committees.[3]

Changes in committee practice and procedure often arise by evolution or gradual increment rather than formal decisions. Over extended periods of time such changes may not always be consistent with each other. Solutions to one particular problem may be reused in quite different circumstances. Evolution in nature can be various and unpredictable, and under the right conditions select committee practice and procedure can have similar characteristics. In this sense the right conditions applied, at least to some extent, between 1913 and 1948; they did so far less, if at all, over the following fifteen to twenty years.

This chapter considers three touchstone issues that at the time were of particular interest to Members: access to expert or specialist advice; travel; and staff support. In different ways each illustrates the change of tone after 1948. But we start with a more fundamental question about select committees: are they outward or inward facing? A key source, both for the purpose of this chapter and for generations of committee Clerks, is the 1958 manual *Select Committees: Procedure and Practice*, which was written by the then Clerk of Committees, Louis Abraham. Its approach and its guidance seem to derive from a very

---

[2] *Erskine May's Treatise on the Law, Privileges, Proceedings and Usage of Parliament*, 23rd edn (London, LexisNexis, 2004) 8.

[3] Experiences of the Select Committee on Luxury Duty recorded by Violet Markham and quoted by Dr Mari Takayanagi in *Parliament and Women c1900–1945* (PhD thesis, King's College, London, 2012).

individual, and arguably partial, understanding of the narrative of the development of select committee procedure and practice, as is illustrated by its views on public access to committee proceedings.

'OPEN' OR 'CLOSED'[4]

The standing order permitting committees to admit the public to their evidence sessions was first agreed in 1971. Like many standing orders, it was made to repudiate a 'practice' that had solidified into a rule. It was required because it had become an accepted practice that committees could not of their own authority admit the public. In his 1958 manual, Abraham states:

> Strangers if admitted, are admitted only on the assumption that no member will take notice of their presence; there is no formal method by which strangers can be admitted, and the chairman should decline to propose the question on any motion for their admission.[5]

Various committees in the 1960s were granted power to admit the public. But the assertion that they needed this permission itself post-dates the Second World War. As late as 1952 the Select Committee on Clergy Disqualification formally decided that the public should not be admitted to its evidence sessions,[6] which surely would not have been necessary if Abraham's ruling had by then become established practice. In both 1932 and 1945 the minutes of proceedings of a committee record that the room was cleared after an evidence session.[7] In 1942 a motion to exclude strangers (the public) was defeated on a vote in the Select Committee on Equal Compensation.[8] In 1920, the Select Committee on Increase of Wealth (War), which examined allegations of profiteering during the First World War, decided that its inquiry should be held in public except when it should determine otherwise.[9] The chairman explained that this was in order to encourage press coverage of their proceedings in order to promote public understanding of the issues and more general approval of their recommendations.[10] A memorandum to the Select Committee on Publications and Debates in 1937, written by Orlo Williams, states:

> Unless a select committee decides to sit in private, members of the public, including press reporters, are admitted to the Committee room while the evidence is being taken.[11]

---

[4] According to Samuel Hoare in 1931, select committees could choose to be either open or closed in how they proceeded; the former involved admitting the public and press to all evidence sessions.

[5] LA Abrahams, *Select Committees Procedure and Practice* (1958, privately published for official use only by the House of Commons) 16. Such motions, not infrequently passed by committees in the years before the Second World War, are described by Abraham as 'irregularities which cannot be relied on as precedents'.

[6] HC (1951–52) 246, Minutes of Proceedings, 15 May 1952.

[7] Select Committee on Police Forces (Amalgamation), HC (1931–32) 106, Minutes of Proceedings, 14 June 1932; Select Committee on Library (House of Commons), HC (1945–46) 99, Minutes of Proceedings, 28 November 1945.

[8] HC (1942–43) 53, Minutes of Proceedings, 10 December 1942.

[9] HC (1920) 102.

[10] *Hansard*, 8 June 1920. cc 283–84.

[11] HC (1936–37) 74, 127, 160, para 39.

PUBLISHING EVIDENCE

Williams's memorandum was prepared to assist the committee's consideration of what was seen as an anomaly under which the public could hear and the press could report evidence given to a committee, but that evidence could not be published by the committee or anyone else during the course of an inquiry. Instead it was published only once it had been reported to the House at the end of the inquiry alongside the report to which it related.

The practice under which evidence could be reported by those who had heard it was long-standing. Williams's research in the course of preparing his memorandum showed that press reporting of select committee evidence sessions was well established by 1875. The ban on publication was based on a resolution of 1837 which stated that

> evidence taken by any Select Committee of this House and documents presented to such Committee and which have not been reported to the House, ought not to be published by any member of such Committee or by any other persons.[12]

This resolution is still in force today. Its requirements, together with those of the Parliamentary Papers Act 1840, govern the current treatment of oral and written evidence by select committees. It seems odd to the modern reader that no reference to the 1840 Act was made during the course of the select committee's inquiry and a little surprising that the committee concluded that there were not sufficient grounds to recommend any change to the existing practice.[13] The committee did, however, recommend that chairmen of committees had drawn to their attention the power of any select committee to ask the leave of the House to report from day to day the evidence taken before them.[14]

The anomaly had become a matter of controversy through an evolution of practice in the early years of the century (it seems to have been routine by 1914) and which was itself inconsistent with 'strict procedure'. It had long been the practice during inquiries to produce printed copies of uncorrected evidence for the use of members of the committee, to enable witnesses to provide corrections, and to inform prospective witnesses of the evidence which the committee had already received and on which they might be examined. The evolution was that additional copies were produced for, and provided to, persons and bodies outside the committee. The extent of this wider circulation can be inferred from the fact that in 1914 the usual number of printed copies was 125.[15] Up until 1915 the written agreement of the chairman of the committee and the Speaker was required to authorise the practice. It seems to have been routinely given and in 1915 it was dispensed with.

From 1927 several select committees, in response to applications from professional institutions and others who perceived they had a direct interest in the committee's inquiry, introduced more formal arrangements, including the reintroduction of payment for the copies. These developments may have created an expectation that interested parties had a right to receive copies of the evidence. Certainly this was the claim made by certain witnesses to the Select Committee on Sky-Writing in 1932, which led to the Clerk of the committee presenting a memorandum to the Principal Clerk 'on the unsatisfactory

---

[12] 92 CJ 282.
[13] HC (1936–37) 127, para 11.
[14] Report from the Select Committee on Publications and Debates Reports, HC (1936–37) 127, vi.
[15] HC (1936–37) 74, 127, 160, p 44.

conflict between the Resolution of 1837 and the existing, but uncertain, practice in regard to the issue of evidence to outside persons, in which he asked for a decision whether the Resolution of 1837 was to be adhered to or to be regarded as null and void' (in other words, superseded by 'practice').[16]

The Principal Clerk took the memorandum to the Speaker, who, in December 1932, issued the following instruction:

> I am informed that there is a growing tendency on the part of Committees to ignore the rule prohibiting the issue of copies of evidence during the progress of an inquiry. The rule must be strictly observed except in cases where a Committee, which holds its sittings in private, considers it desirable to issue copies to a Government Department.[17]

The suggestion of the 1937 committee that chairmen of select committees could ask for leave to report their evidence from day to day does not seem to have been taken up at the time, although it is now a power routinely granted to select committees. The 1958 manual states that evidence is usually reported at the end of an inquiry, but that a committee, if not otherwise empowered, may seek leave from the House to report it from time to time.

The Select Committee on Sky-Writing is also notable for recording abstentions in its minutes of proceedings. The other committee known to have done so, the Select Committee on the Architects Registration Bill, was the first to employ the more formal arrangements for the publication of evidence described above.

SPECIALIST SUPPORT

By the early twentieth century the Committee of Public Accounts already had a long history of working in partnership with the Comptroller and Auditor General (C&AG) to examine what the government had spent. By contrast, as discussed in Colin Lee's chapter on financial procedure (chapter 10), the House had established no mechanism for similar examination of the Estimates. The first steps down the long and at times tortuous path of select committee involvement in the scrutiny of proposed expenditure by government departments and public bodies (as opposed to the overseeing of the auditing of their accounts) were taken by the 1903 Select Committee on National Expenditure, which considered 'whether any plan can be advantageously adopted for enabling the House, by select committee or otherwise, more effectively to make an examination, not involving criticisms of policy, into the details of National Expenditure'.[18] The first Select Committee on the Estimates was appointed in 1912–13. From the outset questions were raised about how it might have access to expert advice analogous to that provided by the C&AG to the Public Accounts Committee.

These discussions would continue—sporadically at least and without resolution—for more than fifty years. But elsewhere, other committees, faced with their own challenges, were finding ways of attracting the advice and support they needed.

One of the earliest examples was the Select Committee on the House of Commons (Kitchen and Refreshment Rooms) of 1916. The usual role of the Kitchen Committee

---

[16] ibid, 46.
[17] Quoted in HC (1936–37) 127, v.
[18] HC (1903) 242.

(as it was known) was to report to the House the annual accounts of the House's catering operations, for whose supervision it was itself directly responsible. In 1916, at the height of the First World War, with the national economy under unprecedented strain,[19] the level of government subsidy came under challenge. The committee was threatened with the withdrawal of the Treasury grants which amounted to £2,600 per annum, a significant sum in the context of a total turnover of less than £8,000.

The Kitchen Committee (apparently prompted by the Treasury) established by its own resolution an 'Advisory Committee' of three of its members and two external experts: the Managing Director of the Savoy Hotel and a former hotel manager for the Midland Railway.[20] The Advisory Committee, in effect a sub-committee of the Kitchen Committee, took exhaustive evidence from managers of the House's Kitchen and Refreshment Rooms, going in great detail into the composition and costs of individual meals, including in one evidence session the physical examination of a chicken (faithfully recorded in the Minutes of Evidence as 'Mr Willsher produced a fowl').[21] The conclusion of the experts, and of the committee, was that the subsidy could not be entirely done away with, but, if prices were increased a little (too great an increase would drive customers away), it might be reduced.[22]

This procedure might have been no more than a one-off peculiarity: the Kitchen Committee stood in the unique position of having direct responsibility for the management of the House's refreshment facilities, including the employment of staff. But in fact, whether consciously or not, it was a precedent that was followed by others. Ultimately it evolved into the modern practice of giving select committees power to appoint specialist advisers. But that is to get ahead of ourselves.

The next step in the story was the establishment the following year of the Select Committee on National Expenditure. The Committee's task was essentially the same as that given to the Estimates Committee in 1912: to examine expenditure and 'to report what if any economies consistent with the policy decided by the government may be executed therein'.[23] The reference to expenditure rather than estimates was in recognition that 'in time of war it is impossible for the full Estimates, to which we are accustomed, to be presented with respect to all the Departments'.[24] But unlike the Estimates Committee, the National Expenditure Committee was given 'power to appoint from outside its own body such additional persons as it may think fit to serve on any Sub-Committee which it may appoint'.[25] At that time select committees in the House of Commons were sessional, so that those with a continuing existence (such as the Committee of Public Accounts), or whose work extended over a sessional break, were reappointed at the start of the new session. The National Expenditure Committee was reappointed in successive sessions up to 1920 with the same power.

At least two other committees appointed in those years were given similar powers: the Select Committee on Luxury Duty and the Select Committee on Transport, both appointed

---

[19] See, for example, First Report of the Select Committee on National Expenditure, HC (1917–18) 151, para 7.
[20] HC (1916) 198, vii.
[21] ibid, 11.
[22] ibid, vii.
[23] HC (1917–18) 125.
[24] *Hansard*, 29 January 1918, c1447. During the war spending was authorised by a Vote of Credit rather than by individual Estimates.
[25] HC Journal, 25 July 1917.

in 1918. The latter appointed a sub-committee, to examine ports and canals of Ireland and co-opted onto it Mr WA Lindsay, a member of Parliament but not a member of the committee, and Mr PJ Hannon, both of whom took a full part, indistinguishable from that of the other members of the sub-committee, in the sub-committee's eighteen-day round trip of evidence-taking in Ireland, starting and finishing in Dublin.

The experience of the Select Committee on Luxury Duty (see above) was perhaps less successful. The committee's task was to prepare a list of articles and places to be classed as articles of luxury and places of luxury for the purposes of the proposed Luxury Duty. The committee appointed four sub-committees to consider categories of article and place and appointed three ladies to sub-committee 2 and two each to sub-committees 3 and 4. The sub-committees took evidence, none of which, unfortunately, was reported or printed. The sub-committees made reports to the main committee that were the basis for its report to the House.

The minutes of proceedings of the committee set out in full a memorandum from Miss Violet Markham and Mrs Vaughan Nash, appointed members of one of the sub-committees, which records, in more moderate terms than those quoted above, their view that the sub-committee's lack of access to the official information and advice necessary to inform decisions on a schedule of items to be subject to the proposed tax together with the multiplicity of trade questions raised in evidence from their witnesses left them unable to recommend any schedule. They accordingly withdrew from further involvement. The committee nonetheless continued its work and in due course agreed a set of recommendations. These, however, were not taken up by the government and no Luxury Duty was introduced.[26]

In 1921 the Select Committee on Telephone Services was given power 'to appoint from outside its own body such persons as it may think fit for the purpose of obtaining special expert or scientific information or advice upon the subject matter of their order of reference'.[27] It did so in the person of Mr WW Cook, who was described in the minutes of proceedings of the committee as an Assessor, and whose presence was minuted. He provided advice during committee meetings. He sat next to the Chairman, who clearly on occasion asked questions proposed by him. He also played a full part in the committee's efforts to learn from international experience (see below). He was not, however, remunerated. To modern ears, Mr Cook sounds very like a Specialist Adviser, but Specialist Advisers do not appear until the 1960s, and however helpful he may have been to the committee, the House did not grant a similar power to select committees in the following years.

The next example seems to be the Select Committee on House of Commons (Rebuilding) which was appointed in December 1943, and in January 1944 was empowered 'to invite any specially qualified person whom they may select to attend any of their meetings in an advisory capacity.'[28] The committee used the power to appoint Mr EN de Normann, Deputy Secretary of the Ministry of Works, who acted as 'a combination of perpetual witness, source of technical information and liaison officer with the Ministry of Works'.[29]

Liaison officers, appointed from that part of government which was responsible for the matters into which a committee was inquiring, were a common feature of select

---

[26] *Hansard*, 17 October 1918.
[27] Journal, 10 March 1921.
[28] Journal, 20 January 1944.
[29] HC (1943–44) 109, para 2.

committees at this time. They acted as a cross between a minder and a facilitator. Between 1927 and 1939 the Estimates Committee had the expert assistance of a civil servant from the Treasury who attended meetings and received all papers.[30] On many occasions the relationship seems to have worked well, particularly perhaps during wartime when committees saw their work as contributing directly to the war effort. But suggestions that this role could develop into one which provided expert advice to a committee or even that a committee might look to civil servants for such support were explicitly rejected by members.[31]

The role was also criticised by the C&AG in evidence to the Procedure Committee in 1931. He is a far from disinterested witness: of the Public Accounts Committee he says: 'Of the value of its work there can, I submit, be no question'; of the Estimates Committee on the other hand his view is that: '[I]t has effected no substantial economies, and its results have surely been achieved by disproportionate expenditure of time and labour by Members and witnesses.'[32] But he does point to a fundamental problem with the analogy between specialist support for the Estimates Committee and his own role with respect to the Public Accounts Committee:

> I think that the objections to, or difficulties inherent in such an appointment were not envisaged by the Select Committees [ie successive Estimates Committees]. The analogy is to my mind fallacious. The Comptroller deals with Accounts which are matters of fact. Estimates are matters of opinion. It is extremely difficult to see how any officer of the House of Commons, however able, could formulate or express any opinion as regards the requirement of the Public Service which would be better than that of the Department responsible or than the conclusion of the Treasury on behalf of the House after minute and often prolonged discussion of the detail.[33]

The issue came to a head again in the Select Committee on Nationalised Industries. A Select Committee on Nationalised Industries was first appointed in 1951–52 and was reappointed in following sessions. Almost from the outset they made efforts to secure additional expert support. Their proposals were variously for more assistance from the statutory auditors of the industries, or for their own professional accountant, or for the creation of an officer of the status of the C&AG. This latter proposal was a direct parallel to the recommendations of successive Estimates Committees for the appointment of an officer to assist in the analysis of the Estimates on the same basis as the C&AG assisted with the Accounts.

The Nationalised Industries Committee of 1959 noted that none of their predecessors' recommendations had been implemented, but was not content to leave it there. They believed time had shown that the unprecedented remit of the committee meant that their task was both novel and different. The Leader of the House, Rt Hon RA Butler, agreed with this diagnosis:

> I think that what we are saying is that in the old days a Select Committee of Parliament dealt either with political matters which as Members they were more than competent to deal with, or questions of procedure on which they had the expert help of the Clerks of the House, or with matters with which the Clerks were familiar. Now, we are attempting to combine politics and economics and we find, especially in a complicated field like this, that the new demands on the human brain have

---

[30] See Abraham memorandum to Select Committee on House of Commons Accommodation etc, HC (1953–54) 184, p 140.

[31] HC (1953–54) 184, Q548; HC (1958–59) 276, para 11.

[32] HC (1930–31) 161, Q3686.

[33] ibid.

outstripped the traditional panoply of clerks which was provided for us; and whilst they can still give us guidance on the grounds of commonsense, I, who was trained in the traditional humanities should be quite hopeless in advising you on the details of accounts; so that it is the new world which is catching up with the old, and we therefore have to think very deeply how we can help you, at the same time preserving your integrity. That is what matters. I am not referring to your moral integrity; your independence is a better word, your independence as a Select Committee.[34]

And having thought further after his evidence session about what he described as a very difficult problem, the Leader concluded that the best course of action for the committee would be to appoint an assessor on the model of the 1921 Telephone Services Committee who would be paid a fee for the work he did.[35] The Leader's conclusion chimed with the evidence given to the committee by the Clerk of the House, Sir Edward Fellowes. Sir Edward had actually been appointed Clerk of the 1921 committee, but was moved to another office before it got going.[36]

He cited three examples of committees that in different ways had acquired access to external expertise, namely the National Expenditure Committee, the Select Committee on Telephone Services and the Select Committee on House of Commons (Rebuilding). These were apparently the only examples of which he was aware.[37] The power given to the National Expenditure Committee, 'which permitted outside people actually to act as Members of the Committee', he regarded as 'rather undesirable'.[38] However, he reserved more severe criticism for the actions of the Telephone Services Committee in apparently endorsing first of all a plan for the Chairman and Mr Cook to travel to the USA to make inquiries on the committee's behalf and then agreeing, when the Chairman fell ill, that Mr Cook could make the visit on his own. Sir Edward's opinion was that 'the whole proceeding was really strictly irregular from the procedural point of view'.[39]

Before moving on to look in more detail at developments in committee travel, it is worth noting that, despite the support of the Leader of the House, when the Select Committee on Nationalised Industries was reappointed in the next session, it was not given a power to appoint an assessor or any other form of adviser; nor was it in the succeeding sessions.

TRAVEL

As well as Mr Cook's 'irregular' visit to the USA, members of the Telephone Services Committee, sometimes accompanied by their Assessor, also visited Sweden, Norway, Denmark and Switzerland. In the same year members of the Select Committee on Training and Employment of Disabled Ex-Servicemen visited France, Belgium, Italy and Germany as well as relevant institutions within the UK.[40] At least one sub-committee of the National Expenditure Committee visited France during the First World War.[41]

---

[34] HC (1958–59) 276, Q267.
[35] ibid, 49.
[36] HC (1958–59) 276, Q1.
[37] ibid, Q2.
[38] ibid, Q1.
[39] ibid, Q2.
[40] HC (1922) 170, Minutes of Proceedings.
[41] The Army Sub-Committee in 1917; Drennan letter, 4 January 1940; First Report of the National Expenditure Committee of 1917–18 (referred to in Metcalfe, evidence to Estimates Committee in 1951).

When in 1940 a National Expenditure Committee on a similar model was appointed, and it discussed its programme of work, it also considered whether to travel, but it seems to have decided not to (at least at that stage) partly from a reluctance on the part of its chair and partly in response to signals from the government. There is evidence that the government view was that a National Expenditure Committee in a blitzkrieg would be 'more of a hindrance than a help' and that Winston Churchill, who had just been appointed Prime Minister, actually wanted it closed down.[42] Although they may not have travelled abroad during the war, sub-committees, or members of them, certainly did travel pretty extensively within the UK. For example, Kay Midwinter, one of the women Clerks appointed during the war, took her sub-committee on transport to Glasgow in April 1941.[43] And in 1946 a sub-committee of the Estimates Committee travelled extensively through Germany, including to Berlin and Hamburg, taking formal evidence on several occasions.[44] In 1948 a sub-committee visited Nigeria and 'went all round the country taking evidence'.[45]

But in 1951 travel suddenly became a whole lot more difficult. Sub-committee F of the Estimates Committee, responsible for considering the estimates for the Foreign Service, decided that it wanted to travel to certain embassies and consulates in order to understand better how public money was spent in and by them. It was advised, however, by the Clerk of the House, Sir Frederick Metcalfe, that to do so as a committee was not possible and that it would in fact exceed the powers of Parliament for the House to purport to authorise a committee to function beyond the territorial extent of its own jurisdiction.[46] It is apparent from the transcript of his evidence to them that the members of the sub-committee struggled to understand both the grounds of the argument itself and how it was consistent with the various precedents, some of which were from just a few years before and within the memory and experience of the Members present.

At the heart of Sir Frederick's argument was the contention that committees could be permitted to function only in circumstances where the House could properly protect them and their proceedings and enforce any exercise of their powers. As Sir Frederick put it: 'I always envisage the figure of the Serjeant at Arms with his Mace.'[47] This objection could not be overcome by a committee choosing to conduct itself in a way which would not engage the use of its powers. When challenged, for example, that a committee might wish to make a visit without exercising any powers, such as a visit of inspection to embassies abroad, his response was:

> I do not think that is one of the functions of a Parliamentary Committee of the House of Commons. I cannot recall any such visits of inspection. I had imagined that the duties of a select committee were always to take evidence.[48]

Sir Frederick was quite willing to characterise the visit of the 1917 National Expenditure sub-committee as unconstitutional, not only for the reasons already given, but additionally because the House had given it no power even to adjourn from place to place, which

---

[42] Drennan letter, 20 June 1940.
[43] Drennan letter, 30 April 1941.
[44] Drennan letter, 7 July 1946.
[45] HC (1951–52) 242, Q2341.
[46] HC (1951–52) 242, QQ2338–40, 2355.
[47] ibid, Q2360.
[48] ibid, Q2332.

should have limited it to meeting only in the Palace of Westminster. He described the sub-committee actions as 'quite inexplicable apart from the fact that in 1917–18 a very large number of our staff had gone to the war and these committees were all staffed by civil servants'.[49]

Sir Frederick does not seem to have been aware of the activities of the Telephone Services Committee and its Assessor, but he was familiar with the Select Committee on Training and Employment of Disabled Ex-Servicemen. He described how it had operated in his memorandum to the 1951 inquiry:

> The members of that Committee went abroad in an unofficial capacity, in three groups, one to France and Belgium one to Italy and one to Germany. Each group produced a report on the information gained, which it presented to the Committee. These three unofficial reports were printed as appendices to the Report of the Committee. The expenses of the Members were paid by the House, each group being supplied beforehand with the necessary cash.[50]

It was this approach which he recommended that the 1951 sub-committee might follow. He conceded that in effect it amounted to a subterfuge to get round the objections he had raised, and he had, he said, no doubt that it had been understood in that sense by the then Clerk of the House, Sir Lonsdale Webster.[51] In many respects it seems very similar to the arrangements under which most overseas select committee visits take place today.

The issue does not seem to have been further pursued in 1951 (the sub-committee did not travel, apparently because the Estimates Committee thought it would be undesirable for the sub-committee to adopt such a method),[52] but it was returned to two years later when it was considered by the full Estimates Committee. Many of the same arguments were made, and Sir Frederick again confirmed that there would be no obstacle to an informal group of members travelling abroad, even going so far as to say: 'If they happen to be the same persons as form the sub-committee it would seem to most people that they were the same, but they would not be acting in the same capacity.'[53] Responding to a question about whether such a group could take a civil servant as a secretary, he said 'certainly they can take whom they will'.[54] He also confirmed that it was his view that such a group would not need the leave of the House in order to travel, or indeed before incurring expenditure associated with that travel.[55] And he retracted his description of such a course of proceeding as a subterfuge: '[I]t was not a subterfuge; it was an absolutely proper way.'[56] Armed with this advice the sub-committee began planning its inquiry. It held its first evidence session on 15 December 1953, just six days after Sir Frederick's appearance before the Estimates Committee. Towards the end of March 1954 it decided it would have to visit Rome because

> [w]hile it would have been possible although extremely expensive to have summoned high-ranking Foreign Service officers and members of their staffs to Westminster, it would have been

---

[49] ibid, Q2312.
[50] ibid, 1.
[51] ibid, QQ2356–58.
[52] HC (1953–53) 290, iv.
[53] HC (1953–54) 149, Q72.
[54] ibid, Q9.
[55] 'I am quite sure this Committee has the inherent right to spend money on pursuing the enquiries which it deems necessary for its task, and if it thinks it is necessary to send you to Belgium obviously we should pay all expenses, and as accounting officer I should deem it proper' (ibid, Q 102).
[56] ibid, Q 9.

quite impossible to transport to British soil buildings, or as in the case of Rome, alternative sites for a new Chancery.[57]

On 29 March the sub-committee instructed its Clerk to make the necessary arrangements for the visit.

It was at this point that a new and apparently hitherto unforeseen problem arose. The committee had evidently (and perhaps not surprisingly) come away from its evidence session with Sir Frederick with the unanimous impression that by his answers he had given sanction for a Clerk to accompany the delegation of members.[58] But this was not the case: it transpired that, when Sir Frederick agreed that such a group of members could travel, with a shorthand writer and even accompanied by a civil servant

> he did not mean that a Clerk from the Committee Office could go with them. ... It appears that the only way for these Members to be able to avail themselves of the services of a Clerk is for the House itself by a motion to give leave of absence for them to go to certain places to make inquiries on behalf of the House.[59]

Having discovered this on 6 April, the committee made a Special Report on 12 April recommending that the House adopt the proposed procedure.

According to the committee, the Foreign Office had welcomed the idea of the visit, but the government as a whole it seemed did not. No time was found for a debate in the House either on the Special Report or the proposed motion. The chairman of the committee wrote to the Leader of the House setting out the arguments in favour of the motion, but in reply the Leader told the chairman that the government had concluded that: '[I]t would be unconstitutional for the House to make an order granting leave of absence to certain Members of [the] Committee to make an official inquiry abroad.'[60] The basis for this conclusion was apparently the contention that 'the mere taking of a clerk makes it into a committee'.[61] And purporting to authorise the overseas travel of a committee was, of course, what the Clerk of the House had previously insisted to be beyond the power or authority of the House. The committee was clearly very unhappy with this outcome. On the one hand it did not agree that 'the presence of a Clerk automatically converts an unofficial group of Members into a Committee';[62] on the other it was not prepared to travel without the services of its Clerk:

> The Clerk is a servant of the House who gives valuable assistance to a Committee and especially the Chairman, in the course of an inquiry. It is clearly laid down in the present instructions of the Principal Clerk of Financial and Miscellaneous Committees that 'a clerk must obtain a complete grasp of what may be a complicated subject'.[63]

STAFF SUPPORT

Basil Drennan started as an Assistant Clerk in the House of Commons in 1926. For most of his career (he resigned in 1960) he worked in the Committee Office. During that time

---

[57] HC (1953–54) 290, vi.
[58] ibid, v.
[59] HC (1953–54) 149, iv.
[60] HC (1953–54) 290, vi.
[61] ibid, vii.
[62] ibid, vii.
[63] ibid, v.

he wrote to his parents, with what seems now, but perhaps was not then, extraordinary frequency. What is, however, extraordinary is that many, probably most, of those letters were preserved and are now held in the Parliamentary Archives. Alongside the more formal records, they give a fascinating personal perspective on the experience of being a committee Clerk.

The Clerk's Department he joined was already a long way from Orlo Williams's grey frock-coated idlers. Recruitment was by a process described as selection rather than pure competition, under which the principal universities were each year invited by the Clerk of the House to propose suitable candidates for a clerkship. From the returns the Clerk would select a number for a preliminary interview. Those who passed the interview would then take the Civil Service entry exam. Whoever did best in that was offered a place. Following a report from the Maclean Committee (an unofficial committee of Members appointed by Mr Speaker to 'consider the method of appointment, conditions of service, and scale of remuneration and allowances of the Clerks and other Officers of the Department of the Clerk of the House') in June 1918, a system of circulation of Clerks between the several offices of the Department was established so that 'at the end of ten or twelve years' service, [they will] have acquired a knowledge of all the work of the Department, with advantage to their general efficiency, and to the service of the House'.[64]

As noted above, many members of House staff, including Clerks, left to join the armed forces during the First World War. The consequences were significant, not only in the use of civil servants as Clerks, but also in the effect that 'war casualties' had on the establishment. In what was until recently the Main Committee Office at the north end of the Committee Corridor in the Palace of Westminster a memorial plaque records that five committee Clerks were lost in action.[65] The Maclean report records six current vacancies (out of a total of 31 Clerk positions). With what strikes a contemporary reader as a certain callousness, it describes this situation as offering 'an opportunity for re-organisation of the Department which should not be let slip'. At about the same time, the role and responsibilities of a committee Clerk were given more formal expression. Clerks had in all probability assisted with the drafting of reports before 1918, but the practice became an instruction in 1921. From that date and up to at least the 1950s, the Principal Clerk of Committees issued an instruction to all committee Clerks to the effect that 'the chairman of a committee now usually expects the Clerk to assist him in the preparation of the draft report, or even to write it for him'.[66]

Certainly that was Basil Drennan's experience on his first select committee: the Select Committee on Shop Assistants appointed in November 1930. In March 1931, he writes to his parents that: 'I had a letter from my Chairman on Friday night to say that he wanted me to help him with the report and telling me which parts he wanted me to tackle.'[67] This came, apparently, after the chairman (Roden Buxton, an ascetic, internationalist Labour Member, who would lose his seat at the 1931 General Election) had initially asserted that he would write the report himself. In the end it seems that Drennan wrote most, if not all, of the draft: '[N]ow he's faced with it, he's shirking it.' But, like many of his successors, he

---

[64] Printed as Appendix H in HC (1953–54) 184.
[65] Robert WT Cox, Victor WD Fox, Francis Seymour, Horace S Green and Robert NM Bailey.
[66] Quoted by L Abraham at HC(1953–54) 184, Q 675.
[67] Drennan letter, 22 March 1931.

appears to have enjoyed the challenge, not least drafting a 'very interesting historical section involving original research'.[68] The first five sections of the report were sent to committee members on 14 May 1931; the committee began paragraph-by-paragraph consideration on 1 July and, after seven further sittings and much procedural toing and froing agreed the report unanimously on 18 September, just a couple of weeks before the end of the Parliament (the General Election was on 27 October). The report's principal recommendation was for a maximum forty-eight-hour working week for shop assistants. It was published on 16 November, allowing the *Morning Post* to describe it as 'one of the last relics of the Socialist Government', a charge hotly contested by Drennan on the grounds that most of the recommendations had been unanimously agreed.

The Shop Assistants Committee is notable for several procedural innovations recorded in its minutes of proceedings. They are not referred to in Drennan's letters, but it seems unlikely that someone clerking their first select committee would not have sought advice on such matters in advance from his colleagues and seniors. They include explicit recognition in the text of the report that certain key recommendations are supported by only a majority of the committee (regarded as a shocking procedural solecism in recent times): 'With two important exceptions these are the unanimous recommendations of your committee. The exceptions are (i) ... and (ii) which are the views of six out of the eleven members of your committee.' On several occasions decisions to agree to certain paragraphs are rescinded at a later meeting to allow the committee to return to the issue, apparently in order to maximise consensus. Again, a young Clerk in recent years might well have been instructed (on a parallel with the rule against 'going back in the bill') that this was procedurally impossible.

It is clear, both from the standing instruction to committee Clerks quoted above and from Drennan's experience, that during the inter-war years committee Clerks were expected to engage as much with the subject-matter of their committee's work as with the procedure. This is not to assert that every select committee report was drafted by the Clerk, something which even if true would probably be incapable of proof. The report of the Select Committee on Capital Punishment of 1930–31, for example, includes an extensive, and somewhat idiosyncratic, history of the subject-matter and various philosophical and ethical discursions which do not seem consistent with a clerkly approach to drafting. And in 1941 the chair of the Navy sub-committee of the National Expenditure Committee is reported by Drennan (its Clerk) to be determined to write a report himself 'nothing daunted by the awful flop of his last one'. Drennan and a colleague supplied him with extensive material on which to draw, but 'vanity is one of his weaknesses and we suspect he will try not to use it'.[69]

With this experience it might seem a natural development that, as committees became more demanding of support on the subject of their work, committee Clerks would respond by increasing the effort and importance given to this component of their roles. But, in an extraordinary intervention, the then Principal Clerk of Committees, Louis Abraham, not only resisted any such development but seemed to attempt to retreat from any commitment to the levels of support which committee Clerks were already customarily giving. In a memorandum to the Select Committee on House of Commons Accommodation etc, Abraham argued firstly that it was not a function of a committee Clerk to get information

[68] Drennan letter, 21 April 1931.
[69] Drennan letter, 14 March 1941.

required by Members or to present the information otherwise provided 'in an informative way' and, secondly, that committee Clerks drafted reports for their chairs only as 'a matter of courtesy rather than of obligation'. This was because the Clerk was obliged to carry out instructions from the chairman only 'where the chairman may be assumed to be speaking on behalf of the committee and to be merely anticipating its wishes'. 'No such presumption,' he argued, 'can arise as regards an instruction to draft a report because every member of a committee has a right to submit a draft report for its consideration.'[70]

These arguments did not go unchallenged by the committee or by other members. The issue had arisen because the Estimates Committee had (again) concluded that it needed additional support. It decided that it would not be appropriate for that support to come (as it had before the war) from the Treasury and therefore sought it from the House itself. The terms of reference of the Accommodation etc Committee included 'the amenities necessary to enable Members to carry out efficiently the services required of them' and 'the methods of appointment of the staff at all levels in the employment of this House'.[71] The concerns of the Estimates Committee were accordingly raised with the committee. Its questioning of Abraham was courteous, but confused. First, there was no common understanding of the role of the chairman of a committee. Members seem to have had no sympathy for and little understanding of the limitations which Abraham was trying to place on their authority within the committee. Members drew on their experiences outside the House to argue that the chairman had a leadership role in which he should be supported by the Clerk. Second, Abraham seems to be arguing that the Clerk's responsibilities are properly limited to recording formal proceedings and providing procedural support. At one point he even seems to suggest that providing procedural advice is only a relative recent requirement, since in the past (the early 1920s) committees had experienced chairmen, but that nowadays they did not.[72] Members, on the other hand, clearly saw Clerks as staff of the committees and were appreciative principally of their support and assistance on the subject matter of the committee's work.[73] Some of Abraham's defensiveness may be on behalf of the Clerks for whom he was responsible, arguing that the committee seems to be asking that every committee Clerk should not only be 'a person with great mental ability but also an "Admirable Crichton"'.[74] But overall he comes across as old-fashioned, pedantic and unhelpful. His constant reference to precedents from before the Second World War (and sometimes before the First) as if they are the only possible guides to present practices and behaviours clearly irritates a number of Members, leading one to interject: 'I think we ought to come up to date. We really must consider the matter at the time that we are sitting, in the light of modern usage.'[75] An assertion that might have gladdened the heart of Thomas Erskine May.

The committee's report makes no reference to the evidence session. It recommends that the Estimates Committee should be empowered, with certain conditions, to secure the assistance of an accountant, actuary or other qualified person. On the subject of committee

---

[70] HC (1953–54) 184, 141.
[71] House of Commons Journal, 4 November 1953.
[72] HC (1953–54) 184, Q595.
[73] eg, HC(1953–54) 184 Q548.
[74] ibid, Q605.
[75] ibid, Q600.

Clerks, it quotes the instruction issued by the Principal Clerk of Financial and Miscellaneous Committees:

> The Chairman usually expects the Clerk to assist in the preparation of the Draft Report and even to draft it. The Clerk must therefore obtain a complete grasp of what may be a complicated subject, and must adapt his knowledge to the general lines which the Chairman wishes to be followed, with a careful appreciation of the views of individual Members of the Committee. Should the Chairman instruct the Clerk to draft the Report, the Clerk before proceeding to do so, should ascertain from the Chairman what general lines he would propose to adopt in the recommendations.

It concludes that 'This … clearly recognises the present requirements of committees and adequately provides for their being met.'[76] The then Principal Clerk of Financial and Miscellaneous Committees was Basil Drennan.

CONCLUSION

The period covered by this chapter was not a golden age for select committees. In 1935 Gilbert Campion, then Clerk Assistant, said in evidence to a committee: 'Of course the normal fate of a Report of a Select Committee is for it simply to lie on the Table.'[77] In 1932 the Select Committee on Procedure passed a pretty damning verdict on the record of the Estimates Committee:

> [E]fforts to make the Estimates Committee an effective instrument for the control of public policy have failed … the difficulties in their way arise from the fact that they are powerless to deal with policy … and no definite days are allotted for a discussion of their reports in the House.[78]

That assessment, however, was in stark contrast to the self-assessment of members of the National Expenditure Committee appointed during the First World War. Its chairman told the House in January 1918 that of the fifty-two recommendations it had so far made, thirty-four had been accepted, eleven were under consideration and just seven had been rejected.[79] Perhaps unsurprisingly since so much of its work, including reports and recommendations, were conducted in private, there seems to be no similar assessment of the National Expenditure Committee of the Second War, but, despite Churchill's initial reservations, it was extremely active throughout the war years: by the end of the 1943–44 session it had produced ninety-two reports.

It was a period of considerable innovation in practice and procedure. Sometimes, these changes were undoubtedly inspired by a desire to avoid the party political splits that had been so damaging before the First World War, and whose memory was clearly alive after the Second War when, as Drennan records, a sub-committee chairman of the newly appointed Estimates Committee was very agitated that the new Conservative Members intended to take a party line in it, so as to split it from top to bottom and ruin its influence.[80] Very often, however, innovation seems to have come simply in response to individual committees' ambitions, and often to have been inspired by pragmatic flexibility on the part of Members

---

[76] ibid, xii.
[77] Select Committee on Witnesses, HC (1934–35) 84, Q217.
[78] HC (1931–32) 129, 13.
[79] *Hansard*, 29 January 1918.
[80] Drennan letter, 26 November 1948.

and Clerks. Possibly it was easier to make such changes at a time when committees were perceived to be less influential than they once had been. But we should be cautious about making such assumptions. Select committees were still important components of the parliamentary armoury. The Select Committee on Training and Employment of Disabled Ex-Service Men, for example, was appointed by means of an amendment to a motion criticising the government's record on the matter.[81]

In the decades since 1960, the status of select committees has, of course, shifted dramatically, not only in the Commons but in the Lords as well. They are far better known and more widely observed by the public than any committee on a bill, and their proceedings are probably more familiar to television watchers than any other aspect of the House's work apart from Prime Minister's Questions. This transformation of the procedural landscape of the Commons began with the decision of the House in 1979 to establish 'departmental select committees', in effect to have a permanent system of committees scrutinising government departments on a one-to-one pattern. In 1983, the National Audit Act created the National Audit Office financed directly by the Commons, supporting and again transforming the work of the Committee of Public Accounts and other select committees. Around the turn of this century, a radical and engaged Leader of the House in the shape of Robin Cook, urged on by the newly activist Liaison Committee (the committee comprising the chairs of all select committees in the Commons) negotiated greater resources to support the select committees. The 2010 reforms of the Committee on Reform of the House of Commons (the 'Wright Committee') brought in whole-House elections for the chairs of most committees by secret ballot, and these newly mandated figures have in turn further raised the profile of the select committees. The select committees have become probably the most studied, as well as the best known, organs of the House. Those committees have themselves been the engine of a further transformation in the resources supporting them—the House of Commons Committee Office, which once fitted in a single room, now has around 250 staff supporting over thirty select and joint committees. In the first session of the 2015 Parliament, these committees produced over 350 reports between them.

But in the years after 1948, activities which had almost become routine were suddenly halted, procedural variety was clamped down on, and the doors were closed on committee evidence sessions. Why did the House seem to lose faith in select committees as instruments of scrutiny? Can the responsibility be laid at the door of the newly appointed Principal Clerk of Committees, Louis Abraham? Certainly many of the new restrictions have his name associated with them. He was clearly not universally popular with his colleagues. Drennan describes him as 'the dreadful Abraham who combines the manners of a dictator with a persecution mania' and claims that many people have had rows with him.[82] On the other hand the Clerk of the House (Metcalfe) was the source of the advice which effectively prevented overseas travel by committees; and the actions of the government whips, in failing to make time for the leave of absence motion which Metcalfe advised was necessary, might indicate a wider shift in attitudes to committee activities. Whatever the reasons, the consequence was a calcification of committee practice and a restriction on the scope of their activities which lasted at least until the late 1960s and, despite the post-1979 renaissance, in some respects persists to this day.

---

[81] House of Commons Journal, 26 April 1922.
[82] Drennan letter, 6 February 1948.

15

A Road not Taken

Select Committees and the Estimates, 1880–1904

COLIN LEE

INTRODUCTION

THE DEVELOPMENT OF select committees in the House of Commons has been marked by the same tensions that have characterised debates and measures to reform the House's procedures more generally. One source of tension lies in the conflict between the perceived needs and interests of the Executive and those of the House as an institution. Another lies in the divide between procedural conservatism and procedural radicalism—a divide visible in the past within the ranks of clerks and described in chapter 14 by Mark Hutton. This chapter explores these themes in consideration of the role select committees could play in the House's examination of public money in the period up to the turn of the nineteenth and twentieth centuries. Although a route was mapped to integrate select committees in the business of approving the government's annual expenditure, this road was not taken.

SELECT COMMITTEES AND THE ESTIMATES PRIOR TO 1880

The examination of Estimates by select committees was an intermittent feature of the work of the House of Commons in the first half of the nineteenth century. Finance committees which had operated in 1782, 1786 and 1791 and from 1797 to 1798 had begun to strengthen parliamentary knowledge of public spending. The last of these, under the chairmanship of Charles Abbot, had suggested 'measures ... either for diminishing the Expense, controlling the Expenditure, or regulating the Establishments' of government, and pressed for clarity about changes in levels of expenditure.[1] Committees constituted in each session between 1807 and 1811 helped to expose improper practices and to point the way to

---

[1] Reports from Committees 1715–1801, Volume IX: Sixteenth Report from the Select Committee on Finance ... Secretaries of State, 305; Twenty Second Report from the Select Committee on Finance ... The Exchequer and Concluding Remarks, 452. See also JED Binney, *British Public Finance and Administration 1774–92* (Oxford, Clarendon Press, 1958) 17–18, 142–43.

savings achievable in peacetime.[2] However, it was the finance committee established in 1817 that began close scrutiny of the Estimates, identifying scope for reductions beyond those already planned.[3] The work of its successor in 1818 smoothed the path of the Estimates, with ministers able to refer to the reports to explain recent changes.[4] The committee of 1819 undertook a comparison of changes between the current and previous Estimates.[5]

The committees of 1817 to 1819 were referred to in Estimates debates during the 1820s and radicals pressed the case for a successor committee until the principle was conceded during Canning's brief premiership.[6] Wellington's subsequent administration honoured the commitment.[7] The committee appointed in 1828 only found time to report specifically on the Ordnance Estimates, but advocated the case for stronger Treasury control over spending Departments and also highlighted 'striking instances' where the House had, through its own actions, prevented 'very wise and salutary measures of retrenchment' proposed by government.[8] According to a historian of the Treasury, the 1828 committee made 'the first authoritative demands for joint financial control by a responsible Treasury and a watchful House of Commons', representing 'landmarks of the first importance'.[9]

Although the redoubtable radical Joseph Hume pressed the case for a new committee on expenditure on several occasions in the 1830s and 1840s,[10] it was only in 1848 that two such committees were appointed, one on the Miscellaneous Estimates and another on the Army, Navy and Ordnance Estimates. The former provided guidance on areas of expenditure where it felt the government 'might use the pruning knife' and proposed a clearer distinction between temporary objects of expenditure and the ordinary civil estimates, leading to the emergence of the Civil Estimates along modern lines, with Votes linked to Departments.[11] The latter proposed reductions in naval expenditure and pinpointed instances of voted limits being exceeded.[12] Nine of its ten recommendations were adopted within two years and it was a valuable tool for the Prime Minister Lord John Russell in persuading reluctant Navy

[2] HC Deb, 30 June 1807, cols 692–715; Report from the Committee on the Public Expenditure, &c of the United Kingdom: the Pay Office, HC (1807) 61; Third Report from the Committee on the Public Expenditure, &c of the United Kingdom: Offices, Places, Sinecures & Pensions, HC (1807) 109; Third Report from the Committee on the Public Expenditure, &c of the United Kingdom: Pensions, Sinecures, Reversions, &c, HC (1808) 331; HC Deb, 29 June 1808, cols 1098–1102.

[3] Second Report from the Select Committee on Finance, HC (1817) 162.

[4] Seventh Report from the Select Committee on Finance, HC (1818) 57; Eighth Report from the Select Committee on Finance, HC (1818) 97; Ninth Report from the Select Committee on Finance, HC (1818) 133; HC Deb, 2 March 1818, cols 701–10; HC Deb, 3 March 1818, cols 756–69; HC Deb, 16 March 1818, cols 1102–09.

[5] Second Report from the Select Committee on Finance: Army, HC (1819) 206; Third Report from the Select Committee on Finance: Navy, HC (1819) 257; Fourth Report from the Select Committee on Finance, HC (1819) 289.

[6] HC Deb, 4 May 1826, cols 852–53; HC Deb, 20 February 1827, cols 591–99; HC Deb, 1 June 1827, cols 1098–1130.

[7] HC Deb, 15 February 1828, cols 424–25; HC Deb, 21 February 1848, col 1007.

[8] Second Report from the Select Committee on the Public Income and Expenditure of the United Kingdom: Ordnance Estimates, HC (1828) 420, 4, 5, 6, 10; HC Deb, 20 February 1829, cols 445–48.

[9] H Roseveare, *The Treasury: The Evolution of a British Institution* (London, Allen Lane, 1969) 137.

[10] HC Deb, 16 March 1835, col 1036; HC Deb, 20 March 1843, cols 1135–36; HC Deb, 29 November 1847, cols 269–70.

[11] Report from the Select Committee on Miscellaneous Expenditure, HC (1847–48) 543, ix–x, viii; V Cromwell, 'The Problem of Supply in Great Britain in the Nineteenth Century', in *Études sur l'Histoire des Assemblées d'États* (Paris, Presses universitaires de France, 1966) 1, 6.

[12] Report on the Navy Estimates from the Select Committee on Navy, Army and Ordnance Estimates, HC (1847–48) 555, xxxvii, xv, xxxiii, xxxv.

professionals of the need to make reductions.[13] The committee was re-established in two subsequent Sessions, arguing for a reprioritisation of the Ordnance Survey on large urban areas to assist in identifying the need for sanitary improvements and highlighting errors in the preparation of the Estimates which had the effect of misleading the Commons.[14]

To some degree, the committees that considered Estimates between 1817 and 1850 represent an element of what has been termed the 'heyday' of select committees.[15] However, there were a number of factors which help to explain why they had few successors for some decades. First, the establishment of such committees was associated with governmental weakness. The committees of 1817–19 were created by a government keen to engage backbenchers with the need to make severe economies in peacetime. One observer noted early in 1819 that the government was 'so completely paralyzed, that they dare do nothing; and it becomes a Government of Committees of the House of Commons'.[16] At the time of the appointment of the 1828 committee, one Member argued that 'such committees were, in general, a delusion on the public. They were appointed only to get over the difficulty of the moment, and were never resorted to, until ministers were driven as it were into a corner by their own extravagance'.[17] The two committees in 1848 arose from a minority government desperately trying to regain its equilibrium after the House had made clear its determination to reject the Estimates initially presented and the associated increase in the rate of income tax.[18] Ministers were keen to stress the temporary nature of such committees. Castlereagh was clear in 1819 that he viewed the committee first established in 1817 and subsequently re-established each session as a temporary response to particular post-war circumstances, and 'to be an abuse of one of the most important powers of the House, which ought only to be exercised upon particular and special occasions', a view echoed by Robert Peel in agreeing to the 1828 committee.[19]

Committees assigned to examine the whole of the Estimates were hamstrung by the breadth of their task. The Whig opposition leader George Tierney cautioned that the committee risked becoming 'a repository for all the evils afloat … a drag-net for all grievances'.[20] The chairman of the 1828 committee reported that, by mid-May, it had held forty-seven meetings with thirty-eight witnesses, ordered the production of 337 accounts, and produced 2,000 sheets of letterpress. The government Chief Whip, however, felt the committee had 'sat nearly three months and have done nothing, and the longer they sit the more confused they get'.[21] The 1848 Committee on the Miscellaneous Estimates also worked hard, meeting on thirty-seven days, but still admitted its work was 'incomplete'.[22]

[13] HC Deb, 12 April 1850, col 271; S Walpole, *The Life of Lord John Russell* (London, Longmans, Green & Co, 1889, 2 vols), II, 28–29.

[14] Second Report from the Select Committee on Army and Ordnance Expenditure, HC (1849) 499, lxiv, lxxi, l.

[15] S Gordon and TGB Cocks, *A People's Conscience* (London, Constable, 1952) 8. See also O MacDonagh, *Early Victorian Government 1830–1870* (London, Weidenfeld & Nicolson, 1977) 6.

[16] HC Deb, 7 February 1817, cols 255–56; B Hilton, *Corn, Cash and Commerce: The Economic Policies of the Tory Government, 1815–1830* (Oxford, Oxford University Press, 1977) 69–70.

[17] HC Deb, 22 February 1828, col 623.

[18] L Strachey and R Fulford (eds), *The Greville Memoirs 1814–1860*, vol 6 (London, Macmillan, 1938) 16–19; Walpole (n 13) 24–25; HC Deb, 18 February 1848, cols 900–981; HC Deb, 23 February 1857, col 1074; HC Deb, 10 March 1857, cols 2158–9.

[19] HC Deb, 8 February 1819, cols 359–60; HC Deb, 15 February 1828, cols 424–25.

[20] HC Deb, 7 February 1817, cols 278–79.

[21] HC Deb, 16 May 1828, col 737; History of Parliament Online, 1820–32 (<http://www.historyofparliamentonline.org/research/members/members-1820-1832>), biographies of Parnell and Holmes.

[22] HC (1847–48) 543, ix–x.

Committees at this time were seldom established before February, and the Session ended in the summer.[23] Lord John Russell argued that the 1848–50 committees on the armed forces Estimates had spent too long taking evidence, and only came to consider their recommendations 'at a time when a considerable proportion of the Members have left town, and, worn out by the public business they have been engaged in, are not able to attend', leading to recommendations which did not command the support of the whole committee.[24] Delay also meant that reports were seldom produced in time to inform debate in the Committee of Supply.[25] If their recommendations could not influence the House's own consideration, committees became dependent on government acceptance of their recommendations, a recipe for disillusion as contemporary committees know only too well. In 1850, Joseph Hume cited many instances of the 'uselessness' of reports from committees which 'could do no good, unless Government went along with them'.[26]

The golden age of select committees was also drawing to a close more generally, with governments preferring the continuity, professionalism and impartiality (or perhaps malleability) of Royal Commissions and departmental committees.[27] Select committees also succumbed to the growing emphasis on the role of the Committee of Supply, with all Members able to attend, as the most suitable place for detailed consideration of spending proposals, including what amounted to cross-examination of ministers.[28] Thomas Erskine May exhibited no interest in referral of Estimates to standing committees or select committees. When the former proposition was put to him in 1871, he said: 'I think a Committee of Supply should certainly be a Committee of the whole House, and nothing short of that.'[29]

The most significant advance in the select committee system made during the Gladstonian era focused not on understanding Estimates during their passage, but on the subsequent examination of the accounts, with the creation of the Committee of Public Accounts in 1861.[30] Calls for the establishment of select committees on the Estimates, usually emanating from Hume's successors on the radical wing of what had become the Liberal Party, including from John Bright,[31] were repeatedly rebuffed by ministers. The notion of scrutiny was not recognised as a proper function of the Commons. Although Gladstone had contemplated that there might eventually be a case for 'a permanent Finance Committee' if supplementary Estimates became the norm,[32] he argued that the idea of an annual select committee to examine the Estimates 'would be a decidedly bad one. It would begin with taking away from the Executive its proper responsibility, and would end by resolving all responsibility into pure vapour.'[33] This view was shared by Disraeli, who viewed the

[23] N Chester, *The English Administrative System 1780–1870* (Oxford, Clarendon Press, 1981) 103.

[24] HC Deb, 5 May 1851, col 538.

[25] See, for example, HC Deb, 12 July 1849, cols 261–63, 264–65 and HC Deb, 18 July 1849, cols 516–18.

[26] HC Deb, 12 April 1850, cols 248–55.

[27] Gordon and Cocks (n 15) 8–10; Chester (n 23) 103–05; J Parry, *The Rise and Fall of Liberal Government in Victorian Britain* (London, Yale University Press, 1993) 115.

[28] HC Deb, 19 June 1857, col 65.

[29] Report from the Select Committee on Business of the House, HC (1871) 137, Q 98.

[30] B Chubb, *The Control of Public Expenditure: Financial Committees of the House of Commons* (Oxford, Clarendon Press, 1952) 32–37.

[31] HC Deb, 19 June 1857, cols 64–65; HC Deb, 26 February 1866, col 1107.

[32] Minutes of Evidence taken before the Committee of Public Accounts, 2 June 1862, Q1571: published with the First, Second and Third Reports from the Committee of Public Accounts, HC (1862) 220, 414, 467.

[33] HC Deb, 2 February 1860, col 472.

Estimates as 'the embodied opinion of the Government upon a great branch of the Public service', and thought that it should be for the government to stand or fall on its judgements on the Estimates. A minister who invited the opinion of a select committee 'authorises no opinion, commits himself to none, and calls upon the House of Commons to perform his work'.[34] Reginald Palgrave, Clerk Assistant under May and his eventual successor, writing anonymously in 1876, praised the work of the Committee of Public Accounts, but criticised 'the constant appeal of economic reformers to subject the yearly estimates to the revision of Select committees'. He considered the idea 'attractive', but 'specious' because 'the action of those Committees must clash with the executive responsibility of the Government'. He thought that even the most zealous advocates of this idea only envisaged such committees being appointed every ten years.[35]

SELECT COMMITTEES AND 'THE CHAMPION OF ECONOMY', 1884–88

The revival of committees to examine the Estimates is due principally to one man—Lord Randolph Churchill. He brought to the task techniques by which he helped to revive Conservative Party fortunes in the lead up to the 1885 General Election—parliamentary persistence, forceful advocacy with colleagues, a willingness to forge alliances across the House and memorable speech-making across the country. His partial success foreshadowed key aspects of the modern select committee system, but his chances of a legacy of an enduring select committee system fell victim to some of the flaws which contributed to the failure of his career as a whole.

Churchill had regularly participated in Supply debates and he used that experience to argue in a speech in Blackpool in January 1884 that 'year by year the control of the House of Commons over the expenditure is getting more slender and more feeble'. He viewed Departments as presided over not by ministers but by permanent officials who 'cared nothing for the House of Commons'. He then said:

> I should like to turn the House of Commons loose into our public departments on a voyage of discovery. I should like to see every one of our public departments rigorously inquired into by small committees of about seven experienced and practical Members of Parliament.[36]

Churchill's speech was not novel in arguing for multiple committees to examine administration and expenditure. The need for such had been made by Tierney in 1817 and Hume had been met with laughter when he said ten or eleven committees would be required in 1828.[37] Gladstone had also suggested in 1860 that at least six committees would be needed to make select committee scrutiny effective.[38] Churchill's originality lay in his advocacy of a *departmental* structure to committees as the best way to secure sustained and rigorous scrutiny.

---

[34] HC Deb, 12 April 1850, cols 231–46.

[35] R Palgrave, 'Parliament and the Public Moneys' (1876) 141 *Quarterly Review* 224, 232.

[36] LJ Jennings (ed), *Speeches of the Right Honourable Lord Randolph Churchill MP, 1880–1888* (London, Longmans, Green & Co, 1889, 2 vols) (hereafter *Speeches*) II, 105–06.

[37] HC Deb, 7 February 1817, cols 278–79; HC Deb, 15 February 1828, col 440.

[38] HC Deb, 2 February 1860, col 472.

In August 1884 Churchill repeated his proposal in the House of Commons, contending that: '[T]here will be no possibility of checking the regular and rapid growth of the public expenditure until the Government of the day allow every single Department to be brought under the rigid examination of a Select Committee of this House.'[39] Attempts to create a single Estimates Committee in 1884 seemed to have frontbench support, but fell foul of disputes between the parties, with each blaming the other for inaction.[40] Late in 1884, Gladstone committed his government to propose at least one committee in the following Session, and they prepared motions for two, one on the Army and Navy Estimates and one on the Miscellaneous Estimates, at the start of the 1885 Session.[41] However, there was no agreement on the establishment of the first, and the second was not nominated due to a dispute over its party composition.[42]

Churchill suggested to an audience in Bow in June 1885 that a Tory government 'would have to set on foot ... a thorough and exhaustive investigation by the House of Commons of the expenditure and management of every government department'.[43] By November, he was a member of such a government, as Secretary of State for India, and he submitted a detailed memorandum to the Prime Minister, Lord Salisbury, with far-reaching proposals for procedural reform, including the following:

> That Committees of the House of Commons be appointed to examine and report upon the constitution, staff, work performed, comparative costs of all public departments, with a view to the effecting of economies and the rearrangement of salaries, promotions and retirements.[44]

These radical proposals commanded little support in Cabinet and the Tory government itself proved short-lived.[45] The idea of 'Select Committees to inquire into the Administration and Expenditure of the great Spending Departments of the State' was kept alive by radicals during Gladstone's third administration, even though soon overshadowed by the divisions on Home Rule that brought the government down.[46] However, Churchill's own prospects for taking the idea forward seemed greatly improved when he was appointed Chancellor of the Exchequer and Leader of the Commons in Salisbury's second administration in July 1886. The *Pall Mall Gazette* recalled Churchill's commitment to departmental committees in his Blackpool speech, but prophesised 'his certain repudiation in office of every principle of economy and of that policy of inquiry which he had so elegantly professed in Opposition'.[47]

Churchill defied forecasts that he might abandon economy, pushing back on demands for increased Estimates from the War Office and the Admiralty and winning glowing reviews

---

[39] HC Deb, 12 August 1884, col 615.

[40] HC Deb, 12 August 1884, col 626; *The Times*, 17 September 1884, p 6.

[41] HC Deb, 17 November 1884, col 1887; HC Deb, 19 February 1885, col 858.

[42] CJ (1884–85) 111; HC Deb, 18 March 1885, cols 1586–88; HC Deb, 17 April 1885, cols 124–28.

[43] *Speeches* (n 36) II, 250.

[44] WS Churchill, *Lord Randolph Churchill* (London, Macmillan 1907) 434.

[45] ibid, 446–47.

[46] HC Deb, 15 March 1886.

[47] *Pall Mall Gazette*, 29 July 1886, p 1; R Rhodes James, *Lord Randolph Churchill* (London, Weidenfeld & Nicolson 1959) 250.

from Treasury officials.[48] This admiration was shared by few of his Cabinet colleagues, who found him 'alarming on economy'.[49] It was on the matter of reductions in the Army and Navy Estimates that Churchill tendered his resignation, but his frustrations extended to procedural reform. After writing his resignation letter at Windsor Castle in December 1886, he sat at dinner with the Queen and, as she recorded, 'talked with me … about the *procedure*, offering to *send me* the proposed rules for me to see!'[50]

Churchill renewed his campaign for economy, of which the case for select committees formed an integral part. Early in January 1887, he wrote to the Head of the Treasury's Finance Division, claiming that his 'main object and hope in going out was to direct public attention in the most forcible manner to the growth of expenditure, and to the carelessness of Ministers and MPs to that growth'.[51] On 31 January, he made the case in the House for a select committee to examine the Army and Navy Estimates 'to get all the necessary information' to determine whether the increases at which he had baulked in office were warranted. He saw such a committee as 'a Parliamentary arbitrator' on the matter, indicating his intention to abide by subsequent decisions.[52] On 21 February, WH Smith, until recently one of the spending ministers with whom Churchill had clashed and now his successor as Leader of the House, agreed to support Churchill's proposal for a select committee on the Army and Navy Estimates, perhaps thereby hoping to call Churchill's bluff on the notion that there was 'extravagance or … unnecessary expenditure' in the Estimates.[53] However, the motion to appoint the committee was blocked and then remained on the notice paper for some weeks, with the government unwilling to provide time for it until prodded by Churchill.[54] Smith then performed a masterstroke by inviting Churchill to chair the committee, expressing confidence in Churchill's 'absolute impartiality', an invitation that Churchill could not resist.[55] There was then a further delay in appointing the members of the committee; he wrote to Smith terming the delay 'scandalous and inexcusable' and, in a speech in Wolverhampton on 3 June, tried to stoke public outrage about the matter:

> This committee, which might have done great work, which might have gone into see things and sifted them, cannot now be usefully appointed this year, as the year is, I am afraid, too far advanced and the committee can hardly in the time which remains to Parliament hold more than twelve or thirteen sittings. All this is very discouraging, very disheartening, and I feel that in these matters I cannot do anything without the help of the English people.[56]

The committee was finally nominated on 6 June and Churchill duly elected chairman. It managed to hold eighteen sittings by early August, but were 'quite unable to complete the

[48] Rhodes James, ibid, 266–68; RF Foster, *Lord Randolph Churchill: A Political Life* (Oxford, Clarendon Press, 1981) 289–93; DWR Bahlmann (ed), *The Diary of Sir Edward Walter Hamilton* (Hull, University of Hull Press, 1993) (hereafter *Hamilton Diary*) 51; British Library (hereafter BL), Add MS 68645, f 68. This and the numerically succeeding manuscripts are the original diaries of Hamilton, including much relevant material not in the printed edition.
[49] Rhodes James (n 47) 266–69, 275–78.
[50] ibid, 302 (emphasis in original).
[51] *Hamilton Diary* (n 48) 52.
[52] HC Deb, 31 January 1887, cols 293–95.
[53] HC Deb, 21 February 1887, col 179; HC Deb, 27 January 1887, col 73.
[54] HC Deb, 5 April 1887, col 602; HC Deb, 9 May 1887, col 1277; HC Deb, 12 May 1887, col 1713.
[55] Churchill (n 44) 677–78.
[56] *Speeches* (n 36) II, 198–99.

work devolved upon them', confining themselves to a recommendation for reappointment in the next Session.[57] Churchill had sufficient time to persuade himself at least of what Edward Hamilton termed 'his great idea'—'to place increased responsibility & control on the professional men'.[58] He pursued this idea with Gladstone, and was encouraged by signs of support.[59] Churchill ended the Session convinced that 'the country was with him on the question of Economy' and in September asserted that there was a 'strong disposition in Parliament to initiate and sustain a vigorous campaign against the extravagant expenditure of public money' so that he 'would look for great results next session'.[60]

In the Session that followed, the government made concessions to Churchill's conception of departmental committees, proposing the establishment of separate committees on the Army, on the Navy and on the Revenue Department Estimates.[61] The last of these, chaired by a Liberal, produced a relatively non-controversial report, which eschewed an opinion on a proposed merger of the Customs and Inland Revenue Departments.[62] The Navy Estimates Committee had a difficult start when Churchill's ally, Robert Hanbury, contested the chair, which went to the official candidate, the Liberal Henry Campbell-Bannerman.[63] Campbell-Bannerman's draft Reports faced consistent opposition from Hanbury and others, but Campbell-Bannerman could rely on government support. The committee eventually produced what Lord George Hamilton, the First Lord of the Admiralty at the time, later called 'a balanced, humdrum' report with no strong line on levels of expenditure or the role of civilian administration.[64] The committee's most lasting achievement was probably the admission it secured from Sir Arthur Hood that it was not possible to say what size of fleet was needed, as he did not know what enemies it might have to fight, which acted as a spur to the development of the two-power standard which was embodied in the Naval Defence Act of the following year.[65]

Churchill chaired the Committee on the Army Estimates, but did not have things his own way. Ministers on the committee fought him at every turn, partly succeeding with amendments to draft Reports which blunted criticism or argued that increases in spending were 'productive of increased efficiency'.[66] It remained an unhappy experience for the government: Lord George Hamilton later recollected that he and the Secretary of State for War had 'deplored to one another the procedure' that Churchill's committees adopted, 'which resulted in the total disorganisation of our two Departments, and which, so far from

[57] Fifth Report from the Select Committee on Army and Navy Estimates, HC (1887) 259, iii.
[58] BL Add MS 64646, ff 96–97.
[59] ibid, ff 95–96, 106–07,116–17; *Hamilton Diary* (n 48) 62–63.
[60] BL Add MS 64646, ff 116–17; *Speeches* (n 36) II, 217.
[61] HC Deb, 13 March 1888, col 1187.
[62] Report from the Select Committee on Revenue Department Estimates, HC (1888) 272, iv and passim.
[63] First Report from the Select Committee on Navy Estimates, HC (1888) 272, iv. On Hanbury's support for Churchill, see HC Deb, 4 August 1887, cols 1179 et seq and *Speeches* (n 36) II, 353.
[64] HC (1888) 272, vii–viii; Fourth Report from the Select Committee on Navy Estimates, HC (1888) 328, xiii–xxiii; Lord George Hamilton, *Parliamentary Reminiscences and Reflections* (London, John Murray, 1922) 105.
[65] Hamilton, ibid, 105–06; CI Hamilton, *The Making of the Modern Admiralty: British Naval Policy-Making 1805–1927* (Cambridge, Cambridge University Press, 2011) 209–10; P Smith, 'Ruling the Waves: Government, the Service and the Cost of Naval Supremacy, 1885–99', in P Smith (ed), *Government and the Armed Forces in Britain 1856–1990* (London, Hambledon Press, 1996) 21, 36.
[66] Second Report from the Select Committee on Army Estimates, HC (1888) 212, xv–xvii; Fourth Report from the Select Committee on Army Estimates, HC (1888) 269, xxiii–xxvii; Fifth and Final Report from the Select Committee on Army Estimates, HC (1888) 285, xvi–xviii.

promoting economy, put forward proposals which very largely increased the expenditure of both Departments'.[67] Churchill had become disillusioned by the enterprise, telling an audience in Hanbury's constituency that the majority of MPs 'appear to be somewhat callous and apathetic regarding public expenditure'. Although Hanbury was an exception, 'there seems to be a kind of determination, an invincible resolution, in the part of the majority of the House of Commons to permit or to support the reckless expenditure of money'.[68] The military reformers whom Churchill had come to support had little faith in his work, the Adjutant General predicting privately that the findings would not be 'worth the paper on which [they] write their reports'.[69] Churchill had highlighted some important issues, but could not command a political consensus on solutions, and it would be for a Royal Commission which sat between 1888 and 1890 to do so.[70]

COMMITTEES AND THE REFORM OF SUPPLY PROCEEDINGS, 1880–96

Select committees of a predominantly investigative character provided additional ammunition to be fired in the Committee of Supply, but they were not intended by and large to supersede the functions of this Committee. The prevailing orthodoxy was affirmed by Palgrave in 1888 when he said that: 'Lord Farnborough [Erskine May] and Mr Speaker Denison have condemned in the strongest possible manner the proposal to submit, not the Estimates, but the actual Votes of Supply to any form of Select Committee.'[71] However, there was a growing willingness to question the view that the formal consideration of Estimates should not be delegated.

The first such challenge came during Cabinet exchanges in response to Gladstone's memorandum in October 1880 proposing to devolve legislative functions to Grand Committees to counteract the delaying effects of obstruction. Gladstone's own scheme for devolution, derived as it was from May's ideas, did not cover Supply proceedings, but this did not stop a proposal being made by John George Dodson, then President of the Local Government Board. Dodson had previously held the posts of Chairman of Ways and Means, Financial Secretary to the Treasury and Chairman of the Committee of Public Accounts. Dodson advanced a separate scheme to facilitate business by referring the Army, Navy and Civil Service Estimates to a select committee and to sweep away the Committee of Supply. It was his intention that the new committee would have the same powers as the Committee of Supply to approve and reduce Votes. The government would have a power to require separate votes in cases where the select committee proposed a reduction, but otherwise each class of estimates, after examination by the select committee, would be 'voted *en bloc* in the House with the Speaker in the Chair'.[72] This scheme was too radical for Gladstone's Cabinet, which

[67] House of Commons, Papers of the Clerk of the Journals (hereafter PCJ), Reform of Parliamentary Procedure, 1902, f 35, Lord George Hamilton to Balfour, 30 November 1901.

[68] *Speeches* (n 36) II, 353.

[69] Hamilton (n 65) 207; BL Add MS 48748, ff 95–96.

[70] WS Hamer, *The British Army: Civil–Military Relations, 1885–1905* (Oxford, Clarendon Press, 1970) 113 et seq.

[71] Report from the Select Committee on Estimates Procedure (Grants of Supply), HC (1888) 281, Q408.

[72] The National Archives (hereafter TNA), CAB 37/3/60, Cabinet papers on Devolution and Obstruction, Dodson to Gladstone, 9 November 1880, 11.

did not advance any proposals along these lines even when faced with the intensification of obstruction in 1881.

Similar proposals were advanced in subsequent years. In 1884, a Liberal backbencher, Henry Fowler, proposed that the Army, Navy and Civil Service Estimates should each be referred to a committee at the start of a Session 'in the same way that Bills were now referred to Grand Committees', saving 'a great waste of time in Committee of Supply, and a considerable amount of labour, which, as a rule, produced very trifling and unsatisfactory results'.[73] In 1886 the Cabinet agreed to take forward proposals for the Estimates to be referred to Standing Committees.[74] A Procedure Committee packed with Cabinet Ministers was appointed and the Chairman sought agreement to a proposal for the three Estimates to be so referred, with the resolutions of those Standing Committees to take the place of resolutions of the Committee of Supply. Although supported by the Cabinet ministers on the committee, it was defeated.[75]

In January 1888, Fowler came forward with a new proposal for select committees which would in effect sift and help to manage the business of the Committee of Supply. He envisaged three select committees being established at the start of each session to which the Army, Navy and Civil Service Estimates would be referred. The committees would identify Votes which, in their opinion, required omission, reduction or further investigation. The Committee of Supply would still be able to consider any disputed item, but Civil Service Votes would otherwise be taken by Class, and then amalgamated for consideration on report.[76] Fowler then secured government agreement for a motion to establish a committee to examine Estimates procedure, whose members included Fowler himself, Churchill, Churchill's successor as Chancellor, George Goschen, and the two other Liberal Unionist heavyweights, Joseph Chamberlain and Lord Hartington, the latter chairing the Committee.[77]

The most fully worked and radical proposals that came before that committee came from Archibald Milman, the Clerk Assistant.[78] Milman acknowledged the reluctance to delegate the Estimates to select committees 'in old times', but considered that 'it would be a great advantage, and a great saving of time' if a strong and permanent select committee could consider Votes and propose those that could be agreed to without separate debate in Committee of Supply. Although he allowed for the select committee's proposal to by-pass the Committee of Supply to be over-ridden by twenty Members acting in concert, he felt adoption of his proposal would save up to fifteen days a session: 'My scheme is to save ... the unnecessary tedium of pretending to go through the whole Estimates which are voted every year in exactly the same way.'[79] Milman envisaged the select committee developing a track

---

[73] HC Deb, 17 November 1884, col 1882.

[74] TNA, CAB 37/18/48, Resolutions proposed by the Chancellor of the Exchequer to the Select Committee on Procedure, 22 March 1886, pp 3–4; HC Deb, 26 March 1886, col 40.

[75] Report from the Select Committee on Parliamentary Procedure, HC (1886) 186, p xxvi.

[76] *The Times*, 18 January 1888, 6 (reprinted in HC (1888) 281, 62–63).

[77] HC Deb, 8 March 1888, col 685; HC (1888) 281, iii.

[78] On the wider development of Milman's views up to 1888, see C Lee, 'Archibald Milman and the Procedural Response to Obstruction' (2015) 83 *The Table: The Journal of the the Society of Clerks-at-the-Table in Commonwealth Parliaments* 22–44.

[79] HC (1888) 281, QQ 459–72, 479, 506.

record over several years so that its judgement on what merited further debate would be trusted by the House and 'would create a confidence between the Treasury, the Departments, and the House of Commons, which would tend to facilitate business'.[80] He submitted the text of a motion to give effect to his proposal, but it was met with some scepticism from the Chairman of Ways and Means and members of the Committee.[81] The Committee rejected the Fowler and Milman proposals for select committees and was so divided on the few proposals they did make that they did not serve as the basis for progress.[82]

In 1894, Milman prepared a revised version of his proposal, which he explained in an anonymous article. To overcome the risk that a small group of Members could overturn the attempt to prevent debate in Committee of Supply, he proposed that the motion to recommit Votes to the Committee of Supply could only be moved by a minister.[83] In 1888 he had described the committee's functions predominantly in relation to its sifting role: in 1894 he stressed that the committee could examine official witnesses and prepare reports which highlighted new expenditure or other matters which warranted further debate in the Committee of Supply.[84] An undated draft of a motion, almost certainly prepared by Milman around this time, proposed further modifications, including limiting the committee to the Civil Service Estimates and providing for members of the Committee of Public Accounts to be included within a larger membership.[85]

Milman argued for the more rational apportionment of time in the Committee of Supply,[86] and these suggestions became more important when Arthur Balfour proposed early in 1896 to limit the number of days in Committee of Supply and to provide for all outstanding questions to be put at the conclusion of the allocation. Palgrave, the Clerk of the House, had already softened his position somewhat on select committees to manage the business of Supply when questioned by Fowler in 1888,[87] and, faced with Balfour's proposals, he advanced his own which drew upon those of Fowler and Milman. In a memorandum prepared for the Cabinet at the end of January 1896, Palgrave made what he labelled a 'tentative' proposal for all Estimates to stand referred to an Estimates Committee composed of all members of the Committee of Public Accounts and twelve other Members. The Estimates Committee would then report within a week on how the allotted days should be allocated between Army, Navy and Civil Service Estimates. It would also identify those Supply resolutions that could be put forthwith or after half an hour of debate or be amalgamated for debate or be referred to a Standing Committee.[88] The proposals for which Balfour secured the House's agreement made no concession to the ideas of select committee involvement envisaged by Fowler, Milman and Palgrave, retaining the role of the whole-House Committee of Supply in return for a guaranteed end point for its work.

---

[80] ibid, Q533.
[81] ibid, 64 and QQ 677, 691.
[82] ibid, iv, ix–xii.
[83] A Milman, 'Parliamentary Procedure *versus* Obstruction' (1894) 178 *Quarterly Review* 486, 499.
[84] ibid.
[85] PCJ, Miscellaneous Precedents and Memoranda on Procedure, vol 3, f 230.
[86] Milman (n 83) 500.
[87] HC (1888) 281, QQ 277–307.
[88] PCJ, Miscellaneous Precedents and Memoranda on Procedure, vol 3, ff 225 and 226v.

A CHURCHILLIAN REVIVAL, 1901–04

Proposals for select committees on the Estimates in the last two decades of the nineteenth century had taken two main forms: those that emphasised the value of scrutiny separate from the Committee of Supply and those that sought to replace or improve the procedures of this Committee. In 1901, a new set of proposals emerged which combined the various strands. They were first made by Robert Hanbury, who had been an ally of Churchill in 1888 and had been a party to the development of Balfour reforms of Supply procedure as Financial Secretary to the Treasury. He was very likely to have been familiar with the proposals that had emanated from Milman and Palgrave, not least because he was Milman's brother-in-law.[89]

Balfour had mooted, late in 1901, the possibility of removing debate on the report of Supply. Hanbury feared the proposal would lessen the House's control over expenditure and would be a 'dangerous step'. He conceded that a great deal of time in debate on Supply was wasted, but felt this was a consequence of the lack of information available to Members under 'the present absurd system'. He argued that Royal Commissions or departmental committees could not perform the role that could be undertaken by 'steady, persistent watching of the expenditure of the various Departments'. He thought that the Treasury could not undertake this role, as its focus was always on new expenditure. The Committee of Public Accounts was concerned with retrospective consideration only, and often it was 'occupied upon the merest technicalities'. Even political chiefs could not fully oversee departments, because they were 'a bird of passage', subject to the strains of parliamentary life and concerned with current challenges. He concluded with the first element of his proposal:

> The only way of securing intelligent and non-partisan and business-like criticism of the Estimates is … by setting up again the kind of Select Committees which Randolph Churchill first started in the 1886 Parliament. There information can be got at first hand—and that information is printed, and at the service of the whole House, and of the country, and would … be of considerable use, even to the Treasury and the Government itself. Business men whose special talents are now never properly utilised, could be specially useful on such Committees, and younger Members, who cannot be expected to be mere voting machines, would gain a large amount of insight into the Government of the country, and have the opportunity to show their fitness for, and to gain knowledge of, the work of administration.

He then went on to propose a further 'radical change' which probably drew on the proposals by Fowler and Milman, but also had echoes of Dodson's submission to an earlier Cabinet:

> I should hand over the work now done, or not done, by the Committee of the whole House to three or four of these Select Committees, and thus increase the real control of Parliament over expenditure, and simultaneously save twenty or more days of the time of the House.

He suggested that the House's direct involvement could be provided through the report stage of Supply, which he wished to retain.[90]

---

[89] *Speeches* (n 36) II, 353; HW Lucy, *A Diary of the Home Rule Parliament 1892–1895* (London, Cassell, 1896) 87–92; BL Add MS 49760, ff 17–18v, Sandars to Balfour, 16 September 1895; C Lee, 'Archibald Milman and the 1893 Irish Home Rule Bill' (2016) 84 *The Table: The Journal of the the Society of Clerks-at-the-Table in Commonwealth Parliaments* 28, 41.

[90] TNA, CAB 37/59/121, Cabinet correspondence, 1–2, Hanbury to Balfour, 10 November 1901.

In reply, Balfour expressed concern at the pressure on ministers if they had to prepare themselves for 'a detailed—and possibly prolonged and hostile—cross-examination … upon minute expenditure'. He thought that 'nothing so disorganises the work of a Department as these parliamentary inquiries'.[91] His scepticism was partly shared by Lord George Hamilton, partly drawing on his 'vivid recollection' of the committees of 1887 and 1888. He thought committees would have a tendency 'to enquire into and examine witnesses upon questions of policy which can only be settled by the Government of the day'. However, he concluded that 'the experiment … might fairly be adopted, if it be in the first instance attempted in a restrictive and tentative form'.[92]

The most forthright criticism came from an official, Edward Hamilton, who was asked to give his opinion by Balfour's political secretary, Jack Sandars. Hamilton began by expressing sympathy for the second element of Hanbury's proposition: 'I have often myself thought that the most effectual way of reforming Supply procedure would be devolution on Select Committees of what the Committee of Supply does now.' He felt that the Committee of Supply 'signally fails' to exercise control over expenditure. He went on to argue that the time saving would not be as great Hanbury suggested, because an outlet would be needed for debates on policy and administration, so that the saving would be ten to twelve days rather than twenty. He acknowledged the benefits of the Committee of Public Accounts and protested, perhaps a little too much, that he had no concern about the demand the committees would place on officials, who were paid by the House and so 'have to be at their beck and call.' Rather, he was concerned that ministers would be asked as witnesses and thus 'the burden on Ministers would … be seriously aggravated and become intolerable'. Worse still, the committees might 'venture upon recommending radical changes in the Estimates', thus 'aggravating an existing tendency on the part of Parliament to usurp the functions of the Executive, which is destructive of all good administration'. Committees might not act as a check on expenditure, but 'foster extravagance' and thus give Parliament a power that it did not have to make additions to the cost of government. Thus, 'the conclusion to which I reluctantly come is that the disadvantages and drawbacks decidedly outweigh the advantages and attractions'.[93]

Although Balfour did not think that there was a basis for an immediate proposal, he sought Cabinet views on whether the matter should be referred to a select committee.[94] In January 1902, Balfour told the House that: 'I myself should like very much to see something done … with regard to that aspect of Supply which consists in the discussion not of questions of policy but of details of expenditure.' He thought it probable that the House would wish to see the matter referred to a select committee for consideration.[95] In February, he implied that he was willing to establish a committee,[96] but that action was taken was due to the campaigning zeal of Lord Randolph's son.

Winston Churchill had been elected in 1900. From the outset he seemed concerned to vindicate his father's memory. Churchill was researching his father's biography and he

[91] ibid, 2–3, Balfour to Hanbury, 17 November 1901.
[92] PCJ, Reform of Parliamentary Procedure, ff 35–37, Lord George Hamilton to Balfour, 30 November 1901.
[93] ibid, ff 31–34, Sir Edward Hamilton to Sandars, 21 November 1901.
[94] ibid, f 38, Balfour's Cabinet submission, 16 December 1901, 9.
[95] HC Deb, 30 January 1902, cols 1372–73.
[96] HC Deb, 17 February 1902, col 208.

consciously sought to emulate his campaigns. *Punch* magazine listed Winston's interests as 'the House of Commons—and its reform. The British Army—and its reform. The British Navy—and its reform. The Universe—and its reform'.[97] Churchill's biographers have concentrated on the second of these interests, which led the Secretary of State for War to accuse him of a 'hereditary desire to run Imperialism on the cheap'.[98] Little attention has been paid to Churchill's campaign on reform of the House of Commons.

In April 1902, Churchill followed up a speech attacking the growth of expenditure by tabling a motion to establish a Committee on National Expenditure. His request for government support was firmly rebuffed by Balfour in early May,[99] but Churchill then wrote to Balfour, restating his case for a substantive parliamentary investigation on the growth of expenditure. Balfour rejected that case, but restated his support for a committee to investigate reform of parliamentary machinery for considering expenditure, and informed Churchill that a motion to establish that committee had been tabled.[100] The House agreed to create a committee 'to inquire whether any plan can be advantageously adopted for enabling the House, by Select Committee or otherwise, more effectively to make an examination, not involving criticisms of policy, into the details of national expenditure'.[101] Early in July the members were nominated, with Churchill among their number.[102]

Churchill prepared a detailed memorandum outlining his own proposals. He drew a distinction between 'policy, merit, and audit' and accepted that '[p]olicy is the province of the Cabinet and of the House of Commons itself', but distinguished between that and the 'merit' or 'value for money' aspect of expenditure of which 'no real Parliamentary control at present exists'. He acknowledged that the task of examining the merits of expenditure lay beyond a committee of the House working alone, but—reflecting the 'satisfactory results' for audit of the combined work of the Committee of Public Accounts and the Comptroller and Auditor General—proposed that the House's examination of Estimates should be assisted by officials within the Comptroller and Auditor General's office 'trained for that very purpose'. He envisaged replacing the Committee of Public Accounts by a Public Finance Committee with two sub-committees—'the Accounts Committee' and 'the Estimates Committee'—both supported by the Comptroller and Auditor General's Department. The Estimates Committee would report on the Estimates for the previous year, in good time to inform debate in Committee of Supply on the current year's Estimates.[103]

The committee completed its evidence-taking in the 1902 Session, but was unable to consider a substantive Report.[104] It was reappointed in April 1903 and in mid-June set about considering the Chairman's draft Report.[105] That draft supported the establishment of an Estimates Committee, but only to undertake a 'post-mortem examination of a branch

---

[97] R Rhodes James, *Churchill: A Study in Failure 1900–1939* (London, Weidenfeld & Nicolson, 1970) 16, 18; M Shelden, *Young Titan: The Making of Winston Churchill* (London, Simon & Schuster, 2013) 49.

[98] HC Deb, 13 May 1901, cols 1562–79; HC Deb, 14 May 1901, cols 94–95; HC Deb, 16 May 1901, cols 308–10.

[99] HC Deb, 14 April 1902, cols 228–42; HC Deb, 24 April 1902, cols 1205–06; HC Deb, 5 May 1902, cols 633–35.

[100] RS Churchill, *Winston S Churchill*, vol II, companion part I: *1901–1907* (London, Heinemann, 1969) 127–30.

[101] HC Deb, 28 May 1902, col 879.

[102] HC Deb, 2 July 1902, cols 538–39; HC Deb, 8 July 1902, cols 1087–88.

[103] Churchill (n 100) 130–34.

[104] ibid, iii.

[105] HC Deb, 26 February 1903, col 937; HC Deb, 18 May 1903, cols 936–37; Report from the Select Committee on National Expenditure, HC (1903) 242, ii, ix.

or branches of the Estimates, or of a particular Vote or item of expenditure of the nearest preceding year of which it can obtain an account' in order to offer 'lessons in economical administration'.[106] Churchill immediately pinpointed the weakness of this proposed Committee, whose work 'would be so little different from that already discharged by the Public Accounts Committee as scarcely to justify the creation of a fresh body'.[107] Instead, Churchill sought support for the proposal 'made to us by Mr Gibson Bowles that at the beginning of each Session one Class of the Estimates should be referred to a Select Committee for examination and report precedent to the Votes being discussed in Committee of Supply'. Because the Committee would be reporting information for subsequent use by the Committee of Supply, 'there could be no question of interference either with ministerial responsibility or with Parliamentary control'.[108] Churchill secured a narrow majority for his amended text of the Report, so that the final Report supported the establishment of an Estimates Committee along the lines proposed by Gibson Bowles, with some overlap of membership with the Public Accounts Committee and with the latter Committee influencing the choice of Estimates to be considered in the following Session.[109]

The Report met with firm resistance from the government. In March 1904, Balfour acknowledged that the recommendations were 'very ingenious', but doubted they would prove acceptable to the House, restating the classic arguments on the timing difficulties and the creation of upward pressure on expenditure.[110] Churchill and Gibson Bowles then badgered Balfour to provide time for a debate. Balfour initially hid behind the need to consult the Leader of the Opposition, Henry Campbell-Bannerman, a consultation which he mysteriously took some time undertake.[111] When they finally spoke, he found that he and Campbell-Bannerman 'were agreed in having some doubts as to the efficacy or practicability of the scheme advocated by the majority of the National Expenditure Committee'.[112] Although Campbell-Bannerman 'urged' the government to set aside a day for debate on the Report, Balfour declined to respond, and, when the matter was raised in August by Churchill, Balfour bluntly said he was 'sure the Leader of the Opposition will agree with me that neither he nor I greatly desire to stay for that discussion'.[113] Churchill regretted the failure to provide for a debate,[114] although his advocacy of the case for an Estimates Committee continued,[115] and he was a Cabinet minister in the Liberal government that supported its eventual creation in 1912.[116]

CONCLUSIONS

The history of select committees in the nineteenth century has largely focused on their contribution to social policy reform in the early part of that century and on the creation and

---

[106] ibid, xii.
[107] ibid, xiv.
[108] ibid, xv.
[109] ibid, xv–xvii, viii.
[110] HC Deb, 1 March 1904, cols 1365–66.
[111] ibid, cols 1366–67; HC Deb, 7 March 1904, cols 324–25; HC Deb, 17 March 1904, cols 1410–11.
[112] HC Deb, 19 April 1904, col 537.
[113] HC Deb, 1 August 1904, cols 282–83.
[114] HC Deb, 2 August 1904, col 570.
[115] HC Deb, 26 July 1905, cols 441–44.
[116] Chubb (n 30) 90–91.

development of the Committee of Public Accounts in the closing decades of the century. The significance of the select committees that examined the Estimates and of the ideas for a more extensive use of the select committee system to improve the House's understanding of, and control over, planned expenditure has been largely neglected. However, the ideas and proposals considered here have enduring importance. They showed an appreciation within the House of the value of examining expenditure at the planning stage rather than simply after the event as a way to gain insight into administration and the merits of policy, an appreciation which has been central to what success has subsequently been achieved. They involved an assertion of the value of select committees best encapsulated in words inserted in the Report of the 1902 Committee by Winston Churchill:

> We are impressed with the advantages, for the purposes of detailed financial scrutiny, which are enjoyed by Select Committees, whose proceedings are usually devoid of party feeling, who may obtain accurate knowledge collected for them by trained officials, which may, if so desired, be checked or extended by the examination of witnesses or the production of documents; and we feel it is in this direction that the financial control of the House of Commons is most capable of being strengthened.[117]

The radical thinking and forceful advocacy by the two Churchills, father and son, charted the direction which was belatedly followed in the twentieth century. This was true not only in relation to the Estimates Committee established in 1912 and its successors up to 1979. Lord Randolph Churchill was the first to identify the value of Departments as the best unit for determining the organisation of committees, foreshadowing the creation of departmental select committees in 1979. Winston Churchill's memorandum of 1902 identifies the importance of auditors considering not simply the accounts but questions of value for money, an idea enshrined in the National Audit Act 1983.

Some of the ideas promoted from the 1880s to the turn of the twentieth century thus bore fruit late in the twentieth century. However, the vision of proposals to connect and even integrate the House's formal proceedings to authorise expenditure with the value of select committee fact-finding, interrogation and analysis has never fully been realised, and this remains a challenge to which the House's procedures and the select committee system have not adequately responded to this day.

---

[117] HC (1903) 242, xix, vii.

Part V

The *Lex Parliamentaria* Revisited

16

Privilege: The Unfolding Debate with the Courts

EVE SAMSON

INTRODUCTION: WHY PRIVILEGE?

PARLIAMENTARY PRIVILEGE IS one of the ways of maintaining balance between the different constitutional players in the United Kingdom. There is broad agreement about the privileges that Parliament requires in principle, as articulated by the Joint Committee on Parliamentary Privilege in 1998:

> Parliament makes the law and raises taxes. It is also the place where ministers are called to account by representatives of the whole nation for their decisions and their expenditure of public money. Grievances, great and small, can be aired, regardless of the power or wealth of those criticised.

> In order to carry out these public duties without fear or favour, Parliament and its Members and officers need certain rights and immunities. Parliament needs the right to regulate its own affairs, free from intervention by the government or the courts. Members need to be able to speak freely, uninhibited by possible defamation claims.[1]

There is far less certainty about how such rights and immunities should operate in practice. As the relationship between the key constitutional players, and indeed, the general understanding of their different roles is not fixed, here, as elsewhere, there is the tension between the clarity of codification and the pragmatism of an approach which leaves room for evolution, for common sense and common understanding. The first has the risk of inflexibility in the face of changing systems; the second the risk that assumptions about common understandings turn out not to be generally agreed.

MAY AND PRIVILEGE

Although we commonly speak of 'parliamentary privilege' Parliament itself is not a unitary body. May confidently set out in his first edition that:

> The Imperial Parliament of the United Kingdom of Great Britain and Northern Ireland is composed of the King or Queen and the three estates of the realm, viz the Lords Spiritual, the Lords Temporal, and the Commons. These several powers collectively make laws that are binding on the

---

[1] Joint Committee on Parliamentary Privilege, Report, Session 1998–99, HC 214-I/HL 43-I, Executive Summary.

subjects of the British Empire; and as distinct members of the supreme legislature, enjoy privileges and exercise functions peculiar to each.[2]

May's description of the composition of Parliament remains, in some sense, correct; today it also appears alien and outdated. The central governing concept described by May, the 'Crown in Parliament' remains but is now largely overlooked. It makes some sense at state opening, but the other occasion on which the Crown appears in Parliament (though not in person since 1854) is the piece of theatre immediately before prorogation. It is seen as either a ridiculous anachronism or a triumph of tradition. This ritual meeting of three disparate yet inextricable power sources—government, apparently hiding behind the Queen, the Lords, and the Commons, now the main source of the government's power—has lasted for centuries. The struggle to keep a proper balance between them is equally ancient; indeed May follows the Elizabethan line that the popular character of the Saxon councils was subverted for a time by the Norman overlord, but gradually reasserted itself. Sometimes the struggle between the constituent parts of the Crown in Parliament has been expressed through war: more usually it has been between through exercise (and limitation) of the royal prerogative, parliamentary procedure, legislation and law suits.

May's description of Parliament includes the judiciary only as useful advisers to the House of Lords. Despite that, even in his day the tension between courts and Parliament was central to any discussion of privilege. The physical separation of law from Parliament since the establishment of the Supreme Court may be new, but it is an extreme manifestation of an old tension: in a parliamentary system of government, what is the proper role of judges and what of Parliament? This question has often been addressed, but there is as yet no definitive answer—and no appetite to give one in statutory form, even though in 1844 May himself concluded:

> The present position of privilege is, in the highest degree, unsatisfactory. Assertions of privilege are made in Parliament and denied in the courts; the officers who execute the orders of Parliament are liable to vexatious actions, and if verdicts are obtained against them, the damages and costs are paid by the Treasury.

May saw a remedy in the shape of legislation:

> It is not expected that Parliament should surrender any privilege that is essential to its dignity, and of the proper exercise of its authority; but the privileges of both houses should be secured by a legislative definition; and a mode of enforcing them should be adopted which would be binding on the courts.[3]

THE DEBATE

The set of problems around parliamentary privilege has changed little since the *Treatise* first appeared in 1844: how to balance the rights of elected MPs, the private citizen, the press, the courts and each House of Parliament as a collective body—but no legislation has been forthcoming.

---

[2] TE May, *A Treatise upon the Law, Privileges, Proceedings and Usage of Parliament*, 1st ed (London, Knight, 1844) 2.

[3] ibid, 129–30.

In part this is because parliamentary time is too precious to deal with a subject widely seen as arcane, and rarely seen as urgent. And in part it is because answering the questions raised would move a key part of the constitution from the realm of common sense, the evolutionary and pragmatic, to the realm of the defined, codified and potentially rigid. How can the proposition that each House has the right to order matters relating to its own proceedings as it considers best, which includes the right to ensure those proceedings are not disrupted, be reconciled with the courts' function of protecting individual rights (a function that long pre-dates the Human Rights Act)? Can one have self-regulation without the right to deal with outsiders whose actions interfere with each House's ability to carry out its functions? Can Parliament effectively make the law, if the courts interpret it? Is the right to speak freely only a matter of avoiding legal liabilities, or is it desirable to have a broad exemption from judicial evaluation? And can parliamentary rights and immunities be entrenched without, for practical purposes, ceding supremacy to the courts? In principle, each House has its own privileges. In practice the most pressing issues have tended to arise in relation to the House of Commons, the arena in which the government is sustained or defeated. This chapter accordingly has a Commons focus.

THE BEGINNINGS: *STOCKDALE v HANSARD*

It was the struggle between courts and Parliament or, more properly, the courts and the House of Commons, which prompted May to recommend legislation to settle the matter of privilege. His frustration was born from an epic: the case of *Stockdale v Hansard*,[4] and the related proceedings in *Howard v Gosset*. In the first case, Stockdale brought an action against an allegation, which was contained in a report printed by order of the House, that he was printing pornography. In the second set of cases, the House attempted to take various retaliatory steps against Howard, Stockdale's solicitor. At the centre of those cases were the following issues: how far did parliamentary freedom of speech extend? How could the penal powers of the Commons be exercised? Who should decide the extent of privilege? And in a showdown, did courts or each House of Parliament have the upper hand?

MPs were bit players in *Stockdale v Hansard* itself: the report which famously accused Stockdale of issuing pornography was simply printed by the House printers, Messrs Hansard, on the order of the House. It was not in issue that the House had the right to have papers printed for the use of Members, or that papers so printed might contain matters which would otherwise be actionable. The point on which the courts and Parliament disagreed was whether the House had power to order those papers to be printed for wider circulation and, by that order, attach the same privilege to them.

The particular issues in *Stockdale v Hansard* were resolved resoundingly in favour of the courts.[5] After a series of cases in which Stockdale took on Hansard, sometimes from prison, and in which the House of Commons attempted to take retaliatory action against Stockdale's solicitor, Howard, the House resolved the situation by passing the Parliamentary Papers Act 1840. This provided protection for papers published by order of either House of

---

[4] *Stockdale v.Hansard* (1839) 9 Ad & Ell 96.
[5] The House had one small win, over whether a Speaker's warrant should be treated as if emanating from the lower or higher courts.

Parliament—the model commended by May for wider use. It also implicitly recognised that legislation was the only the way in which Parliament could tell the courts about its powers.

Stockdale v Hansard is noteworthy for the level of contention between the House of Commons and the courts, and the 'gloves off' nature of the arguments. The case centred on who should hold power, and how that power should be checked. This was an argument about the respective role of the House and the judiciary as fierce as any modern arguments over the European Court of Human Rights. It was central to the House of Commons' position that at some point, however wise and well balanced a constitution is, however much there is a framework for avoiding and correcting abuses of power, ultimately there will be institutions which can exercise their powers without hindrance. As the Attorney General, Sir J Campbell, put it:

> In every balanced government there must be powers so constituted as to check each other, powers which have their respective limits, but for the abuse of which there can be no remedy.[6]

The argument was not confined to the abstract. The Attorney General noted that judges themselves had not been beyond criticism, citing examples of judges behaving badly. Most importantly, he noted the judicial decision of 1637 in favour of the legality of ship money (ie Charles I's claim that the prerogative right to levy this charge on the people extended to times of peace even without the consent of Parliament); a decision on the wrong side of the political argument, and hence, in the long term, on the wrong side of the legal argument. The judges gave as good as they got. Lord Denman declared:

> The independence of parliament is the corner stone of our free constitution. The Judges who invaded it in the reign of James the First and his son have justly shared with those who betrayed the rights of the people in the case of ship money the abhorrence of all enlightened men. But a mean submissiveness to power has not been always confined to the Judges; the same dispositions belonged to Parliament itself, and to both houses.[7]

Mr Justice Patteson considered that the House began to order papers to be printed for general circulation in 1641 'a most suspicious time in the history of this country for the acquisition of a new power by the House of Commons'. The papers so printed dealt with the relations between King and Parliament and 'surely it is impossible to contend that a practice arising out of the unfortunate and violent state of the times can be supported, unless other reasons applicable to quiet and ordinary times can be assigned for its continuance'.[8] Mr Justice Littledale attacked the Attorney General's proposition there was a public interest in Parliament communicating with constituents:

> As to the general information to be given to the public of all that is going on in Parliament, I cannot conceive upon what ground that can be necessary. I do not consider as a matter of right that the public should know all that is going on in Parliament.[9]

However ill articulated, underlying these acid exchanges are deep questions about the relationship between law and politics, and about the communications between Parliament and the public. The core question was who defined privilege. May quotes Mr Justice Littledale:

> It is said the House of Commons is the sole judge of its own privileges: and so I admit as far as the proceedings in the House and some other things are concerned; but I do not think it follows that

---

[6] *Stockdale v Hansard* (1839) 9 Ad & Ell 96.
[7] ibid.
[8] ibid.
[9] ibid.

they have a power to declare what their privileges are, so as to preclude enquiry whether what they declare are part of their privileges.

The Attorney-General admits that they are not entitled to create new privileges; but they declare this to be their privilege. But how are we to know that this is part of their privileges, without enquiring into it, when no such privilege was ever declared before?

May sourly adds: 'To this argument however, it is an obvious answer that assuming the House to be judge of its own privileges, it is its province to determine whether a privilege be new or not, from an examination of the Journals and other authorities.'[10] However, an attempt to cow the courts by reaffirming the Commons' view of its privileges through a series of resolutions failed.[11] The response was that if Parliament wished to change the law, it should do so by statute: without that, it was for the judiciary to interpret the law.

May pointed out that the logical consequence of the House's assertion '[t]hat for any court or tribunal to assume to decide upon matters of privilege inconsistent with the determination of either house of Parliament thereon, is contrary to the law of Parliament and is breach and contempt of the privileges of Parliament' would be a wholesale attack on the officers of the law 'and so great would be the injustice of punishing the public officers of the law for administering the law according to their consciences and their oaths, that Parliament would shrink from so violent an exertion of privilege'.[12] As May shrewdly remarked, the failure to take action against the judges who repeatedly denied the House's assertion of its privilege 'is inconsistent in principle, and betrays hesitation on the part of the house— distrust of its own authority, or fear of public opinion'.[13]

It would be surprising for there to be such a robust exchange between a modern Attorney General and the judiciary in the context of a particular case, but the sense of politics and judiciary approaching the same questions from radically different directions has, if anything, increased. There can be a sense of mutual incomprehension about matters such as the way in which decisions are properly reached and communicated. There has even been a recent attempt to use a Resolution of the House of Commons to clarify the law, and this twenty-first-century attempt to define what Parliament meant through resolution was as unsuccessful as the nineteenth-century one.[14] The assertion by the House of judicial 'no-go' zones, and the contrary determination of the judges to examine where boundaries of those zones should be set, continues. The Commons' distrust of its own authority and fear of public opinion has increased.

---

[10] *Treatise* (n 2) 119.

[11] 'That the power of publishing such of its reports, votes and proceedings as it shall deem necessary or conducive to the public interests, is an essential incident to the constitutional functions of Parliament, more especially of this house, as the representative portion of it. That by the law and privilege of Parliament, this house has the sole and exclusive jurisdiction to determine upon the existence and extent of its privileges; and that the institution or prosecution of any action, suit or other proceeding, for the purpose of bringing them into discussion or decision before any court or tribunal elsewhere than in Parliament, is a high breach of such privilege, and renders all parties concerned therein amenable to its just displeasure, and to the punishment consequent thereon. That for any court or tribunal to assume to decide upon matters of privilege inconsistent with the determination of either house of Parliament thereon, is contrary to the law of Parliament and is breach and contempt of the privileges of Parliament' (see Commons Journal, 31 May 1837, CJ 92, 419).

[12] *Treatise* (n 2) 130.

[13] ibid.

[14] On 19 June 2012, in connection with the Statement on Changes to Immigration Rules (HC 194), the Commons debated the motion: 'That this House supports the Government in recognising that the right to respect for family or private life in Article 8 of the European Convention of Human Rights is a qualified right and agrees

PARLIAMENTARY PRIVILEGE: THE COMMONS COMMITTEES

Even at the time of *Stockdale v Hansard*, parliamentary privilege was not an entirely statute-free zone. Article IX of the Bill of Rights of 1688/89 codified earlier claims to free speech into a prohibition against 'impeaching or questioning' proceedings in Parliament 'in any court or place out of Parliament'. Other statutory provisions were enacted after the 1840 Parliamentary Papers Act, notably the Witnesses (Public Inquiries) Protection Act 1892, which included investigations by select committees among the public inquiries whose witnesses gained automatic protection, and the Parliamentary Witnesses (Oaths) Act 1871, which read in conjunction with the Perjury Act 1911 makes giving false witness under oath before a committee of Parliament a criminal offence (incidentally appearing to drive a coach and horses through Article IX). But May's ambition of a general legislative definition of the privileges of Parliament remains foreign to UK law. In contrast, other commonwealth jurisdictions in the Westminster tradition have now legislated on privilege—the Australian Federal Parliament enacted a Parliamentary Privileges Act in 1987 and the New Zealand Parliament made similar provision in 2014. Canada, for example, has not.

The lack of UK legislation does not mean privilege has rested unexamined. As the nineteenth century progressed, the penal powers of the House were exercised increasingly infrequently. The last person committed (put under detention) by order of the House was Charles Bradlaugh in 1880[15] (in connection with his refusal, as an avowed atheist, to swear the oath of allegiance before being permitted to take his seat, despite being properly returned at an election).[16] By the twentieth century, complaints of privilege were most frequently made against journalists or the press. Although the Committee of Privileges rarely recommended action, and in many cases did not uphold the complaint, the press considered that the boundaries of privilege were uncertain, and that complaints of contempt had a chilling effect. Certainly, the procedure in use at that time encouraged high-profile and hasty action: complaints had to be made on the floor of the House, after Questions, as soon as practicable after the MP became aware of the alleged contempt. The Committee of Privileges most frequently found no contempt had been committed, or recommended that no action should be taken, either because an apology had been made, or because the matter was trivial. These considered judgements, issued in print, could never have the impact of the denunciations which led to a matter being referred to the Committee in the first place.

---

that the conditions for migrants to enter or remain in the UK on the basis of their family or private life should be those contained in the Immigration rules' (see HC Deb, 19 June 2012, cc 760–823; in *Izuazu (Article 8—new rules) Nigeria [2013]* UKUT 45 (IAC) (30 January 2013) the Upper Tribunal rejected arguments that the approval of HC 194 in this way was an approximation of a statutory assessment of the balance between competing interests. Mr Justice Blake noted: '[I]t has long been the law that a resolution of the House of Commons is not given supremacy akin to primary legislation by the court: see *Stockdale v Hansard* (1839) 9 A & E 1.'

[15] He was committed to custody of the Serjeant on 23 June 1880 (CJ (1880) 235); a few months earlier, on 3 March, Mr Charles Edmund Grissell had been committed to Newgate for refusing to obey an order to attend the House in the previous Session (CJ (1880) 77).

[16] See Bryan Niblett, *Dare to Stand Alone: The Story of Charles Bradlaugh, Atheist and Republican* (Oxford, Kramedart Press, 2010).

THE 1967 AND 1977 COMMITTEES

In 1967 a Select Committee on Parliamentary Privilege was established and reported. This was a solely Commons Committee since privilege was clearly more problematical for the lower House than for the Lords. The Committee's witnesses could be categorised as falling into one of three categories: lawyers; MPs and officials of the House; and the press and television companies, who were the most urgent in pressing for change.

The Committee considered that the term 'parliamentary privilege' should be abolished, and that the House should speak of 'rights and immunities' rather than 'rights and privileges'; this uneasiness about the way in which term privilege 'has in modern times acquired a meaning different from its traditional Parliamentary connotation' has frequently resurfaced, as has the assertion of

> the fundamental principle that 'privilege' is not the prerogative of Members in their personal capacities. Insofar as the House claims and Members enjoy those rights and immunities that are grouped under the general description of 'privileges', they are claimed and enjoyed by the House in its corporate capacity and by its Members on behalf of the citizens whom they represent.[17]

The proposal to focus not on 'privileges' but on 'rights and immunities' had implications that could have gone beyond simple nomenclature. The Committee considered the Strauss case in 1957. Mr Strauss had written a letter to a minister criticising certain alleged practices of the London Electricity Board. The Board had threatened to bring proceedings for libel against Mr Strauss after the minister had asked for its comments. Mr Strauss complained of breach of privilege. The Committee of Privileges had focused on the status of Mr Strauss's letter, concluding that it was a 'proceeding in Parliament', and the action of the Board was a breach of privilege. The House, by a narrow majority, held that the letter was not a 'proceeding in Parliament'.

The 1967 Committee considered that the Committee of Privileges had misdirected itself. In its view, the proper question was not one about the status of a particular document, but rather: 'Is this threat, maintained as it has been, a contempt of Parliament, that is an improper obstruction which is likely substantially to interfere with the parliamentary duty of the Member affected?'[18] The Committee considered that: '[T]he House in that case failed to ask itself a question which was material to its powers and which might possibly have been answered in a manner favourable to the Member's complaint.'[19] In rejecting the focus on whether a particular matter had the status of a 'proceeding' in favour of a system in which question was whether Member had been obstructed, the Committee implicitly invited the House to extend the protections enjoyed by Members to any activity undertaken in their official capacity. This invitation to consider privilege more broadly has been consistently ignored, even by the Committee that first extended it.

Despite this emphasis on the broad question of obstruction rather than the narrow definition of proceedings, the Committee recommended legislation to extend and clarify the scope both of absolute and qualified privilege. Its analysis of matters which should be absolutely privileged largely replicates current assumptions about what is so privileged: everything said or done in the Chamber or in a Committee, documents published or printed

---

[17] Report from the Select Committee on Parliamentary Privilege, Session 1967–68, HC 34, para 12.
[18] ibid, para 81.
[19] ibid, para 82.

by order of the House, or documents necessary for the performance of the business of the House or a Committee, unless published without the authority of the House; and questions and notices of motions, or drafts of the same, provided they were published no more widely than is reasonably necessary. The Committee would have extended privilege to any group of Members appointed by the authority of the House, such as a Speaker's Conference, and to informal meetings, and would also have extended it to any communications between Members and Ministers.

In its consideration of whether legislation was necessary, the Committee noted that the House's rights and immunities would be given effect by the courts 'to the extent, and only to the extent, that the courts recognize them as part of the law of the land'.[20] It also noted that:

[T]he claim of the courts to interpret and to define the rights and immunities of the House and of its members, insofar as they form part of the common law of the land and are consequently possible in the courts, has led to a history of fruitless, and, in the past, often undignified conflicts between the courts and the House.[21]

Nonetheless, the Committee was of the opinion 'that this power of the House [to interpret its own rights and immunities] cannot be surrendered since it is essential to the exercise by the House of its control over its own procedure and to the protection which its penal jurisdiction provides'.[22]

The Committee rejected the proposition that categories of contempt should be codified, both because 'new forms of obstruction, new functions and new duties might all contribute to new forms of contempt', and because it was satisfied that 'only under statutory authority can the House lawfully be divested of its powers in such manner as to bind its successors. Codification, if desirable at all, could be effective only if embodied in legislation.'[23] Later in the Report the Committee raised a further objection to transferring jurisdiction to the courts, resting on the Commons' political nature:

[I]n deciding whether a contempt has been committed the tribunal concerned must decide a number of questions which involve delicate balance between freedom of the individual and the essential protection of House, its Members and Officers to enable them to perform their various functions and duties. Such functions and duties are in a constant state of alteration and development and your committee are firmly of the opinion that it must be the prerogative of the House, and of the House alone, to determine what at any time are their limits.

This balance between the freedom of the individual and essential protection of the House involves considerations of a political character which may vary according to the circumstances of the day. It is right that the House, which is responsible to the electorate, should make such decisions rather than that they should be made by an appointed tribunal, whether or not of a judicial character.[24]

Instead, the Committee recommended changes to the procedures of the Committee of Privileges to ensure fairness, including the right for the complaining member and the subject of the complaint to attend hearings, to apply to be represented by Counsel, and to examine witnesses and make submissions to the Committee. The Committee also considered that

[20] ibid, para 70.
[21] ibid, para 71.
[22] ibid, para 71.
[23] ibid, para 40.
[24] ibid, paras 141–42.

the Committee of Privileges should be empowered to authorise legal aid for those involved in its proceedings.

The Committee was nervous of conflict with the courts. Its proposed solution was a mixture of assertion, legislation to confer power to imprison for a fixed period rather than until the end of the next session and to give the power to fine, and, most importantly, encouragement to self restraint:

> Whilst the House cannot be deprived of its right to interpret where such interpretation is essential to its powers of control over its own procedure and in particular to its penal powers, the more often it exercises that right, the more frequently will it find itself in conflict with the courts on matters of interpretation. ... The more closely the House confines the exercise of its penal jurisdiction to its own essential protection, the less likely will it be that conflict will occur in future.[25]

The Committee proposed that where a Member had a remedy in the courts, he or she should not be permitted to invoke the penal jurisdiction of the House.[26] Most strikingly, it recommended that the penal jurisdiction should be exercised

> (a) in any event, as sparingly as possible and (b) only when the House is satisfied that to exercise it is essential in order to provide reasonable protection for the House, its Members or its Officers, from such improper obstruction or attempt at or threat of obstruction as is causing, or is likely to cause, substantial interference with the performance of their respective functions.[27]

The Committee also proposed transferring decisions about whether to pursue complaints of contempt to the Committee of Privileges rather than the House.[28] Taken together, these recommendations would have removed much of the chilling effect complained of by the press, by requiring Members to bring defamation cases, rather than to denounce the journalist concerned on the floor of the House.

No decision was taken on the major recommendations of the 1967 Committee's report, although recommendations to deal with historic anomalies, such as the resolution banning reporting of the House, were accepted.[29] On 16 July 1971 the government brought forward motions to implement the proposals that the House should use its privileges sparingly, and that Members should not raise grievances as a matter of privilege if they had a legal remedy, but it withdrew those motions after the debate. The concerns expressed in that debate were ones of principle: that the privileges involved were those of the House, not of the individual MP; and of practicality: many MPs would not be able to afford the costs of proceedings for defamation.[30] The debate contained a clash of ideas that resonates to this day. Supporters of the Committee considered that MPs should be no different from other citizens in terms of their rights to take action against defamatory statements. Opponents considered that MPs

[25] ibid, para 79.
[26] ibid, para 48.
[27] ibid, para 17.
[28] ibid, paras 162–70. The proposals include a power for the House as a whole to override a committee decision *not* to take up a particular case.
[29] Recommendations relating to the position of resolutions prohibiting the reporting debates, the adoption of rules for the readmission of strangers to committees, permitting the publication of Members' actions and intentions in advance of the appearance of the Notice paper, and permitting the wider publication select committee evidence were implemented.
[30] See HC Deb, vol 821, cc 922–94.

were in a special position, both because they were far more in the public eye than ordinary citizens, and because of their status as elected representatives.

Ten years later, the 1967 Report was referred to the Committee of Privileges for reconsideration. In its 1977 report, that Committee did not explore the radical assertion that the proper focus should not be on whether a particular document fell within the definition of 'proceedings', but on whether an MP's work had been impeded by the action of the alleged contemnor. Instead it focused on the earlier concerns about the status of 'proceedings in Parliament', and recommended a statutory definition of proceedings, echoing the proposals of its predecessor. That statutory definition should cover both those matters which were currently assumed to be proceedings, and correspondence with ministers and constituents.[31]

Like its predecessor, the Committee of Privileges recommended the House should have a power to fine, but this Committee considered that the House's power to imprison should be extinguished. These proposals, it believed on advice, would have required legislation. Still more significantly, it recommended that the House should agree to the recommendation of the 1967 Committee that its penal powers should be exercised sparingly, and only when essential.

The Committee rejected its predecessor's proposal that the Committee of Privileges should decide on the admissibility of complaints, but proposed that such complaints should be submitted to Mr Speaker, who should have the responsibility of ruling on whether they should be put to the House. On 6 February 1978 its Report was endorsed by the House of Commons, although legislation was not forthcoming.

Between them, the 1967 and 1977 committees set out the principles in operation today. The House agreed to the proposition that its penal jurisdiction should be exercised sparingly, and only when essential. Complaints have to be made first to the Speaker, who decides whether the matter complained of is capable of being a contempt. Motions on the floor of the House raising matters of privilege are rare, and referrals to the Committee of Privileges are still rarer; there were only three such in the 2010–15 Parliament, and two in the 2005–10 Parliament. The definition of proceedings which enjoy absolute privilege without change in the law has become accepted as a matter of practice, even though the committees themselves were tentative about this.[32] Ultimately, it would be for the courts to rule on the matter, but the assumption is that formal parliamentary proceedings such as questions, and matters immediately antecedent to them, enjoy absolute privilege, while more general correspondence, such as letters to ministers or constituents, is not so protected.[33]

COMITY AND MUTUAL SELF-RESTRAINT

While both the 1967 and the 1977 committees agonised over the meaning of the term 'proceedings in Parliament' neither Report discussed the way in which those proceedings might

---

[31] See Third Report from the Committee of Privileges, Session 1976–77, Recommendations of the Select Committee on Parliamentary Privilege, HC 417.

[32] HC Deb, 6 Feb 1978, vol 934, cc 1155–98.

[33] The Australian Parliamentary Privileges Act adopts this definition, as does the New Zealand Act.

be 'impeached or questioned' in the courts. This is not surprising. In the first instance, the courts themselves excluded the use of parliamentary material. The courts' self-restraint was mirrored by the House's application of the sub judice rule, preventing reference to matters before the court. The House changed its procedures over the course of the nineteenth century, to reduce the danger that it would usurp the functions of the court. The first editions of May contain no reference to the sub judice rule. Indeed, in 1844, when Lord John Russell was asked whether he would bring forward a motion relating to the state of Ireland while trials were not concluded, he confirmed that he would do so since

> while he quite concurred in the propriety of having no discussion in that House, which might influence the decision of the jury, ... he did not think it was at all necessary that they should be acquainted with the decision of the jury before entering on his motion.[34]

The rule first appears unambiguously in the tenth edition (1893) of May (edited by Sir Reginald Palgrave) in brief: 'A matter, whilst under adjudication by a court of law, should not be brought before the house by a motion or otherwise.'[35] Since then the prohibition has been formalised in resolutions of the House of Commons, the most recent version having been agreed on 15 November 2001.

In the rare cases when parliamentary material was relevant, the practice was to petition the House of Commons for leave to use Commons material in legal proceedings. It was not until 31 October 1980 the House resolved:

> That this House, while re-affirming the status of proceedings in Parliament confirmed by Article 9 of the Bill of Rights, gives leave for reference to be made in future Court proceedings to the Official Report of Debates and to the published Reports and evidence of Committees in any case in which, under the practice of the House, it is required that a petition for leave should be presented and that the practice of presenting petitions for leave to refer to parliamentary papers be discontinued.[36]

The resolution was not passed without a struggle. Initially it was talked out,[37] and the reaffirmation of the status of proceedings at the beginning of the resolution was inserted by amendment to meet concerns that, as Michael English MP said, 'if we pass the resolution ... they will go beyond this narrow boundary of reference to the proceedings and start to question a statement in the proceedings'.[38]

Michael English may have had a point. Since 1980 judicial use of proceedings has increased, and widened. Judgments are carefully crafted to deal with the facts of a specific case: this brief summary, from a frankly House of Commons viewpoint, inevitably compresses the arguments. But this, itself, is part of the difference between the legislative function and the judicial one: the first produces sets of general rules; the second seeks to apply those rules to the subtleties and complexities of individual cases.

The key cases relating to judicial use of parliamentary proceedings go wider than UK law. The role of the Judicial Committee of the Privy Council as the ultimate court of

---

[34] HC Deb, 3rd series, vol 72, cc 489–90.

[35] TE May, *A Treatise on the law, Privileges, Proceedings and Usage of Parliament*, 10th edn (London, Clowes, 1893) 264; the footnotes refer to Lord John Russell's earlier indication that he would not bring forward his motion if the trial were not concluded (HC Deb, 3rd series, vol 72, c 86), but not to his later determination to do so.

[36] Commons Journals (1979–80) 823.

[37] See HC Deb 3 December 1979, vol 975, cc 167–97.

[38] HC Deb 31 October 1980 vol 991, c896.

appeal for many Commonwealth jurisdictions, and the judicial interest in rulings made in similar jurisdictions, mean that Commonwealth jurisprudence is also relevant. Since *Brind* in 1991 it has been accepted that ministerial statements to the Commons (and Lords) can be examined in the course of judicial review, to establish the policy intention behind a particular action or measure.[39] Although this caused some misgiving, it now appears relatively uncontroversial.

The first use of proceedings as an aid to statutory construction was in 1993, in *Pepper v Hart*.[40] In this case the minister's undertakings to a standing committee were examined to establish what Parliament had intended a disputed legislative provision to mean. Lord Browne-Wilkinson made clear that use of proceedings in this way was only permitted when: first, legislation is ambiguous or obscure, or leads to an absurdity; second, the material relied upon consists of one or more statements by a minister or other promoter of the bill together if necessary with such other parliamentary material as is necessary to understand such statements and their effect; and third, the statements relied upon are clear.[41]

The widest use of proceedings has been made by the European Court of Human Rights, which has looked at parliamentary proceedings to assess the degree to which parliamentary debates demonstrate that the proportionality of any measure was taken into account in making legislation. In the case of *Hirst v UK* the Court explicitly assessed the quality of parliamentary debate:

> As to the weight to be attached to the position adopted by the legislature and judiciary in the United Kingdom, there is no evidence that Parliament has ever sought to weigh the competing interests or to assess the proportionality of a blanket ban on the right of a convicted prisoner to vote. … It may be said that, by voting the way they did to exempt unconvicted prisoners from the restriction on voting, Parliament implicitly affirmed the need for continued restrictions on the voting rights of convicted prisoners. Nonetheless, it cannot be said that there was any substantive debate by members of the legislature on the continued justification in light of modern-day penal policy and of current human rights standards for maintaining such a general restriction on the right of prisoners to vote.[42]

The UK courts have generally been more cautious in their use of proceedings in this way; in *Wilson v First County Trust* the House of Lords rejected the Appeal Court's use of parliamentary material to assess the human rights compatibility of legislation, holding that: 'The proportionality of a statutory measure is not to be judged by the reasons advanced in support of it in the course of parliamentary debate', although there could be occasions when *Hansard* might provide background information.[43]

The courts stand firm against impeaching and questioning proceedings in a way that would expose those participating in parliamentary proceedings to legal liability. There have, however, been two Commonwealth cases which have restricted this protection. Although it has long been accepted that a statement made in proceedings was not protected if repeated

---

[39] *R v Home Secretary, ex parte Brind* [1991] 1 AC 696; there were earlier cases in which parliamentary material was used in judicial review; see the judgment of Lord Browne-Wilkinson in *Pepper v Hart* (next reference).

[40] *Pepper (Inspector of Taxes) v Hart* [1993] AC 593.

[41] Lord Browne-Wilkinson, ibid.

[42] Grand Chamber, *Case of Hirst v The United Kingdom (No 2)* (Application no 74025/01), para 79.

[43] Lord Nicholls in *Wilson and Others v Secretary of State for Trade and Industry* [2003] UKHL 40.

outside it, the Privy Council in 2004 ruled in *Jennings v Buchanan* that a simple statement that a New Zealand MP 'did not resile' from accusations he had made in Parliament was 'effective repetition' of those accusations.[44] The second case, in 2011, *Attorney General and Gow v Leigh* held that official briefings to assist a minister in answering parliamentary questions were not covered by parliamentary privilege.[45] Neither of these cases are binding in the United Kingdom, although they are persuasive.

Judicial use of proceedings has recognised that, in the words of Lord Browne-Wilkinson, Article IX is part of 'a long line of authority which supports a wider principle … viz that the courts and Parliament are both astute to recognise their respective constitutional roles'.[46] Nonetheless, despite the reassurance that '[s]o far as the courts are concerned they will not allow any challenge to be made to what is said or done within the walls of Parliament in performance of its legislative functions and protection of its established privileges',[47] there has been some disquiet about these developments. The flexibility and adaptability which the 1967 Committee saw as one of the great advantages of an uncodified system has been applied by the courts to their use of parliamentary material as well as by each House of Parliament to its own proceedings.

THE TWO JOINT COMMITTEES ON PARLIAMENTARY PRIVILEGE

Whereas in the 1960s and 1970s privilege was seen as a House of Commons matter, Joint Committees on Parliamentary Privilege have been established twice in relatively recent years. One motivation for the use of Joint Committees may have been that even as early as 1997 the pressing questions in privilege had changed from the relationship between the press and the House of Commons, or the protections given to individual Members, to broader questions about the increasing readiness of the courts to examine what was said in Parliament in ways that they considered did not infringe the Article IX ban on impeaching or questioning, but which Parliament itself might consider doubtful. There may have been other factors, such as the growth in concept of Parliament as antithesis to government, a desire to access the legal expertise in the House of Lords, and the erosion of the previous assumption that the Attorney General could be called on to advise any committee of the House.

The first such Committee was established in July 1997 (remarkably quickly after the general election bringing in a Labour administration) and reported in 1998. The high judiciary were then part of the House of Lords, and the Committee was chaired by a Law Lord, Lord Nicholls. The Committee also contained two former law officers, two former Home Secretaries and a former liberal Chief Whip, who was both barrister and politician.[48] The Commons Members of the Committee were Mr Joe Benton, a government backbencher, Sir Patrick Cormack, then the Opposition Deputy Leader of the House of Commons,

---

[44] *Jennings v Buchanan* [2004] UKPC 36.
[45] *Attorney General and Gow v Leigh* [2011] NZSC 106.
[46] *Prebble v Television New Zealand Ltd* [1994] UKPC 4 (27 June 1994).
[47] ibid.
[48] Lord Archer of Sandwell, former Solicitor General, Lord Mayhew of Twysden, former Solicitor General and Attorney General, Lord Merlyn-Rees, former Home Secretary, Lord Waddington, former Home Secretary and Chief Whip, and Lord Wigoder, a Crown Court recorder.

Mr Bill Michie, a government backbencher, Mrs Ann Taylor, the then Leader of the House of Commons, Mr Paul Tyler, the Liberal Democrat Chief Whip, and Mr Alan Williams, a government backbencher and, incidentally, the Father of the House. Sir Patrick Cormack, Ann Taylor and Paul Tyler were all also members of the Modernisation Committee, appointed to consider how the practices and procedures of the House of Commons should be brought up to date (see chapter 13).

It is perhaps not surprising that such a Committee, chaired by a Law Lord and reporting at a time when there was a perceived need to modernise Parliament, should have recommended radical change, in the form of a Parliamentary Privileges Act. As well as setting out a series of specific recommendations for such an Act, the Committee went far beyond its predecessors in recommending that the whole of parliamentary privilege be codified:

> Codification has advantages and disadvantages. The advantages are clarity and accessibility. At present, there is no sense of a coherent framework or structure, because the period over which privilege has developed is so long: the earliest privilege case cited in Erskine May was decided 700 years ago. Many of the old court cases were decided in the days of long forgotten legal procedures. To the ordinary lawyer, let alone non-lawyer, these cases are difficult, if not impossible, to understand. All this combines to make the subject obscure. A short statutory code would be an enormous improvement.

> The main fear of codification is that it will reduce flexibility for the future. This consideration need not weigh heavily in the case of parliamentary privilege, provided the legislation is drafted in the form of statements of principle, followed by particular examples. ... The underlying rationale is that the two Houses and their members and officers must have the rights and immunities needed to enable them to carry out their parliamentary functions effectively. The structure comprises two broad headings: parliamentary freedom of speech, protected by article 9, and control by Parliament over parliamentary affairs.[49]

The proposals of the Joint Committee would have entailed a radical shift of power from Parliament to the courts. In place of the difficult, obscure and contestable privileges which Parliament asserted, there would be a new statute, which the courts themselves would interpret. The Committee recommended that the courts should be able to use parliamentary proceedings so far 'as they relate to interpretation of an Act of Parliament or subordinate legislation or judicial review of government decisions or the consequences of government decisions, or the non-critical use of statements where no legal liability is involved'.[50] Parliamentary control over its own affairs should only extend to 'activities directly and closely related to proceedings in Parliament. As to other activities, statutes should be assumed to bind both Houses in the absence of contrary intention.' Although the Joint Committee did not explore the matter, the precedent of *Stockdale v Hansard* makes it clear that it would be for the courts to decide whether particular activities were indeed 'directly and closely related to proceedings in Parliament'.

The new government quickly learnt that legislative time in Parliament is limited, and an overambitious programme invites defeat. Although the Leader of the House promised legislation at some point, the time never came. Nonetheless, the Joint Committee report was

---

[49] Joint Committee on Parliamentary Privilege, Report of Session 1998–99, HC 43-I/HC 214-I, paras 378–79.
[50] ibid, para 376.

influential, and frequently cited in judgments.[51] The judges did not appear to consider that, apart from updating the sub judice resolutions in each House, none of the recommendations about the relationship between the courts and Parliament had been implemented.

Apart from a brief flurry over the search by police of the office of a Member of the Opposition front bench in 2008–09,[52] privilege became obscure again, until the expenses scandal overwhelmed the House of Commons. Three of those facing trial for dishonestly claiming expenses claimed that since the expenses system rested on resolutions of the House of Commons, parliamentary privilege meant that the case could not continue. The courts eventually ruled that there was no bar to the trial (noting, inter alia, that the House had not sought to intervene to assert its privilege). Lord Phillips's judgment noted:

> Submitting claims for allowances and expenses does not form part of, nor is it incidental to, the core or essential business of Parliament, which consists of collective deliberation and decision making. The submission of claims is an activity which is an incident of the administration of Parliament; it is not part of the proceedings in Parliament.[53]

Lord Phillips concluded that 'extensive inroads have been made into areas that previously fell within the exclusive cognisance of Parliament';[54] neither Article IX nor exclusive cognisance shielded MPs from the law.

The Chaytor judgment came after an election in which the Conservative party pledged that if privilege prevented the trial of MPs accused of financial misdemeanours, privilege should be changed. In 2013 the Coalition government accordingly produced a Green Paper on Parliamentary Privilege.[55] Since it was now established that privilege did not provide a general shield against the law, the Green Paper was a miscellaneous and half-hearted affair. It raised a number of questions about freedom of speech, reporting of parliamentary proceedings and committee powers. The first consultation question gives its flavour: 'Do you agree that the case has not been made for a comprehensive codification of parliamentary privilege?'

A Joint Committee on Parliamentary Privilege was duly appointed to consider it. This Committee was chaired by Lord Brabazon of Tara. The 2013 Committee, far less dominated by lawyers and far more oriented to the backbenches than the 1997 Committee, took a diametrically different line from its predecessor. It accepted that the courts ultimately defined the boundaries of privilege, but it rejected codification. It embraced the virtues of evolution and adaptation:

> Absolute privilege attaches to those matters which, either because they are part of proceedings in Parliament or because they are necessarily connected to those proceedings, are subject to Parliament's sole jurisdiction or 'exclusive cognisance'.

> The extent of Parliament's exclusive cognisance changes over time, as the work of Parliament evolves: it would be impracticable and undesirable to attempt to draw up an exhaustive list of those matters subject to exclusive cognisance.

---

[51] See, for example, *R v Chaytor and others* [2010] UKSC 52.
[52] Report of the Committee on an Issue of Privilege: Police Searches on the Parliamentary Estate, House of Commons Paper 62 of Session 2008–09.
[53] *R v Chaytor and others* [2010] UKSC 52, para 62.
[54] ibid, para 78.
[55] Cm 8318.

Where there is uncertainty in a case brought before the courts, the extent of Parliament's exclusive cognisance will be determined by the courts.

Parliament cannot establish a new privilege or extend an existing privilege by resolution; if Parliament were to consider that its privileges had been reduced to the extent that it could no longer effectively perform its core work, it could in the last resort change the law.

We do not consider that comprehensive codification is needed at this time. This does not mean that we reject all legislation; but legislation should only be used when absolutely necessary, to resolve uncertainty or in the unlikely event of Parliament's exclusive cognisance being materially diminished by the courts.[56]

The Committee took evidence from both the Australian and New Zealand Parliaments and the experience of these countries resonated in its report. The 1987 Australian Parliamentary Privileges Act provided an example of established law. At the time of the inquiry, New Zealand was considering following Australia's example, which it did in 2014.[57] In both countries, the legislation was precipitated by judgments which Parliament considered reduced the scope of privilege so much that legislation was necessary. The Joint Committee dealt with two key New Zealand judgments in its report, regretting the decision in *Attorney General and Gow v Leigh*,[58] and making it clear that it expected briefings to ministers to enable them to respond to parliamentary questions to continue to enjoy parliamentary privilege in the United Kingdom. The Committee also recommended legislation to clarify the law relating to reports of parliamentary proceedings, and, as part of that legislation, to limit the chilling effects of *Jennings v Buchanan* by making clear that MPs had the same protection as non-Members in repeating or broadcasting extracts or abstracts of proceedings.[59]

Both the Australian and New Zealand Parliamentary Privileges Act confirm the Parliament's penal jurisdiction, rather than transferring it to the courts. The Joint Committee itself rejected suggestions that the courts should be given jurisdiction to take action against contempts because this would ultimately lead to the courts having power to decide whether a committee or the House was justified in using its coercive powers. Unlike earlier committees, it swept aside doubts about the House's penal powers, asserting: 'The first and most important challenge is to assert the continuing existence of each House's jurisdiction over contempt. This is, fundamentally, a test of institutional confidence.'[60] Nonetheless, the Committee recognised that:

Modern concepts of fairness in the judicial process have radically changed since either House last used its penal powers. While there is an external imperative, in that the United Kingdom could potentially be challenged in the European Court of Human Rights, we consider that this is a secondary consideration. Parliament itself would expect to comply with modern expectations of fairness and due process, which are very different to those which applied in the late nineteenth century.[61]

---

[56] Joint Committee on Parliamentary Privilege, Report of Session 2013–14, Parliamentary Privilege, HL 30, HC 100, para 47.
[57] Parliamentary Privilege Act 2014, Public Act 2014 No 58.
[58] *Attorney General and Gow v Leigh* [2011] NZSC 106.
[59] *Jennings v Buchanan* [2004] UKPC 36.
[60] HL Paper 30/HC (2013–14) 100, para 77.
[61] ibid, para 78.

The New Zealand legislation introduced as a result of *Gow v Leigh* and the debate which preceded it emphasised the importance of comity: the principle that each party, court and Parliament, should recognise and respect the other's authority in its particular sphere. The implication in New Zealand, despite respectful denials in debate, was that the courts no longer respected the principle of comity and needed a statutory reminder. There is a thread of concern throughout the Joint Committee's own report. The reference to 'the unlikely event of Parliament's exclusive cognisance being materially diminished by the courts' can be read as a warning to the courts against pushing the United Kingdom to follow Australia and New Zealand as much as a sign of confidence.

PRIVILEGE NOW

So what has changed in the years since May first raised the question of legislation, and what has remained the same? All institutions evolve. It would no longer be possible for the most constitutionally conservative judge to consider that the public did not have a right to know what was going on in Parliament, once matters had progressed beyond private discussions. And while it is recognised that within the United Kingdom each House can control its own procedures, the United Kingdom is signatory to a number of treaties which mean that parliamentary practice can be scrutinised by judicial or quasi-judicial bodies. Ultimately, Parliament could decide to resile from such international bodies, but unless and until it does so, both courts and Parliament are part of an international dialogue about the boundaries of justiciability, and what particular freedoms, if any, are needed to ensure a democratically elected legislature can function.

The increasing prominence of the international framework for the rule of law has also resulted in a shift toward seeing the courts as the guardians of rights, and a shift to regarding legally enforceable rights, defined through a process of legal argument and enforced through legal judgment, as the norm. The very different ways in which a political body containing a wide variety of opinions, some irreconcilable, comes to agreement do not sit easily in this norm. There is dispute over what areas should be susceptible to judicial accountability, what to political accountability and where the two jurisdictions may overlap.

The sharing of territory by courts and Parliament has been hastened by the growth of judicial review, not because the courts are in any way consciously or improperly trespassing on properly parliamentary territory, but because the courts and Parliament each have an ambivalent relationship to the executive. Executive, courts and Parliament are all, in the widest sense, part of the governing apparatus of the country, and yet courts and Parliament are each, in in very different ways, a check on government power. In a system of constitutional evolution, the different functions of courts and Parliament are not always clearly expressed. The first sub judice resolutions were subsequently amended to relax the prohibition on discussing matters before the courts in cases of national importance or 'where a ministerial decision is in question'—that is, in judicial review.[62]

---

[62] The initial resolution of 23 June 1963 barring reference to matters awaiting decisions in the court was supplemented by a further resolution on 28 June 1972, permitting such reference, subject to the discretion of the chair.

DISCIPLINARY POWERS

One of the issues in *Howard v Gossett* was whether the power to arrest and imprison on the order of the House could also permit trespass in an attempt to execute the order. The existence of the House's penal powers was not in question. Indeed, although Erskine May noted that the House had not fined since 1666 and the right to fine might be in doubt, he also noted that since the House released its prisoners on payment of fees,

> it cannot fail to be remarked that this condition of the payment of fees still partakes of the character of a fine. The payment of money forms part of the punishment, and it is compulsory; nor could any limit be imposed upon the amount fixed by order of the house.[63]

The extent to which penal powers are consistent with current legal norms has been repeatedly raised.[64] Yet, despite the difficulties in theory, this is not yet a problem in practice, even though it may become one. For many years, before it became obvious that the standards of fairness in the European Convention on Human Rights might apply to parliamentary disciplinary proceedings, each House has exercised its penal powers against third parties very circumspectly indeed.

Those powers are now most frequently used for internal disciplinary purposes. While there is no parliamentary immunity in the United Kingdom and criminal matters are dealt with by the police,[65] each House has its own disciplinary procedures to deal with Members who breach their Codes of Conduct. There is no statutory power to fine, but financial penalties can be imposed: suspension from the Commons entails loss of salary, and those suspended from the Lords cannot claim allowances. The Commons has withheld resettlement grants from retiring members, and recommended repayment of monies by others—with the implicit threat of suspension, if the recommendation is not complied with. The Commons' use of its disciplinary powers has indeed been challenged at the European Court of Human Rights—without success.[66]

When and how to exercise penal powers against non-Members is perhaps most pressing in the Commons. Not only has it traditionally been the focus of more adverse media attention than the Lords, its committees have perhaps been more inclined than those in the House of Lords to become players in unfolding political dramas, rather than to provide magisterial analysis based on evidence freely given. As May shrewdly recognised in 1840, public opinion has been a very real constraint on Parliament. In most cases involving the press, the Commons backed down. Even when the Committee of Privileges investigated, it rarely recommended any punishment. On the rare occasions when it recommended action, the House declined to support it.[67]

---

[63] ibid, 74.

[64] See, for example, Richard Gordon and Malcolm Jack, *Parliamentary Privilege: Evolution or Codification?* (London, Constitution Society, 2013).

[65] One exception was the treatment of Ron Brown MP, who damaged the Mace in a political protest made during a sitting of the House of Commons in 1988. In this case, the House dealt with the matter entirely through its own processes, rather than referring the matter to the courts. The event was closely related to proceedings, there was no doubt as to what had happened, and the House had power to discipline the offender by imposing a financial penalty. In contrast, in 2011, when Jonathan May-Bowles attacked a witness before the Culture, Media and Sport Committee, the matter was left to the courts to deal with.

[66] *Hoon v The United Kingdom*, App 14832/11.

[67] See CJ (1985–86) 374.

That has not been an end to the external jurisdiction of the House of Commons. Committees still use their powers to compel evidence from third parties, and to compel witnesses to attend to give evidence. This jurisdiction often passes unnoticed, for two reasons. First, in most inquiries, committees are simply scrutinising a government policy, or the way in which it has been implemented, rather than finding facts. For these purposes, there is no point in examining a reluctant witness. Second, in the rare cases where committees wish to hear from a reluctant witness, the explanation of committee powers is usually sufficient to compel attendance. In two recent cases where witnesses have been inclined to test the powers involved, committees have stood firm. Despite initial reluctance, on 15 June 2016 the Business, Energy and Industrial Strategy Committee and the Work & Pensions Committee took evidence from Arcadia Group's Chairman, Sir Philip Green, as part of their inquiries relating to the BHS pension fund deficit and the sale of BHS to Retail Acquisitions Limited.[68] The Business, Energy and Industrial Strategy Committee had earlier had to exercise pressure on Mr Ashley to attend in connection with its inquiry into employment practices at Sports Direct.[69] The clear public interest in the committees' inquiries meant that neither witness was prepared to risk the reputational consequences of defiance, and the question of sanctions did not have to be addressed.

The question remains about what would happen in a case in which the House felt it needed to take action against a serious breach of privilege, and the existence of that breach, or the legitimacy of its action, was contested. The two notable points here are that public opinion—or the anticipation of public opinion—has shaped the way in which the Commons exercises its jurisdiction. The reluctance to take action against the press who 'are only doing their job' is long-standing. Conversely, as demonstrated, committee power is strengthened when the press and public back their action.

The second is that, in discussing disciplinary powers, the courts and the Houses now speak in similar, if not identical, terms. When the Committee of Privileges was considering the case of those alleged to have misled the Culture, Media and Sport Committee about phone hacking it did so on the basis of a clearly set out process, designed to be fair.[70] That process was clearly parliamentary, rather than legal, and the Committee rebutted numerous complaints by lawyers:

> The Committee's policy on all these matters has been quite clear: documents were disclosed to those to whom they were of relevance but general disclosure was resisted on the grounds of confidentiality and to provide a degree of privacy to the victims of phone-hacking and persons not in the public eye whose personal data is included in the documents; case management meetings were refused because they are not applicable to parliamentary proceedings; and we have not released our internal legal advice because it is subject to parliamentary and legal privilege. The Committee has further been criticised for deliberating in private which is in fact a requirement for all parliamentary committees. Complaints that this approach is 'bewildering' reflect the extent to which legal representatives have drawn false analogies with court processes to come to mistaken conclusions.

---

[68] See Work and Pensions Committee, First Report, and Business, Energy and Industrial Strategy Committee, Fourth Report, Session 2016–17, BHS, HC 54.

[69] See Third Report of Session 2016–17, HC 219, paras 4–9.

[70] See First Report from the Committee of Privileges, Session 2016–17, Conduct of Witnesses before a Select Committee: Mr Colin Myler, Mr Tom Crone, Mr Les Hinton, and News International, HC 662.

The role of our Committee is quite clear. It is to consider the matter referred to us and to report to the House on our conclusions.[71]

Nonetheless, the Committee's report makes it clear that its process was designed to conform to the recommendation of the 1999 Joint Committee on Parliamentary Privilege that it should follow procedures providing safeguards at least as rigorous of those of the courts, including: a prompt and clear statement of the precise allegations; adequate opportunity to take legal advice and have legal assistance throughout; the opportunity to be heard in person; the opportunity to call relevant witnesses at the appropriate time; the opportunity to examine other witnesses; the opportunity to attend meetings at which evidence is given; and to receive transcripts of the evidence.[72]

The Committee of Privileges recommended that 'the Leader of the House take steps as soon as possible to address the issues identified by the Joint Committee on Parliamentary Privilege in 2013, particularly in respect of the penal powers of the House and select committees and contempt'.[73] In response, the House resolved that 'the matter of the exercise and enforcement of the powers of the House in relation to select committees and contempts be referred to the Committee of Privileges', and an inquiry into the powers of select committees was launched. The Committee published a paper by the Clerk of the House and sought evidence on the options identified therein—to do nothing, to reassert the House's existing powers by amending Standing Orders or by Resolution, or to legislate to provide a statutory regime—all strangely familiar to those who followed the Joint Committees' work.

It is notable that the terms of reference for Committee of Privileges inquiry focus on powers and penalties, rather than on fairness. There may be arguments about whether Parliament's contempt jurisdiction would in all circumstances constitute the sort of obligation which would engage ECHR Article 6 rights. There may be arguments about whether the particular processes used are proportionate or fair. But the arguments are ones which the courts would recognise, and the values of courts and Parliament are similar: both have to deal with possibly unwilling witnesses; both are concerned, in various ways, with fairness. We have come a very long way from the 1967 Committee's assessment that the House would and should be swayed by considerations of a political nature in deciding how to exercise its penal jurisdiction.

COMITY AND IMPEACHING AND QUESTIONING

Things become more troubled when one moves to judicial use of words spoken in Parliament. Here, too, there has been a gradual evolution. There has been no erosion of the right to speak freely in Parliament, even when to do so entails direct defiance of the courts.[74] The danger, if it exists, lies in the more subtle use of proceedings.

---

[71] ibid, para 62.
[72] ibid, para 50.
[73] ibid, para 330.
[74] See Report of the Committee on Super-Injunctions, Super-Injunctions, Anonymised Injunctions and Open Justice, May 2011, Summary of Conclusions and Recommendations, 9(i): 'Article 9 of the Bill of Rights 1689 recognises and enshrines a longstanding privilege of Parliament: freedom of speech and debate. It is an absolute privilege and is of the highest constitutional importance. Any attempt by the courts to go beyond that constitutional boundary would be unconstitutional. No super-injunction, or any other court order, could conceivably restrict or prohibit Parliamentary debate or proceedings.'

When he appeared before the 2013 Joint Committee, the then Lord Chief Justice, Lord Judge, was emphatic that parliamentary material should be used in the courts only in very rare cases, such as those envisaged in *Pepper v Hart*, and that:

> If these things do slip under the wire, they should be treated as what they are: a moment of aberration, and of no consequence whatever by way of a threat or challenge to Parliament. They are mistakes; that is all they are.[75]

Yet there have been suggestions that human rights jurisprudence is developing in ways which permits courts to look at the extent to which Parliament considered human rights issues when assessing proportionality. Aileen Kavanagh considers:

> Much hinges on the possibility of distinguishing between assessing the quality of the decision-making process from the quality of the individual reasons. By adopting a minimalist approach, I think the UK courts have succeeded in drawing a line between these two types of inquiry, one which keeps them out of the forbidden territory.[76]

She welcomes the change on the grounds that the

> indirect consideration of parliamentary deliberation could enhance and support Parliament's primary role as legislator, rather than undermine it. It could provide a way in which the court can respect and uphold Parliament's legitimate role in protecting Convention rights and its ability to take a lead in this regard. In turn, this may give Parliament an added incentive to take rights seriously during the legislative process.[77]

The difficulty with such an approach is that it does not give due weight to the fact that the Commons is, as the 1967 Committee recognised, a political arena. Individuals choose what part they will play. The House can collectively establish mechanisms to scrutinise matters it considers need particular focus, such as the Joint Committee on Human Rights. It can ensure that explanatory notes on bills and explanatory memoranda on statutory instruments are available to individual MPs. But the House cannot go beyond this. Whether or not a wide range of views on a particular legislative proposal is presented on the floor of the House in debate is not within its collective control. Parliamentary time is valuable, and debates in which nothing but agreement is expressed are usually brief and reserved for the retirement of distinguished officials, or tributes to former colleagues. Assessment of the quality of parliamentary engagement by the length of debate, or the range of views expressed would have a perverse effect. If the aim is for the legal system to defer to the democratic mandate it would be logical (though undesirable) for fully debated and hotly contested measures to receive more sceptical assessment than those which passed unscrutinised.

Judicial use of parliamentary proceedings could risk distorting those proceedings, and reducing Parliament's ability to perform the constitutional function which it alone can carry out. There are already signs that the erosion of Article IX has changed Parliament. The *Guide to Making Legislation* recommends that legal advisers clear speaking notes before they are passed to ministers, saying: 'The importance of this is due to the ruling of *Pepper v Hart* where parliamentary material may be used to assist in the interpretation of legislation

---

[75] Minutes of Evidence taken before the Joint Committee on Parliamentary Privilege, 5 March 2013, HC JCPP-OE-v, Q 265.

[76] Aileen Kavanagh, 'Proportionality and Parliamentary Debates: Exploring Some Forbidden Territory' (2014) 343 *Oxford Journal of Legal Studies* 443.

[77] ibid.

in cases where such legislation is ambiguous or obscure.'[78] Such guidance could have the effect of inhibiting proper debate, as ministerial replies become cautious. On at least one occasion a Secretary of State has declined to answer a question put to him by a select committee on the grounds that that answer might be used in judicial review.[79]

Attempting to evaluate parliamentary debate as if it were judicial reasoning fundamentally misunderstands the way in which each House of Parliament plays its part both in holding government to account, and in upholding that government. Parliament's functions include the day-to-day business of ensuring the government has the support it needs to carry on, as well as the high-minded scrutiny of government proposals. The Commons is about party solidarity, as well as individual views. It is about speaking to the electorate, as well as speaking to colleagues in the Chamber. A great deal of negotiation and agreement takes place in the parliamentary hinterland, where judicial assessment cannot reach, such as those occasions when the 1922 Committee of Conservative backbenchers or the Parliamentary Labour Party makes clear to its leaders that certain proposals will not be carried, or proposals are modified to meet the concerns of the House of Lords. All of that is beyond the courts' reach, and inappropriate use of parliamentary proceedings may be a factor in pushing more negotiation and debate into that hinterland.

CONCLUSION

The separation between courts and Parliament may have been finalised by the Constitutional Reform Act 2005, but long before that it had become increasingly uncommon for MPs to move into the judiciary (or even vice versa).[80] In recent years, though, there has been more dialogue. Judicial seminars have been addressed by the Clerks.[81] Judges are increasingly coming to give evidence before select committees; Lord Judge's appearance before the 2013 Joint Committee on Parliamentary Privilege was not a one-off. The House of Commons has its Justice Committee, and the two Houses share the Joint Committee on Human Rights.

Looking back at the first edition of the *Treatise*, some things seem very familiar. Freedom of speech is recognised by all as essential. There is still no agreement on legislation to entrench parliamentary privilege. There is a renewed emphasis on Parliament's penal powers.

But perhaps what resonates most of all is the continued tension between the House and the judiciary. We may have progressed from Lord Mansfield's vigorous view, quoted by Lord Denman in *Stockdale v Hansard*, that:

---

[78] Cabinet Office, *Guide to Making Legislation* (July 2014).

[79] In oral evidence to the Transport Committee on Wednesday, 21 May 2003, Alistair Darling refused to be drawn on whether the government would honour an undertaking not to develop Gatwick before 2019, saying: 'I am determined not to be judicially reviewed again if I can help it, which is why I am not getting drawn into it [discussion of the issue].' HC 454 (2002–03) II, Q 1985.

[80] See David Howarth, 'Lawyers in the House of Commons' in D Feldman (ed), *Law in Politics, Politics in Law* (Oxford, Hart Publishing, 2013) 41–63.

[81] Minutes of Evidence taken before the Joint Committee on Parliamentary Privilege, 5 March 2013, HC JCPP-OE-v, Q 251.

Declarations of the law ... made by either House of Parliament, were always attended with bad effects: [Lord Mansfield] had constantly opposed them whenever he had an opportunity, and in his judicial capacity thought himself bound never to pay the least regard to them.

In 2013 Lord Judge even told the most recent Joint Committee that the judiciary would pay heed to a resolution on privilege. Nonetheless, he was careful to qualify his position. And as the Attorney General said in 1844:

In every balanced government there must be powers so constituted as to check each other, powers which have their respective limits, but for the abuse of which there can be no remedy.

The constitution gives both courts and each of House of Parliament such powers—and while neither side can intervene in individual cases, there is hope that informal dialogue will enable comity between the two to reign, without recourse to statute.

17

Is the Lex Parliamentaria *Really Law?*

The House of Commons as a Legal System

DAVID HOWARTH

INTRODUCTION

T HE INTERNAL WORKINGS of Parliament are crucial for the way our democracy works, but they receive very little attention from lawyers. The main reason lawyers are uninterested in Parliament seems to be that, as a result of each House's exclusive cognisance over its own proceedings, reinforced by Article IX of the Bill of Rights 1689, Parliament's internal decisions are not reviewable by the ordinary courts. Common lawyers tend to equate the boundaries of the law with the boundaries of case law, and a field in which no cases can ever arise is one that lies outside the law as they understand it.

Academic lawyers, whose vision ought to be broader, have their own reason for ignoring the internal procedures of Parliament. They tend to treat what happens in Parliament as entirely 'political'.[1] They usually conceive of Parliament as a freewheeling institution constrained only by 'constitutional conventions', the standard view of which is that they are vague principles rather than rules, established by practice and tradition rather than by enactment and enforced by social pressure and criticism rather than by compliance with the judgments of a specific authoritative decision-maker.[2]

In previous times, Parliament's internal rules and practices were said to constitute a '*lex parliamentaria*',[3] but lawyers both in the universities and in the professions have long abandoned that phrase and have followed Dicey in treating the rules or principles governing Parliament's internal working as 'not in reality laws at all'.[4]

---

[1] eg, Adam Tomkins, *Our Republican Constitution* (Oxford, Hart Publishing, 2005).

[2] See, eg, P Morton, 'Conventions of the British Constitution' (1991–92) 15 *Holdsworth LR* 114. See generally David Feldman, 'Constitutional Conventions' in Matt Qvotrup (ed), *The British Constitution: Continuity and Change—A Festschrift for Vernon Bogdanor* (Oxford, Hart Publishing, 2013) 93–120. Tomkins (n 1) 3–4 treats Prime Minister's Questions as a 'tradition'.

[3] eg George Petyt, *Lex Parliamentaria: or a Treatise on the Laws and Customs of the Parliaments of England* (London, Timothy Goodwin, 1690). Petyt treats Parliament as 'the highest Court in England' and the King, Lords and Commons as 'judges' (2), a reflection of the 'High Court of Parliament' theory, the medieval roots and subsequent fate of which were famously traced by CH McIlwain, *The High Court of Parliament and its Supremacy: An Historical Essay on the Boundaries between Legislation and Adjudication in England* (New Haven, CT, Yale University Press, 1910). Nothing in this chapter turns on that theory.

[4] AV Dicey, *Lectures Introductory to the Law of Constitution* (London, Macmillan, 1885) 25.

Regardless of whether the Diceyan view of constitutional conventions is correct in general, however, the idea that the internal procedures of the Houses of Parliament are vague principles established by tradition and enforced only by criticism seems wrong. Each House operates a set of procedural norms, many of which are precise, established by specific decisions and enforced through recognised mechanisms. For example, in the Commons procedural rules may be consciously created or altered by resolution of the House and are enforced by the Speaker and the Clerks. Enforcement occurs not just through criticising those who violate the rules but through sanctions against individuals and, more importantly, through the institutional fact that attempts to make decisions in ways not authorised by the rules have no effect.[5] Matters might seem more Diceyan in the Lords, where rulings on procedural issues are made by the House itself by means of resolutions rather than by its Speaker (indeed the whole concept of a 'point of order' is not recognised in the Lords),[6] but nevertheless one can point to specific, enforceable rules that have real effects.

It is true that in both Houses the rules are not codified and the rules written down in the form of resolutions are not the whole story. As we have seen in chapter 11, the standing orders of the House of Commons fail to mention the most basic rules of procedure, for example that bills go through three readings. The standing orders do not describe the House's procedures but rather regulate a process presumed already to be known and accepted on all sides. But that does not mean that these rules are vague or enforceable only by social pressure. On the contrary, a bill that has not completed its stages will not be sent to the Lords or to the sovereign for assent and so will not be enacted. The situation is similar to that of the common law itself. The fact that the common law is not codified and that the origins of many of its most basic rules are difficult to track down does not make it any less applicable and enforceable.

A LEGAL SYSTEM

More generally, one can make a case that Parliament, especially the Commons, operates its own legal system, albeit one largely uninfluenced by the legal system operated by the judges.[7] Parliament, especially the Commons, operates systems of decision-making based on previously announced rules in which decision-making proceeds by reasoning about those rules. These decisions are not managerial or 'political', in the sense of decisions taken solely on the basis of what seems most to the advantage of the decision-maker. They are taken on the basis of what the rules appear to demand.

---

[5] See Malcolm Jack (ed), *Erskine May's Treatise on the Law, Privileges, Proceedings and Usage of Parliament* 24th edn (London, LexisNexis, 2011) 418, 426.

[6] ibid, 72.

[7] In *Stockdale v Hansard* (1839) 112 ER 1112, 1200 Coleridge J moved away from the previous fiction that the judges were 'ignorant' of the 'Law of Parliament' and some judges have ever since sought to assert the supremacy of judicial law over parliamentary law (eg *R v Chaytor* [2010] UKSC 52). For the most part, however, the separation established by the Bill of Rights still holds. The converse, of course, does not hold. The judges system is heavily influenced by the parliamentary system. See further David Howarth, 'The Politics of Public Law' in Mark Elliott and David Feldman (eds), *The Cambridge Companion to Public Law* (Cambridge, Cambridge University Press, 2015).

Calling the system of decision a legal system is not to say that the process of reasoning it employs is solely about the meanings of words. The reasons for a decision might include consideration of the consequences of deciding one way or another. But that is true in the courts too. 'Policy' reasons, 'purposive' interpretations and judicial pragmatism are hardly unknown in the courts.[8] It might also weigh heavily with decision-makers in the Commons that their conclusions can be overturned by resolutions of the House passed by simple majority and that prospect might discourage making decisions that will immediately be repudiated. But even so, decisions of the Speaker are far from invariably convenient for the government. One thinks immediately of the ruling of Mr Speaker Bercow, technically sound but politically very unwelcome for the government, that motions put to the House to approve the draft Criminal Justice and Data Protection (Protocol No 36) Regulations 2014 and related matters did not cover the issue of opting into the European Arrest Warrant.[9] In any case, because of the doctrine of parliamentary supremacy, the situation of common law judges within their legal system is not very different from that of the Speaker in the Commons. Parliament can (and does) reverse the effect of court judgments of which it disapproves.[10] All legal systems exist in the time that elapses between making a decision based on the existing rules and those rules being changed.

One might even argue that Parliament's internal procedural rules, and especially those of the Commons, possess the characteristics of a legal system in more precise senses. They contain, for example, the full panoply of HLA Hart's secondary rules, the rules Hart claimed turned a collection of rules into a legal system: a rule of recognition, which distinguishes between rules that are part of the system and rules that are not; a rule of change, which lays down how recognised rules are altered; and a rule of adjudication, which lays down how authoritatively to resolve uncertainties about how recognised rules apply in particular cases.[11] The parliamentary rules of change and adjudication are quite straightforward. Each House has a rule of change, that resolutions carried by majority can create new rules and abolish or alter old ones. As for rules of adjudication, in the Commons the rule is that the Speaker decides what the rules mean and in the Lords the House itself acts as adjudicator, fusing the legislative and judicial roles.[12] The parliamentary rule of recognition is more complex but still capable of being formulated. Rules are recognised as procedural rules of the House if they have been created by a resolution of the House or if they have been

[8] See, eg, John Bell, *Policy Arguments in Judicial Decisions* (Oxford, Oxford University Press, 1983); Lord Bingham of Cornhill in *Reyes v R* [2002] UKPC 12 at 7 (purposive interpretation).

[9] HC Debates, Official Report, 10 November 2014, cc 1199–1200.

[10] eg, Compensation Act 2006 s 3, attempting to reverse the effect of *Barker v Corus UK Ltd* [2006] UKHL 20, [2006] 2 AC 572; Criminal Evidence (Witness Anonymity) Act 2008, reversing the effect of *R v Davis* [2008] UKHL 36; Terrorist Asset-Freezing (Temporary Provisions) Act, reversing the effect of *HM Treasury v Ahmed* [2010] UKSC 2; and Police (Detention and Bail) Act 2011, reversing the effect of *R (Chief Constable of Greater Manchester Police) v Salford Magistrates' Court and Hookway* [2011] EWHC 1578. There might be some limit to this kind of legislation when it involves the government acting as a judge in its own cause. See *R (on the application of Reilly (No 2) and Hewstone v Secretary of State for Work and Pensions* [2014] EWHC 2182 (Admin), holding that the Jobseekers (Back to Work Schemes) Act 2013, which reversed the effect of *R (on the application of Reilly and another) v Secretary of State for Work and Pensions* [2013] EWCA Civ 66, [2013] 1 WLR 2239, was incompatible with Art 6 of the European Convention of Human Rights.

[11] HLA Hart, *Concept of Law*, 2nd edn (Oxford, Clarendon Press, 1994) 94–99.

[12] In the Commons the Speaker may refer an issue to the House to decide itself, but the power is now rarely, if ever, used. See *Erskine May* (n 5) 455.

recognised or would be recognised as a rule in the course of adjudication by the authoritative adjudicator for that House. Thus not only resolutions and standing orders are recognised rules but also the practices and usages of the House that in the Commons the Speaker and in the Lords the House itself uses or would use to resolve disputes. One might object that it might not be entirely clear in advance of any particular dispute what will eventually count as a rule of the House, but the rule recognition used by the common law similarly has to incorporate common law rules and principles whose origin, scope and formulation are also not entirely clear in advance.

DIFFERENCES FROM THE COMMON LAW

In other ways, however, what happens in the Commons diverges markedly from the common law. Speakers of the House do not operate a very strict theory of precedent. In the words of May's *Treatise*, Speaker's rulings constitute precedents by which subsequent Speakers 'are guided'.[13] They are 'an important source' for future rulings.[14] That is not the language of *stare decisis* as the common law understands it. In the courts, precedents are binding and constitute the law itself. Even more different is the form and content of judgments. Speakers have developed a rule, only occasionally departed from, that they give no reasons for their decisions. They simply announce the result. The process of reasoning behind the Speaker's decision is usually known only to the Clerks who advised on it. If a Member wants to know the reasons for a decision, the Member has to find and talk privately to the right Clerk (who will reveal 'what Mr Speaker might have had in mind'). But nothing will ever appear in the Official Report beyond the bare decision. In addition, before judgment very little in the way of argument is permitted. Members raise points of order in the Chamber in the form of short questions, and are usually cut short if they try to argue at length for a particular ruling. A more elaborate form of argumentation can be attempted by writing a letter to the Speaker giving notice of the point of order before raising it in the Chamber, but any attempt to put the text of such a letter on the record will almost certainly be cut off by the Chair, for example by making reference to the (otherwise rarely enforced) rule against 'reading' speeches.[15] After rulings are made, contesting the result or the reasoning by which it might have been arrived at is treated as challenging the authority of the Chair, a rule members only occasionally manage to evade by prefacing their remarks with the words 'without in any way challenging your ruling, Mr Speaker'.

The laconic form of rulings and the lack of argumentation prior to and after judgment seem designed to preserve a high degree of mystery around the process and thus to maintain the authority of the chair by the rather crude mechanism of cutting off the possibility of rational debate about the rules. But minimising discourse around the rules brings with it the disadvantage that reasons for the rules will not be understood and thus the rules themselves will not be understood. Moreover, decisions unsupported by reasons can look random and irrational even when they are not. One of the functions of the *Treatise*,

---

[13]   ibid, 62.
[14]   ibid.
[15]   See, eg, HC Debates Official Report, 29 January 2008, c 236.

therefore, is to put these decisions into some kind of order and to give, or at least imply, the reasons that led to them. That is the logic behind making the Clerk of the House of Commons its editor and other Clerks the editors of its chapters. The Clerk is the Speaker's senior adviser for procedural issues. Indeed for some Speakers one suspects that little in the way of independent judgment occurs between the Clerk's advice and the announcement of the result to the House. The *Treatise* is thus no ordinary textbook. It is a peculiarly authoritative account of the rules, written by people whose advice on the meaning of those rules is almost invariably accepted.

Another difference between Parliament's internal legal system and the common law is its relationship to statute law. The courts frequently claim to have certain inherent powers, for example to dismiss actions as an abuse of process,[16] but if a statute takes away or limits those powers, the courts are bound to and will follow the statute. Parliament, even though it is the source of all statutes, takes a different view. Although normally it would follow its own statutes, where statutes contradict Parliament's own rules, Parliament reserves the right to follow its own rules on internal procedure in preference to the statute. The courts have accepted that Parliament can do this. In *Bradlaugh v Gossett*[17] the Commons resolved not to allow Charles Bradlaugh, the duly elected member for Northampton, to take the oath (Bradlaugh was an atheist to whose presence in Parliament a great number of members vociferously objected). The court took the position to be that the law, the Parliamentary Oaths Act 1866, required the oath to be taken (admittedly not the only possible interpretation of the Act), and proceeded on the basis that the House had resolved to exclude Bradlaugh in contravention of the Act. Nevertheless, the court refused to take any action against the House. In the course of controlling its own procedures the House was entitled to interpret statutes in any way it chose, even in ways that were plainly erroneous. The court would not even inquire as to whether the House had interpreted the statute at all. Outside Parliament statutes take precedence over resolutions of the House. Inside Parliament, the opposite can obtain.

TOO DIFFERENT TO COUNT AS A LEGAL SYSTEM?

Do these differences make Parliament's procedural rules any less a legal system? Two possible lines of argument might be taken. The first concerns whether the rules are sufficiently stable to count as 'previously announced'. Not having a system of strict precedent is no bar in itself. Many countries outside the common law world have no formal system of precedent—indeed the French Code civil explicitly forbids 'general and regulatory' decisions by judges[18]—and yet they have legal systems. But lacking both a strict system of precedent and a comprehensive written code might be thought to create a problem. If unwritten practices can come in and out of validity as rules by the unfettered discretion of

---

[16] See, eg, IH Jacob, 'The Inherent Jurisdiction of the Court' (1970) 23 *Current Legal Problems* 23.

[17] *Bradlaugh v Gossett* (1883–84) LR 12 QBD 271.

[18] Code civil, Art 5. In reality French law does have a de facto system of precedent, treating previous cases as guidance though not as binding, and as a source of argument though not as a source of law. See, eg, John Bell, Sophie Boyron and Simon Whittaker, *Principles of French Law*, 2nd edn (Oxford, Oxford University Press, 2008) 25 et seq.

the Speaker, how can the rules be known in advance? The answer to that point, however, lies in the special status of the *Treatise*, as an authoritative account of the rules produced by people on the inside of the decision-making process. Although, in theory, a Speaker called upon to make a decision in which unwritten practices and background assumptions are in play could ignore the past and start again, those advising the Speaker on the basis of the writings of their own predecessors are unlikely to propose unstable switchbacks of position. As a consequence one can expect switchbacks to occur no more frequently than in a common law system.[19]

In the case of the House of Lords an additional problem exists. The fusing of legislative and adjudicatory functions in the House of Lords, by which the House itself both lays down rules and says what they mean, could lead to a situation in which it matters not at all what the rules say. The House can effectively ignore its own rules whenever it interprets them. The problem is not entirely theoretical. In November 2010, for example, the Lords decided whether to refer the Parliamentary Voting Systems and Constituencies Bill to examiners on the question of hybridity after a debate and vote that divided almost purely on party lines.[20] In practice, however, the House of Lords has not yet descended into arbitrariness.

The second objection concerns the process in the Commons by which decisions are made. There can be little doubt that reasoning about the rules takes place and that it bears some relationship to the result reached. Members who ask for an explanation of a ruling in the privacy of the Clerk of Legislation's office invariably receive one that bears a strong resemblance to legal reasoning. It might not be an explanation that satisfies the Member and the Member might suspect that the result determined the reasoning rather than the other way round, but the same is often also true of litigants contemplating the judgments of courts. The important point is that an explanation in terms of the rules is felt to be necessary at all. When a member asks for an explanation, the decision is not clothed in the language of pure power but instead in some form of reasoning.

The trouble, however, is that in the public aspect of the process, the ruling as announced to the House, no reasoning based on the rules, or indeed reasoning of any kind, usually appears. Can a system of decision operating without offering any public reasons count as a legal system? The answer, however, is that it can. Juries give verdicts without reasons and in many countries, especially in the highest courts of civil law countries, judgments can be very short. In France, for example, the Cour de cassation renders judgment in a single, admittedly very long, sentence, consisting of little more than a statement of the facts, a list of the relevant provisions of the codes and the result. Not giving reasons might be bad

---

[19] Sometimes switchbacks can happen in the course of the same decision, but usually only in the interests of restoring longer-term consistency. See, eg, HC Debates Official Report, 2 December 2009, cc 1234–49. A Member moved the previous question, a procedural motion that 'the question be not now put', the effect of which is, if passed, the House moves on to its next business without resolving the question under consideration; or, if negatived, the House moves immediately to a vote of the question under consideration. The practice of the House is entirely clear: such a motion can be moved without notice and has to be put to the House. The Deputy Speaker in the chair, however, was unaware of that practice and, believing that the situation was identical to that when a Member moves the closure, purported to reject the motion. He then called to speak a Member who purported to move an amendment that it was the whole point of moving the previous question to prevent being debated. The situation was resolved by the Deputy Speaker being replaced in the chair by the Speaker, who then allowed the previous question to be debated as if the amendment had never been moved.

[20] HL Debates Official Report, 15 November 2010, c 522.

practice. It might even amount to an illegal practice.[21] But it arguably remains a bad practice of a legal system, not a practice that takes the system beyond the boundaries of the legal.

DEFICIENCY OF REASONS AND ITS CURES

The situation remains, however, that the mode of rendering judgment in the Commons is far from satisfactory, a position that might stand in the way of acceptance of the idea that the Commons has its own legal system. In 2008, during the committee stage of a bill to give parliamentary approval to the provisions of the Treaty of Lisbon, a point of order was raised several times as to why before resolving itself into committee the House was not asked, as seemed required by Standing Order No 66, to dispose of an instruction to the committee, notice of which had been duly given. The point of order was brushed aside without explanation. Then, suddenly, without more than a few hours warning and again without explanation, the Speaker called a debate on the instruction.[22] One day the Standing Order did not apply. The next day, it did. Both decisions looked equally baffling. In private, however, some explanation was offered. The trouble was that the explanations kept changing and none of them made no sense to the Members who heard them.[23] Indeed they made so little

---

[21] See, eg, Mark Elliott, 'Has the Common Law Duty to Give Reasons Come of Age Yet?' [2011] *Public Law* 56. Where judicial decisions are concerned, and thus where Art 6 of the European Convention of Human Rights is engaged, failure to give reasons might even amount to a violation of human rights: *Hadjianastassiou v Greece* (1993) 16 EHRR 219.

[22] HC Debates Official Report, 4 March 2008, c 1598.

[23] The painful detail is perhaps not worth reliving, but for the sake of the historical record some account of it should be given. Originally (see HC Debates Official Report, 29 January 2008, c 236) the explanation for the refusal to allow a debate on the instruction was that although the instruction was in order it had not been selected under a power granted by Standing Order No 32(4), which says that the power to select amendments applies to notices of instruction. The trouble with that explanation is that Standing Order No 66 requires that where the instruction is to a committee of the whole House, the instruction has to be 'disposed of' before the House goes into committee. It is far from clear how merely not selecting an instruction can count as 'disposing of' it. If anything the opposite is the case. The alternative interpretation is that Standing Order No 32(4) is limited by Standing Order No 66, so that the power to select does not apply to instructions to committees of the whole House at the point just before the House goes into committee (although it does apply otherwise). After the reversal of fortunes (which followed an act of civil disobedience by an aggrieved member, see HC Debates Official Report, 26 February 2008, c 925), another explanation was offered to the author, namely that the instruction could not be called because the House had passed a timetable motion defining an 'allotted day' as a day on which 'the first business is a motion in the name of the Crown to approve the Government's policy towards the Treaty of Lisbon [or a motion in the name of a minister amending the timetable order]'. It was claimed that this order excluded taking an instruction as first business. How that worked, however, was very unclear. A definition is not the same as a prohibition. A definition, moreover, cannot suspend standing orders. The argument seemed to be a very elaborate four-stage one: (1) applying Standing Order No 66 would mean making the instruction 'first business', so (2) according to the definition of 'allotted' the day would no longer count as 'allotted', which meant (3) the timetable motion would not apply and chaos would ensue and so (4) since the House could not possibly have intended chaos to result, Standing Order No 66 could not apply. The sudden reversal of the fate of the instruction, it was explained, resulted from the House's decision to pass an amendment to the timetable order that excised the reference to 'first business' and replaced it with a reference to the business 'including' a government motion on the Lisbon Treaty. Oddly, the minister who introduced the amendment somehow forgot to mention that it would have the effect of resurrecting the instruction. If he had mentioned that effect, different Members might have voted for his amendment. But the trouble with this whole line of argument is that it is entirely unnecessary if one had quite reasonably interpreted 'first business' as meaning 'first government business'. It is also worth mentioning that the 24th edition of *Erskine May* seems to make no reference at all to Standing Order No 66.

sense that if they had been offered in public, it is difficult to believe that they could have withstood scrutiny. The problem with not having to explain the reasons behind a decision in public is that it allows weak reasoning to survive.

The best way to improve the situation would be for the Speaker to give detailed reasons for procedural decisions. If the point is one that needs to be decided immediately, the Speaker could adopt the judicial practice in urgent cases of announcing a decision straightaway without reasons, but giving full reasons later. The prospects of such a reform seem distant, however. Many would advise against it on the ground that giving detailed reasons would invite debate and thus would threaten the Speaker's authority. That is a bad argument as a matter of principle—authority that fears discussion seems peculiarly ill-suited for the chair of a democratic assembly—but experience suggests that it will probably prevail.

Assuming that the forces of institutional conservatism succeed, one other way forward exists that could possibly increase the system's level of rationality without committing the Chair to argumentation that might not stand up later. That would be for academic lawyers to start to treat the decisions of the Speaker as cases and to write about them as they already write about the decisions of the courts. The starting point would be to compose case notes in the form familiar to readers of the standard legal journals. Case notes in that tradition describe and discuss a single decision, explaining how it fits, or does not fit, with previous decisions and discussing its implications for the future. The absence of reasoning is no bar to such an exercise since the minimum material needed to underpin a case note is a set of facts and a decision. Eventually, when many case notes exist, one might be able to move on to producing compilations of them in various forms. One form, which would mirror the style of case reports in civil law jurisdictions, would be a simple chronological series of decisions and notes.[24] Another form would be a case-book, a collection of cases and commentary selected for their significance and arranged by theme, extended by adding other materials (for example, the Standing Orders, academic articles, extracts from the *Treatise*). The classic use of a case-book is as an aid to teaching, but case-books can also stand as reference works in their own right. It would amount to a kind of *Erskine May* upside down, in which the material usually relegated to the footnotes becomes primary and the text becomes secondary. Another possibility is to use the cases to underpin an account of the system as a whole, as the basis of an anthropology of Parliament, not so much in the form of an ethnography such as we have an example of from Emma Crewe in this book (chapter 3) as that of a functional account of how Parliament solves problems.[25]

AN EXAMPLE

What would such case notes look like? To illustrate the concept we might turn to a decision of Mr Speaker Bercow, delivered in the House on 10 July 2012, during proceedings on

---

[24] I am informed that the Journal Office of the Commons used to produce a series of decisions of the Chair (albeit without academic commentary) until fairly recently. Perhaps as a first step this publication could be revived.

[25] For an excellent ethnography of parliament, see Emma Crewe, *The House of Commons: An Anthropology of MPs at Work* (London, Bloomsbury, 2015). For a classic of functional legal anthropology, see Karl Llewellyn and E Adamson Hoebel, *The Cheyenne Way* (Norman, Oklahoma University Press, 1941).

the ill-fated House of Lords Reform Bill. As undoubtedly a bill of 'first rate constitutional importance' the bill was to be referred, by a resolution proposed by the government, to a committee of the whole House. In order, however, to protect the bill from attempts to wreck it by endless extension of debate in committee and to avoid having to assemble daily major-ities for closure motions, the government put down a motion to programme the bill, under Standing Order No 83A, proposing to restrict debate to a specific number of days (in this case ten in committee and two on report) and specifying in the normal way which clauses and schedules were to be discussed on which days. But after having given notice of moving their programme motion, the government came to the conclusion that the motion had no chance of being carried. Despite the fact that the government could expect a large majority for the second reading of the bill itself, the programme motion faced a hostile combination of the official opposition and a very considerable number of rebels on the government's side. The government therefore announced that when the time came later that evening to move the programme motion, it would simply not move it.

The question then arose of what would happen next. Standing Order No 63 says that, unless the House resolves otherwise, bills are automatically referred to a Public Bill Committee, usually a small committee of around fifteen members, but occasionally larger. That would plainly be unsatisfactory for a constitutional Bill, and so Members began to focus on Standing Order No 63(2), which says that a motion to commit a bill to, inter alia, a committee of the whole House

> may be made by any Member and if made immediately after the bill has been read a second time shall not require notice, and, though opposed, may be decided after the expiration of the time for opposed business, and the question thereon shall be put forthwith.

Could that provision be used at least to commit the bill to a committee of the whole House? We can quote the point of order and the ruling in full.

Mr Peter Bone (Wellingborough) (Con): On a point of order, Mr Speaker. The media have announced that there will not be a programme motion. According to Standing Order No 63, by rights the Bill should not be committed to the whole House, but should go to a Public Bill Committee upstairs. Will that procedure apply in this case?

Mr Speaker: I do not think that Standing Order No 63 applies in this case, given that the programme motion has been tabled. I am happy to take further advice on the matter, and to consider whether the hon Gentleman's point is valid.[26]

That might be taken to be the Speaker's preliminary view. Full judgment followed shortly:

Mr Speaker: Order. Before I call the first Back-Bench speaker, may I, for the benefit of the House, now respond substantively to the point of order raised with me earlier by the hon Member for Wellingborough (Mr Bone)? Standing Order No 83A provides that, where notice is given of a pro-gramme motion, Standing Order No 63 shall not apply. That means that, if the Bill is read a Second time this evening, it will not be possible for Ministers or others to move to commit the Bill, whether to Committee of the whole House or elsewhere. The Bill will remain uncommitted for the time being. I hope that that information is helpful to the House.[27]

---

[26] HC Debates Official Report, 10 July 2012, c 187.
[27] HC Debates Official Report, 10 July 2012, cc 204–05.

In other words, the Bill was to be left in limbo—Members could not move its referral to a committee of the whole House, but it was not automatically referred to a Public Bill Committee either. Standing Order No 83A was taken to disapply Standing Order No 63 in its entirety.

Mr Speaker Bercow's ruling appears to turn on a literal interpretation of Standing Order No 83A(1), which, as he intimated, says that, if before the second reading of a bill, a minister gives notice of a programme motion, 'the motion may be made immediately after second reading, and Standing Order No 63 (Committal of bills not subject to a programme order) shall not apply to the bill'. The crucial word is 'notice'. The decision is that Standing Order No 83A disapplies Standing Order No 63 as soon as the minister declares an intention to move the programme motion, an event evidenced by the motion's appearance on the Order Paper. It is not necessary actually to move the programme motion for the disapplication to take effect.

Speaker Bercow's interpretation of Standing Order No 83A(1) has the remarkable effect that a minister can limit the rights of all other Members to move a motion not by persuading them to pass a different motion, or even by moving a different motion, but merely by announcing that a different motion will be moved. That matters not just because it shifts the balance of power between the government and the House in favour of the former on government bills, but also because it provides yet another weapon by which the government can destroy private Members' bills. Standing Order No 83A(1) is not limited to the government's bills. It applies to any bill. The effect is that a minister could stop any private Member's bill in its tracks by the simple method of giving notice of a programme motion about it and then failing to move that motion. The bill would then enter permanent limbo unless the government moved the programme motion and released it.

That result, however, is not inevitable. Another way of reading Standing Order No 83A(1) is that the interposition of the words 'the motion may be made immediately after second reading' before the disapplication clause implies that if, in the event, the motion is not made, the disapplication ceases. The reasoning behind Standing Order No 83A(1), as far as it can be rationally reconstructed, is that it would be very inconvenient if any Member could jump up before the programme motion has been moved and propose a committal without a programme. That is also why the programme motion may be made 'immediately'. But if it is not made, the reason to exclude Standing Order No 63 disappears and so the disapplication should also cease. That interpretation is reinforced by the way Standing Order No 83A(1) refers to Standing Order No 63 as the standing order about 'Committal of bills not subject to a programme order'. If a programme motion is not moved, the bill is at that point 'not subject to a programme order' and so Standing Order No 63 should once more apply.

One might also ask what precisely Standing Order No 83A(1)'s disapplication of Standing Order No 63 achieves. The original version of Standing Order No 63 was passed in 1907, by a government anxious to provide more time for its legislative programme on the floor of the House and irritated by long debates about committal. Before then, any Member could, immediately after second reading, move without notice any form of committal and a debate would then ensue. Standing Order No 63 did not create the right to move committals. It rather removed the ability of the House to debate such motions and provides for an automatic default option if no committal motion is moved. Disapplying it therefore might produce its own paradoxical effect of reviving the previous position under which committal motions were debatable. The problem for Members wanting to move a committal would then not be Standing Order No 83A but Standing Order No 9(6), which provides that no further unexempted opposed business can be taken after the moment of interruption. A committal could indeed have been moved but could have been blocked by any Member voicing an objection. Sadly neither Mr Bone nor any other Member attempted to move a committal after the moment of interruption and so this theory remains untested.

CONSEQUENCES

What difference would it make if we began (or began again) to treat Parliament, and in particular the House of Commons, as operating a legal system? Two consequences come to mind. First, it would improve academic understanding of Parliament. Some historians have understood the importance of parliamentary procedure, as have some political scientists.[28] But many, including lawyers, have not. To treat everything that happens in Parliament as a black box marked 'political' is to miss much of what happens there. Parliamentary politics takes place within rules, is influenced by rules and sometimes consists of arguments about what the rules should be. The system for deciding what the rules are and what they mean matters. The rules are not, of course, the only thing that matters. It is possible that they matter only a little, that they provide a bare framework that helps to structure daily routines but nothing else. But it is also possible that they are fundamental to the acceptance by Members of Parliament of the legitimacy of Parliament itself. Further research might reveal the answer to the question of which of those views is correct, but the question can only be asked at all if we take the system of rules seriously to begin with.

The second consequence is that it would help to focus more attention and effort on reforming Parliament. Thinking of Parliament's procedures as misty traditions that somehow float up without any conscious design from the dank atmosphere of the ground floor of the Palace of Westminster tends to discourage putting effort into reform. If current practice is ultimately ungraspable and tied up in intricacies we can only guess at, how can we be sure that change will be for the better? And thinking of procedure as 'political' also discourages reform by giving the impression that political convenience will always outrank the rules and so changing the rules is futile. If, however, we think of the system as a type of legal system we should be able to see it as designed for certain purposes and capable, as are all modern legal systems, of having its purposes changed.

No doubt some will raise as an objection to treating parliamentary procedure as a legal system a third possible consequence, that it will encourage and embolden that least popular group of Members of Parliament, namely lawyers. The stereotype that lawyers are pointlessly argumentative and pernickety persists as much in Parliament as in the outside world, perhaps even more.[29] The prospect of more wrangling over small points is not attractive.

---

[28] See, eg, Steven Watson, 'Parliamentary Procedure as a Key to Understanding Eighteenth Century Politics' (1962) 2 *Burke Newsletter* 108 and Herbert Döring, 'Parliamentary Agenda Control and Legislative Outcomes in Western Europe' (2001) 26 *Legislative Studies Quarterly* 145.

[29] I should record that shortly after my own election I was offered the (genuinely friendly) advice that it would not be a good idea to be identified as a lawyer and that I should try always to let others know that I was an academic.

But even if that were to happen—and one might counter that Members of Parliament, whether lawyers or not, are already so argumentative that very little room exists for more wrangling—its inconveniences would be outweighed by setting lawyers both inside and outside Parliament to work on what they really do best, using or designing formal structures of rules to achieve specific purposes.[30] Perhaps it might even attract different, and possibly better, kinds of lawyer into Parliament, those who see their role not as causing problems but as solving them.

---

[30] See generally David Howarth, *Law as Engineering: Thinking about What Lawyers Do* (Cheltenham, Edward Elgar, 2013).

Index